# Schott's Significa

PENGUIN MICHAEL JOSEPH

UK | USA | Canada | Ireland | Australia
India | New Zealand | South Africa

Penguin Michael Joseph is part of the Penguin Random House group of companies whose addresses can be found at global.penguinrandomhouse.com

Penguin Michael Joseph, Penguin Random House UK,
One Embassy Gardens, 8 Viaduct Gardens, London SW11 7BW

penguin.co.uk

Penguin Random House UK

First published 2025
001



Acknowledgements, references, and full image credits may be found on pp. 295–303.



Printed and bound in Dubai

The authorized representative in the E.E.A. is Penguin Random House Ireland,
Morrison Chambers, 32 Nassau Street, Dublin, D02 YH68

A CIP catalogue record for this book is available from the British Library

I.S.B.N.: 978-0-241-73660-9

Penguin Random House is committed to a sustainable future for our business, our readers and our planet. This book is made from Forest Stewardship Council® certified paper.

FSC www.fsc.org MIX Paper | Supporting responsible forestry FSC® C018179

# Schott's Significa

*Conceived, written, & designed by*

BEN SCHOTT

MICHAEL JOSEPH
PENGUIN
Est. 1935

One of the difficulties in making the present study
has been that, since this work has no true predecessor,
we had first to find out what there was to find out,
before we knew whether there existed a subject to study.

IONA & PETER OPIE
*The Lore and Language of Schoolchildren*

Colloquial language is a part of the human
organism and is not less complicated than it.
... The silent adjustments to understand
colloquial language are enormously
complicated.

*The limits of my language* mean
the limits of my world.

LUDWIG WITTGENSTEIN

Tickets — bus, train, or theater tickets — are a typical form of ephemera, vital when they are needed, wastepaper immediately afterwards. They flourish for a moment and are done. As with the mayfly (the *ephemerid*), which lives but for a day, theirs is a brief and modest glory.

MAURICE RICKARDS

Give the people a new word,
and they think they have a new fact.

WILLA CATHER

Each way of looking at the world
had a language of its own.

JACOB BRONOWSKI

Everyone knows that when individuals
in the presence of others respond to events,
their glances, looks, and postural shifts carry
all kinds of implication and meaning ...
So it remains to microanalysts of interaction
to lumber in where the self-respecting
decline to tread. A question of pinning
with our ten thumbs what ought to be
secured with a needle.

ERVING GOFFMAN

Slang is the most sour poetry. It does
not wish you well ... It's the spoken, and
very occasionally written invention of
the tap-room, the bar-room, the work-
place, the barracks ... the private place.

JONATHAN MEADES

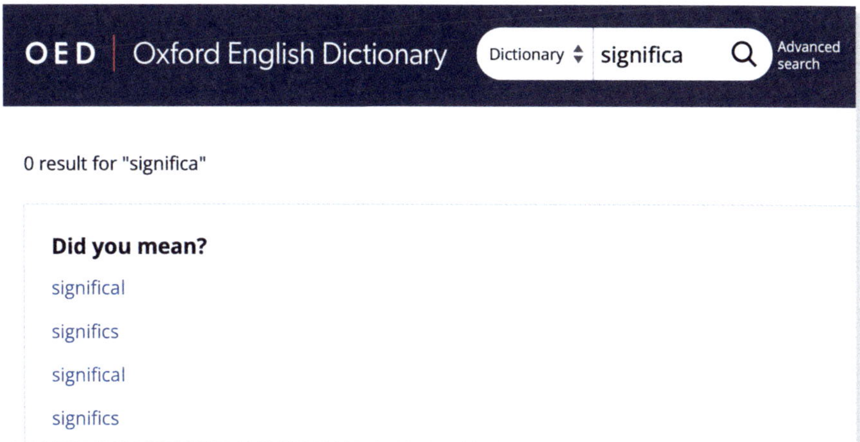


## SIGNIFICA

/ sɪɡˈnɪfɪkə / *noun*

That which is overlooked, yet essential;
marginal, yet meaningful; ephemeral, yet enduring.

# Contents

# Gondola! Gondola!

*Whereas once some 10,000* **GONDOLAS** *coursed through the veins of Venice, now just some 440 licensed* **GONDOLIERI** *service an annual tsunami of over 30 million visitors.*

Prior to mass tourism, the gondola season was relatively short: **I SETTANTA GIORNI DEL GELATO** [the 70 days of ice cream] ran from the *Festa del Redentore* in July to the *Regata Storica* in September. Outside these dates most gondoliers returned to their day-jobs as labourers, coalmen, or Murano glass blowers.

But now, as the tour groups stream endlessly in from around the globe, being a gondolier is a full-time (and often well-paid) job, and the updated expression — **I NOVANTA GIORNI DEL GELATO** — describes just the especially hectic 90 days between June and September.

The topography of Venice is much disputed, but some facts are appropriate, if approximate:

There are 121 **ISOLE** [islands] connected by 435 **PONTI** [bridges] — of which ~72 are privately owned — crossing 177 **RII** [tributaries] and **CANALI** [canals] — of which only three are truly canals: Canal Grande, Canale della Giudecca, and Canale di Cannaregio.

(Over time, a number of canals have been converted into streets: **RIO TERÀ** indicates a canal that has been filled completely, e.g., Via Garibaldi, or paved over so as to preserve the tidal flow below, e.g., Rio Terà dei Gesuati.)

The dimensionality of Venice's ~26-mile canal network varies extensively: The Canal Grande is 30–70 metres wide, with an average depth of 5 metres, whereas the narrowest *rii* can be 3 metres wide and 1.5 metres deep. This unique topography inspired both the gondola and its characteristic style of rowing — **VOGA ALLA VENETA**: The tightest of *rii* mean that the **RÈMO** [oar] must be held almost vertically, and the deepest *canali* preclude the use of traditional punt poles.

*"I am afraid I study the gondolier's marvellous skill more than I do the sculptured palaces we glide among... He makes all his calculations with the nicest precision, and goes darting in and out among a Broadway confusion of busy craft with the easy confidence of the educated hackman. He never makes a mistake."* — MARK TWAIN[1]

## GÓNDOLE

Gondolas are hand-built from ~280 pieces of fir, larch, lime, mahogany, cherry, elm, oak, and walnut. Some 35.5 feet long and 4.5 feet wide, they are artfully asymmetrical ("*banana shaped*"), listing gently to starboard to allow a lone gondolier to steer, propel, and brake with a single, unfastened oar.

Gondolas are constructed using the traditional Venetian units of measurement where:

1 **PIÈ(DE)** = 12 **ONCE** = 347.74 mm / 13.69"

Over the centuries the number of **SQUÈRI** [gondola shipyards] has dwindled from more than 50 to just four, with a consequent impact on the number of **SQUERARIÒLI** [shipwrights], *A.k.a.*, **MAESTRI D'ASCIA** [masters of the axe]. That said, gondolas require also the expertise of a range of craft specialists, e.g.:

**INTAGIADÓRI** .......... wood carvers
**FRAVI** .......... blacksmiths
**FONDIDÓRI** .......... metal workers
**INDORADÓRI** .......... gilders
**REMÈRI** .......... oars and **FÓRCOLE**
**SARTÓRI** .......... tailors
**BARETÈRI** .......... hat makers
**CALEGHÈRI** .......... cobblers

**NERO DA GÓNDOLA** · A high-gloss, jet-black, water-resistant paint. Traditionally each *squèro* would concoct its own secret recipe; now various synthetic marine paints are used.

Why gondolas are black is disputed: some point to the formal mourning that followed the 1348 Black Death; others to "sumptuary laws," which limited displays of ostentation. The most likely explanation is a mix of poetry and Henry Fordian practicality.

**BATÌZO** [baptism] · A formal ceremony, attended by a priest, to bless every new (or substantially renovated) gondola. (By tradition, a new gondola's first pilot is its **SQUERARIÒL**.)

☜ *A gondolier turns past the San Zaccaria vaporetto station toward the Grand Canal*

**GARANGHÈLO / RINFRÈSCO** [snack / refreshment] · A post-**BATÌZO** party held (in the *squèro*) to celebrate a new launch.

**OPERA MORTA / OPERA VIVA** [dead work / living work] · The parts of the gondola above and below the waterline, respectively.

**FÓRCOLA** · A wonder of deceptively simple engineering, this contorted wooden oarlock limb offers gondoliers eight points of leverage with which to manoeuvre. Fast, slow, forward, back, wide, narrow — every movement, including gliding to a halt, is achieved through the subtlest shifts of posture and hinge.

Carved by hand from a block of walnut, cherry, pear, or maple by an expert **REMÈRO**, each *fórcola* is designed to suit the height, weight, and style of the gondolier and the shape and form of his vessel.

**FÈLZE** · A covered passenger cabin in the centre of the gondola that offers protection from the elements and privacy for lovers, prostitutes, and fleeing criminals.

(Some *fèlze* had heaters to keep women warm, and their slatted window shades are said to be the first Venetian blinds.)

Once a common sight, the *fèlze* has all but disappeared from the canals.

**GÓNDOLA DA LÙSSO** · A *luxury gondola* with (highly) elaborate **MÙA** [furnishings] used for weddings and other grand occasions.

**GÓNDOLIER DE CASÀDA** · The now archaic position of a privately employed gondolier, who lived in the family *palazzo* so as always to be on call. Both gondola and gondolier would be decked out in the colours of the house.

Less onerous was to be **IN SERVIZIO** [*in service*] to a specific patron, the most famous of whom, in modern times, was Peggy Guggenheim, whose **GÓNDOLA DE CASÀDA** is displayed at Venice's *Museo Storico Navale*.

**NASTRI DE OTÓN** 📷 · *Brass ribbons* (now usually steel) set at the gondola's bow and engraved with phrases, quotes, or the names of loved ones. Since gondolas are not christened, *nastri* often become the boats' de facto name.

**SÀCO DA PÒPE** · A (usually ornate) cloth draped over, e.g., unsightly luggage.

**FÈRO DA PRÒVA / DOLFÌN** 📷 · The characteristic metal blade at the gondola's *pròva* [bow] is both use and ornament.

Functionally, the *fèro* acts as a counterweight to the gondolier standing at the stern — even if the modern steel and aluminium versions are significantly lighter than the original iron.

Symbolically, the blade's curious details have (romantically, if dubiously) become linked to Venetian topography and iconography.

As various legends have it:

- The six forward *denti* [teeth] or *rebbi* [tines] depict the city's six *sestieri* [districts]
- The rear-jutting tooth depicts the Giudecca
- The three inter-dental *chiodi* [nails] depict either three islands (Murano, Burano, Torcello); three bridges (Rialto, Accademia, Scalzi); or the nails of Christ's crucifixion
- The bulbous comb-head depicts the *Corno Ducale* [Doge's cap]
- The empty semicircle below depicts both the Rialto Bridge (the curve) and the San Marco basin (the void)
- The overall silhouette depicts the curves of the Grand Canal and/or the mane of the Lion of Venice

Because of the hazard of passing under low bridges during **AQUA ALTA**, some modern *fèri* are detachable, or hinged, to avoid damage.

**MÉTAR LA BARCA IN TÈRA** · *To put a boat onto land*, for storage at the end of a season, or for routine cleaning, especially in summer when the warmer water causes more fouling.

**SECÀR LA BARCA** · *To dry out the boat* (e.g., with a **SÈSOLA** [bailer]) to prevent it sinking during heavy rain — notwithstanding the protection of its **COPRIFIUBÓNI**.

**VÈRZER LA BARCA** · *Readying the boat* for the day, which may involve **NETÀR LA BARCA** · *Cleaning the boat* using a **SPONZA** [sponge], often undertaken by **SOSTITÙTI**.

*A* FÈRO DA PRÒVA *in front of the Ponte dell'Accademia dei Pittori*

NASTRO DE OTÒN *engraved with Robert Benchley's telegraphic joke: "Streets full of water, please advise"*

## VOCAL CALLS

**PÒPE** · Both a general term for a gondolier, and a warning call — deployed like a car horn — to alert other boats in poor visibility, or when approaching a corner or canal crossing.

**ÒE!** · A warning cry similar (or in answer) to PÒPE, bellowed with more or less volume depending on the character of the gondolier and the exigency of the situation. Often augmented with additional information, e.g.:

**ÒE PREMÀNDO!**................I'm turning left!
**ÒE STAGÀNDO!** .............. I'm turning right!
**ÒE DE LONGO!**..........I'm going straight on!

**DRIÀN!** [behind] · Hence, "*Mì sarò driàn de ti!*" [I will follow you].

**GÓNDOLA! GÓNDOLA!** · The age-old street cry, deployed when trade is slow.

## TIDE & TECHNIQUE

**ANDÀR CONTRÀRIA** · To go against the tide.

**ANDÀR A SECONDA** · To go with the tide.

**ANDÀR TORZIO / SCAROSSANDO** · To go where the waters take you. *Also*, **CON LA FIACA** · To row sweetly without haste.

**ANDÀR IN BANDA** · Tilting the gondola to safely pass under low bridges at high tide.

**VOGÀR IN CAVATA** · To row (and, more generally, to hustle) with maximum speed and effort; vital in high season.

**ANDÀR A FONDI** · *To sink*; metaphorically, to get caught in the rain, or to sweat profusely.

**MOTO ONDOSO** · *Wave movement* (i.e., wake) caused by marine traffic, which makes rowing harder. More common in open water and busy canals than in tight *rii*.

*Similarly*, **RESTÌA** · A *wild* and hazardous wave caused (at low tide) by a fast or big boat, e.g., police launch, vaporetto, or cruise ship.

The increasing roughness of the water has cut the longevity of a gondola from 25–30 years to 13–15. *Hence*, **BARCA DA BRÚSO** · A boat fit only for firewood [*bruciare*, to burn].

**ACQUA ALTA** · *High water.*

**ACQUA STANCA** · *Tired water* between tidal phases. *Also*, **ACQUA MORTA** · *Dead water*, with no difference between high and low tide.

**ANDÀR A MORTI** · To row as part of a funeral procession.

## NICKNAMES

Bestowing **NOMINÀNSE** [nicknames] is an ancient tradition for gondoliers, and the majority have an appropriate **SOPRANNOME** based on a physical characteristic, family tradition, or quirk of personality, e.g.:

**NIAGARA**, who fell into the water three times in one day; **GIRASOLE**, who has the metaphorical height of a *sunflower*; **CHICCHIRICHÌ** [*cock-a-doodle-doo*], who is as ebullient as a cockerel; **MANOVRA**, because of an inability to *manoeuvre*; **IL MAESTRO**, *the master*; and **SORRISO**, who always *smiles*.

**SBESARIOL** [penniless] · An aspiring or boatless gondolier who helps out other gondoliers.

**NOL PÀRLA** [he doesn't speak] · A novice gondolier too focused on perfecting his craft to banter with colleagues.

**TROVÀI** [foundlings] · Gondoliers who cannot boast family links with the profession.

**DEL CEPPO** · One descended from a long line of gondoliers. [A *ceppo* is a stump of wood, hence a "(chip) off the old block."]

**INRUSENÌO** [rusty] · A nickname for gondoliers, given their weather-beaten suntans.

**GHÈBI** .......... police
(*Also*, a small network of neighbourhood canals)
**CARAMBA** .......... Carabinieri
**GRIGI** .......... Guardia di Finanza
(named after their grey livery and uniforms)

## MUSIC

Contrary to cliché (and ice-cream ads) very few gondoliers sing while they row. If a large group, special occasion, or elaborate client is to be serenaded, then professional *cantanti* [singers] and *musicisti* [musicians] are hired.

There is an extensive songbook of traditional *canzoni da battello* [boat songs] including *Venezia La Luna e Tu* [Venice, the Moon, and You]; *La Biondina in Gondoleta* [The Blonde in the Gondola]; and *Il Gondoliere*, which is sung by Venezia F.C. fans at the local Stadio Pier Luigi Penzo — Italy's second oldest football stadium, constructed in 1913.

Classically minded passengers may select **BARCAROLE**, which use tempos and time signatures (e.g., 6/8, 9/8, 12/8) that mimic a gondola's rhythmic passage — notably Offenbach's *Belle Nuit, ô Nuit D'amour* or Chopin's *Barcarolle in F-sharp major*.

Opinion divides on the suitability of *'O Sole Mio*, the famously Neapolitan folk song.

## TRADE

Gondoliers are attached to one of ten stations:

DANIELI · MOLO · DOGANA · TRINITA
SANTA MARIA DEL GIGLIO
SAN TOMA' · SAN BENETO · CARBON
SANTA SOFIA · SAN MARCUOLA

Each **STÀSIO** has several smaller, peripheral **RIVE** in the neighbourhood that are manned by gondoliers on a rotational basis.

**BANCÀL** · The senior gondolier at each *stàsio* (elected for a two-year term) who runs operations, sets schedules, and litigates disputes.

**PRESIDENTE DEI BANCÀLI** · The head of all the **BANCÀLI** who helps settle serious disputes and coordinates with municipal authorities.

**BALOTÀR** · A *ballot* to decide which shifts gondoliers will work for the year ahead. Shifts vary by *stàsio* and season, and are colour-coded for clarity: white, yellow, red, blue, or green.

**TABÈA DE VÓLTA** [table of turns] · A narrow wooden board with a ladder of slots, used in some larger *stàzi*, to indicate which gondoliers are working, and the order of job assignment.

Gondoliers each have a **STECHÈTO** [*toothpick*] inscribed on both sides with their licence number (and nickname), and on one side with the letter V [*volta*, turn] that, when inserted into the *tabèa*, indicates they are available.

**SERVIZIO DI NÒLO** · The *hire service*, where passengers are taken on an agreed tour of the sites, or to a specific destination.

**SERVIZIO DI PARÀDA** · The *parade service* that takes passengers straight across a canal — usually known as the **TRAGHETTO** [ferry].

In centuries past, scores of *paràda* routes operated at all hours and in all weather. Now only a handful remain, offering a limited (and sometimes haphazard) schedule across the Canal Grande at locations not usefully served by bridges: Santa Sofia, Carbon, San Toma, Santa Maria del Giglio, and Trinita.

The **GÓNDOLA DA PARÀDA** is actually a **BARCHÉTTA**, an unadorned *little boat* with two rowers: one forward, one aft. {☞ p.236} It is larger (and more symmetrical) than the **GÓNDOLA DA NÒLO** [gondola for hire].

Tourists are currently charged €2 per ride; locals pay 70¢ and, unless infirm, take pride in standing.

**CAROVÀNA** [caravan] · The term for dividing large tourist groups into multiple gondolas, and ferrying them en masse around the sites. Not undertaken by all *stàzi*, and deprecated by some gondoliers (and many Venetians) because of the chaos and noise it can cause.

(In 2020, in response to the ever-increasing obesity of tourists, the maximum capacity of a gondola was reduced from six to five.)

**BUTTO** · A one-way fare. Because journeys traditionally start and end at the same place, gondoliers negotiate a **CONTRÀTO** [contract] for *butti* to defray the cost of their return.

Gondoliers will not usually pick up passengers at a *stàsio* that is not their own, even if there are no other gondoliers waiting.

**CASÒTO** · A (hexagonal) wooden hut that serves as the headquarters for each *stàsio*, and the courtroom for any internal dispute.

(Back in the day, gondoliers would sleep in their *casòto* during night shifts.)

**FRÀGIA** · The *fellowship* at each *stàsio*; and the deep fraternity of gondoliers generally.

**LÈVO DE VÒLTA** [skip a turn] · Gondoliers who violate the rules in some way may be suspended for one or more shifts, or days.

Those so punished may request a **BÀNCA AGIUNTA**, an appeal to neighbouring *bancali*.

**GIORNÀDA** · The plan for the day — chalked up on a blackboard **TABÈA** — which specifies the day's bookings and other details. More common in *stàzi* that offer **CAROVÀNE**.

**SOSTITÙTO** · A young *substitute* gondolier who is still learning the trade, of which there are currently ~180.

Although many *gondolieri* are firmly **DELL CEPPO** (and all but ~14 are male) the profession is open to anyone over 18 and, in 2009, Giorgia Boscolo became Venice's first licensed *gondoliera*.[2]

To qualify, candidates must pass not just extensive theory exams and rowing tests, but also be proficient in English and French, first aid, local history, and swimming.

**GANSÈR** · One who helps gondolas dock, and assists passengers board and disembark.

Historically, the *gansèri* were gondoliers who had retired due to old age, infirmity, or accident — as a result of which they were sometimes derided as *l'ultimo pelo della coda della mucca* [the last hair of the cow's tail]. Now the job is usually undertaken by *sostitùti*, whose pay is augmented by tips, traditionally hustled via a doffed (or artfully placed) hat.

Larger *stàzi*, especially those who provide **CAROVÀNE**, may have more than one *gansèr*.

**GÀNSO** · The **GANSÈR**'s boat hook, *A.k.a.*, **RAMPIN / MESOMARINER**.

**PALÀNCOLA** · A *plank* used for boarding.

**PASÉTO** · The *short walk* from gondola to bridge that *gansèri* take with passengers.

**PIGNATÈLA** [small saucepan] · A home-prepared meal eaten at work, because it is cheaper and healthier, or because work is too hectic to stop and eat **IN TÈRA** [on land].

**I XE TEGNA** [they are miserable] · Bad tippers. *Conversely*, **I XE SPLENDIDI**.

**HO REALIZZATO UN SOGNO** [I fulfilled a dream] · The clichéd (yet cherished) sentiment of many tourists after a gondola journey.

**MÉTER LA BARCA DA NÒTE** · *To put the boat to bed*, by removing its **PARÉCIO** [seating &c.] and protecting it with a navy blue **COPRIFIUBÓNI** [waterproof "jacket"]. ⊙

☞ **MÉTER LA BARCA DA NÒTE** *at Santa Sofia, seen from room 41 of the Venice Venice hotel*

# Where Credit's Due

*The blurb at the bottom of a* **MOVIE POSTER** *is the* **BILLING BLOCK**. *And while it might look like a barcode of haphazardly packed type, it is in fact the product of detailed legal agreements and intense contract negotiation. Below is the billing block for a fictional film —* "All the Presidents" *— and opposite, an explanation of how it was constructed.*

(1) PAUL REVERE FILMS AND (2) OVAL OFFICE PICTURES / FOUNDING FATHERS

PRESENT IN ASSOCIATION WITH (3) EAST INDIA CO. A (4) 10 DOWNING ST. PRODUCTION

AN (5) ABRAHAM LINCOLN FILM (6) GEORGE WASHINGTON (7) "ALL THE PRESIDENTS"

(8) JOHN ADAMS DOLLEY MADISON WITH (9) MOLLY PITCHER

(10) AND JAMES K. POLK AS (11) "11" INTRODUCING (12) "TAD" LINCOLN

(13) CASTING BY JOHN Q. PUBLIC, (14) CSA (15) MUSIC BY JOHN STAFFORD SMITH

(16) ORIGINAL SCORE BY J. P. SOUSA (17) COSTUMES BY BETSY ROSS (18) EDITED BY ROSE MARY WOODS, (19) ACE

(20) PRODUCTION DESIGNER BENJAMIN LATROBE (21) DIRECTOR OF PHOTOGRAPHY ABRAHAM ZAPRUDER, (22) ASC

(23) ASSOCIATE PRODUCER ABIGAIL ADAMS (24) CO-PRODUCERS THOMAS JEFFERSON JAMES MONROE

(25) EXECUTIVE PRODUCER BENJAMIN FRANKLIN (26) PRODUCED BY FREDERICK NORTH, (27) p.g.a.

CHARLES WATSON-WENTWORTH, (27) p.g.a. (28) BASED ON CHARACTERS CREATED BY KING GEORGE III

(29) STORY BY ALEXANDER HAMILTON (30) & JAMES MADISON (31) AND JOHN JAY

(32) SCREENPLAY BY THOMAS PAINE (33) DIRECTED BY ABRAHAM LINCOLN

## INTRODUCTION

On the facing page is the **BILLING BLOCK** for an (imaginary) studio-financed American theatrical motion picture **ONE-SHEET**: in layman's terms, the small print on a poster you might see in a cinema lobby. The content, order, and format of the billing block are governed by two things: **PERSONAL SERVICE CONTRACTS** with cast and crew, and **INDUSTRY-WIDE AGREEMENTS** with professional guilds — notably the Directors Guild of America (D.G.A.) and the Writers Guild of America (W.G.A.). Thus, while some elements of the billing block remain consistent, others depend on the type of film and on individual negotiations. That said, there has been a marked inflation in billing block credits. An *Ocean's 11* poster from 1960 credited three non-cast individuals; the 2001 remake poster credited, coincidentally, 11.

The billing block is distinct from the **CREDITS** (the on-screen "main titles" at the start of a movie) and the **CRAWL** (the cast and crew listed on-screen in the "end titles"). Furthermore, different rules and conventions apply to other forms of communication, like **TEASERS** (posters on which the film title is deliberately not shown); **ADVANCE ONE-SHEETS** (posters that show only the names of star actors); **WILD POSTING** ("guerrilla" pasting of posters in urban locations, often unlicensed) as well as billboards, taxi tops, online ads; &c.

## TYPE & DESIGN

The design of modern billing blocks illustrates the tension between two intersecting interests: Studios want uncluttered marketing materials, and industry organizations want their members prominently and fairly credited.

Thus, it is neither accidental nor for aesthetics that the text in most modern billing blocks is tall and highly condensed. To ensure that the credits are legible, the D.G.A. and W.G.A. require that their members' names be at least 15 percent of the size of type used for the **ARTWORK TITLE** (i.e., the name of the movie, as set in the main body of the poster). If the **ARTWORK TITLE** has words of varying size, the height of every letter is measured, and an average calculated. The D.G.A. and W.G.A. also mandate that the credit titles (e.g., **STORY BY** or **DIRECTED BY**) be no less than half the size of the names to which they refer. This explains the vertical stacking of job titles (e.g., ⓭).

There is no official billing block typeface, but because of the unique requirements of the design, a few fonts are frequently used — including Univers Std 39 Thin Ultra Condensed, employed here.

## OPENING CREDITS

The first name in a billing block is usually the **PRESENTATION CREDIT** ❶ — which generally recognizes the film's **DISTRIBUTOR**. (This credit can be shared ❷, for example when one company distributes domestically, and another abroad.) The **IN ASSOCIATION WITH** credit ❸ is usually given to a body that helps finance the movie, though it can also credit others, like the management of a star. The **PRODUCTION CREDIT** ❹ generally recognizes the producer's or director's own company.

The "possessory credit" **A ××× FILM** (or **A FILM BY ×××**) ❺ is negotiated as part of the director's personal service agreement. Such credits give additional prominence to the director — to the annoyance of some writers — and they do not negate the requirement of a final **DIRECTED BY** ㉝ credit. (Some directors, like Martin Scorsese and Jonathan Demme, use the **A ××× PICTURE**; Spike Lee famously uses the credit **A SPIKE LEE JOINT**. The D.G.A. does not usually allow such bombastic credits on a director's first feature film.)

## CAST

Although the Screen Actors Guild (now SAG-AFTRA) plays a part in how actors are credited on-screen, credits in billing blocks are separately negotiated.

Actors' agents strive to get their clients into the billing block — citing the significance of a role as justification, or past inclusion as precedent. For obvious reasons of space, though, only key names are credited. Major stars sometimes appear before ❻ the title ❼; others are listed directly after ❽ — alphabetically or in a descending order that reflects the importance of each role and the clout of each actor.

The ranking of an actor (**FIRST POSITION**, **SECOND POSITION**, &c.) is the subject of negotiation before shooting, and it is occasionally renegotiated if the scope of a role expands — or "pops" in the edit. (A dispute over first billing for *Outrageous Fortune* in 1987 was settled by the creation of two sets of prints and publicity material; half gave the lead to Shelley Long, half to Bette Midler.)

Actors can negotiate to have the word **WITH** ⑨ or **AND** ⑩ before their names; such words tend to be used when a major star has a small but significant role. There can be more than one **WITH** credit, and more than one **AND** — though **WITH** usually comes before **AND**. (**AND** has been called the "third best credit," because of its prominence at the end of a list.)

The credit **AND** XXX **AS** XXX ⑪ is used to highlight a notable cameo, give additional emphasis to an actor, or differentiate it from other **AND**'s.

The word **INTRODUCING** ⑫ is used to promote a young actor's major film debut. (For example, in 1973, Tatum O'Neal had an INTRODUCING credit on *Paper Moon*.)

Parenthetically, in the poster **ARTWORK** (i.e., outside the billing block), disagreement over first position can be solved by **STAIRS** — where actors' names are arranged horizontally and vertically. In the example below, either "Actor A" or "Actor B" can have **FIRST BILLING**, depending on how you read the layout.

| ACTOR A | ACTOR B | ACTOR C |

**CREW** Convention and "deal memo" negotiations generally dictate which credits follow actors in the billing block, and the order in which they are listed — though **CASTING BY** ⑬ is commonly first. (Members of the Casting Society of America may add the post-nominal letters **CSA** ⑭.)

The credits **COSTUMES BY** ⑰, **EDITED BY** ⑱, and **PRODUCTION DESIGNER** ⑳ usually follow. (Members of the American Cinema Editors society use the post-nominal letters **ACE** ⑲.)

A wide range of other credits may be added to a billing block if they are especially significant — such as **MUSIC BY** ⑮, **ORIGINAL SCORE BY** ⑯, **STUNT COORDINATOR**, **SPECIAL EFFECTS**, **VISUAL EFFECTS**, &c. (In 1986, the poster for *Aliens* had **ALIEN EFFECTS CREATED BY** Stan Winston.)

Although many directors of photography (**D.P.**) prefer the title **CINEMATOGRAPHER**, the credit **DIRECTOR OF PHOTOGRAPHY** ㉑ was hard won in the days of the studio system, and it still predominates in billing blocks. The placement of the **D.P.** credit is individually negotiated, with an eye to being as close to the director as possible. (The members of the American Society of Cinematographers are entitled to include the post-nominal letters **ASC** ㉒.)

**PRODUCTION** Unlike writers and directors, producers have no collective-bargaining agreement with the major studios. Thus no rules govern the allocation, placement, or meaning of the various production credits in the billing block or elsewhere. (Hence the proliferation of "unearned" producer credits for managers, financiers, friends, and relatives.)

In 2004, the Producers Guild of America (P.G.A.) began a "truth in credits" campaign to ensure that the **PRODUCED BY** ㉖ credit was given to bona fide producers; a year later, the Academy of Motion Picture Arts and Sciences adopted the P.G.A.'s criteria to determine who should be eligible to collect a best-picture Oscar. (Eyebrows arched in 1999 when five producers stepped up to collect the Academy Award for *Shakespeare in Love*.)

Both organizations now limit to three the number of people who can share a **PRODUCED BY** credit, except in "rare and extraordinary circumstances."

In 2010, the P.G.A. launched a voluntary certification mark (the lowercase letters **p.g.a.** ㉗) to indicate that an individual performed a majority of the **PRODUCED BY** duties. Rob Reiner's 2012 film *The Magic of Belle Isle* was the first movie to feature this certification.

While there are no formal job descriptions for the various production titles, the P.G.A. offers these guidelines: **PRODUCED BY** ㉖ credits the initiation, coordination, supervision, and control of all aspects of the production process (creative, financial, technological, and administrative) from inception to completion — including the coordination of all other talents and crafts. **EXECUTIVE**

**PRODUCERS** ㉕ are those who have made a significant contribution to the movie, by securing no less than 25 percent of the financing and/or by developing the literary property (for example, by securing rights to the source material). **ASSOCIATE PRODUCERS** ㉓ perform any producer functions delegated by a producer. **CO-PRODUCERS** ㉔ are usually those with primary responsibility for the day-to-day logistics of the production process. Other heads of departments report to the **CO-PRODUCERS**, who in turn report to the holder of the **PRODUCED BY** credit.

## WRITING

Writers are usually credited just before the director in the billing block — though the number and complexity of writing credits varies considerably. For example, if a movie is based on existing material, credits might include **BASED ON CHARACTERS CREATED BY** ㉘, **FROM A PLAY BY**, **FROM A NOVEL BY**, &c.

The **STORY BY** ㉙ credit is used for any writing contribution distinct from the actual screenplay and consisting of "basic narrative, idea, theme, or outline indicating character development and action." The **SCREENPLAY BY** ㉜ credit is used for the final script, as represented on-screen, with individual scenes, full dialogue, and other material. (The credit **WRITTEN BY** is used when the same author has written both the story and the screenplay; it is not interchangeable with the **SCREENPLAY BY** credit.)

The W.G.A. limits the number of writers who can receive a credit. **WRITING TEAMS** are counted as a single writer, even though they can have two or three members. (Larger teams must be approved by the W.G.A.) The **STORY BY** credit is generally not shared by more than two writers (or six people, assuming two writing teams of three). The **SCREENPLAY BY** and **WRITTEN BY** credits are generally not shared by more than three writers (or nine people, assuming three writing teams each with three members).

Writers within teams are connected with ampersands (i.e., &) ㉚; individual writers are connected with the word **AND** ㉛. The most substantial contributor in each writing credit will usually be named first, although teams can decide how to order their names — and some swap the order with each movie.

## DIRECTION

The **DIRECTED BY** ㉝ credit comes at the end of the billing block. Although the D.G.A. has a policy of "one director to a picture," there are a number of scenarios in which the credit may be shared — for example, Jim Abrahams, David Zucker, and Jerry Zucker each received a director credit for *Airplane!* (1980).

The D.G.A. prohibits any other credit from using the words "director" or "direction" — with the exception of the historical titles **DIRECTOR OF PHOTOGRAPHY** and **ART DIRECTOR**.

When the same person is writer and director, the credits can either be combined (e.g., **WRITTEN AND DIRECTED BY**) or listed as two separate credits. But the **DIRECTED BY** element must appear just before the director's name as the final credit of the **BLOCK**.

## BUGS & RATING

A billing block can include a range of **BUGS** (the logos of distribution and production companies and technical partners), as well as details of a movie's website, social media, and release date.

The Motion Picture Association of America (M.P.A.A.) **RATING BLOCK** {see below} is generally incorporated into the billing block — though it can be placed anywhere on the poster provided that all of its elements (rating, definition, and reasons) are fully legible.

Once completed, the poster (and billing block) will be approved by a range of bodies, including the studio's legal department (to ensure compliance with contracts), the D.G.A., the W.G.A., and the M.P.A.A. ⊙

**PG-13** PARENTS STRONGLY CAUTIONED

SOME MATERIAL MAY BE INAPPROPRIATE FOR CHILDREN UNDER 13

SCENES OF WAR, BRIEF NUDITY, TOBACCO USAGE, AND POWDERED WIGS

# Sign Dining

*The 3-Michelin-starred New York City restaurant* **ELEVEN MADISON PARK** *uses discreet hand signals to communicate across its imposing Art Deco dining room — demonstrated below by the Director of Operations,* ***Andrew Chandler****.*

**PIN TOUCH**
Indicates to a colleague that they are needed.

**PLEASE REPEAT**
Requests the maître d' to restate the name of the party.

**I'VE GOT THIS**
Indicates that the signaler will be the one to explain the menu.

**TABLE NOT READY**

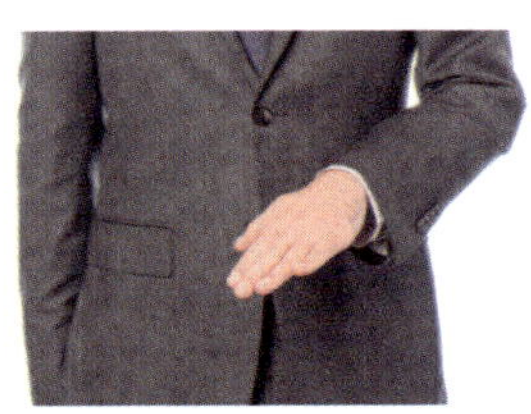

**STILL WATER**

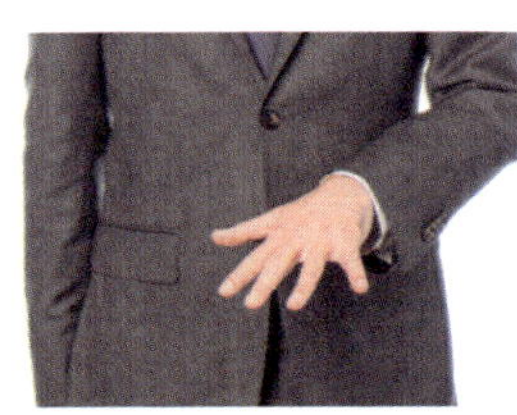

**SPARKLING WATER**

**CLEAR THIS PLACE**
Indicates from where a table should be cleared.

**LOCKED IN**
Signals you are occupied with an urgent task.

**STALL**
Informs a colleague that you need more time.

*The dining room of Eleven Madison Park, Manhattan*

**SEAT GUESTS IN LOUNGE**

**SEAT GUESTS IN BAR**

**A WALK-IN PARTY**

**MORE INFORMATION**
E.g., reservation name, or how many of a party are still to arrive.

**CONFIRM № IN PARTY**
The size of the party is indicated by the number of fingers, e.g., four.

Indicates that a **DINING ROOM TABLE IS SITTING IN BAR.**

E.M.P. also has "traffic" rules to regulate movement in the dining room. Staff **WALK CLOCKWISE** around the room, and must always **KEEP TO THE RIGHT**. At intersections, staff will **YIELD** to traffic in the following order: **GUESTS** or someone **LEADING A GUEST** have the right of way, followed by **HOT FOOD**, **COLD FOOD**, **EMPTY PLATES**, and, finally, **EMPTY-HANDED** colleagues.

# Heat in Hand Grails & Straight to Feet Kicks

**SNEAKERHEAD** *slang.*

## SNEAKERS

*A.k.a.*, **KICKS / CREPES**

**GRAIL** · A "Holy Grail" dream shoe; a shoe with an extremely limited release; and/or a shoe acquired only after considerable questing. ("*Rock a* ROTATION, *keep grails on the shelf.*")

**G.O.A.T.** · Greatest Of All Time · An iconic, O.G. shoe and/or a personal **GRAIL**.

(**HIGH**) **HEAT** · A personal favourite and/or a shoe that turns (sneaker)heads.

**HYPE SHOE** · One with pre-DROP buzz.

**HYPEBEAST** · A dedicated follower of fashion and/or a fashion victim who follows the herd. *A.k.a.*, **HYPESHEEP**.

**BEATERS** · Sneakers worn **DAILY** with no concern for their wear and tear.

(**SUPER**) **COZY** (**BOYS**) · Unashamedly comfortable kicks. ("*Feet sweaters.*")

**DAD SHOES** · Chunky-soled, mass-market, and blissfully comfy, e.g., New Balance 992.

## ROCKING & FLEXING

**W.D.Y.W.T.?** · What Do You Wear Today? · Online invitation to share what kicks you are **ROCKING**. *Similarly*, **W.O.Y.F.T.?** · What's On Your Feet Today?

**IN HAND** · How a shoe looks and feels when handled (as opposed to in a photo). ("*Man, these Sambas are fire in hand!*")

**BABYING** · Ensuring kicks remain FRESH for longer, e.g., by inserting protective **CREASE SHIELDS**, DUCK WALKING, &c.

**DUCK WALK** · A constipated, flat-footed gait, used to prevent CRISP kicks from creasing.

**STRAIGHT TO FEET** · Instantly wearing a newly acquired pair, rather than **BABYING**.

**ON ICE** · Waiting before wearing: to build anticipation; because of an inclement season; for a special occasion; or so they look CRISP after everyone else's are COOKED. ("*Hold 'em till you rock 'em!*") Some **ICED** shoes are *never* worn.

**ROTATION** · The selection of one's collection that gets worn: changes by season, mood, or fashion, and to delay wear / allow for drying. ("*Working this* L.P.U. *into my rotation.*")

**DRIP** · One's (sartorial) style and **SWAGGER**. ("*Cash is fleeting, drip is forever.*")

**FLEXING** · "Casually" showcasing your style, e.g., by rocking extremely HEAT sneakers.

**AIRPORT FLEX** · A trend of wearing (and 'gramming) your fiercest kicks when flying.

**SNEAKER WHEEL** · Posting pictures of your shoes in a (colour-coordinated) circle; a flex.

**FIT** · The outFIT you rock with your kicks. ("*Shoes, then fit.*") *A.k.a.*, **GARMS** (garments).

**PINROLLING** · Rolling up your trouser cuffs to showcase your KICKS.

**MISMATCHING** · Flexing with contrast, e.g., wearing a different model (or colourway) on each foot; tying different laces on each shoe; or wearing contrasting brands, e.g., Adidas shoes with Nike socks.

**ROCK, STOCK, BURN** · The sneakerhead equivalent of the game "Fuck, Marry, Kill." *Also*, **DRIP, FLIP, SKIP** · Wear, resell, SLEEP.



*Michael Jordan in Air Jordan 13* BREDS *at Game 2 of the 1998* N.B.A. *Finals* ☞

**LACE SWAP** · Adding swagger with new (and contrasting) laces.

**STEEZY** · Stylish + Easy.

**COKE WHITE** · Whiter-than-white; dazzling.

**L.P.U.** · Latest Pick Up · The most recent **COP**.

(**SUPER**) **CRISPY** / **CLEAN** / **FIRE** / **LIT** · All indications of approbation.

**BOMBPROOF** · Kicks that can handle heavy **ROTATION** and/or inclement weather.

**BURNING THROUGH** · Wearing shoes to the point that they are **COOKED** (i.e., destroyed).

## BUYING & RESELLING

**COP** · To buy, or acquire. *Hence*, **INSTACOP** / **MUST COP**. *Also*, **SNAG** / **SCOOP** / **GRAB**.

**W** / **L** · To Win or Lose when **COPPING**. ("*The rush when you score a W on such hyped shoes.*")

**S.E.** · Special Edition.

**D.E.** · Deluxe Edition · One made with especially luxurious materials.

**P.E.** · Player Exclusive · A shoe designed for an athlete; if it is also released for retail sale, it becomes a **PLAYER EDITION**.

**O.G.** · Original (Gangster) · The first release of a new shoe, or colourway.

**RETRO** · A **1:1** (i.e., faithful) **RETROSPECTIVE** release of an **O.G.** shoe, or colourway.

**REIMAGINED** · A **RETRO** release with a twist.

**PACK** · A set of shoes released as a series. E.g., the 2013 Air Max 90 Independence Day pack came in a **TONAL** trio of red, white, and blue.

(**B.**)**N.I.B.** · (Brand) New In Box.

**DEADSTOCK** (**D.S.**) · An unworn pair that is no longer in production. Does *not* include any that have been **TRIED ON** or **ONLY WORN INDOORS** (not that anyone can usually tell), which are (**V.**)**N.D.S.** · (Very) Near Deadstock.

**UNDSING** · Unboxing (and wearing) a **D.S.** pair (which might have been long **ON ICE**). ("*Undsing those* **BOXFRESH** *grails is a flex.*")

**N.W.T.** · New With Tags.

**N.O.S.** · New Old Stock · The (increasingly) rare discovery of **FIRE** sneakers languishing overlooked, say, in forgotten stockrooms.

**FACTORY LACING** · How shoes are laced when **N.I.B.**; an (unreliable) indicator of **D.S.**

(**SHOCK**) **DROP** · A (surprise) new release.

**QUICKSTRIKE** · An unannounced, limited-edition (Nike) release. *Also*, **HYPERSTRIKE** · An absurdly limited release, often just to …

**F. & F.** · A release limited to ~~**FRIENDS AND FAMILY**~~ influencers.

**TIER ZERO** / **T.Z.** · A retailer bestowed the privilege of limited-release Nike allocations.

**G.R.** · General Release · Mass-market shoes.

**RESTOCK** · When a sold-out shoe reappears.

**F.C.F.S.** · The (antiquated) retail tradition of First Come First Served, which necessitated a lengthy **CAMPOUT**, or the endless refreshing of websites, for **DROPS** that were sold **ONE PER CUSTOMER**. Many **HEAT** releases are now orchestrated via online **RAFFLES** that randomly grant applicants the chance to buy.

**BOTTING** · Using automated software agents to secure limited edition shoes in online sales. ("*Reseller bots are killing the game.*")

**RESALE** · From bootstrap beginnings in the 1980s, the sneaker resale market is now a global phenomenon, with sites like StockX, GOAT, and Grailed acting as stock exchanges.

Although reselling boomed during Covid's lockdowns, at the time of writing, the talk was of a market bust, caused by high inflation, consumer exhaustion, and the (cynical) over-saturation of new releases and endless colourways.

**BACKDOORING** · When retail staff covertly divert (part of) their store's limited-edition allocation to private resellers, who can then manipulate scarcity and price.

**SLEEPING** · Passing on a release. *Or*, being amazed that kicks you **COPPED** are **SITTING**. ("*Y'all sleeping on these!*") *A.k.a.*, **SNOOZING**.

**TEAM EARLY** · Who **COP** before the **DROP**.

**SITTING** · When a **G.R.** shoe gathers dust on the (virtual) shelf.

**DOUBLE UP** · Buying a second pair of shoes. ("*One to rock, and one to stock.*")

**FLIP FLOP** · When sneakerheads suddenly decide a **BURN** is actually a **MUST COP**.

**W.T.B. / W.T.T. / W.T.S.** · Online abbreviations for Want To Buy / Trade / Sell.

**COOK GROUPS** · Exclusive sneakerhead communities (on platforms like Discord and Slack) that share release and restock information, and work together to secure heat kicks.

**PLUG** · A **CONNECT**; one who scores highly prized, limited-edition kicks (for a price).

**BRICKS** · Shoes that don't (re)sell, even when listed **BELOW RETAIL**. *Or*, a disliked design.

**FLIPPING BRICKS** · Reselling run-of-the-mill (i.e., **UNHYPED**) shoes, purchased below retail price; a volume strategy.

**B-GRADE** · Shoes with manufacturing flaws.

**REPS** · Replica fakes, of mixed quality. While some assert "*real sneakerheads don't wear reps*," many take a "*you-do-you*" attitude to copping bargains, objecting only if reps are (re)sold as real. There exists a somewhat spurious informal grading quality for replicas:

**A.A.A.** → **SUPER PERFECT** →
**SUPERMAX PERFECT** →
**UNAUTHORIZED AUTHENTIC** (**U.A.**)
*supposedly made with original materials and in the same factory, but for some curious reason not authenticated by the brand*
→ **1:1** · *As close to authentic as possible*

**FUFU** · Fake; possibly derived from **FUGAZI**. *Also*, **FEEZY** · Fake Yeezy. Many resellers claim to **AUTHENTICATE** their stock, and sneakerheads use online communities (and apps like CheckCheck) to get a **LEGIT CHECK** (**L.C.**).

## MISCELLANEOUS

**COLLABS** · Much sneaker hype is driven by brand collaborations, with musicians (Travis Scott × Air Jordan 1); athletes (Steph Curry × Under Armour); designers (Salehe Bembury × New Balance); celebrities (Anna Wintour × Nike); beauty brands (Fenty × Puma); &c.

**COLOURWAY** · A shoe's colour scheme; some have specific nicknames, e.g., **WHEAT** · Chestnut brown; and **BRED** · Black and red.

In April 2023, the **BRED** Air Jordan 13s that Michael Jordan wore {📷} for Game 2 of the 1998 **N.B.A.** Finals sold at auction for $2.2m.

**TONAL** · A monotone (e.g., all red) colourway.

**SIZE RUN** · The sizes in which a shoe was manufactured. A **FULL SIZE RUN** (**F.S.R.**) usually means men's 6–12. ("*Cries in size 14.*")

**T.T.S.** · True To Size · As opposed to those that **RUN LARGE** *or* **SMALL**.

| | | | |
|---|---|---|---|
| **M** | Men *sizes* | **G.S.** | Grade school |
| **W** | Women | **P.S.** | Preschool |
| **U** | Unisex | **T.D.** | Toddler |

**BRICK SIZES** · Those on the periphery of the normal distribution curve that tend to **SIT**.

**SILHOUETTE** · A shoe's trademark shape.

**3M** · Reflective material stuck to shoes, originally to protect runners, now for decoration.

**DEUBRÉ** · Originally Nike's term for the decorative shoelace tag, now widely used. *A.k.a.*, **LACE LOCK** / **SNEAKER CHARM**.

**AGLETS** · Metal or plastic lace-tips.

**110** / **ONE-TENS** · British nickname for the Nike Air Max 95, which used to retail for £110.

**ICY SOLE** · One that is (semi) transparent.

**GLITTER** *or* **LEATHER BLOOM** / **SPEW** · When shoes are disfigured by fungus, bacteria, or crystallization from within the leather.

**WHEN YOU SEE THE FOAM, YOU'RE IN THE ZONE!** · A paean to shoe cleaning based on Miguel "The Shoe Doc" Solorio's slogan.⊙

Bounty
Since 1916
FAMOUS

# A Game of Crumbs

*In 8 minutes, a human can consume: 3 lb of haggis; 9.75 lb of Spam; 10 lb of spaghetti with red sauce; 10.5 lb of ramen noodles; 10.8 lb of key lime pie; 17.75 bagels with cream cheese; 87 glazed doughnuts; 91 Chinese dumplings; 126 3-inch tortilla tacos; 128 oz of mayonnaise; 141 hard-boiled eggs; 165 pierogies; 275 pickled jalapeño peppers; 338 pistachios; 390 shrimp wontons; and 564 oysters ...*

*... and this is merely a taste of the indigestible world of professional* **GURGITATORS.**

## CONTESTS

There are almost as many eating **CONTESTS** as there are foodstuffs (and sponsors) — from watermelon, phở, and matzo balls to lobster, chocolate, and cow brains.

Most contests fall into one of two categories: **FIRST TO FINISH** (e.g., 3:04 minutes for 50 hard-boiled eggs) or **EAT ALL YOU CAN** (e.g., 1.75 lb of butter in five minutes).

Additionally, there are **STEEPLECHASES**, like the DraftKings "Big Game Snackdown," which offers a **MEDLEY** of: 1 pepperoni pizza; 32 oz chilli; 25 blanketed pigs; 100 cheese balls; 32 oz 8-layer dip; 25 boneless wings; 12" sub; and 25 jalapeño poppers — all of which was eaten in 2021 in just 5:43 minutes.

The "Super Bowl of competitive eating" is **NATHAN'S FAMOUS INTERNATIONAL HOT DOG EATING CONTEST**, which has been held annually(ish) on New York's Coney Island every July 4th since the early 1970s. From humble origins, Nathan's has grown in popularity ... and gluttony: In 1972, Jason Schechter won by eating 14 hot dogs and buns (**H.D.B.**) in 3½ minutes; in 2021, Joey Chestnut won by eating 76 in 10.

Two events catapulted Nathan's into the mainstream. In 2001, Takeru Kobayashi ate 50 H.D.B. in 12 minutes, obliterating the previous record of 25⅛, and re-framing what was thought physically possible. And in 2003, E.S.P.N. began broadcasting the contest to an audience that regularly tops a million.

While **CHOMPETITIONS** strive (ironically?) to present themselves as sports (calling players athletes; awarding trophies and belts; deploying red and yellow cards) they are essentially an extension of the carnival side show, with barkers dressed in patriotic colours, sporting boaters, and egging on the crowd.

## CHALLENGES

Until relatively recently, food **CHALLENGES** were predominantly publicity gambits by local restaurants — open to all, and run on the basis of free-if-you-finish / pay-if-you-fail.

(For example, the Big Texan Restaurant in Amarillo boasts that only 10,413 of the 94,705 people who have tried to eat its 72 lb steak in under an hour have succeeded, i.e., 11%.)

Such tourist-trap tests shot to fame in 2008, when the Travel Channel began airing *Man vs Food*, in which Adam Richman traversed America to take on the most gut-busting tests, including San Francisco Creamery's "Kitchen Sink Challenge" — a vast 2-gallon sundae with "3 bananas, 8 regular size scoops of ice cream, 8 toppings, whipped cream, nuts, and cherries."

Everything changed with the mass adoption of social media and the astonishing popularity of **EATING INFLUENCERS**, who film themselves taking on restaurant challenges and devising feats of their own. E.g., Matt Stonie's 2019 attempt to eat 15 packs of Korean fire noodles has been seen on YouTube more than 148 million times. {☞ MUKBANG p.277}

**STUNT EATING** · Food feats as click bait, e.g.: **BLINDFOLD** eating; eating the **ENTIRE MENU**; **HANDS FREE EATING** (e.g., face-to-food consumption of pies) 📷; **MOUTHFUL CHALLENGES** (e.g., how many cupcakes can be crammed); mad physical excess ("*I tried to gain 20 POUNDS in ONE HOUR!*"); and **STUNT LOCATIONS** (e.g., eating your way out of a 60 sq. ft. popcorn sarcophagus).

**GALLON CHALLENGE** · Drinking a gallon of various liquids (lemonade, water, ice-tea, gravy) as quickly as possible. *Similarly*, **MILK CHUGGING** · Drinking a gallon of milk in under an hour without vomiting.

☞ *Joey Chestnut eats 76* H.D.B. *in 2021, to set a new Nathan's record*

**CALORIE CHALLENGE** · E.g., attempting to consume 100,000 calories in 100 hours.

**BUFFET DESTRUCTION** · When influencers film themselves "breaking the bank" of an "all you can eat" restaurant buffet, sometimes in the hope of being **SLOW PLATED**, **CUT OFF**, **KICKED OUT**, or **BANNED** so they can feign consternation for clicks.

**DOUBLING** · When influencers attempt to complete a challenge twice at the same sitting. (Easier if the second round is served fresh.)

**HOME CHALLENGES** · When influencers make, attempt, and film eating feats at home.

## HEAT

Eating absurdly hot food is a feature of many contests and challenges — probably because the outward suffering of participants is more entertaining than their internal (in)digestion.

This is the premise of the YouTube show *Hot Ones*, where celebrities are interviewed while attempting to eat ten chicken wings dipped in increasingly spicy sauces. The show both humanizes (i.e., humbles) celebrities and obtains revealing answers to probing questions while interviewees are physically distracted.

**CHILLI EATING** · Tests the ability to eat a quantity of one hot chilli type, or to sequentially ascend the Scoville Scale, e.g., *Bird's eye* → *Scotch bonnet* → *Naga viper* → *Carolina reaper*.

**HOT SAUCE** · Involves either **SWISHING** shots of hot sauce like mouthwash, or racing to **CHUG** entire (and multiple) bottles.

**HOT FOODS** · Eating either specialist red-hot snacks (chocolate, popcorn, jerky) or restaurant dishes (wings, pizza, ramen) coated in hot sauce or chillies.

Some Indian restaurants challenge customers to consume their version of **PHALL**, a British frankencurry, even hotter than vindaloo.

Spicy food events often enforce an **AFTER-BURN PERIOD**, where contestants who have finished eating must wait in pain for a set number of minutes before drinking anything, or washing their face and hands.

Some challenges penalize participants for every swig of water they take and/or prohibit (or require) the use of gloves.

## TRAINING

In addition to general **CARDIO** and **WEIGHT** training, competitive eaters (claim to) undergo any number of pre-event preparations, e.g.:

**STOMACH STRETCHING** · **MAXING OUT** belly capacity before an event, e.g., by **WATER LOADING** with gallons of $H_2O$ and/or eating large quantities (5–10 lb) of vegetables.

**JAW & NECK** · Masticating **CHEW BALLS** of gum and/or hanging heavy weights between gripped teeth to strengthen mouth and throat.

PRE-CHEWING *a* FRY BALL

HANDS-FREE *pie-eating at the 25th annual Goleta Lemon Festival, 2016*

**SUPPRESSION TRAINING** · Acclimatizing the body to overcome its instinctive defences, e.g., by tooth-brushing near the uvula to dampen the **GAG REFLEX**.

**MENTAL FOCUS** · Preparing the mind via meditation, breathing, pre-visualization, &c.

**STRATEGY** · Studying videos of record holders to glean the most effective techniques.

## TECHNIQUE

**TECHNIQUE FOODS** · Those that require dexterity to eat (e.g., pistachios, crawfish). *Conversely*, **CAPACITY FOODS**, which can be scarfed without too much finesse (e.g., eggs).

**DEBRIS FOODS** · Those that must be weighed before and after an event to calculate what has been consumed (e.g., corn, wings, ribs).

**PICNIC STYLE** · Requiring participants to eat the food as it's presented, i.e., without mashing, DUNKING, DECONSTRUCTING, &c.

**DUNKING** · Immersing bready foods (e.g., buns, pizza crust) in liquid to create a **MUSH**. Some competitions enforce a **NO DUNK RULE**, others limit dunking to five seconds.

**DECONSTRUCTING** · Disassembling a challenge to make it easier (or possible) to eat, e.g., separating dogs from buns, or **UNSTACKING** a monstrous, multi-patty hamburger tower.

**PRE-CHEWING** · Vigorously squeezing or tearing foods (e.g., deep-fried asparagus) before eating, to reduce **JAW STRAIN**. *Hence*, **FRY BALL** · A fist of crushed French fries. 📷

**LUBRICATION** · Wet and greasy foods are easier to swallow than those that are hard or congealed. (Hence pizza is simpler to scarf when hot.) In addition to (hot or room temperature) water, eaters may sip flavoured beverages to add a new taste. Of course, drinking excessively reduces the space left over for food.

**MULTI-TEXTURED** · Foods that combine consistencies (e.g., cake and icing).

**SEQUENCE** · The order in which challenges are eaten varies by competitor and event. E.g., faced with a stack of burgers, many will eat the proteinaceous patties before the carbohydrate baps — unless FLAVOUR FATIGUE inspires them to mix things up.

**HEADPHONES** · Some competitors use music to channel their focus from crowd to plate — **EATING TO THE BEAT**, or using specific songs to help keep to a **TIMING STRATEGY**.

**GLOVES** · A few eaters opt to wear gloves to ensure that greasy hands do not slow the pace. Some heat-based events ban gloves to maximize the pain, others require them for safety.

**POSTURE** · Most eaters prefer to stand while competing, though some may kneel to vary their posture.

**VALSALVA MANOEUVRE** · Pinching your nose and exhaling against a closed mouth (as if "popping" your ears); said to aid peristalsis. [1]

**PACE** · Whereas long-duration challenges call for a steady eating rhythm, speed contests usually require eating as much as you can, as fast as you can — before you hit **THE WALL**.

**KOBI SHAKE** · A trademark series of jumps and twists, popularized by Takeru Kobayashi, and used in the final stages of a contest, to ease the food's transit.

**CHIPMUNKING** · Packing your cheeks with as much food as possible, just before the bell. Permitted at many contests; most require contestants to swallow within, say, 30 seconds and **PRESENT AN EMPTY MOUTH**.

**FLAVOUR FATIGUE** · A common complaint, which competitors overcome by: sipping (or dunking foods into) flavoured beverages; adding (spicy) CONDIMENTS; or alternating between contrasting elements of a dish.

**CONDIMENTS** · Pros avoid adding sauces ("*Why eat more than you need?*"), though they can help mitigate **TEXTURE NAUSEA** or FLAVOUR FATIGUE, e.g., Tabasco-ing oysters.

**ICE** · To combat nausea toward the end of an event, some pack ice around their neck.

## FOODS

**HOT DOG & BUN (H.D.B.)** · Up until 2001, most competitors either ate each **H.D.B. PICNIC STYLE**, or dunked the bun while eating the dog. Takeru Kobayashi's record-smashing technique was to eat *two* dogs simultaneously, chased down by two well-dunked buns.

Known now as the **SOLOMON METHOD**, Kobayashi's simple innovation had an impact on hot-dog contests as revolutionary as Dick Fosbury's backwards "flop" which, after it won him gold at the 1968 Mexico City Summer Olympics, forever changed the high jump.

**PIZZA** · Some deploy the **REVERSE FOLD**, flipping each slice so top and bottom surfaces enter the mouth coated with lubricious cheese ⓞ. Others **ROLL THE TIP** of the pizza in the form of a mini-burrito.

**WINGS** · While **DRUMSTICKS** are best eaten with a horizontal **ROLL AND TWIST** chomp, **FLATS** *or* **PADDLES** can either be gripped at the base, inserted into the mouth, and **STRIPPED** out between the teeth, or pushed down against the plate to form a **MEAT UMBRELLA**. Since flats have meat:bone ratio of 0.66, and drums a ratio of 0.49, most will eat all of the paddles first, though some alternate.

**OYSTERS** · Usually served in dozens, either loose in cups, or the half-shell — where forks are required to avoid facial lacerations. Some consume their oysters **ONE BY ONE**, others deploy the **FOUR-IN-ONE** swallow.

**CORN ON THE COB** · Various methods are used, including: the boustrophedon (i.e., left-right-left) **MANUAL TYPEWRITER**; the downward **STRIPPER** against the bottom teeth; the upward **RAKE** against the top; or rapid **RABBIT** *or* **RACCOON NIBBLES**.

**ICE CREAM** · Competitors will often mush the scoops, or squeeze the carton, to help melt the challenge. To overcome sphenopalatine ganglioneuralgia (i.e., **BRAIN FREEZE**) some will invert their spoons (to keep the ice cream from the roof of the mouth), and/or drink warm water or hot coffee. [2] To prevent physical chills, eaters come prepared with extra layers.

## PHYSICAL CONSEQUENCES

**CATCHING A BURP** · Belching is both an inevitable consequence of speed eating and a useful way to free up space for more grub.

**THE ROMAN METHOD / REVERSAL OF FORTUNE / URGES CONTRARY TO SWALLOWING** · Vomiting mid-contest; usually a disqualifying act. ("*If you heave, you leave.*")

**PULLING THE TRIGGER** · The controversial practice of inducing vomiting after an event has finished, to **PURGE** excess (or spicy) food.

**CHOKING** · The most immediate and potentially lethal risk of eating too much, too fast.

According to press reports, there have been at least a dozen choking deaths associated with eating competitions, including a 37-year-old woman who, in 2023, died stuffing marshmallows into her mouth.

*The* REVERSE FOLD

**MEAT SWEATS** · When rapid overconsumption of meat (and cheese) leads to sudden and excessive perspiration. Science is oddly silent on the term, though it seems to be a form of "diet-induced thermogenesis."[3]

**HEAT** · In addition to headaches, diarrhoea, chest pain, nausea, and vomiting, chilli eating presents unique risks, such as: **HICCOUGHS**;[4] abdominal **CAPSAICIN CRAMPS**;[5] and the dermatological **HUNAN HAND SYNDROME** (*A.k.a.*, **CHILLI BURN**).[6]

The **AFTER EFFECTS** of spicy food (*A.k.a.*, **THE RING OF FIRE**) can be exacerbated by pre-existing anal fissures and haemorrhoids.[7]

**RUINING FOODS** · Professional eaters often report being (temporarily) repulsed by specific foods after a particularly noisome challenge or only eating certain foods at contests.

## MISCELLANEOUS

**CHEATING** · Rumours occasionally float of eaters using **MUSCLE RELAXANTS** to loosen their throats, or **CANNABIS** to induce the **MUNCHIES**. More prosaically, cheats will simply try to **DUMP** or **PALM** uneaten food.

Restaurants are sometimes accused of cheating on challenges e.g., by under-cooking food; over-serving by weight; and adding excessive condiments or unreasonably hot chillies.

**LEAVE NO DOUBT** · Completing a challenge with time to spare and no meat on the bones.

**PRIZES** · Whereas public contests offer media exposure and cold, hard cash, local restaurants incentivize challengers with **MERCH** (hats, T-shirts, &c.), **CERTIFICATES**, and **FREE** or **DISCOUNTED MEALS**.

**THE WALL (OF FAME)** · Where restaurants post victorious pictures of challenge winners. *Conversely*, **WALL OF SHAME** · Featuring failures with the food they could not finish.

**BELLY OF FAT THEORY** · The belief that overweight eaters are hampered by excess fat around the abdomen (i.e., a **BEER BELLY**).

Spectators are often surprised that professional eaters are so (comparatively) slim and athletic — erroneously confusing sporadic binging with quotidian excess.

**MESSY EATING** · Both an eyesore and, if it (deliberately) obscures the quantity of food consumed, a cause for disqualification.

**JUDGING** · The majority of pro contests come down to tiny differences in consumption, forcing judges to sift through **SLURRY** and **DEBRIS** before declaring a winner. As Crazy Legs Conti said: "If football is a game of inches, competitive eating is a game of crumbs."

**MEANWHILE IN AFRICA** · The oft-repeated criticism that competitive eating squanders food that might otherwise feed the starving.

[Many of the activities described above are at best foolish and at worse hazardous; do not attempt.] ⊙

# One, Two, Three: Let's Go, Bitch!

*Not since Beatlemania has a musical fandom erupted like that which engulfs* **TAYLOR SWIFT**. *Across the globe, legions of* **SWIFTIES** *obsess not just over her songs, but her every act and word. Whether Swift's music survives time's test remains to be seen. But, as a master-class in content creation, fan engagement, and viral marketing,* **SWIFTMANIA** *is a milestone for the ages.*

## AUNT BECKY

Born on 13.12.1989, in West Reading, P.A., U.S., Taylor Alison Swift's singer-songwriter career began in the world of country music, though her debut album, *Taylor Swift* (2006) enjoyed a pop crossover popularity that would set the trajectory for the stellar success to come.

Since then (and to date) T.S. has recorded ten further albums — *Fearless* (2008); *Speak Now* (2010); *Red* (2012); *1989* (2014); *Reputation* (2017); *Lover* (2019); *Folklore* (2020); *Evermore* (2020); *Midnights* (2022); and *The Tortured Poets Department* (2024) — which together contain 264 songs, 12 of which hit № 1 on the *Billboard* Hot 100 (59 made the Top 10).

T.S.'s statistics are striking: 14 Grammys; 40 A.M.A.S; 30 V.M.A.S; and 118 Guinness World Records, including the first and only artist in history to claim all top ten entries on the *Billboard* Hot 100 in a single week. Her global sales exceed 200m units; she has over 91 m monthly Spotify listeners; and her Eras Tour became the highest-grossing concert tour of all time. In a May 2023 poll, 53% of U.S. adults described themselves as fans of T.S.

**NICKNAMES** · Most of T.S.'s monikers need no decoding (**TAY** / **TAY-TAY** / **T. SWIZZLE** / **T-SWEEZY** / **BLONDIE** / **CAT LADY**), but a few are part of the EASTER EGG hunt.

E.g., the nickname **BECKY** derives from a random 2014 Tumblr post that joked that an old photo of T.S. was a girl called Becky who had died snorting marijuana. When a commenter said, "pretty sure that's Taylor Swift," the poster replied, "no, its becky." T.S. ran with the meme, wearing a "No, it's Becky" T-shirt, and calling herself **AUNT BECKY**.

The fan-applied nickname **MOTHER** dates to the underground queer ballroom scene of '60s New York, and has been associated with other successful independent women, including Rihanna, Jennifer Lopez, and Lady Gaga.

## MUSIC/BUSINESS

**T.V.** · A defining pivot in T.S.'s ascent came in 2019, when she failed to buy the masters of her first six albums from her original label, Big Machine Records. After the masters were sold to Scooter Braun (her "worst case scenario"), T.S. began re-recording these albums and releasing them as **TAYLOR'S VERSIONS**.

T.S.'s reclamation of her music is central to the "girl power" the Spice Girls could only sing about. Indeed, her re-recorded songs generally out-stream the original recordings — which some fans deride as **STOLEN VERSIONS**.

(The success of TAYLOR'S VERSIONS has prompted many record companies to tighten their contracts, preventing artists from re-recording their tracks for up to 30 years after they have left the label, or even in perpetuity.) [1]

**VAULT TRACKS** · Songs **FROM THE VAULT** that did not make it onto the original albums but are included on TAYLOR'S VERSIONS to offer both an insight into her creative journey and an incentive to (re-)purchase.

**VOICE MEMOS** · Brief audio notes that T.S. releases to contextualize her work and share contemporaneous moments of creativity.

**PEN-TYPE LYRICS** · Accepting the 2022 Songwriter-Artist of the Decade honour at the Nashville Songwriter Awards, Taylor revealed three "secretly, established genre categories": [2]

› **QUILL** · "If my lyrics sound like a letter written by Emily Dickinson's great grandmother while sewing a lace curtain." (E.g., "Ivy")
› **FOUNTAIN PEN** · "Confessions scribbled and sealed in an envelope, but too brutally honest to ever send." (E.g., "All Too Well")
› **GLITTER GEL PEN** · "Frivolous, carefree, bouncy, syncopated perfectly to the beat ... the drunk girl at the party who tells you that you look like an angel ..." (E.g., "Shake It Off")



*A young Swiftie outside Wembley Stadium for an Eras Tour concert, 2024* ☞

SHAKE IT OFF
SPARKS FLY
SWIFT
LOVE
LOVER
1989
HATE IT
KARMA
CLEAN
WHITE
13

**REAPPROPRIATION** · After being slammed as **QUEEN OF SNAKES** (following a 2016 "feud" with Kim Kardashian), T.S. responded with snake-themed references, designs, and merch. Similarly, her 2023 single "Slut!" was a confident reappropriation of being stigmatized as a "boy-crazy psychopath."

**PAYBACK** · That T.S. settles (romantic) scores in her work is all too evident in songs like "I Bet You Think About Me"; "The Smallest Man Who Ever Lived"; "Karma"; "Vigilante Shit"; "Better Than Revenge"; &c.

**VARIANTS** · Releasing multiple versions of a record (e.g., with bonus tracks or novel art) to a fanatical, **COMPLETIONIST** fanbase is not new, but T.S. takes it to extremes, e.g., with 36 variants of *The Tortured Poets Department*.

Critics claim such ecocidal excess exploits her fans, artificially juices sales, and "blocks" other (female) artists from topping the charts.

**SWIFTONOMICS** · The fiscal heft of **SWIFT INC.** is felt from local retailers (restaurants, tattoo parlours, bead shops, hotels) to nation states (the 20-city U.S. leg of the Eras Tour may have boosted the economy by >$5 bn). The leaders of Canada and Chile both implored T.S. to perform in their countries, and Singapore gave "certain incentives" to ensure Eras toured in no other Southeast Asian nations.

**SWIFTFLATION** · Price gouging relating to T.S. tickets, merch, &c. Seemingly part of the post-Covid **FUNFLATION** trend where (young) consumers eschew durable goods in favour of (TikTok-able) experiences.

## EASTER EGGS & CLOWNS

**EASTER EGGS** · For decades T.S. has teased and tantalized fans, detractors, and the media:

> The best messages are cryptic ones ... when you plan something that far in advance, you're kind of just flexing on planning. That's what an Easter egg really does. [3]

Such Easter eggs range from references hidden in liner notes and music videos to meaningful manicure colours and costume designs.

This gambit of clue-dropping (reminiscent of cults like QAnon) is central to T.S.'s complex connection with her most loyal fans, who react to the sophistication of her machinations with the online squeal: **HER MIND!!**

**CLOWNING / REACHING** · When **EASTER EGG** hunting stretches the credulity even of die-hard Swifties. (*"Call the circus, there's a clown on the loose!"*)

**TRISKAIDEKAPHILIA** · As Taylor explains:

> I was born on the 13th. I turned 13 on Friday the 13th. My first album went gold in 13 weeks. My first #1 song had a 13-second intro. Every time I've won an award I've been seated in either the 13th seat, the 13th row, the 13th section or row M, which is the 13th letter ... basically whenever a 13 comes up in my life, it's a good thing. [4]

As a consequence she, and legions of her concert-goers, regularly draw "13" on their hands.

Such **NUMEROLOGY** is also evident in **FAN THEORIES**, e.g., that T.S. strategically **DROPS** music (or announcements) every **112 DAYS**. After fans commented that the **FIFTH TRACK** on her albums seemed to be the most emotionally raw, T.S. ran with the ball:

> So because you noticed this, I kind of started to put the songs that were really honest, emotional, vulnerable, and personal as track five. [5]

**TAYLURKING** · T.S.'s habit of lurking on her fans' social media feeds, posting comments, likes, and direct messages.

**GAYLOR SWIFT** · A fan theory that debates Taylor's sexuality and searches for L.G.B.T.Q.+ codes in her music, interviews, clothes, &c. *Conversely*, **HETLORS** argue that **#GAYLOR** conjecture is disrespectful and dangerous.

Related is the phenomenon of **SHIPPING**, where fans speculate (or invent) relationships for their idol {☞ p.208}. Over the years Swifties have **SHIPPED** T.S. with a veritable armada of men and women.

(**DROPPED**) **HAIRPIN** · "Dropping hairpins" is an age-old gambit where L.G.B.T.Q.+ people hint at their sexuality to test the waters of tolerance and signal to an interlocutor that it is safe to follow suit. T.S. mentioning "hairpins" in two songs sends **GAYLORS** into a whirl.

*Swifties at Wembley Stadium make a* **HEART HANDS** *emoji that* T.S. *signs when she plays "Fearless"*

## FANS

**FRIENDSHIP BRACELETS** · Ever since T.S. mentioned them in her 2022 track "You're on Your Own, Kid," Swifties have been fervently making, wearing, and swapping letter-based friendship bracelets that reference T.S. albums, songs, and lyrics. Trading bracelets with new-found fan-friends is now a core component of T.S. concerts, parties, and TAYLOR-GATING.

**TAYLOR-GATING** · When ticketless Swifties gather *outside* stadia to hear the concert over the wall and join in the party.

In 2023, 20,000 fans met outside Philadelphia's Lincoln Financial Field — an additional ~30% of the venue's capacity.

**INITIALISMS** · To facilitate their Byzantine dissection of Taylor's oeuvre, Swifties use a profusion of song title initialisms, ranging from the simple — **C.P.** ("Champagne Problems") to the downright preposterous — **A.T.W.T.M.V.T.V.F.T.V.S.G.A.V.R.A.L.P.S.** ("All Too Well" [Ten Minutes Version] [Taylor's Version] [From The Vault] [Sad Girl Autumn Version] [Recorded At Long Pond Studio]).

**SLEEP STREAMING** · When fans set Spotify to play Swift songs all night (or 24/7) so that, at the end of the year, Spotify Wrapped declares them to be a "Top 0.001% listener."

**TAYVOODOO** · (Humorous?) fan theory that those who malign T.S. suffer instant karmic retribution. {☞ CURSE OF GNOME p.140}

**CONCERT RITUALS** · While many bands have a song or two that inspires a specific fan reaction during gigs, Swifties literally compile spreadsheets. E.g., during "You Belong With Me" they double clap *en masse*; during "Delicate" they yell *"One, two, three: Let's go, bitch!"* following a spontaneous mid-concert holler by a 15-year-old fan in 2018; and during "Marjorie" (written in memory of her grandmother) they illuminate their cellphone torches, or hold up photographs of the dead woman.

**GATEKEEPING** · A side-effect of neurotic fandom; when Swifties become jealous that *their* secret has been discovered by **BANDWAGON** fans, e.g., those who like "Shake It Off" but not obscure VAULT TRACKS.

**PARASOCIAL** · An artificial, unreciprocated intimacy that fans attach to celebrity. Coined in 1956 to explain, for example, the impact of Liberace, the term has exploded in popularity to describe the pathological need of some Swifties to connect with their heroin(e).[6] E.g., **STANS** (i.e., serious fans) of T.S.'s 2012–13 relationship with Harry Styles (still) refer to themselves as **CHILDREN OF DIVORCE**.

**POST-CONCERT AMNESIA** · Some Swifties attending 3+ hour Eras Tour concerts reported an inability to remember parts of the show.

This is the 21st-century iteration of **PARIS STENDHAL,** *and* **JERUSALEM SYNDROME,** where sensitive neophytes become physically overwhelmed by the beauty and magnificence of culture, art, or religion, respectively.

# Agit-Prop Z–A

*The alphabet's unexpected role in radical protest and realpolitik.*

Z · President Vladimir Putin's February 2022 invasion of Ukraine found an unlikely symbolic straw man in the shape of the letter Z — which was daubed on Russian tanks, trucks, and armoured vehicles as they shattered Europe's peace.

Despite various claims that this symbol was an initialism of *Za pobedy* [for victory], *Zapad* [west], *Zhopa* [ass], or even Ukrainian President Volodymyr Zelenskyy, it seems likely the letter was an arbitrary identifier to prevent friendly fire, since Cyrillic has no letter Z.

Given that the Russian Ministry of Defence Instagram account only began dropping dark Z-themed memes on 2 March, a week after the assault began, it looked like the Kremlin was rushing to retcon Z into a propaganda campaign.

X · Widely attributed to the British street artist ESP, the Extinction Symbol transforms the letter X into an hourglass (to signify time running out) that is set within a circle (to symbolize the globe).

Devised in ~2011, the symbol began gaining notoriety in 2018, when it was adopted by the environmental group Extinction Rebellion, whose direct actions and mass arrests have made ESP's design the most widely recognized icon of "climate emergency" politics.

V · Perhaps the most universally known agit-prop letter is the **V FOR VICTORY** [*Victoire* in French and *Vrijheid* in Flemish], which was suggested by the Belgian politician Victor de Laveleye in a 1941 radio broadcast:

> Let the occupier, by seeing this sign, always the same, infinitely repeated, understand that he is surrounded, encircled by an immense crowd of citizens eagerly awaiting his first moment of weakness, watching for his first failure. [1]

Almost immediately, Vs sprang up across Europe: printed on posters, chalked on walls, beamed by searchlights, snapped from matchsticks, and propagated sonically via the letter's ···— Morse Code which, fortuitously, echoed the rousing opening notes of Beethoven's Fifth Symphony in C Minor.

Of course, it was Churchill's fondness for the *gestural* V that gave the letter its imprimatur of authority, and countered — in a rock-paper-scissors way — the "Hitler Salute," especially as Winston delighted in rotating his hand to signal a far more vulgar meaning.

☜ *A C.N.D. banner at an anti–Gulf War demonstration in Trafalgar Square, London, 1991*

QAnon is an ultra-right American conspiracy that posits a "deep state" cabal of pederastic and cannibalistic Satanists. Mad as it is, the cult has destroyed families and friendships, and a January 2021 YouGov poll showed that 30% of American Republicans and 12% of independents who had heard of QAnon held a favourable opinion of it.

Significantly, QAnon is not a blunt-force "big lie" like the "false flags" of domestic terror or the "crisis actors" of school shootings. Nor is it a tin-foil "chemtrail" conspiracy like "the Moon landing was faked" or "Elvis lives." Instead, QAnon acolytes follow an infinitely unwinding "breadcrumb" trail "dropped" by a "shadowy insider" identified only as Q.

As Walter Kirn wrote in *Harper's Magazine*:

> Q is part fabulist, part fortune-teller, holding up a computer-screen-shaped mirror to our golden age of fraudulence. He composes in inklings, hunches, and wild guesses, aware that our hunger for order grows more acute the longer it goes unsatisfied. [2]

This hunger is precisely what makes Q's convoluted memes, myths, numerology, and synchronicity so pernicious. QAnon warps the dopamine pleasure pulse of Easter egg hunts

into a gibberish grail quest where obvious drivel {COVFEFE p.250} is imbued with (faux-)serious significance.

Although QAnon shows signs of fading, the lure of conspiratorial Easter eggs is likely to endure, further to poison the well of rational debate. As Jared Holt told *Vox* in 2021:

> Even if Q posts and Trump gradually take a backseat role in the movement, many of the tagalong theories — on topics including 5G, vaccines, and alternative medicine — will produce significant risks to the public. [3]

It's no accident that Russian disinformation tactics {p.122} rapidly evolved from creating novel topics of dissent to amplifying existing domestic divisions — seamlessly switching its target from pro-Trump to anti-vax, and back.

CND · The world's most famous peace sign was devised in 1958 for the Campaign for Nuclear Disarmament by the graphic designer Gerald Holtom — a devout Christian and passionate pacifist.

Rejecting the traditional (and historically problematic) symbolism of the Christian cross and the pacific dove, Holtom drew from two inspirations. The first was artistic:

> I was in despair. Deep despair. I drew myself: the representative of an individual in despair, with hands palm outstretched outward and downward in the manner of Goya's peasant before the firing squad in his painting, *The Third of May 1808*. I formalized the drawing into a line and put a circle around it ... It was ridiculous at first and such a puny thing. [4]

The second was typographical: Holtom decided to represent the initials of Nuclear and Disarmament with the British navy's semaphore signs for N and D:

N D CND

The symbol received its first mass outing on the lead banner of the 1958 four-day C.N.D. march from London to the Atomic Weapons Establishment at Aldermaston, Berkshire. From that protest on, Holtom's deceptively complex design began to represent not just nuclear disarmament but an end to all war.

*View of the entrance to the main camp of Auschwitz (Auschwitz I), 1945*

B · Above the main gate of the Auschwitz I concentration and extermination camp is a 16-foot wrought-iron sign that declares *Arbeit Macht Frei* [work sets you free] — a diabolically sadistic slogan seemingly bastardized from the Bible: "And ye shall know the truth, and the truth shall make you free" (John 8:32).

The sign was forged from water pipes by prisoners in the camp's "locksmith's workshop," and its letters were designed by the master blacksmith Jan Liwacz — a Polish political prisoner (inmate № 1,010) who had been arrested in 1939 for burning an effigy of Hitler.

A closer inspection of the sign suggests that Liwacz's defiance may not have been quashed by incarceration: the B in *Arbeit* appears to be inverted, so that the heavier, lower bowl is uppermost. There is debate as to whether this inversion was deliberate, accidental, or even

stylistic (given the shape of the preceding R, and the typography of the period).

No matter: Over time, the "upside-down B" has become an icon of creative defiance in the face of cruel injustice. In 2010, the International Auschwitz Committee began awarding a reproduction of the letter "to personalities who act in the spirit of the Auschwitz survivors' key concept: Never again!" [5]

A · The "encircled A" of the anarchist movement is often linked to the French philosopher Pierre-Joseph Proudhon who, in 1840, wrote: "As man seeks justice in equality, so society seeks order in anarchy." In this way, the A of anarchy is said to interact with the O of order to form a new, defining unity.

However, the symbol likely dates back no further than 1964, when it appeared on the cover of a "bulletin" issued by the anarchist activists *Parisian Groupe Jeunes Libertaires*. Months later, the symbol was adopted and adapted by the theorist Tomás Ibáñez and the designer René Darras, who used it in an article for the newspaper *Action Libertaire*. [6]

The power of the now globally recognized symbol lies in the ease of its reproduction (as graffiti) and the dynamism of its message — especially when the A bursts aggressively out of its containing circle. ⊙

# Stacking Aces in the Court of King George

*Nothing on the floor of a* **LAS VEGAS CASINO** *happens by chance. Every action and word has been choreographed to maximize two key factors:* **SECURITY** *— to safeguard staff and patrons and minimize loss — and* **SPEED** *— because the House always wins ... eventually.*

The traditional hierarchy of a Las Vegas casino gaming floor is as follows:

**C.E.O.**

**VICE PRESIDENT**

**CHIEF GAMING OFFICER**
*Oversees table games and slot machines*

**CASINO MANAGER**
*The director of table games*

**SHIFT MANAGER**

**PIT MANAGER**
*Manages a number of* PITS *(gaming areas), each of which include a number of* SECTIONS

**FLOOR SUPERVISOR**
*Manages a* **SECTION**, *which varies by the complexity of the games included — e.g., four blackjack tables; one craps table; or two roulette wheels and one blackjack table*

**DEALER**

Dealers work in a four-person **STRING** (cards and roulette) or **CREW** (craps) — with three dealing at any given time, and one **RELIEF** rotating between them every 20 minutes.

A new dealer signals she is ready to take over by **TAPPING OUT** her colleague on the left shoulder (*A.k.a.*, **PUSHING IN**). This allows the active dealer to complete all the remaining transactions in a game before **CLAPPING OUT**, i.e., demonstrating their empty hands to players, managers, and security. (Dealers are similarly expected to **CLEAR THEIR HANDS** before touching their body, covering their mouths, reaching into their pockets, or placing their hands behind their backs.)

The outgoing dealer then introduces his or her replacement, and may pass on intelligence about the state of tipping, either with an aside ("*Look out for* GEORGE *... Sorry, Bill at* FIRST BASE") or, less subtly, by spreading the cards not into an arc, but an S-shape — for **STIFF**.

A range of signals is used by dealers to alert colleagues that **HEAT** / **BRASS** (senior management) is on the floor, e.g., tapping the craps stick on the ledge of the table.

Dealers instinctively assess the calibre of every player — sometimes by how they are dressed, but more often by how they play. A dealer will instantly **CLOCK** those exhibiting **GAME KNOWLEDGE** or **STRATEGIC PLAY**.

Dealers can invariably spot off-duty dealers (and other pros) by certain (unconscious) **TELLS**, e.g., encouraging other players to tip; RIFFLING or DROP-CUTTING chips; and, in poker, PITCHING their hand into the **MUCK** of discarded cards when they fold.

Dealers are instructed to **TALK THE GAME** — verbalizing the action for the benefit of players and supervisors, as well as their own concentration.

A call of **CASH CHANGE**, for example, will alert the pit bosses that money is being exchanged for CHECKS; and **COLOUR UP** or **COLOUR DOWN** that CHECKS are being exchanged for larger or smaller denominations.

If asked for advice, dealers are cautioned only to quote what **THE BOOK** advises (e.g., "*Always split eights at blackjack*").

**HUSTLING THE TOKE** / **BUZZING** / **STRONG-ARMING** · Attempting to persuade players to tip. **SOFT HUSTLES** include paying out a winner with low-denomination CHECKS to encourage a gratuity; a **HARD HUSTLE** is when a dealer says, *"Hey, that check would look great as a dealer bet!"*

Blatant **TOKE HUSTLING** is prohibited by management and frowned upon by most dealers (who pool their tips) as unprofessional and generally counter-productive.

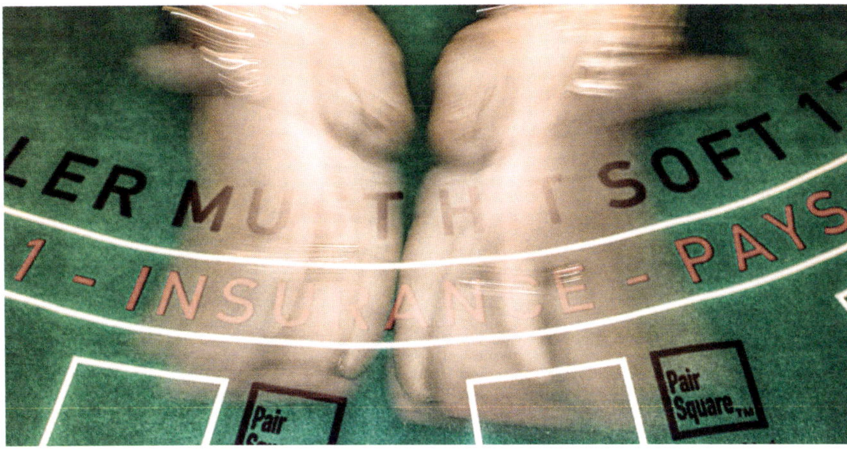


CLAPPING OUT

**DEAD GAME** / **DEAD SPREAD** · An **OPEN TABLE** with no players. Dealers are told to stand at dead tables, the cards arced in front of them, with their hands either side, and a welcoming look on their face. Those hoping for a quiet shift avoid making eye contact with passing customers to discourage any action.

**CROSSFIRE** · When dealers chat with colleagues at nearby tables; disliked by management, especially when in a foreign language.

**BREAK-IN HOUSES** · Casinos that hire and train **BREAKER** (i.e., inexperienced) **DEALERS**, often straight from **DEALER SCHOOL**.

## PLAYERS

**GEORGE** · The most admired player in any casino: a good tipper. *Hence*, **KING GEORGE**, **TRIPLE GEORGE**, and **JORGE**. Some managers dislike generous Georges, reckoning that a $5,000 dealer tip is **DEAD MONEY** that might otherwise be gambled (and lost).

**STIFF** · A reluctant or non-tipper; the kind of player who brings his own food and drink to avoid tipping the waitstaff. Stiffs will tip a buck and then say **CHOP** to get 50¢ back. *A.k.a.*, **TOM** · Tight Old Man.

**DONK** · An unskilled player.

**CHAMELEON** · A **DONK** who mimics the playing or betting patterns of nearby winners.

**FLEA** · Annoying, ill-mannered, tight-fisted. ("*Watch out, that table's got fleas.*")

**VULTURE** · One who prowls the floor looking for dropped money or un-cashed vouchers.

**STEAMER** · A (reckless) player for whom speed is the motivation, win or lose.

**FISH** · A fool. In poker, one exploited by other players; in craps, a clumsy **RAIL-HOGGER**.

**TAKE THE HOOK** · When a player **CHASES** wins (or losses) and can be **REELED IN** by an experienced dealer.

**ROCKS** · Poker players who bet only when they have **THE NUTS** (i.e., the strongest hand).

**FACCE** [Italian] · *Faces* in need of a slap.

(**ON**) **TILT** · A (poker) player gambling recklessly, usually to recover from a losing streak; a player who has his **NOSE OPEN**.

**ACORN** · A newbie; one who can be taught and moulded, e.g., by a good dealer.

**GRINDER** · One who sits at the same table for hour upon hour, staking paltry sums, rarely changing betting patterns, and neglecting to **TOKE** the dealers. *Hence*, **GRIND JOINT** · A casino with low-limit games.

**SCARED MONEY** · Money players can't afford to lose. ("*Scared money don't make money!*")

## CARDS, SHUFFLES, & DEALS

Most dealers will be fluent in the **CORE** card games, such as blackjack (**SNAPPER; 21; B.J.**) or baccarat (**BAC**), as well as a range of **SPIN-OFF, NOVELTY**, or **CARNIVAL GAMES** (e.g., Big Six, Let It Ride, Three Card Poker, &c.).

Although the basic techniques of shuffling, dealing, and CHECK-handling remain consistent, shuffles vary by casino and between games; the challenge for the House is to ensure **GAME PROTECTION** while maximizing the number of deals (or spins) per hour. The faster the **GAME PACE**, the more the House wins.

A (somewhat elaborate) shuffle might be:

WASH → RIFFLE → RIFFLE → STRIP
→ RIFFLE → BOX → CUT → BURN

**WASH / SCRAMBLE** · Randomly mixing the cards face down on the layout.

**RIFFLE** · Bisecting and interleaving a deck.

**STRIP** · A series of cuts (usually three to seven) stacked one on top of another.

**BOX** · Placing the bottom third of a deck on the top, sometimes with a 180° rotation.

**BURN** · Discarding the top card.

**PITCHING** · Dealing **FROM THE HAND**, rather than from a (multi-deck) **SHOE**.

**SHORT PITCH** · A card that doesn't make it across the **FELT** to the player.

**CARD DOWN** · Any card dealt off the table.

**HELICOPTERING** · Pitching the cards high above the table, risking **EXPOSURE**.

**FLASHED** · A card whose value has been (accidentally) **EXPOSED**.

**BOXED** · A card accidentally face-up in a deck.

**STUB** · Whatever the dealer is left holding after the first hand has been dealt.

**LAYING BRICKS** · The brutally repetitive nature of dealing blackjack.

## ROULETTE

Roulette dealers **PICK** and **FLICK** the **PILL** in various ways, e.g., **SNAPPING** it between their fingers, or **WHIPPING** it round the wheel.

Casinos require dealers to vary their actions to prevent players **CLOCKING / TRACKING** patterns, and to counter claims of **SECTION SHOOTING**: the theory that dealers can cause the pill to land in specific areas of the wheel.

(**WHEEL WATCHERS** believe that certain dealers have a **SIGNATURE** method of flicking the pill that can be tracked.)

The ball must make at least **THREE REVOLUTIONS**, but since many won't bet until it is in motion, dealers often **SLING THE PILL** with vigour to allow more time for chips to be placed. (That said, more spins means more profit, and dealers are under pressure to keep the game moving.) Personable dealers will add some character to the game with a gentle flow of (tip) encouraging badinage: "*Place 'em, don't waste 'em ... Congratulations in advance!*"

Dealers signal the end of betting by **WAVING OFF THE TABLE** (i.e., sweeping an arm across the layout), and declaring "**NO MORE BETS**."

Once the ball has **DROPPED**, its number is marked on the layout with a **DOLLY** (*or* **CROWN**), and the losing chips are **PULLED** or **SWEPT** away to **ISOLATE** the winning bets, which are then **PAID OUT**.

Some dealers learn **PICTURE BETS** to help them calculate odds at speed. For example, the bet below (two **CORNERS**, one **STRAIGHT UP**) is called the **MICKEY MOUSE**; it pays 51.

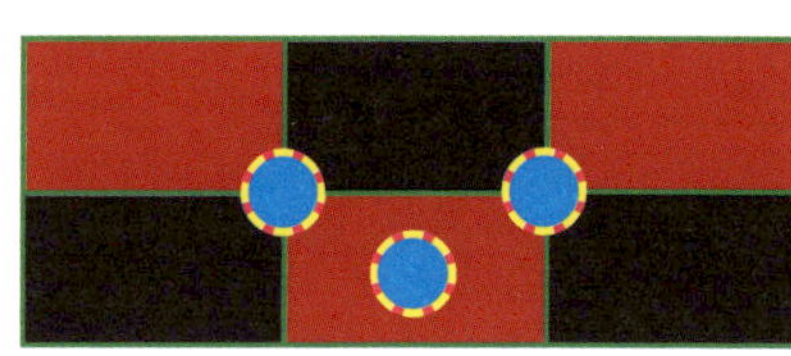

And this combination of **STRAIGHT UP**, four **CORNERS**, and four **SPLITS** is called the **PICTURE FRAME**; it pays 135.

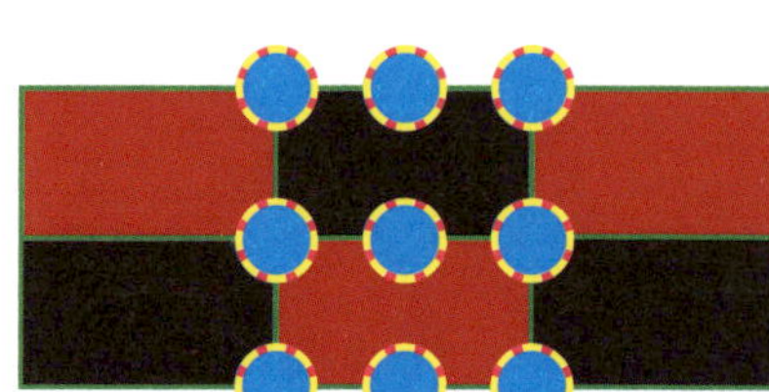

## CRAPS

The four-man **CRAPS** (*or* **DICE**) **CREW** comprises a **STICKMAN**, two **BASE DEALERS** (who place and supervise bets), and a rotating **RELIEF**. They are supervised by a **BOXMAN** who sits opposite the stick man, in front of the **CHIP RACK**. The stickman's jobs are:

› Check the dice after each throw
› Return the dice to the shooter with the **STICK** (**MOP** / **WHIP** / **POLE**)
› Hustle up action by **SELLING PROPS** (i.e., encouraging and placing high-risk **PROPOSITION BETS** in the centre of the layout)
› **CALL** the rolls as they land

Rolls are called loudly to announce the total and how it was made (i.e., **EASY** or **HARD**), and to help dealers **PAY OUT** accurately. They are designed to eliminate ambiguity, e.g.: "*Five, five, no-field five*" ensures the roll is not confused with "*Centre field nine*"; and "*Yo*" or "*Yo-leveen*" is called when the total is 11, to avoid any confusion with the dreaded seven.

Many stickmen take pride in amusing or risqué **BARK-UP CALLS** which are designed to keep the game entertaining, attract passing players, and encourage **TOKES**: "*Ten, hard ten ... girl's best friend!*"

## WAITRESSES

By charming guests and sustaining the flow of **COMPED** alcohol, the mainly female cocktail waitstaff is vital to a casino's ecosystem. At the start of each shift, waitresses will swap intel on players ("*Handsy George on table 2*"), before setting out on their **ROUNDS**.

Once collected, orders are filled at backstage **SERVICE BARS**. Here waitresses prepare their own glasses, ice, and garnishes ready for the barmen, before **CALLING** the drinks in a set order, e.g., beers, followed by mixed drinks and shots (in order: vodkas, gins, whiskeys, &c.), and then wine, soda, and juices. (Smart waitresses **TIP OUT** the barmen to ensure faster service and more generous pours.) Standard orders are dispensed via guns or machines, which have key codes for different drinks and brands of liquor. 📷 (House liquor is served unless a premium brand is requested.)

Because waitresses keep their own tips (unlike most dealers), getting the busiest shifts in

*A drinks gun preloaded with spirits and cocktails*

the best sections is crucial: Working **GRAVEYARD** in penny slots can be financially disastrous, whereas the craps pit on Super Bowl weekend makes it near certain to **MAKE BANK**.

Shifts and sections are allocated by seniority based on longevity; at the top of the ladder are **DAY ONE** waitresses, who joined when a casino opened. (This explains the popularity of joining new establishments.)

Slots players usually tip cash or vouchers; table players usually tip **CHECKS**. Some waitresses linger at a table to develop a rapport with players, others are "*all business*," figuring "*you're just dropping off a drink*." But you're crazy if you don't think waitresses are comparing the colour of your stack with the tip you drop.

If a shift has been profitable, waitresses say they **MADE BANK**; if especially good, they **MADE YELLOW** (i.e., $1,000), or even "*Get the milk ready! I got a* **CHOCOLATE CHIP**" (i.e., $5,000). **GEORGES** are sometimes referred to by the value of their toke ("*Mr. Black on table 3*"). Collegiate dealers will often encourage **STIFFS** and **TOMS** to pony up: "*Hey, now! Don't forget your waitresses!*"

Given the stereotypes about waitresses (and the uniforms they are obliged to wear) many consider gentle flirtation to be part of the job. But dealers, supervisors, and security are all alert to when "banter" becomes abusive. Some single waitresses wear engagement or wedding rings to keep pests at bay; some married waitresses work ring-less to inspire hope. That said, waitresses will be sure to acknowledge (and compliment) the female in a couple, knowing that she is often the key to a good (or bad) tip.

19-36

2to1
26
23
24
18
16
25
19
20
26
27

## CHECKS, CHIPS, & CASH

Although many use **CHECK** and **CHIP** interchangeably, there is a difference. **CHECKS** have a fixed monetary value and are all colour-coded (though colours can vary by casino):

| $ | COLOUR | NICKNAME |
|---|---|---|
| 1 | *white* | **BIRD DROPPING / WHITE** |
| 2 | *yellow* | **YELLOW** |
| 2.50 | *pink* | **PINK** |
| 5 | *red* | **NICKEL / RED** |
| 25 | *green* | **QUARTER / MINT** |
| 100 | *black* | **BUCK / BLACK** |
| 500 | *purple* | **PURPLE** |
| 1k | *yellow/orange* | **PUMPKIN / BANANA** |
| 5k | *brown/grey* | **CHOCOLATE** |

**CHIPS** — commonly used in roulette — have no set value until a player **BUYS IN** and denominates them according to their bankroll. (Some players request colours they consider lucky.) When players buy in, they place their bills on the felt and the dealer sorts them by denomination before **BREAKING THEM DOWN** in a pattern visible to the **CAMERAS**.

The largest-denomination bills are placed nearest the wheel (roulette) or the shoe (cards) to prevent them being snatched. Then the number of chips or checks is manually **PROVED** to the player (and to the EYE IN THE SKY), before being **PUSHED** (**SENT / PASSED**) across the table with the dealer's outside hand (in roulette, the hand farthest from the wheel).

Standard **TWENTY STACKS** are PUSHED across the table toward the player using the established formations illustrated below.

With table games, the House's checks are stored in a **RACK** (**BANK / TRAY / WELL**) in front of the dealer, and are arranged by colour in the various **TUBES**. (Larger denominations are stored on the inside of the rack, for added protection.) Dealers use various techniques to remove checks from the rack, such as **PLUCKING / PICKING** · Taking chips one at a time, at speed.

**SHORT STACK** · Any stack of chips under 20, but still in a House-approved format.

**DIRTY STACK / BARBER'S POLE** · A stack of different-value checks.

**CUTTING** · Separating checks from a stack, or dividing a stack into smaller units.

**SPLASHING / SPREADING** · **WIPING** (sliding) a stack of checks (usually four or five) into a line along the layout to **PROVE** (demonstrate) the number to the player, and security.

**DROP CUT** · Skilfully releasing a set number of checks from the bottom of a stack by feel.

**SKIPPING** · A DROP CUTTING technique that results in a neat, tight stack.

**STAMPING OUT** · Rapidly and accurately laying out bets and paying winners.

**COLOUR FOR COLOUR** · Paying a winning bet by matching the checks a player staked. *Also,* **CONVERTING** · Paying a winner with a larger-value check and taking change (in order to make the winnings more manageable).

**DIRTY MONEY** · Checks collected from a losing bet. Some think it bad luck (and bad manners) to pay winners with dirty money — and many casinos think it bad game security.

**CLEAN MONEY** · Checks taken directly from the dealer's tray. (The act of putting DIRTY MONEY into a tray magically cleanses it.)

## STACK-PUSHING FORMATIONS & NICKNAMES

→ *pushed toward player*

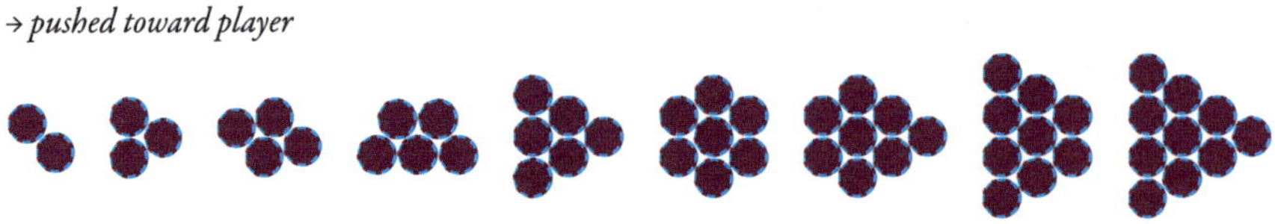

**2** **3** **DIAMOND** **5** **6** **FLOWER** **XMAS TREE** **9** **PYRAMID**

*$86,360 of* CHECKS *secured in a locked* RACK *before the opening night of The Fontainebleau*

**COLOUR UP** · Exchanging low-denomination checks for fewer checks of a higher value. *Conversely,* **CHECK CHANGE.**

**MUCKING / CHIPPING (UP)** · Gathering chips from the layout into stacks of 20: a test of skill and speed examined when auditioning as a dealer. Mucking can be assisted by a colleague (**MUCKER**) or **CHIPPING MACHINE.**

**TIGHTENING THE POT** · Rearranging a pile of chips (in poker) for neatness, security, or so they can be easily PUSHED.

**HAND TO HAND** · Passing chips, cash, or anything else by hand without placing it first on the layout; a breach of game protection.

**TAPPING TOKES** · When the dealer knocks a check they've been tipped against a hard surface before dropping it into the **TOKE BOX.** This notifies supervisors and security of a gratuity, and soft-hustles others to **ZUKE** (tip).

**TOKE COMMITTEE** · An elected group of dealers who collect the tips each shift/day, and complete the paperwork to distribute the money according to any local regulations.

## PROPS & SHILLS

**PROPOSITION PLAYER** · A person paid a fixed sum by a casino to participate in a card game. **PROPS** use their own money, keeping any winnings and absorbing all losses.

**SHILL** · An employee paid and financed by a casino to initiate and/or maintain a sufficient number of players in a card game.

Nevada places various restrictions on the use of such **STOOGES.** E.g., no more than four shills and prop players may play in any card game; shills may not collude to disadvantage real players; and shills and proposition players must be identified by management on request.

## SLOTS

Although less glamorous than table games, slot machines are a Vegas cash cow, generating 70% of all gaming revenue across Nevada. In 2023, slots brought in $10.5 billion — a rate of $258.26 per casino room per day (when the average daily room rate was $203.73).[1]

Slots are a star attraction at some casinos — not least El Cortez, which has 237 traditional coin-operated machines and one of the last remaining **HARD COUNT** rooms in Vegas to handle all of the change.

Players develop affections for specific machines ("*You can move 'em, but they will find 'em*"), which can make decommissioning certain games problematic.

**VOLATILITY** · The risk/reward ratio. High-volatility slots make infrequent payouts of larger sums, low-volatility slots the opposite.

**TASTE** · Small wins that keep players playing (*A.k.a.*, **INTERMITTENT REWARD**).

**TILT** · Traditionally an attempt to joggle or tip a machine which triggered a **TILT ALARM**; now, an indication that a machine has been tampered with; is out of paper; or has a fault.

**CANDLE** · The light atop a machine that illuminates when a jackpot is won; an error has occurred; a player needs assistance; or a **HAND-PAY** is required.

**HAND-PAY** · To pay a player at the machine (or cage), when the winning sum exceeds the limit of the game's automatic pay dispensers.

**ATTRACT MODE / BEG CYCLE** · A sequence of sounds and lights deployed by vacant machines to beguile passing trade.

**ROLL-UP** · An **ATTRACT MODE** that aggressively broadcasts a jackpot win.

**APPOINTMENT GAMES** · Games that draw players into a casino, currently Buffalo and Dragon Link. Casinos hoping to attract the slots crowd will install dozens of such games.

**HOLD** · The percentage of bets kept by the House. Holds can be **LOOSE** (marginally more advantageous to the player) or **TIGHT** (further favouring the House).

**BONUS VULTURES / FLEAS** · Ne'er-do-wells who intimidate (older) players into abandoning a game just before it is due to pay a bonus. Casinos are conscious of the **FLEA FACTOR** when deciding which new games to purchase.

Coin slots are susceptible to a range of cheating techniques, including the **MONKEY PAW** (a metal hook designed to fake a coin) and **SHAVED TOKENS** or **SLUGS**, which register a credit, but fall through the machine. (Experienced slot workers instantly recognize a slug's discordant clang as it falls through a machine.)

## CHEATING, SECURITY, & ADVANTAGE PLAY

In addition to detecting and ejecting pickpockets, gropers, and disorderly drunks, the **EYE IN THE SKY** (surveillance) hunts for cheats, and **ADVANTAGE PLAYERS (A.P.)**. Cheating (breaking laws or casino rules) is illegal; **ADVANTAGE PLAY** (exploiting weak casino procedures, dealers, or equipment) is not — though Houses can and will ask advantage players to stop playing, modify their betting, or leave the property.

**FLAT JOINT / BUST OUT STORE** · A crooked casino.

**BASIC STRATEGY** · The "correct" way to play a game. Cheats are often caught by playing irrationally and contrary to **THE BOOK** (e.g., sticking on a weak hand or taking insurance inappropriately), or simply because they defy the odds and win too often.

Casinos rarely object even to big winners, but an unexpected or sustained winning streak is likely to draw **HEAT** and be investigated.

**TAKING SHOTS** · (Trying) to cheat. *A.k.a.*, **MAKING MOVES**.

**STROKERS** · Players who seek out and hustle weak or inexperienced (craps) dealers, e.g., by placing complex, last minute bets, or aggressively challenging alleged errors.

**PINCHING** · Surreptitiously removing chips from a losing bet.

**CAPPING / PRESSING** · Surreptitiously adding chips to a winning bet.

**PASS POSTING** · Adding chips to a roulette or craps layout after a number has won.

**(HAND) MUCKING / SWITCHING / CARD PALMING** · A variety of techniques to swap cards on a table, or introduce winning cards.

**GAFF** · Any piece of equipment used to cheat. There is a wide array of **GAFFED DICE**, e.g.:

**MIS-SPOTTED / TOPS & BOTTOMS/ TEES** · *Dice mis-numbered in various configurations to avoid or ensure certain rolls*

**LOADED** · *Weighted*

**FLATS** · *Misshapen*

**SHOEBOXES**
*Grossly misshapen, easy to spot with the eye*

**GLIM / SHINER** · A reflective device used to identify cards (e.g., when dealing).

**COLD** *or* **STACKED DECK / COOLER** · A deck or shoe that a cheat has prearranged.

*The* APPOINTMENT GAME *Dragon Link*

**PAPER** · Marked cards (usually aces and tens). A range of methods allow cards to be **READ**:

**CRIMPING** · *Folding or bending a card*

**(THUMB)NAILING / DIMPLING** · *Indenting or* **BUMPING** *a card — sometimes using a* CHECK *that is then* TOKED *to the dealer as a distraction*

**DAUBING / JUICING** · *Applying foreign substances* (**SHADE**) *to the back of a card*

**PINNING/PUNCHING**
*Making small holes or indentations in cards*

**EDGE WORK**
*Shaving or nicking the edge of a card*

**BORDER WORK**
*Marking a card's printed edges*

**SANDING**
*Roughening the back of a card, say with a speck of sandpaper stuck to a finger*

**SLUG** · A block of high-value cards (tens and aces) in a shoe — deliberately introduced, or the result of a lucky or weak shuffle.

**CARD COUNTING** · Where blackjack players keep a **RUNNING COUNT** of the cards dealt and bet big when the shoe is **RICH** with high-value tens and aces.

Counters often work in **TEAMS**, where **SPOTTERS** sit counting at the tables (betting small) before **SIGNALLING** to a **BIG PLAYER** (**B.P.**) who steams in with a significant bet.

**BACK COUNTING** · When card counters play only advantageous hands. *A.k.a.*, **WONGING** after blackjack ace Stanford Wong.

**SMOKE / CAMOUFLAGE / COVER** · Deliberately clumsy moves intended to avert suspicion from card counting, or cheating. E.g., making poor gaming decisions and/or acting like a (drunk) recreational gambler.

**DISGUISE** · A serious form of SMOKE used by pros; encompasses everything from a cheap wig to a professional makeover.

**SQUARE (JOHN)** · A civilian; one not in on any kind of cheating. Acting (and looking) like a JOHN is a key form of SMOKE.

**RED CHIP(PERS)** · Card counters who hope to fly under the radar by betting relatively low sums. *Conversely*, **BLACK CHIP(PERS)**.

**RAT-HOLING / GOING SOUTH** · Sneaking CHECKS off a table to conceal one's winnings.

**PLAYING THE SORTS** *or* **THE TURN** · Exploiting printing errors to identify cards by patterns on their reverse. *A.k.a.*, **EDGE PLAY**.

**CONTROL** *or* **RHYTHM ROLLING** · Attempting to influence a craps roll by setting and shooting the dice in a specific way.

**SLIDING** · "Throwing" **PRE-SET** dice flat across the craps layout, so they neither leave the table nor hit the back wall **ALLIGATOR**.

**SUB** · Anything used by a dealer to conceal stolen checks — from a thick watchband to shoes with hidden cavities in the heel.

*A roulette wheel is checked and balanced at The Cosmopolitan*

**DUMPING** · When a dealer deliberately pays losers, overpays winners, or misplays a hand to benefit an **AGENT** (i.e., collaborator).

**HOP CUT** · A **FALSE CUT** where the cards are returned to their original order.

**FLUTTER** *or* **BUTTERFLY** *or* **STUTTER CUT** · Riffling the cards during the cut to expose their values to an AGENT.

**STEP** · When a dealer misaligns the deck to indicate where an AGENT should make a cut.

**STACKING ACES** · Shuffling to ensure the dealer's first card is an ace.

**MECHANIC** · A dealer who manipulates cards to cheat, e.g., by **BUBBLING** (squeezing) a deck to peek at the top card(s) before **DEUCE DEALING** the second card.

**DUMPING OFF** · Sneaking a card into the discard pile.

**SHORTING** · Removing high-value cards from a deck or shoe to stymie advantage players.

**FRONT LOADING** · When a sloppy or dishonest dealer flashes his hole card.

**FIRST** *or* **THIRD BASING** · Reading the dealer's hole card from the first or last seat.

**SPOOKING** · When a spectator communicates the dealer's hole card to a player **AGENT**.

**SWEATING / THE HEAT** · When pit bosses **HAWK** (i.e., intimidatingly stare down) those they suspect of ADVANTAGE PLAY.

**MILD** (*or* **PRE**) **BACK-OFF** · A selection of **COUNTERMEASURES** pit bosses introduce to disrupt ADVANTAGE PLAY, e.g., insisting on additional shuffles, or cuts of the shoe.

Some casinos will **FLAT BET** suspected card counters, allowing them to wager only a fixed sum for the duration of a shoe.

**THE BACK-OFF / THE TAP** · Stopping a (suspected) ADVANTAGE PLAYER playing blackjack, or any casino game. ("*I know what you're doing, and I don't want to* **BOOK YOUR ACTION**.")

**TRESPASSING** · When a casino instructs an individual to leave. *A.k.a.*, **NRS 207.200** — after Nevada's trespass statute.

Players who return to a property having been TRESPASSED risk arrest.

**BACK-ROOMING** · Legends abound of (suspected) cheats being escorted to back rooms before being **WARNED OFF** ... or worse.

**SELF-EXCLUSION** · A range of procedures allow problem gamblers to reduce their exposure to temptation, e.g., opting out of direct marketing; rendering their bank cards inoperable in casino A.T.M.S; and cancelling loyalty cards. Players can also sign **SELF-TRESPASSING** agreements to ban themselves from a casino's properties.

## SUPERSTITION

**PLAYERS** · In addition to lucky clothes, charms, seats, tables, machines, and dealers — players display a host of bizarre superstitions.

Some buy in for odd amounts, or for sums featuring eights (e.g., $8,880); others think $50 bills are unlucky; and many have a specific way they insert banknotes into the slot.

In craps, saying "seven" is considered unlucky (and ill-mannered), as is applauding your own roll. Some believe that a new stickman will prompt a seven; a left-handed female shooter is lucky; cocktail waitresses **COOL** the action; or changing the dice after a winning run brings bad luck. **VIRGIN SHOOTERS** are lucky if female, unlucky if male. Blowing on dice to bring you luck is commonplace.

Blackjack players believe a strong **ANCHOR** (the last player) prevents the dealer's "destined" card going awry. Others place two bets instead of one to change their luck.

Some (poker) players **RABBIT HUNT**, i.e., attempt (or ask) to see the card they would have been dealt, had they called differently. (Usually deprecated because it slows play.)

Slots players will tap, touch, or caress the machine for luck, or crank the arm rather than push a button to spin the reels. Some believe cash bets win more than voucher bets; that machines are programmed to favour new players; or that standing improves their odds.

Many slots players will talk to their machines, and a few are convinced that turning up the machine's volume to maximum will increase their odds of winning.

Cellphone signals are believed to influence a win positively or negatively, depending on who you ask. And opinions differ as to whether using casino loyalty cards increases or decreases the odds of winning.

Card players sometimes shout **MONKEY** (possibly a corruption of "monarchy") in a bid to encourage tens or **PAINT** (face cards).

**THE HOUSE** · It's curious how irrational even experienced dealers and floor men can be — though inexplicable "runs of luck" may signal a flaw in security.

Supervisors have been known to perform a range of rituals to cool the action: shaking salt behind players or under tables; turning the dropbox paddle around in its slot; standing on one leg; and swapping out winning dice or cards (sometimes for replacements literally chilled in a fridge). One shift manager placed a folded surveillance photograph of a "lucky" player inside his shoe before walking the floor.

Craps is a hotbed of superstition. Pit bosses have been known to place seven ashtrays round a table; spray paint the number seven onto the table when changing out the cloth; and even to have "hot" tables moved an inch or so to disrupt the flow of luck. Unscrupulous dealers throw coins under the table to bring bad luck, or find any excuse to touch the dice, or brush against a winning shooter.

Anxious floor men who **SWEAT THE HOUSE'S MONEY** are known as **BLEEDERS**.

Finally, and splendidly, many on both sides of the layout are convinced that "it's unlucky to be superstitious." ⊙

*"And don't forget to tip your waitress!"*

# Fatto a Mano Con Amore

*A field guide to* **ITALIAN GESTICULATIONS** *(handmade with love).*

**CALMA!**
Stay calm! / Calm down!
*Gently pat a downward palm*

**CHE VUOI?**
What do you want?
*Pinch fingers in exasperation*

**STAI ATTENTO!**
Pay attention!
*Raise a warning index finger*

**DUE SPAGHETTI?**
I want to eat / Shall we eat?
*Rotate index and second finger as if twirling a forkful of pasta*

**PER FAVORE!** [oh, please!]
Plea of exasperation
*Pivot hands pressed together in prayer in front of the chest or face*

**NON LO SOPPORTO!**
[I am against it]
Indicates strong disagreement
*Hit vertical hand against chest*

**CI VOGLIONO SOLDI!**
We need cash! / How much!?
*Rub index and second finger against thumb*

**BUONO!** [good!]
Shows quality or deliciousness
*Press an index finger into the cheek and rotate it*

**RABBIA** [rage]
A (melo)dramatic display of anger or frustration
*(Fake) bite knuckles of a fist*

**ACQUA?**
Water?

**CAFFÈ?**
Coffee?

**BEVANDA ALCOLICA?**
A *drink* drink?

**MAGRO COSÌ** [as thin as]
Indicates that someone
or something is skinny
*Raise a little finger*

**ME NE FREGO!**
I don't give a damn!
*Flick the back of one's fingers*
*out from under the chin*

**PAURA, EH!**
Oh, are you *scared*?
*(Insinuatingly) pinch fingers*
*of one hand open and closed*

**CHE PALLE!** [what balls]
Give me a break!
*Cup immense and*
*imaginary testicles*

**STANNO INSIEME**
They are together ...
in an intimate way
*Bring index fingers together*

**CHE CULO!** [that bottom]
What luck / Lucky bastard
*Hold or waggle open-palmed*
*L-shaped hands admiringly*

**FURBO** [cunning]
Notes a person is sly or sharp
*Draw back of thumb across cheek*

**INTESA** [understanding]
I'm watching you / Stay alert
*Pull the skin below one eye*

**BARBA** [beard]
This is / they are tiresome
*Stroke a long, imaginary beard*

**ANNI FA** [years ago]
Indicates a (long) time past
*Wave hand over the shoulder*

**HO FAME**
I'm hungry / let's eat
*Hold hand vertically at stomach*

**NIENTE** [nothing]
There's nothing left / there
*Waggle L-shaped finger(s)*

**RIMASTO SOLO** [left alone]
To be all on one's own
*Rotate vertically pinched fingers*

**RUBARE** [to rob]
Watch out, thieves about!
*Waggle fingers insinuatingly*

**MATTO** [crazy]
This is / they are nuts
*Tap index finger against temple*

**È DAVVERO PERFETTO**
It's utterly perfect / exquisite
*Draw an inward-facing O.K. sign across one's body or face*

**POCHE CHIACCHIERE — FATTI!** Less chat, more facts!
*Hit the back of one's hand against one's palm*

**VAI VIA!**
Get lost!
*Dismissively flick one's upturned palm*

**CHE BELLO** [how beautiful]
Indicates elegance or quality
*Rub palms together*

**PIENO DI GENTE**
Full of people / Crowded
*Pinch fingers of both hands*

**SIAMO D'ACCORDO**
We are in agreement
*Grip clasped hands together*

**CORNA** [horn]
Wards off misfortune
*Points sign of the horn down or horizontally*

**CORNUTO** [cuckold]
Suggests or mocks infidelity
*Raise sign of the horn aloft (or point it at someone)*

**VATTENE!**
Get out of here!
*Strike back of downward facing hand against vertical palm*

**UNA COSA VELOCE**
A quick thing / Something fast
*Open and close fingers of one hand*

**CONTRASTO**
(In) contrast
*(Almost) touch index fingers*

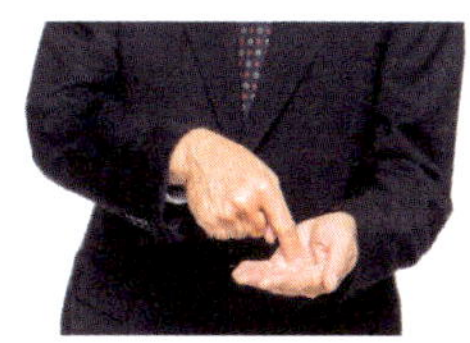

**INSISTO!**
I insist!
*Jab index finger into palm*

**ANDIAMO!** [let's go]
Let's get out of here!
*Flick away a folded palm*

**LO FACCIAMO DOPO**
We'll do it later
*Rotate a horizontal index finger*

**SEI TESTARDO!**
You are stubborn!
*Hit one's palm with a fist*

**BOH!** [Who knows?]
*Shrug in incredulity or indifference*

**ARIANNA ROSATI & ANTONIO FELIZIANI**

# "I'm Not Here to Make Friends!"

*Sixty years after* Seven Up!, *30 years after* The Real World, *and 20 years after* Big Brother *the avalanche of cheap and cheerful* **REALITY TELEVISION** *shows no signs of relenting. Indeed, the construction of* **CONSTRUCTED REALITY** *remains potent and popular despite participants and audiences knowing every trick in this book ...*

## SHOW FORMATS

There are endless taxonomies of **REALITY T.V.** [R.T.V.] — which itself is a sub-genre of **UNSCRIPTED.** Below are some of R.T.V.'s many interlocking descriptors.

**SELF-CONTAINED** · Where each individual **EP**(isode) is complete in itself, and can be viewed in any order, e.g., *Grand Designs.*

**ARCED** · Where **EP**s form a **NARRATIVE ARC** that builds to a finale, e.g., *Below Deck.*

**COMPETITION** · Where contestants vie to win a prize of some sort (financial, romantic, career, &c.), e.g., *The Biggest Loser.*

**DOCUFOLLOW / FOLLOW DOC** · Where the action is fluid and (more or less) dictated by the (celebrity) performers (*The Osbournes*).

When such shows are based on unusual (*Ace of Cakes*) or hazardous (*Ice Road Truckers*) jobs, they are *A.k.a.*, **OCCU-SERIES.**

**SHINY FLOOR** · Glitzy, studio-based talent competitions, e.g., *Dancing With the Stars.*

**HYBRID** *or* **HIDDEN** · Shows that combine formats, e.g., episodes of *Dance Moms* start as DOCUFOLLOW and end in a COMPETITION.

**SPIN-OFF** · When BREAKOUT character(s) from one show are given a show of their own. E.g., *Vanderpump Rules* spun off from *The Real Housewives of Beverly Hills.*

**SOFT-SCRIPTED** · Industry euphemism for semi- (or fully) scripted shows, where participants are briefed by producers about the action and dialogue required for each scene.

Examples of specific format types include:

| | |
|---|---|
| **APPRAISAL** | *Antiques Road Show* |
| **BUSINESS ADVICE** | *The Profit* |
| **CELEBRITY SPOUSES** | *Basketball Wives* |
| **COOKING** | *Top Chef* |
| **CUSTOMIZATION** | *Pimp My Ride* |
| **ETHNIC GROUPS** | *Shahs of Sunset* |
| **FIELD COMPETITION** | *Amazing Race* |
| **GENEALOGY** | *Who Do You Think You Are?* |
| **INVESTMENT** | *Dragon's Den* |
| **KIDSPLOITATION** | *Toddlers and Tiaras* |
| **LEGAL** | *Judge Judy* |
| **MAKEOVER / MAKE BETTER** | *Queer Eye* |
| **MATCHMAKING** | *Love Is Blind* |
| **PARANORMAL** | *Most Haunted* |
| **PHYSICAL QUIRKS** | *The Undateables* |
| **REAL ESTATE** | *Selling Sunset* |
| **RENOVATION** | *Instant Dream Home* |
| **SOCIAL EXPERIMENT** | *Big Brother* |
| **SURVIVAL** | *Man vs. Wild* |
| **TIME TRAVEL** | *Victorian Slum House* |

## FILMING

The style of R.T.V. filming is dictated by the **COVERAGE** a format demands.

DOCUFOLLOWS (*Little People, Big World*) favour a **RUN AND GUN** style where camera operators follow the action kinetically with **P.S.C.**s (Personal Single Cameras).

More **STATIC SHOWS** (*The Circle*) require a **FIXED RIG** of remote control **P.T.Z.** (Pan, Tilt, Zoom) cameras (often with night-vision) for inescapable, panoptical surveillance.

Many shows combine styles, using a range of cameras, e.g., drones, GoPros, cellphones, and miniature "lipstick" cameras. Some shows (*Alone*) give participants cameras so they can **SELF-DOCUMENT** their stories.

☞ *Production shot from* The Real World II: Los Angeles, *1993*

**SHOOTING RATIO** · The quantity of **RAW** footage shot compared to the material shown on screen. E.g., a single season of *The Deadliest Catch* generates ~25,000 hours of footage that takes four days to process before it is edited down to 24 hours of on-screen action. [1]

**EDITING RATIO** · The time it takes to edit an R.T.V. show; this depends on the format and shooting ratio. That said, an average one-hour episode might take 6–10 weeks to edit.

**M.I.V.** · A formal, sit-down Master Interview. Shot at the start of a show to establish personalities, back-stories, and motivations, and then conducted regularly during shooting to provide commentary and **REACTION BITES**.

**O.T.F.** · An informal (hand-held) On The Fly interview conducted **I.T.M.** (In The Moment) during filming to add narrative explanation or show instant emotional reaction (e.g., to being eliminated). *A.k.a.*, **PULL OUT**.

**PRE-CAP / MID-CAP / RECAP** · An O.T.F. conducted before, during, or after a key event (e.g., mission, challenge, date, party, &c.) to record expectation, experience, or reaction.

**CONFESSIONAL** · A sob-story M.I.V. or O.T.F. — in some shows (*Big Brother*) made in front of a dedicated (fixed-rig) **CONFESSION CAM**.

**VERITÉ / REALITY** · Seemingly "real" moments of action, e.g., when contestants chat casually "off camera."

True *verité* occurs when R.T.V. collides with actual reality, e.g., in S.2 E.10 of *The Real Housewives of Salt Lake City*, when a member of the cast was arrested for fraud.

**STEALING** · Covertly capturing **REACTION SHOTS** to be deployed later in the edit.

**MONEY SHOT** · An especially dramatic or emotional moment.

Epic money shots will become the focus of an episode — and can even define a season, e.g., in S.6 E.20 of *The Real Housewives of New York City* when Aviva Drescher removed her prosthetic leg and slammed it on the table.

**HERO** *or* **BEAUTY SHOT** · A mini **SETUP CAMEO**, where participants turn to the camera and give their "signature" **PROFILE** look.

**B-ROLL** · Supplemental footage, usually shot without sound. B-roll has many uses: transitioning from day to night (and vice versa); covering ragged edits or **FRANKENBITES**; or explaining a technical oddity (e.g., a scene with unavoidable road noise may use B-roll to show the offending traffic).

**ESTABLISHING SHOT** · **B-ROLL** that shows viewers where and when action is unfolding. Such shots start wide and get more specific, e.g., city > exterior > reception > office. *A.k.a.*, **G.V. / GENERAL VIEW**.

**CUTAWAY** · Shots that add context to a **BEAT**. E.g., a participant receiving a text may cut away to the message's on-screen content.

**NODDIES** · **CUTAWAYS** that show the (nodding) head of an interlocutor, e.g., to cover **FRANKENBITING**, **CHEATING**, or **A.D.R.**

**HOMETOWN PACKAGE / POP-IN** · Scenes that introduce participants and explore their back-story, often using **ACQUIRED** (i.e., supplied home-) **FOOTAGE**.

**BITES** · Especially clippable dialogue snips.

**SPIKING** · When a performer (accidentally) looks into the lens.

**BREAKING THE FOURTH WALL** · When performers acknowledge the show's existence.

Historically, this was a *faux pas* likely to be edited out; nowadays it is a handy way to develop **VERITÉ**, e.g., when performers bicker with producers on camera, or a contestant requires urgent medical attention.

**PICKUP** · Material shot after the main filming. Used to fill narrative gaps; aid transitions; provide editing options; and correct technical errors (e.g., poor focus, loss of sound, &c.)

**WILD LINE** · An audio-only **PICKUP** that gets **TUCKED UNDER** a visual to explain a plot point, or add a character reaction. Often the result of unsubtle **PROMPTING**. ("*So ... what did you think when she hit you?*")

**A.D.R.** · Additional Dialogue Replacement · When scripted dialogue is (re)recorded after principal filming, to correct technical errors, explain a moment, or re-frame a narrative.

*Nicole Polizzi & Deena Nicole Cortese filming* Jersey Shore *on a Seaside Heights ride, 2010*

## EDITING

If editing scripted T.V. is like tailoring a bespoke suit, editing R.T.V. is like "discovering" a sculpture from within a block of marble.

(It is often said that the same raw footage given to three different editors would result in three very different shows.)

An editor's first task is to go through the raw or **STRINGOUT** footage, developing a sense of character and storyline while organizing the material into **TIME-LINES** and **SEQUENCES**. Editors will also collect **BINS** of useful smiles, smirks, shrugs, grimaces, yawns, eye-rolls, &c. that can be dropped in as **REACTION SHOTS**.

Episodes are usually divided into **ACTS** *or* **PARTS** dictated by the show's format, and by the structure of ad breaks. These acts are broken into **SCENES**, which are in turn comprised of **BEATS**, i.e., individual moments of action or emotion that move a story forward.

**MINING THE FOOTAGE** · Searching through raw material to find a story.

**REVERSE ENGINEERING** · Locating **BEATS** to support a narrative arc. Editors use software tools (e.g., ScriptSync, PhraseFind) to match transcribed dialogue to video footage.

**A-STORY** · The most important narrative line in an episode; followed by **B-** and **C-STORY**.

**CHEATING** · Inserting an out-of-sequence (audio) clip to tell a story or complete an unfinished sentence. Because of discontinuities in location, clothing, &c., editors may **PULL IN** to a tighter shot when cheating visuals.

**FRANKENBITE / FRANKENGRAB** · Assembling a **BEAT** from the body parts of other sequences, including words and even syllables.

At its mildest, frankenbiting is used to tighten story lines, salvage corrupted footage, and remove extraneous verbal tics. At its meanest, it is used to fabricate entire scenes. (Savvy R.T.V. viewers distrust any significant dialogue that takes place **O.O.V.** [**OUT OF VISION**].)

Advances in A.I. are raising the stakes of **FRANKENBITING**, especially as editors have vast archives of participant speech to sample.

**CUTTY / UPCUTTY** · The look and sound of a clumsily edited sequence, or **FRANKENBITE**.

**LIP FLAP** · When the mouth moves after the audio has ended (often a sign of poor editing).

**FLASHBACK** · Using earlier footage to develop a narrative arc or impeach a participant. Often signalled with an audio **SWOOSH** and a unique visual effect (e.g., desaturated colours).

**MONTAGE** · A **B-ROLL** compilation used to accelerate and enliven dull but vital processes (e.g., travelling, training, rehearsal).

**REWIND** · A reverse montage used to go back in time or to an earlier series.

**SPLIT SCREEN** · Used to depict simultaneous action; enliven montages; or visualize conflict.

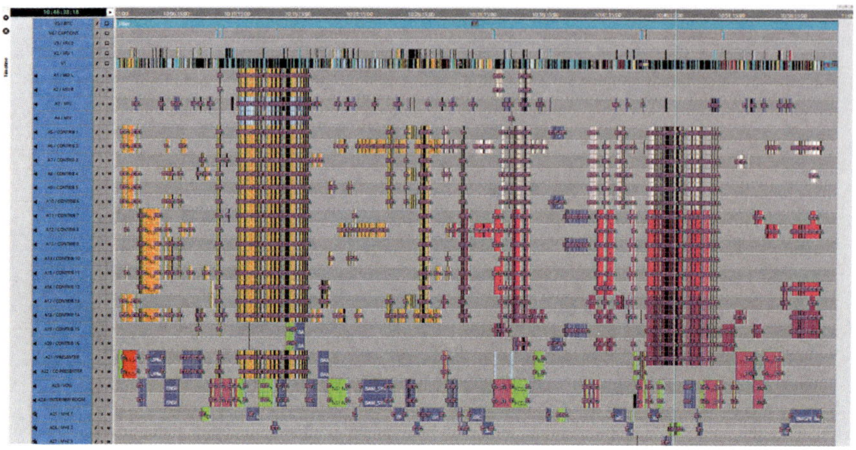

*Screenshot of an Avid edit of a 57-minute reality T.V. show*

**MISDIRECTION** · Tension-raising "red-herring" edits, e.g., cutting away to a contestant who is *not* to be eliminated.

**SPEED RAMPS** · Slowing down (or speeding up) BEATS to create a dynamic stylistic shift.

Footage to be used for ramps (e.g., PROFILE SHOTS) will often be filmed at a higher frame rate to accommodate the technique.

**TRANSITION** · A segue between scenes with a variety of techniques (e.g., **FADES**, **WIPES**, **DISSOLVES**, &c.) to keep viewers engaged.

**ARCHIVE** · A show's entire back catalogue, mined by editors to create inserts and FLASHBACKS and to develop **LOOK BACK** episodes.

**EXIT EDIT** · Where a quick recap (or BACKSTORY) of a soon-to-be evicted participant is compiled to complete their narrative journey.

**PRESENCE** · A participant's time on-screen. Balancing presence in a multi-character show is never easy, since even peripheral players need their moment in the sun.

**FINISHING EDITOR** · Arrives at the end of a project to create a **DRAMA PASS** (PUNCHING UP the action) and/or a **POLISH PASS** (ensuring consistency across a show).

**BLURRING / PIXELATION** · Obscuring young children, **CIVILIANS** (i.e., members of the public), nudity, or artworks for which the production does not have clearance.

(**MAKE IT**) **POP / PUNCH IT UP** · To add drama and pace to a dull sequence with music, S.F.X, graphics, jump cuts, whip pans, &c.

Moments of conflict that fly by too quickly can be drawn out with a range of tricks, e.g., repeating the scene in **SLOW-MO**; **PUSHING IN** for a tighter shot; switching to black and white; and adding (or cutting) audio.

**NOTES** · Every stage of an edit will be submitted for notes to an increasingly senior cast of executives, ending with **NETWORK NOTES** from the commissioning entity.

Such notes range from the infuriatingly vague ("*The music isn't working hard enough here*") to the absurdly specific ...

**FRAME FUCKING** · The act of (leaning over an editor's shoulder and) demanding trivial changes to individual frames in a BEAT.

## EDGIC

A theory devised by fans of *Survivor* to predict the show's winners [edgic = edit + logic].

For each episode, **EDGICERS** give participants: [a] one of five personality **RATINGS** (INVISIBLE / UNDER THE RADAR / MIDDLE OF THE ROAD / COMPLEX PERSONALITY / OVER THE TOP); [b] a descriptor of their **TONE** (PP, extremely positive; P, positive; M, mixed; N, negative; NN, extremely negative); and [c] a ranking of their airtime **VISIBILITY** 1–5. These codes (e.g., UTRP4) are tracked across a season in complex, colourful spreadsheets.

## AUDIO

**MUSIC** performs a range of interlocking roles: establishing pace; bracketing scenes; signalling key moments; and provoking emotion (e.g., melancholy piano chords to introduce a tragic **BACKSTORY** or intense crescendoing strings to hammer home that "*time is running out!*").

Some shows identify teams or characters with specific **CHARACTER MUSIC**, as Sergei Prokofiev did in *Peter and the Wolf* (1936).

**STING** · A (punchy) fragment of audio, used to signal the end of a scene.

**FOLEY** · Additional audio that augments on-screen action, used when **NAT**[ural] **SOUND** is missing or insufficiently dramatic, e.g., the crunch of insects being eaten.

**S.F.X.** · Over the years, a vocabulary of sound effect cues (and clichés) has emerged, e.g.:

| |
|---|
| **BELL** dinged to signal a flash of inspiration |
| **BONGO** paddled for wacky humour |
| **GONG** struck for dramatic impact |
| **SWOOSH** added to cue a (quick) transition |

Occasionally S.F.X. become **BREAKOUT** stars, e.g., the iconic **RATTLESNAKE** woodblock sound that accompanies "shade" on *RuPaul's Drag Race*.

Similarly, the **BOWED CYMBAL** (where a violin bow is drawn across a cymbal's edge) is now a standard marker of (forced) tension.

**SILENCE** · Abruptly cutting the music is an easy way to telegraph moments of conflict.

**NARRATION** · Complex formats require **V.O.** (**VOICE OVER**) to explain the action; other shows use it (as a last resort) to impart information not caught on camera. *Similarly*, a **VOICE OF GOD** intervenes to ask questions or direct participants: "*Paul to the diary room!*"

**CATCHPHRASES** · Many R.T.V. shows aim for memorable and meme-able phrases. Some emerge naturally from the mouths of participants ("Gym, tan, laundry," *Jersey Shore*) or judges ("Soggy bottom," *The Great British Bake Off*); others are scripted for the format ("You're fired!," *The Apprentice*) or hammered in the edit ("Make it work!," *Project Runway*).

## STOCK CHARACTERS

**AUTHENTICITY** · Notwithstanding this industry obsession, few authentic wallflowers are ever cast. Instead, producers look for characters with **BIG ENERGY** who **POP** on-screen.

**SHOWMANCE** · A (seemingly) genuine love interest that blossoms during a series. *Conversely*, an obviously fake **FAUXMANCE**.

**FAN FAVOURITE** · A (breakout) character who (unexpectedly) wins the heart of the audience (i.e., social media) — and will be **GIVEN MORE TIME IN THE EDIT**.

**GOOD COP / BAD COP** · The hero *vs* villain paradigm is as powerful for R.T.V. judges as for contestants. That said, few good cop judges are as memorable as bad cops like Simon Cowell, Gordon Ramsay, or *Judge Judy* Sheindlin.

## STRUCTURAL EDITING ELEMENTS

| | |
|---|---|
| **P.T.T.** (**PRE-TITLE TEASE**) | a **FORWARD THROW** to an episode's upcoming action |
| **PREEV-ON** | a recap of an earlier season, episode, or pre-break scene: "*Previously on …*" |
| **SERIES TEASE** | a sequence used to sell a new series or show; often dropped after a few episodes |
| **COLD OPEN** | launching into the action before the opening credits, to grab viewer attention |
| **TONIGHT ON** | the opening **SIZZLE SEQUENCE** of a (**SHINY FLOOR**) show |
| **SETUP BITE** | a short explanation of what is about to unfold: "*Today the team is …*" |
| **ACT ON** *or* **OUT** | the last scene before an ad break; designed as a mini-cliffhanger |
| **COMING UP ON** | teaser to keep audiences loyal over an ad break |
| **ACT IN** | the first scene after an ad break; often a **RECAP** |
| **CHICKEN COUNT** | briefly checking in on each character after a break |
| **STORYTAGE** | an elaborate **CHICKEN COUNT** that sets up the action to come |
| **RECAP / RESET / RE-RACK** | a scene that catches the viewers up on the story so far |
| **NEXT-ON** | teaser for the next episode: "*Next time on …*" |

*Kim Kardashian filming* Keeping Up with the Kardashians *in 2008*

**VILLAINS** · Some participants enter a show determined to be the villain, others have villainy thrust upon them — supposedly via a Machiavellian **VILLAIN EDIT**.

Although villains are, famously, "*not here to make friends, but to win!*" they rarely do. Yet some succeed in parleying an on-screen persona into real-life profit, e.g., Omarosa Manigault Newman, who went from "reality T.V.'s number one bad girl" in S.1. of *The Apprentice* to one of President Trump's White House assistants (albeit briefly).

Protestations that "*villain edits don't exist*" are undercut by shows like *House of Villains*, which featured ten of R.T.V.'s most notorious villains competing for the title of "America's Ultimate Supervillain" (and $200,000).

**WINNER EDIT** · Depicting winners over the run of a series so that their eventual victory makes sense to the viewers.

*Conversely*, **PURPLE EDIT** · Rendering peripheral characters all but invisible until their eviction, because they don't fit the narrative; don't **POP**; or have somehow shamed the show. (Named after a participant on *Survivor: Nicaragua* who had purple hair streaks.)

(Such thinking is characteristic of **FEEDSTERS** — those who compulsively watch *Big Brother*'s 24-hour **LIVE FEEDS**, and think themselves a cut above **T.V. ONLY** viewers.)

**HOT MESS** · A character who can be relied (or plied) upon to stand out, act up, and kick off — a staple of most castings, and a prerequisite for "can't look away" **TRAINWRECK T.V.**

## TENSION, CONFLICT, & JEOPARDY

Many shows are premised on highly tense subjects, from surviving perilous conditions (*Ice Road Truckers*) to betraying strangers (*The Traitors*). Others require skilful editing to establish jeopardy in the inherently sedate (*The Great British Bakeoff*).

**IN VINO VERITAS** · The (not so) secret sauce of R.T.V. is alcohol, which loosens tongues, relaxes morals, and fuels confrontation — from **SLAPS** and **WIG-PULLS** to full-on **FIGHTS**.

**WINE THROW** · Hurling pinot grigio into a rival's face is now so tired a trope, it has its own nickname: **DRINK SLAPPING**.

**TABLE FLIP** · A clichéd cry for screen time, made famous by Teresa Giudice in the 2009 S.1. finale of *The Real Housewives of New Jersey*.

**HUMILITAINMENT** · The television magic of watching people suffer and (if possible) cry.

**VOW RENEWALS** · An easy way to inject romance and glamour (while simultaneously quashing rumours of infidelity or marital discord). At least 12 *Real Housewife* couples have renewed their vows on the show; at the time of writing only five have since divorced.[2]

**SEQUESTERING** · Quarantining performers in a **BUBBLE ENVIRONMENT** to ramp up conflict and/or protect a **BIG REVEAL**.

**APOLOGY / REDEMPTION** · To satisfy narrative conventions, conflict is expected to resolve in (authentic) contrition or (attempted) apology. A few R.T.V. shows have become vehicles for disgraced celebrities and politicians to atone for their sins and reboot their careers. (Witness the parade of love-rats and lowlifes on *I'm a Celebrity ... Get Me Out of Here!*)

**INTERVENTION** · Confronting participants about substance abuse or bad behaviour is an easy way to spark conflict and occasionally contrition (notwithstanding the irony of one drunken housewife being lectured on restraint by her dipsomaniac pals). So powerful is the trope that it has become a standalone R.T.V. format, e.g., *Intervention* and *Celebrity Rehab*.

**TWISTS** · R.T.V. regularly contrives unexpected events to provoke conflict and/or energize formats. Most twists are stagily provocative (e.g., introducing ex-lovers into *Love Island*) others are simply preposterous: In 2014, 12 American women were persuaded they might wed Prince Harry in, *I Wanna Marry "Harry."*

One of R.T.V.'s darkest moments occurred in *There's Something About Miriam*, where six "red blooded" British men competed to woo Miriam Rivera, a 21-year-old Mexican model who, in the show's denouement, revealed she was born a man. ("*These heroic guys have no idea that Miriam is as much Steve as Eve ... from the waist down, she's a man.*") Sixteen years after the show, Rivera took her own life.

**DRAMATIC REVEALS** · From home makeover shows to weight-loss competitions, the dramatic **BEFORE-AND-AFTER** moment is the **MONEYSHOT PAYOFF** to many formats.

That said, perhaps the most curious reveal in modern R.T.V. was a meta-moment during the final moments of the final episode of the sixth and final series of *The Hills*. Here — likely in response to criticism of the show's unreality — after a tearful Kristin bade farewell to a brooding Brody, the Hollywood-sign background that framed the shot was wheeled away to expose a studio back-lot teeming with crew. As *Entertainment Weekly* responded: "Haters rejoice! It was all fake. Whoa, did *The Hills* just get smart?"[3]

[The above lexicon is an amalgam of American and British editing terms, many of which happily trans the Atlantic, while others may draw puzzled frowns.] ⊙

**EDITING THE KARDASHIANS**

Below is a breakdown of S.14 E.19 of *Keeping Up With the Kardashians*, by content type edit:

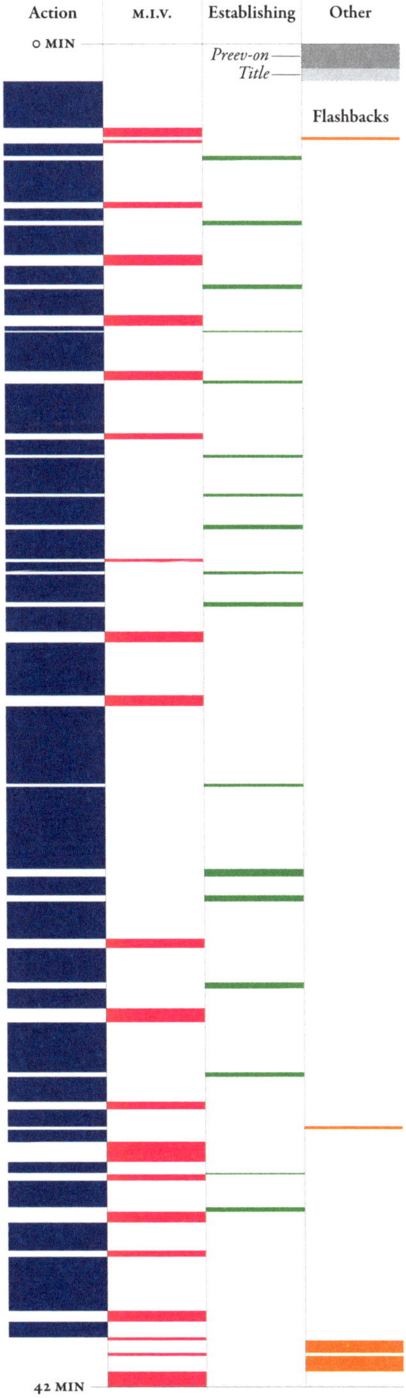

# Quick Foxes, Pig Bristles, Dingbats, & Gadzooks

*A lexicon of* TYPOGRAPHICAL *terminology.*

Although often considered synonyms, **TYPEFACE** describes an overall typographic design, and **FONT** its physical manifestation (metal type, software, &c.) — and, in some contexts, its visual presentation. (In the U.S., typefaces cannot be copyrighted, but font files can.)

**TYPE FAMILY** · A group of **FACES** that variously expresses an overarching theme, e.g., Resistenza Type's Norman includes:

REGULAR / **FAT** / STENCIL

| Acumin | TYPE FAMILY | Roboto |
|---|---|---|
| · Variable | TYPEFACE | Serif · |
| · *Italic* | STYLE | Regular · |
| · Extra Light | WEIGHT | **Bold** · |
| · Extra Condensed | WIDTH | **Extended** · |

**TYPE SYSTEM** · A hierarchy of faces, styles, sizes, &c., used within a publication, e.g.:

› Brunel Deck Black 36 pt ............. headlines
› Georgia Italic 14 pt .................... sub-heads
› Georgia Regular 10 pt ................ body text
› Gill Sans Nova 9 pt ........... image captions

**OPENTYPE** · A highly flexible cross-platform font format (co-developed by Microsoft and Adobe) that allows for >65,000 glyphs.

**PRO FONT** · One with additional glyphs, e.g., Greek or Cyrillic letters, swashes, ligatures, dingbats, &c. *Conversely*, **STD** · Standard font.

**VARIABLE FONT** · A single file that allows the user to adjust a range of traditionally fixed variables, e.g., glyph width, weight, slant, &c.

**DISPLAY FONT** · One designed for use at larger sizes, e.g., with headlines, banners, &c.

**GLYPH** · A single character, e.g., a digit, letter, mark, or symbol.

**DINGBATS** · Ornamental or expressive glyphs (e.g., ❦ / ❧ / ☺); the progenitor of emojis.

**LIGATURES** · Where two or more glyphs are combined — for elegance and readability, e.g., compare the "f/f/i" in "affix" and "affix."

Some stylistic ligatures deploy ornamental **GADZOOKS** to connect letters (e.g., st, ct, sp).

The **AMPERSAND** evolved as a ligature for "et" [Latin for "and"], e.g., & / & / & / & / &c.

**MANICULE** · A pointing hand, e.g., ☞ ☝ ☜

**ALTERNATES** · Substitute glyphs that offer various stylistic options, e.g.: e/e; a/a; Q/Q

**ARABIC NUMBERS** · There are two types: **OLD STYLE** numerals have different heights and interact with the baseline to harmonize with text; **LINING** numerals sit on the baseline, and are often **CAP HEIGHT**, e.g.: 1/1; 9/9.

Additionally, numerals can be **TABULAR** (given a fixed **MONOSPACE** width, for use in tables) or **PROPORTIONAL** (given individual widths to interact elegantly with text). E.g.,

| | |
|---|---|
| Oldstyle tabular | 1234567890 |
| Oldstyle proportional | 1234567890 |
| Lining tabular | 1234567890 |
| Lining proportional | 1234567890 |

**MONOSPACED** · A font where every glyph has the same width (`Monospacing`); used for tables and computer coding. *Conversely*, **PROPORTIONAL** · When glyph widths vary.

**UNICASE** · Where upper and lowercase letters have the same height so they can be combined.

**KERNING** · The spacing between individual pairs of glyphs in a **PROPORTIONAL** font; *Also*, the process of adjusting it for legibility.

(The joke term for poor or unintentionally amusing / embarrassing kerning is "keming.")

## A BRIEF TYPOGRAPHICAL ANATOMY

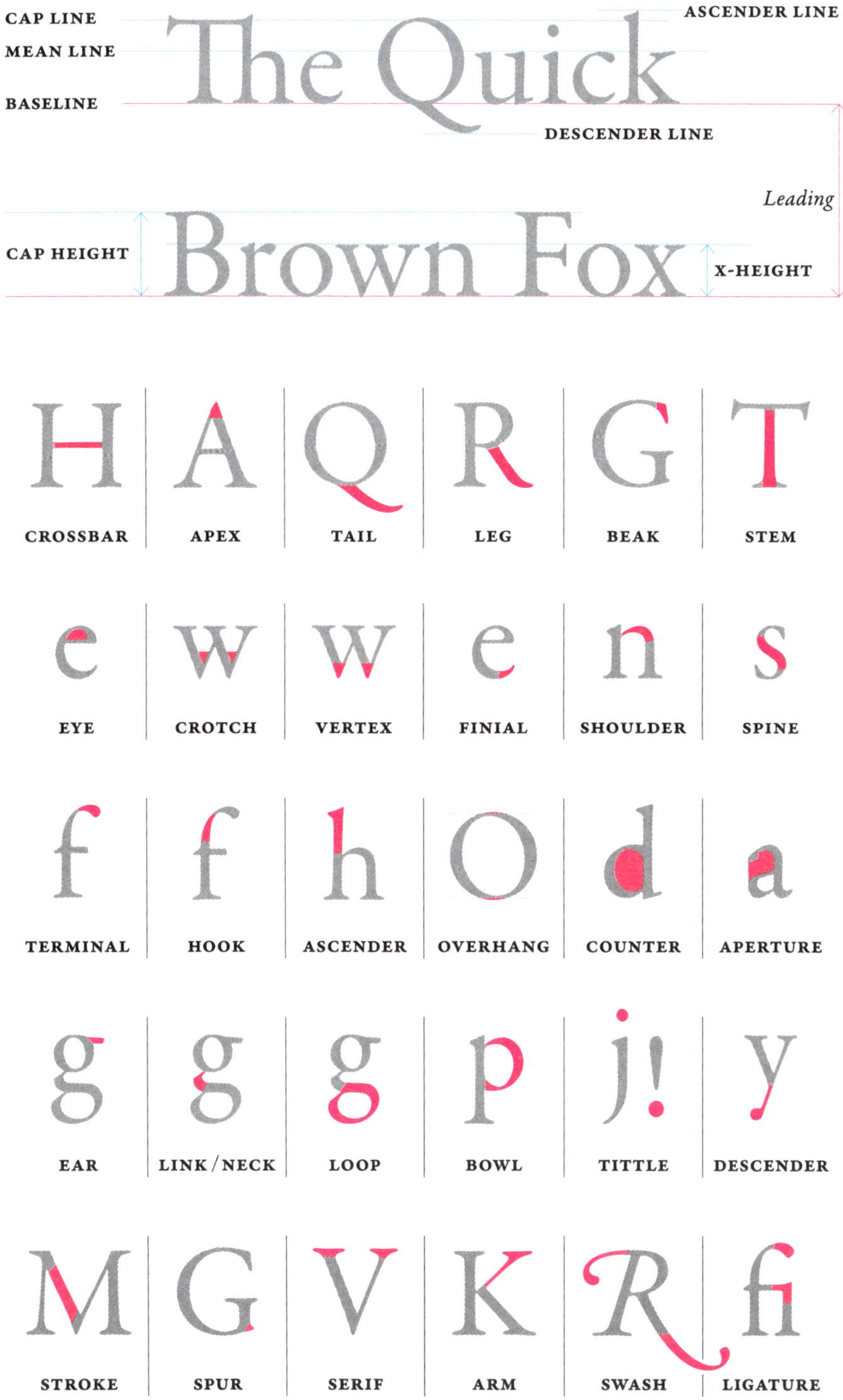

**TRACKING / LETTER-SPACING** · The space between blocks of letters, which can be tightened or loosened to fit text into a specific space, or for visual elegance [☞ COLOUR].

Letter-spacing is more common / acceptable with (uppercase) headlines than body copy, and can be combined with **WORD-SPACING**.

**LEADING / LINE-SPACING** · The vertical spacing of text, from baseline to baseline, adjusted to fit copy; for elegance and legibility; and to prevent letters from crashing vertically.

**BASELINE** · An invisible line on which text rests. **BASELINE SHIFT** · Raising or lowering text, e.g., $^{\text{super}}$ or $_{\text{sub}}$-script; fractions (½); &c.

R**AISED CAP** · *A.k.a.*, **STAND-UP CAP**.

D**ROP CAP** · Where the initial letter(s) of a paragraph are set over two or more lines to introduce a new chapter or section.

**SMALL CAPS** · Capital letters (roughly) as high as the face's X-HEIGHT. Created algorithmically, or designed specially for **PRO** fonts.

**TAB LEADER** · Characters (usually periods) that fill the space between tab stops to guide the eye along a line. (To render them less intrusive, the dotted tab leaders in this book are set three points smaller than the body copy.)

**GUTTER / ALLEY** · The gap between columns.

**POINT** · A standard type measurement, where 1 pt = 1⁄72" or 0.3528 mm.

**EM** · A measure equal to the POINT SIZE of the text; an **EN** is half this width. (An em is sometimes linked to the width of a capital M.)

**SPACES** · Typographers use spaces of varying widths, e.g., **HAIR SPACE** (1⁄24 em); **THIN SPACE** (⅕ em); **PUNCTUATION SPACE** (width of a period or comma); &c.

**WIDOWS / ORPHANS** · Stray words, or short bits of text, that sit inelegantly at the end of a text block or flow over to the top of a new column or page. (The words are often used interchangeably.) *Similarly*, **RUNT** · A solitary word that hangs off the end of text block, like so.

**UPPERCASE** (**U.C.**) ..... *A.k.a.*, **MAJUSCULE**
**LOWERCASE** (**L.C.**) .... *A.k.a.*, **MINUSCULE**

**HANGING INDENT** · When lines following the initial line of a paragraph are given additional marginal padding to create a visual list effect without the use of ...

**BULLETS** · Whereas most lists use heavy mid-line dots [• OPTION+8], the lighter dots [· SHIFT+OPTION+9] are far more elegant.

**MEASURE** · The width of a text block: Too wide, and the eye cannot fluidly track across a line; too narrow, and the eye is constantly snagged by line-breaks and hyphens.

**COLOUR** · The density of text when set as a block, compared to the **WHITE** *or* **NEGATIVE SPACE** around it. Impacted by type WEIGHT, LEADING, TRACKING, SPACING, &c.

**RIVERS** · Distracting vertical lines of white space running through blocks of text, caused by forced justification, poor hyphenation, or awkward repetition of similar words. Ameliorated by LETTER-SPACING, WORD-SPACING, manual hyphenation, and ...

**GLYPH SCALING** · Invisibly shrinking (or expanding) the size of individual glyphs (e.g., by 1–3%) to improve text flow and COLOUR.

**HANGING PUNCTUATION** · Setting certain glyphs (hyphens, quotation marks, brackets, &c.) outside of a text block (i.e., inside the margin or gutter) for stylistic ornament; to balance COLOUR; or to enhance readability.

**PIG BRISTLES** · When two or more successive lines end with hyphens or other punctuation, creating an ugly stacked effect, as above.

**DASH** · Most typefaces offer a trio of dashes:

› **HYPHEN** used to connect words (on-site).
› **EN DASH** used to show ranges (JAN–FEB).
› **EM DASH** used as a form of parenthesis — like so — or to show a pause — or new idea.

**TOFU** · The place-holder box (□) that software inserts when a glyph is missing from a typeface. (Named after the bean-curd food block.)

**ENDMARK** · Signals a section end, like so: ⊙

**TYPE ALIGNMENT** · How type is positioned in relation to the margins in which it is contained:

- ........ **CENTRED**
- ........ **TAPERED CENTRED**
- ........ **LEFT JUSTIFIED / (FLUSH LEFT) RAGGED RIGHT**
- ........ **RIGHT JUSTIFIED / (FLUSH RIGHT) RAGGED LEFT**
- ........ **(FULLY) JUSTIFIED**
- ........ **JUSTIFIED WITH LAST LINE CENTRED**
- ........ **JUSTIFIED WITH LAST LINE ALIGNED LEFT**
- ........ **JUSTIFIED WITH LAST LINE ALIGNED RIGHT**

*Below are some of the* **TEST WORDS** *that* **TYPE DESIGNERS** *use to explore the fundamentals of a new typeface, and fine-tune how letters, digits, and ligatures interact.*

## ROUXEAU EFFIʃʃIENCY CLIʃK FLUET

**SIMON** *by*
Vika Usmanova

"Picking the right word for testing a font is tricky. It depends on the font's style and how I've started working on it. My recent font includes multiple stylistic variations of certain letters (STYLISTIC SETS). To ensure these alternative letterforms harmonized with the base characters, I had to create test words that used all the options. This process helped me evaluate how the different styles complemented each other and determined the overall visual impact they brought to the font."

## धूमिका

**TIFFIN** *by* Salomi Desai

"Devanagari has a lot of different shape groups. I like this combination with a mix of straight and curved characters. Their position next to the straight stems, which appear frequently in text, help in defining spacing. धूमिका means mist, vapour, or fog. I picked it more for the characters than the meaning. Though in hindsight it's a nice word — as if it's slowly unveiling the design!"

## tiếng việt

**VIAODA LIBRE** *by*
Tra Giang Nguyen (Gydient)

"When working with Vietnamese clients, language compatibility is a priority. Before selecting a Latin font, I check for Vietnamese (i.e., *Tiếng Việt*) inclusion. Testing is crucial before proceeding, and sometimes custom Vietnamese fonts are necessary to meet specific needs."

## Squatchee

**EUCHRE** *by*
Jackson Showalter-Cavanaugh

"*Squatchee* is a word baseball geeks invented for the little fabric-covered button on the top of baseball caps. For testing fonts, the most useful feature is the *tc* pair right smack-dab in the middle of a bunch of boring letters. In text sizes, *t* and *c* can start to look similar, so it's always a good idea to double-check."

## Headgowns

**ITC OFFICINA SERIF BOOK** *by*
Erik Spiekermann

"Only nine characters, and all shapes are there."

# tipografia

**SERIGUELA** *by* Sofia Mohr

"I usually use the word *tipografia*, which means typography in Portuguese. This word has the *a* and *g* which are letters I like to start drawing, and also has ascending and descending letters like the *p*, *f*, and *t* that allow me to work on the font's character."

# murciélagos

**AIMÉ** *by* Fer Cozzi

"*Murciélagos* [bat in Spanish] is a word I often use to test typefaces because not only can I see spacing, but it also contains all the vowels and different shapes to check consistency. Additionally, it includes an accented letter, which allows controlling the colour of the project in a more complete layout, checking vertical proportions, and the intended texture in words."

# ইকাতবীক্ষ্ণদ্ধিষ্ঠপ্রবু

**ABP2015** *by* Neelakash Kshetrimayum & Fiona Ross

"The above assortment of Bengali letterforms — base glyphs, conjuncts, ligatures, and vowel signs — are our 'usual suspects'. These give us an idea of proportion, ascender and descender heights, spacing, and the overall relationship between the letterforms."

# AVATAR

**FH PREMIER** *by* Fatih Hardal

"The word *AVATAR* is important for kerning because it tests the interaction of different letter shapes and spaces. It is particularly useful for ensuring balanced spacing between letters like *A*, *V*, and *T*."

# RESSASSER

**RIFUGIO REGULAR** *by* Alex Chavot

"In French, *ressasser* means to harp on about, or turn over in one's mind — which suits the kerning task quite well to me. It is also a palindrome which — in any language — is very useful to inspect any given letter in context and set its metrics and kerning because you can analyse right and left sidebearings at once. Such symmetry is therefore useful as well as pleasing to the eye."

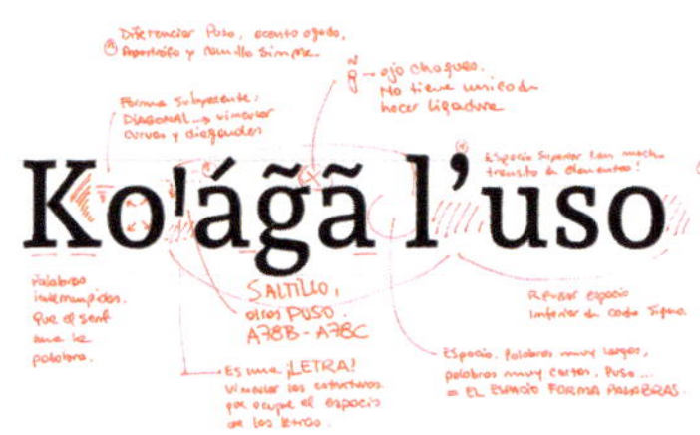


**ANDADA HT** *by* Carolina Giovagnoli

"I don't really have 'test words,' and some words that I use don't even make sense. I try to reproduce the visual form of the language, keeping in mind the underlying forms, the regularities, their diacritics, and the length of the words. It's as if I'm humming the language while typing. In the unconscious part of my projects are the indigenous languages of Latin America. Sometimes it's Guarani, other times it's Tzotzil, Wounaan, Quechua, or Mapudungun. So even if the project is in English, I might test in Guarani."

# Visual!الهوية

**INLINE ARABIC** *by* Tarek Atrissi Design

"I always use a bilingual combination of the term *visual identity*, with *visual* in Latin, and *identity* in Arabic. This allows me to define right from the start the bilingual characteristics of the design. The Arabic word contains the *heh medi* glyph [ـهـ], one of the most challenging glyphs to design. These words work as well when used in presentations for custom typefaces projects."

## *abraqadapra*

**HATTON BLACK ITALIC** *by*
Morgane Vantorre (Pangram Pangram)

"I use the word *abracadabra* and replace certain duplicated letters to get *a*, *b*, *d*, *q*, *p* together, especially in italics. This helps me to test the shape of these letters, which are cousins, and the space/ing between the round and straight shapes. And then, it's like a magic trick!"

## KARAGATAN
## karagatan

**YOR REGULAR** *by*
Jo Malinis (Type West)

"*Karagatan* is the Filipino for 'ocean,' and it allows me to check the flow of negative and positive space between letters. Its upper-case form tests diagonal letter combinations like *KA*, *RA*, *ATA*, and *AGA*, while in lower-case, it helps me balance the counters of *k*, *a*, and *g* better, and assesses the shoulder of *r* in relation to neighbouring letters."

## LAVANDERÍA
## HALAGÜEÑO

**CIUDADELA_LC** *by* Muk Monsalve

"Usually when designing I start testing words in Spanish (e.g., *LAVANDERÍA HALAGÜEÑO*) that fit the rule of having diagonals, rounds, and straight stems plus the diacritic marks that are commonly used in our language (e.g., *é*, *ü*, *ñ*). Also, in this case I considered testing words which contained *similar* characters to evaluate their structure and how they interact together. Testing the contextual alternates for open and closing characters was very important here from an early stage, as well."

## หอกลางฐานจัตุรัส

**GRAPHIK THAI LOOP**
*by* Anuthin Wongsunkakon

"This phrase in Thai roughly translates as 'dorm-middle-base-square.' Although it does not make much sense, it's the equivalent of a Swiss army knife for Thai font testing as it has all of the key shapes, such as straights, curves, diagonals, and basic vowel placements."

## Typeverything

**TALKIE** *by Andrei Robu*

"We can use the word *Typeverything* ... but we do test all the letter combinations possible within the alphabet to eliminate most chances of bad kerning. A single word will only give us an idea of how the letters should be spaced, but for kerning: we test everything."

## Goood
## Typooography

**BRANDON GROTESQUE**
*by* Hannes von Döhren

"A good typeface has to be balanced perfectly in all its details ... but *goood typooography* — the specific emotion I design for — cannot be measured mathematically."

## Laerce

**VICTRY** *by* Frank Adebiaye

"I see a typeface as a voice. And I design it according to what it can speak, depending on the letters available along the way. For instance, with this typeface in progress (working name VICTRY) I am using the name Laerce, which is very good for setting overshoots, spacing, and even kerning based on the letters I now have available." ⊙

# Feeding the Reindeer

*The* **SANTAPRENEURIAL** *secrets of professional* **FATHERS CHRISTMAS.**

**GRAND ENTRANCE** · The initial appearance of Santa at many events — heralded by a ringing bell and a resounding "**HO! HO! HO!**"

Santa's trademark vocalization is considered both a proclamation (similar to a town crier's *Oyez! Oyez! Oyez!*) and the manifestation of his ebullient festive laugh.

**PERSONIFICATION** · Professional Santas do not *impersonate* a fictional character but *personify* a mythological legend, merging historic tropes with local traditions and personal traits. This involves creating a **BACK-STORY** that allows them to "*be their own Santa*" and to improvise convincingly when faced with unexpected **QUESTIONS** and occurrences.

**BEARDS** · The canonical image of Santa with a bushy white beard poses a challenge for the insufficiently hirsute and for those unable to sport festive face-fuzz in their daily lives.

The profession is split into **REAL BEARDED SANTAS** [**R.B.S.**] and Santas who wear **THEATRICAL BEARDS** in synthetic fibres, mohair, yak, or human hair. (The term **FAKE BEARD** is widely considered an insult.)

R.B.S. whose beards show signs of yellow or grey may use temporary whitening pastes and sprays, or resort to more intensive, time-consuming (and hazardous) chemical **BLEACH**.

Even those with natural beards will augment their whiskers with fillers, patches, and extensions as well as exuberant eyebrows and magnificent moustaches to create the fabled …

**STORYBOOK LOOK** · An exaggerated, cinematic effect that suits more statuesque Santas and grander **VISITS** (e.g., **TREE-LIGHTINGS** and **PARADES**). The most elaborate handmade **BEARD SETS** can cost over $1,300.

**YEAR-ROUND SANTA** · An R.B.S. who looks like Santa even out of costume, and is burdened by being **ALWAYS ON** throughout the off-season. Such Santas are careful to sustain an aura of **WONDERMENT** even when kids encounter them in the dullest of daily chores.

**DEFROCKING** · The transition from "*Santa to civilian*" (which can confuse kids, if spotted).

**CHILD TYPES** · Every Santa and Mrs. Claus develops a taxonomy of kids; this list is from Stafford Braxton of **Santas Just Like Me**:

The Ultra Excited · The Nonchalant
The Fearful · The Escape Artist
The Hungry & Exhausted · The № 1 Fan
The Unbeliever · The Curious · The Wiggler
Special Needs · Fur Babies (i.e., pets)

Fearful children need coaxing to counter all they've been instructed about **STRANGER DANGER** or to overcome **POGONOPHOBIA** (a fear of beards, common in kids). It doesn't help when parents wield the threat of Santa's disapproval: "*Father Christmas won't bring any presents if you don't tidy your room!*"

**DROP & RUN** · When parents place a fearful kid in Santa's lap just long enough for a photo.

**CRIERS** · Children — usually from 10 months to 3 years — who are induced to tears either through shyness or sheer terror. Shy criers may be coaxed; terrified criers are handed back.

**TUGGING** · The urge to tug at Santa's beard is, oddly, less common in children than (tipsy female) adults. A sceptical child can sometimes be persuaded of a Santa's *bona fides* by inviting them to **TEST-TUG** — though savvy Santas will lightly hold a lock of a tugging child's hair, promising to tug back with equal force.

**SENSORY** *or* **SENSITIVE** *or* **SILENT SANTAS** · Visits designed for children (and adults) with special needs and learning challenges, e.g., without the long lines, bright lights, loud noises, and exuberance that can overwhelm.

**PREPARATION** · Many Santas will seek background intel to delight a child by knowing, e.g., their birthday, the name of their pet, or what they got for Christmas the year before.



*Santa delivers presents from an abseil line to children in a Barcelona paediatric hospital, 2023* ☞

**TOYS** · Santas are expected to have a working knowledge of current toys (*"It's all about the toys"*). Once, this meant studying catalogues; now it involves staying sharp on social media.

When kids ask if they'll receive the toy of their dreams, Santas deploy evasions (*"It depends if you're naughty!"*) or react to parental cues (*"The elves have run out of Xboxes!"*).

**ELF ON THE SHELF** · Some Santas feel that this irksome supernatural humanoid cheapens the season; others contend that it keeps kids engaged in the build-up to Christmas Day.

**PHOTOGRAPHS** · Even before cellphones, photos with Santa were a selling point; in the age of social media they are an essential. For many Santas, the golden rule when being snapped is *"Always keep your hands visible."*

**DIVERSITY** · Although St. Nicholas was born in Patara, Lycia (now Turkey), and was historically depicted with dark skin, the image of Father Christmas as a ruddy-faced Caucasian has been dominant since an 1863 cartoon in *Harper's Weekly*. In recent decades, a growing cohort of **BLACK SANTAS** and **SANTAS OF COLOUR** has sought to extend the Christmas magic to children across every culture.

(Sadly, this magic is not always welcome, and many Santas of colour suffer the vilest abuse for simply widening the popularity of a much-loved myth, as documented in Avi Zev Weider's 2023 short film, *American Santa*.)

A second trend in diversity is the number of children with same-sex parents, which leads Santas to avoid assuming a "mum and dad."

**PROPS** · In addition to **HANDBELLS** and **GIFT SACKS**, Santas use a range of props to develop their personal narrative, give stories colour, and help answer **QUESTIONS**.

For example, the oversized **MAGIC KEYS** that hang from Santa's thick leather belt might *"unlock the North Pole present vault,"* or explain how presents are delivered to homes without a chimney.

The **MAGIC FINGER** — an illuminating prosthetic digit — is used in various stunts, e.g., transferring lights from one Christmas tree to another; playing "Elf catch"; and testing who is **NAUGHTY OR NICE**. Naturally, no child is ever *irredeemably* naughty, but degrees of naughtiness may be discerned by how long the magic finger takes to glow.

**LOCATIONS** · Santas are hired by an array of organizations, including department stores, hotels, car dealerships, museums, schools, nurseries, garden centres, Christmas markets, high streets, office parties, and even churches (though not without some controversy).

Different locations demand different skills: Shopping mall Santas (who can meet up to 15 families per hour, for 6–7 hours a day) require an indefatigable stamina; home-visit Santas need the skills (singing, story-telling, magic) to sustain a party for several hours.

The most delicate visits are to **HOSPITALS**, where Santas must calibrate their shtick to the condition of each patient, and avoid insensitive questions such as *"How are you doing?"* or *"Where are you spending Christmas?"*

**Q & A** · While some questions demonstrate a sense of awe (*"What's the North Pole like?"*), others suggest a creeping sense of doubt (*"So, where are your reindeer?"*). To all, professional Santas develop a repertoire of answers:

"If you're really Santa, what's my name?"
*"I only know the names of naughty children!"*

"I don't believe in Santa!"
*"Santa believes in you!"*

For tricky questions, Santa can always fall back on **SANTA MAGIC** — or blame the poor memory of their preternatural old age.

The hardest (and not uncommon) question is when a bereaved child asks if Santa can "bring back" a deceased pet, parent, or sibling.

**MRS. CLAUS** · Opinion divides as to whether Mrs. Claus is a co-partner in the global logistics operation, or a *"support act"* wife in charge of baking gingerbread and wrapping gifts.

In recent years, one trend has been to shed her bookish half-moon spectacles and fusty silver-hair bun to present a youthful, "sexy" (and even pole-dancing) **MISS CLAUS**.

**BAD SANTA** · Where Santa is hired to visit drunken adult venues and debauched office parties (accompanied by his **SLUTTY ELVES**). The psychic stress of transitioning *"from nightclub to nursery"* is not for every pro Santa.

**FEEDING THE REINDEER** · A euphemism deployed to cover any off-stage activity, from taking a call to answering the call of nature. ⊙

# Boomerangs Behind Bars

*The* **BARTENDER SLANG** *of some notable drinking establishments.*

## OVERSTORY

MANHATTAN, U.S.A.

**STU** · A problem guest.

**GAZ** · A cocktail enthusiast.

**BIZ / BIZNESS**
Small batch of ingredients used in a cocktail.

**CRANSTON**
A guest who orders like they're stuck in the '80s (Mudslide, Long Island Iced Tea, &c.).

**FLOODED**
The bar is about to get packed and **FLAT SAT.**

**BACK TO BACK**
Sneaking behind someone in a tight space.

**MAGIC** · Going all out to blow a guest's mind; whatever it takes to win them over.

## DIE GOLDENE BAR

MUNICH, GERMANY

**TABLE № 17** · Employee toilet.

**TABLE № 1,000** · To-go drinks.

**DER GERÄT** · The [credit card] device.

**CRACKIES** · Outdoor benches.

**JIZZ** · Homemade lemonade.

**TO JIZZ** · Making juice *mise en place.*

**DARKROOM** · The tiny storage with no light.

**TELEPHONE BOOTH** · Spirit storage.

**BIG MAMA** · The largest glass bin in the house.

**SVENPRESSO** · A shot in an espresso cup (shots are not served officially).

**SHELF OF SHAME** · Hidden shelf for bottles you won't put on the back bar (gifts, samples).

## MILADY'S

MANHATTAN, U.S.A.

**I.L.M.J.** · I Love My Job.

**BUBBLES?** ***BUBBLES!***
Time for **THE BUBBLE GUN.**

**HARD CLEAR** [name of glassware]
"We're running low on a specific glass during a rush, so **PULL** empties from the floor A.S.A.P."

**CHEEKY** · Little shots for V.I.P. / industry pals.

**AQUA HOUR** · Playing Aqua, girlie pop, and dance ballads as a pick-me-up.

**CAMPERS** · Guests who have stopped ordering / paid but show no signs of leaving.

## TRE MONOS

BUENOS AIRES, ARGENTINA

**PERRO** · Rush hour.

**85** · Almost out of stock.

**86** · Out of stock.

**87** · Police are here!

**LLEVO!** · I need [something] A.S.A.P.

**OLD-FA** · Old-Fashioned.

**A COMER** [to eat] · Time for a shot!

**ASCENDIDO A CLIENTE**
[promoted to customer]
When someone on staff makes a big mistake.

## SIDE HUSTLE

AT THE NoMAD HOTEL, LONDON, U.K.

**MISE** · Prepping for a shift.
*Also,* **MARKING** guests with silverware.

**CHEATERS** · Unmarked bottles used for batches, juices, syrups, infusions, and spirits used in smaller quantities.

**PLOUCHE** · A collection of mint sprigs used to create a garnish bouquet.

**MENISCUS** · Filling a jigger to the very top, so convex/concave curve of liquid forms.

**SCANT MEASURE** · Filling a jigger slightly under the top; a touch below a meniscus.

**LEGEND** · Creating a special and personalized moment for a guest.

**PIN TOUCH** · Seeking a colleague's attention, by subtly touching your NoMad lapel pin.

**SOIGNÉ** · Another term for a V.I.P.
*Also,* code for going "above and beyond."

**SOIGNÉ VACUUM** · A reminder not to overcrowd V.I.P. tables, and ensure that all guests feel an equal amount of love.

**BUBBLE** · The invisible perimeter that exists between service professionals and a table of guests. *Hence,* **BREAKING / ENTERING /** *and* **MINDING THE BUBBLE.**

**ONE-INCH RULE** · Performing every action with care, down to the final inch. E.g., placing items down with a soft touch.

**GOLDEN TICKET** · SOIGNÉ guests are informed that their bill will be covered when they unwrap a NoMad chocolate bar and discover a Wonka-esque golden ticket.

*The* QUAD(RUPLE) STIR *at The Clover Club*

## WEATHER UP

MANHATTAN, U.S.A.

**SNAQUIRI / SNACK** · A tiny daiquiri, or daiquiri paired with another daiquiri.

**STRAIGHT UP** · "When *we* say it, it means 'for real.' When a *guest* says it, it means they don't know how to order a drink but they heard this phrase and it sounds good. E.g., '*I'll have a Martini, straight up*' ... you'll have a Martini *served* up, as it comes in a coupe."

**HARVESTING** ◎ · Cutting house-made ice to size from slabs, or removing it from moulds.

**SECRET HANDSHAKE PATRON** · A guest who orders a nouveau classic cocktail (e.g., a Chet Baker) and expects bartender respect.

**STAR-TENDER** · A bartender whose ego exhausts his jaded and expert colleagues.

**IRISH EXIT** · Leaving the bar without saying goodbye (or paying your tab).

**NOT TOO SWEET** · When a guest doesn't know where they are (a classic cocktail bar) and asks for their commonly sugary drink to not be made too sweet. ("*Skinny margarita*")

## THREE SHEETS

LONDON, U.K.

**SCOOSH** · Sanitizer spray.

**TEPACHES** · Bartenders (often nerdy).

**CHICKEN JUICE** · Egg white.

**CHEF JUICE** · Coca-Cola.

**CUSTIES** · Guests.

**CHRISTOPHERS** · Walk-ins.

**CHECK THE DATABASE**
Look at the recipe.

**PUSH PUSH** · Go faster.

## BAR LEONE

HONG KONG

**BIG DOGGOS**
Industry or bar people in the house.

**KK** · Nerdy barfly in the house.

**SITUATIONSHIP**
A girl or a guy hitting on a team member.

**DAI DAI DAI** · Faster! Move faster!

## BROOKLYN SOCIAL

BROOKLYN, U.S.A.

**SOUL STEALER**
A barfly who comes in (usually when it is quiet) and sucks out the barman's very core with his depressing, self-centred rhetoric.

**BOOK CLUB** · A group of (almost exclusively) women who drink (almost exclusively) wine — excruciatingly slowly.

**THE WAVE**
Demanding a bartender's attention, often with cash in hand. **WAVERS** usually begin an order asking, "*Yeah, so what kinda beers do you have?*" — and commonly engage in ...

**ONE-AT-A-TIMING**
The time-wasting habit of ordering a round of drinks sequentially, as each one is made.

**FRICTION!!!**
"A barman's appeal to the cosmos. A call to arms. A recognition that it's absurdly busy, so hold on tight and let's **RIDE THE WAVE**."

**NINO STYLE**
("*Let's take it home, Nino style.*")
Closing early if business is dead. Named after a barman of lore who could eject the few remaining customers by force of will.

## ABRICOT BAR

PARIS, FRANCE

**HOT BITCH**
House spicy margarita with jalapeño syrup.

**NERDY** · A highly technical cocktail, and/or one with obscure ingredients — appeals mainly to enthusiasts.

**AMUSE** [*-bouche*] · A welcome shot that is given to every guest on entry.

**TUTTO BENE?** *or* **ÇA VA?** · Checking staff have all they need; usually asked after a rush.

**I'LL DO TAPS** · When the second bartender helps ROUND BUILD during a rush by pouring tap cocktails and beers.

**ROUND BUILDING** · The art of making drinks in an order so that they all finish at the same time without losing texture or chill.

**BASTA! BASTA!** · When you've overfilled a glass, or are doing too much for one table.

**FRIENDLY FACES**
Regulars, referrals, and industry people.

**HOT** · A cocktail that's tasting very boozy.

## PETER MCMANUS CAFE

MANHATTAN, U.S.A.

**B.I.B.** · Best In Bar (looks-wise).

**CREEPER** · A guy who goes from girl to girl.

**STALKER** · A girl with eyes for the barmen.

**THE TURN** · Crossing over to midnight.

**CINDERELLA** · When business slows early.

**ON THE ROPES** · A crazy night.

**MUSIC MAN** · A customer who spends more at the jukebox than on drinks.

**WE AIN'T SERVIN' HOLY WATER ...**
When a good customer turns bad one night.

## MIRROR BAR

BRATISLAVA, SLOVAKIA

**ITALIAN SPARKLING WATER**
Free prosecco welcome drink.

**MISSED CALL**
A staff shot poured by the barback.

**TOGETHER-PUTTER** · Stapler.

**LET IT GO FASTER** · Turn up the music; *Also*, change the playlist to cocktail-night vibe.

**PROTECTION** · Tapwater for the guests.

**DRIMALDINI** · Exhausted; ready for bed.

**BREWSKI** · After-work team beer.

## THE CLOVER CLUB

MANHATTAN, U.S.A.

**SKANT HALF** · Just under half an ounce.

**SKANT DASH** · A soft dash of bitters, &c.

**HEAVY** *or* **HARD** · The opposite of SKANT.

**TALK TO ME, GOOSE** · A request for help.

**QUAD(RUPLE) STIR**
Stirring four drinks simultaneously.

**WATERFALL SPEC**
Remembering a recipe in descending order of measures (e.g., 1.5, 0.75, 0.5, 0.25 ounces).

**DYING IN THE WINDOW**
Fresh drinks that need to be run to tables.

## TRUE LAUREL

SAN FRANCISCO, U.S.A.

**GHOST YOUR LEMON / LIME GHOST**
To express the oil of citrus upon your cocktail, but not garnish with it.

**CORN! / CORNDOG! / CORNELIUS! / &c.**
Safety call when turning a blind corner.

HARVESTING ICE *at Weather Up*

### MASQUE

MUMBAI, INDIA

**BHASAD** [chaos] · The crazy ruckus behind the bar during peak service hours.

**HEAVY HAND** · A pour a "bit" over 90 ml.

**PANI KAM CHAI** [weak-ass tea] Low-alcohol drinks.

**FIRE** · A very "lit" drink.

**SUPERDRY** · Guests who drink strong, spirit-forward cocktails.

**SWAAD ANUSAAR** [to taste] A guest with strong opinions on how a cocktail *should* have been made.

**FULL TIGHT** · A "sloshed" guest.

**THE PRE-GAMER** · A guest who's already a "few" drinks down before coming out.

**HIT MAN** · A highly skilled and persuasive bartender.

**CHEETAH** · A bartender who outperforms for the day.

**KACCHA NIMBU** [raw lemon] A mocktail-only drinker.

**BANTAI** [brother] · A friend of the bartender's who's a "free" guest for the night.

### LILLI STAR

BROOKLYN, U.S.A.

**MOVES** · Creating an experience tableside *or* serving something with flair.

**DANGLES** · Stir-sticks and fun garnishes.

### ALLEGORY

WASHINGTON, D.C., U.S.A.

**BANGERS ONLY** · Making cocktails that are focused on being delicious. If your drink is complicated from a flavour or technical standpoint then it better taste amazing. *Also*, drinks that you want more than one of.

**INTERESTING** · When you try a cocktail that is overly complicated from a flavour or technique standpoint and the cocktail isn't delicious. Code for: *This drink sucks!*

**I SEE WHAT YOU WERE TRYING TO DO THERE** · Building on **INTERESTING**: a nice way of telling someone their cocktail sucks.

**POP** · A ½ sized shot.

**BABY** · A ¼ sized shot.

**FULL SEND** · A full comp for a bar V.I.P.

**W.W.R.B.D.** · What would Ruby Bridges do? [Bridges is an American civil-rights activist; in 1960 she became the first Black child to attend an all-white school in New Orleans. A mural featuring her story adorns the bar.]

### HERO

NAIROBI, KENYA

*Most of these terms are in Sheng — a Swahili-based slang popular in Nairobi.*

**NG'ANG'O** · Spirits or hard liquor.

**MZINGA** · A 750 ml bottle of wine or spirits.

**WABA** · Water.

**MAFUTANI** · One who's loaded with cash.

**KUOGELEA** · So busy it's swimming.

**JUBILEE** · A non-tipping guest.

**MWERE** · A foolish person.

**MBOGI** · A great team or a group of friends.

**PENGTING / MSUPA** · A beautiful lady.

**KUCHOMA PICHA** · Misbehaving in public.

**NDECHU** · A brand-new item.

**MABESHTE** · Good friends.

**KUZITOKA** · Dancing.

**MBLEINA** · A perennial complainer.

**TEI** · Alcohol in general.

## UBIQUITOUS / ANONYMOUS

*Terms used by a range of establishments, or one establishment that uses it on the* D.L.

**WEEDED / IN THE WEEDS** Backed up on orders; slammed; drowning.

**STAFF MEAL** · A round of team shots taken during a long shift and/or an emergency bar-snack meal (e.g., cucumber, nuts, and olives).

**OUI (CHEF)** · Yes, I understand; I hear you; approved; confirmed; agreed; gottit!

**BARTENDER'S HANDSHAKE** A rococo order that "subtly" indicates you work in the industry, e.g., Jeppson's Malört, Chartreuse, Fernet Branca, or the Ferrari, i.e., equal measures Fernet and Campari.

**86'D** · When an ingredient has run out; *or* when a guest is (permanently) kicked out; *or* when a member of staff storms out.

**BOOMERANG** ⓞ A specially prepared drink that is bottled or sealed (say, with plastic wrap or a rubber glove) and dispatched as a gift to a nearby bar. Of dubious legality, boomerangs are a way of "having a drink" with industry friends during work hours. Boomerangs are often shuttled from bar to bar by regulars, who are thereby identified as **GUESTS OF QUALITY**. Some boomerangs travel across countries.

**THE SKI TEAM** Coked-up customers who show up after 2 A.M. and are difficult to chase out at 4 A.M. *"The ski team is generally reluctant to pay."* ⊙



*A* BOOMERANG *ready to be sent out into the world* ☞

LOVE
YOU!

# Making Money Hand Over Fist

*For generations* **TRADING FLOORS** *around the world operated through* **OPEN OUTCRY** *— a complex system of signals and phrases that dictated the terms of transactions. Below are the hand signals used in the New York Mercantile Exchange, until 2016.*

## MONTHS OF THE YEAR

## BUYING

*A trader signals a purchase by pulling his open hands toward his body. Numerals relating to a buy are made with the palm facing in.*

## SELLING

*A trader signals a sale by pushing his open hands away. Numerals relating to a sell are made with the palm facing out.*

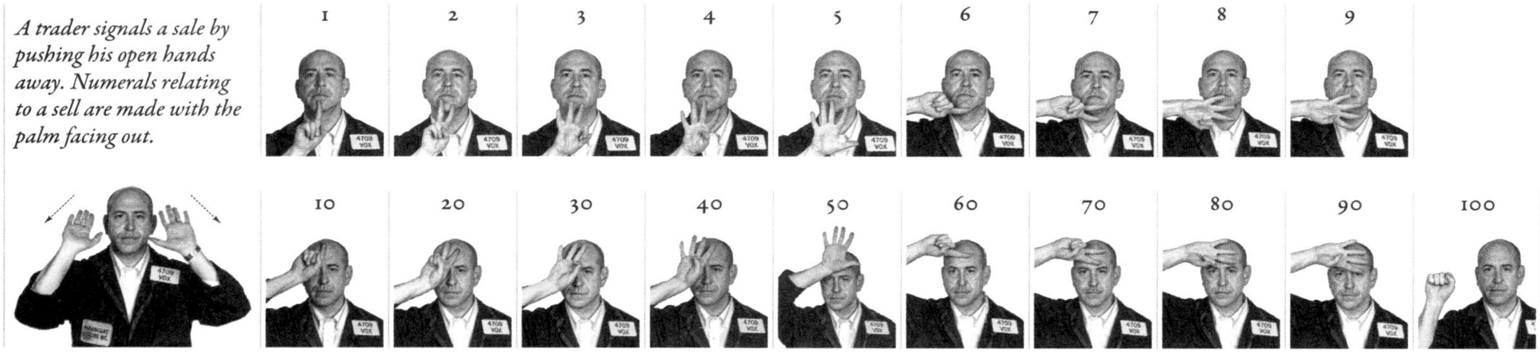


## OTHER SIGNALS

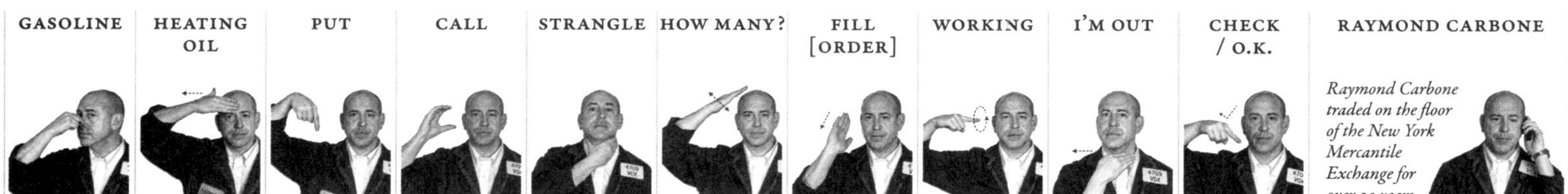


*Raymond Carbone traded on the floor of the New York Mercantile Exchange for over 20 years.*

A **PUT** option is the right to sell a set quantity of an asset, at a set price, on or before a set date. A **CALL** option is a similar right to buy. A **STRANGLE** combines the two, using the same expiration date but with different strike prices for each trade.

Raymond Carbone, who for decades traded energy options on the floor of the Nymex for his company, Paramount Options, explained why open outcry lasted for so long, even after the mass adoption of computerized systems: "I can signal a trade faster than you can type it."

# Fashion on the Out & Back

*"People think* **FASHION WEEK** *is glamorous — but really, it's just like Navy* SEALS *Hell Week."*

## FASHION WEEK(S)

Although **FASHION WEEKS** are held in cities from Berlin to Bangalore, fashion's calendar is dominated by **MILAN**, **PARIS**, **NEW YORK**, and **LONDON**, which each host (at least) two WEEKS a year: **FALL/WINTER** (**F/W**) in January–March; and **COUTURE** and **SPRING/SUMMER** (**S/S**) in July–October.

These weeks focus on four main audiences: **BUYERS**, **EDITORS**, **CELEBRITIES**, and (a recent novelty) **INFLUENCERS**. Each group has its own hierarchy, rivalries, and politics, and each looks, in part, to the others. E.g., at the show of a new designer, buyers will note the presence of major editorial faces (and vice versa). And, at the show of a famous name, the absence of a key buyer may raise eyebrows. That said, given the economics of post-Covid trade (and travel), the obligation to attend every show (or indeed, every week) has faded.

In addition to a whirl of social events and business **APPOINTMENTS**, each week's days are packed from ~9 A.M. to 8 P.M. with 10–20 events in (far-flung) locations across the city.

There are two key types of events:

› **PRESENTATION** · Where (more or less static) models display clothes in an intimate location (hotel suite, gallery, loft, &c.), allowing a relaxed and detailed examination.

› **RUNWAY SHOW** · Where each look is fleetingly paraded in a (spectacular) setting to communicate a collection's narrative theme.

Headline-grabbing runway shows are just the public-facing pinnacle of a complex business ecosystem. E.g., to accommodate manufacturing and delivery **LEAD TIMES**, major labels host **PRE-COLLECTION SHOWS** months before fashion week, where the majority of looks are shown to the trade for pre-order. And, in the day(s) following their runway show, designers host **RE-SEES** where the trade can place (additional) orders, and media stylists can **PULL** which looks they want to feature.

## SEATING

Seating shows involves an artful mix of drama and diplomacy since who is seen in the audience can add significantly to a designer's reputation and the collection's coverage. Juggling friends, enemies, and frenemies in such an intimate world is an exercise in tact.

**BOLD-FACE NAMES** are media catnip, and celebrities of various types can dramatically increase press coverage and social-media virality. **FASHION-FORWARD** actresses (Cate Blanchett) please trade and heavyweight publications; reality stars (Kim Kardashian) please the tabloids and the weeklies; and A-listers (Rihanna, Taylor Swift) please everyone.

In February 2024, Beyoncé "stole" New York Fashion Week when she made a surprise audience appearance at the ("off-Broadway") Bushwick show of Raul Lopez's label, Luar.

To the cognoscenti, only the first three rows of seating count. The **FRONT ROW** is the only place to seat V.I.P.s — which explains the preference for **U-SHAPED** runways that have more front-row seating.

V.I.P.s expect to be seated next to people of equal or greater status, and so the front row becomes integral to the show when captured by the photographers.

**V.V.I.P.s** are seated in **PRIME POSITION** along the front row, e.g., two-thirds down a **STRAIGHT** (**OUT AND BACK**) runway — a vantage point that allows ample time to see the **FRONT AND BACK** of each **LOOK**.

More junior members of an editorial or buying team can be arrayed in the second or third rows, but the rows beyond that — **SIBERIA** — are seldom to be tolerated by anyone with the slightest influence.

Stories abound of people demanding upgrades, refusing seats they deem insulting, or storming out of shows in fits of pique.

Non-V.I.P.s sometimes sneak into vacant front-row seats moments before a show start; similarly **SEAT FILLERS** are drafted in to plug any unphotogenic gaps.

*Models wearing protective shoe coverings are instructed on how to walk Jason Wu's S/S 2013 show*

(Guests seated in the front row may be asked to move their handbags so as not to clutter the runway photographs.)

There is an elite group of highly influential commentators for whom, if they are running late, many designers will **HOLD THE SHOW**.

Traditionally, this meant **ANNA** (Wintour), editor-in-chief of *Vogue*; **SUZY** (Menkes), formerly fashion editor of *The International Herald Tribune*; and key writers from *The New York Times*, *Women's Wear Daily*, &c.

Nowadays, the most influential social-media influencers have joined this group, because of their online following (which often dwarfs even major titles), their immediacy (especially when compared to long-lead monthly magazines), and their (perceived) independence.

## LOOKS & CASTING

Fashion shows are constructed in many ways; the following is but one example.

A **DESIGNER** works with a **STYLIST** to **FOCUS** a **COLLECTION** into a series of **LOOKS** that constitute the **SHOW**.

This process often involves a **LOOK MODEL** upon whom different **COMBINATIONS** of clothes and accessories are **TESTED**. The look model can be the designer's **MUSE**, or a **FIT MODEL** whose proportions suit the designer's style and the character of the collection.

The number of looks in a show varies across designers and seasons; most have between 20 and 40, though some have as many as 80–90.

Integral to a show's creation is the **HAIR AND MAKE-UP TEST**. Here the **LEAD** (*or* **KEY**) hair and make-up artists work with the designer and stylist to establish how the models will look.

While the designer and stylist work with **PRODUCERS** and **TECHNICIANS** to create the look, feel, and sound of the show, the task of locating suitable models falls to the **CASTING DIRECTOR**.

Casting directors generally work on a number of shows and are constantly **SCOUTING** for models to suit a range of designers. Aspiring and established models have **GO-SEES** with casting directors. And, as shows loom, **PRE-CASTINGS** narrow a selection of models to be **PRESENTED** to the designer and stylist.

Casting often involves arbitrage with model agents. Casting directors request an **OPTION** (**FIRST** or **SECOND**) for each model — a tentative booking that allows both sides to hedge their bets. Directors want the best models for their shows; agents want the hottest shows for their models. Fees are negotiated, schedules are juggled, and the shows get cast.

After casting, **FITTINGS** are held to match each look to a model and adjust the clothes accordingly. (Attending a fitting does not guarantee a model will appear in the show.) Fittings conclude with **ROTATION**, where the order of the looks is finalized, both to establish the narrative of the show and to allow **CHANGING TIME** for models with multiple looks. Fittings and re-fittings take place in the days and hours before a show, placing further pressure on the schedules of popular models.

*Anna Wintour, Virginia Smith, and Hamish Bowles at Jason Wu's S/S 2013 show* ☞

## BACKSTAGE

A show's **CALL TIME** is usually 2–3 hours before it starts, though models are regularly delayed by late-starting prior shows, or traffic.

Once **CHECKED IN**, models are **GRABBED** by **HAIR AND MAKE-UP**, whose team of stylists erase any evidence of personal looks or previous shows and re-create the **CONCEPT** that was finalized at the hair and make-up test.

Most shows have a **UNIFORM** hair and make-up style for every model; early-arriving models are used by the lead stylists to **DEMO** the processes to their teams.

During hair and make-up, the models are summoned for a rehearsal, where the show's structure and choreography are explained.

To prevent clothes becoming damaged or creased, **DRESSING** happens only minutes before the show begins, when "**FIRST LOOKS**" is called. Models go to the **RACK** labelled with the **COMP CARD** that displays their name, picture, and vital statistics. There, **DRESSERS** help them **ASSEMBLE** the look to match exactly the **REFERENCE PICTURES** on the **DRESSER CARDS**.

Once attired, the models will usually be photographed for the **LOOK BOOK** that forms the show's archival record. Then they **LINE UP**, in the order they will **WALK**, for **FINAL ADJUSTMENTS** and words of encouragement. Some designers display inspirational posters backstage, e.g., "*you're a confident, sexy, fun woman!*"

Finally, in sync with the music, the models are sent out: **GO! ... GO! ... GO!**

## THE SHOW

Models **WALK THE RUNWAY** in the style they have been given — e.g., "bright," "confident," "stoical," "no smiles" — and, if instructed, will **STOP** in front of the photographers.

The photographers are usually forewarned as to how the models will walk and whether or not they will stop.

Models with more than one look make a **QUICK CHANGE** on returning before going **BACK OUT**. The number of looks shown at any one time depends on the length and layout of the runway and the choreography. The tradition of runway shows is to **OPEN** and **CLOSE** with the **STRONGEST** looks, worn by the strongest (or most famous) models.

The style of **FINALE** varies by designer. Some send out every look at once, others send just a few. If designers take a bow, some are shy, others exuberant; certain designers walk (or cartwheel) down the runway, alone or with their models. Backstage, designers are usually greeted with applause.

Runway shows seldom start on time and are not usually considered late until 20 minutes or so after schedule. For all their planning, pressure, and controlled chaos, most shows last just 10–15 minutes — and savvy spectators will be off to the next event before the applause has died down.

(Anna Wintour is famous for arriving early, because she knows designers may **HOLD** the show for her; that said, she is often the first out of the building once the show is over.)

Once displayed, the clothes that formed the looks become **SHOW SAMPLES** that can be sent around the world for magazine shoots or worn by stars down the red carpet. Emerging designers might sell their samples to raise money; established brands will archive them.

## MODELS

What models are paid for runway shows varies tremendously. Inexperienced models may walk for free (or for handbags and shoes) to gain experience and exposure; A-list models can command more than $50,000 a show.

That said, some designers are notoriously parsimonious and get away with paying little (or nothing) because of their reputation. Conversely, well-known models will walk for free, or at reduced rates, for their friends.

**SUPERMODELS** (**SUPERS**) exist in a different orbit: If they walk runway shows at all, it is usually because they are friends with a designer, contractually obliged by a wider brand relationship, or handsomely remunerated.

Model agents usually take up to 20% from their client and 20% from the designer.

Popular models typically appear in a number of shows, which inevitably creates tight deadlines. While most designers are happy to accommodate models' schedules, some try to **LOCK OUT** the competition with unnecessarily early call times. This brinkmanship is not just an issue within a single fashion week; in years past designers in London became upset when models left the city early for castings and fittings in Milan.

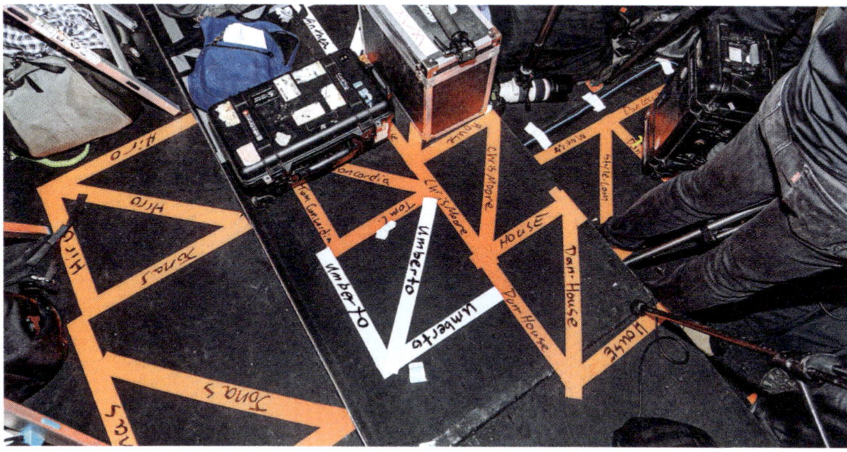


*The photographer's* PIT *at Jason Wu's S/S 2013 show*

## SNAPPERS

**PAPARAZZI** {☞ p.97} and **STREET FASHION** photographers aside, there are three (overlapping) groups of fashion week snapper: those who work **BACKSTAGE**; those who snap the **FRONT ROW**; and **RUNWAY PHOTOGRAPHERS** who shoot the **CLOTHES**.

**HOUSE PHOTOGRAPHERS** document the show for the designer, **SCOUTING** the location to test the brightness and colour temperature of the lights and **MARKING OUT** (with coloured tape) **STANDING POSITIONS** on the floor of the photographers' **PIT**.

Space in these pits is tight, and etiquette demands that photographers remain in their (foot-square) spot, tuck in their elbows, and ensure their lenses do not swing disruptively from side to side.

**MAIN SPOTS** in **PRIME POSITION** (front and centre) are reserved for the **HOUSE** and those shooting for major publications. If territorial skirmishes occur, they are settled by the house photographer or the production team. That said, there is a community of seasoned runway snappers who respect an unwritten pecking order and are accustomed to working in close proximity, show after show.

Unless they are tasked with photographing **DETAILS**, like shoes or accessories, the goal of the runway photographer is to capture **FULL-LENGTH** pictures of every look. The best shot is sharp and uncluttered, and with the clothes and model displaying a **GOOD LINE**. Ideally, the model's eyes will be open and her front foot will be down and flat.

Runway photographers tend to shoot with 70–200mm zooms or 300mm prime lenses — often attached to monopods for stability and to avoid fatigue. Like sports photographers, they shoot at a wide aperture (*f*2.8) to soften the background and a fast shutter speed (at least 1/250th of a second) to freeze the action. Some photographers will pick a spot along the runway and blast the motor drive when each model comes into frame. Others will zoom out as each model walks toward them, taking a picture with every step.

Photographers usually capture 10 to 15 frames per look and can shoot 2,000 pictures in a show. Nowadays, digital cameras are standard; some shoot in the highest-resolution **RAW** format, though — because of limitations in storage and processing time — many shoot lower-res **JPEGS**.

Boxes are used to elevate photographers standing farther from the stage; those who arrive with tripods, flash, or stepladders risk being called **TOURISTS**.

For years **VIDEO** was considered a second-tier medium, but in an age when social media virality is everything, shows are structured, staged, and lit with TikTok, Instagram, YouTube, &c. in mind — to say nothing of (more or less successful) forays in the **METAVERSE**.

In recent years, in addition to live-streaming their runway shows online, major brands go to extraordinary lengths to create highly produced **SHOW VIDEOS** featuring multi-camera coverage of the runway, as well as details that even the attending audience did not see, such as drone overflights or backstage footage.

# Tic-Tac & Racing Talk

*For generations, British horse races were enlivened by a band of* **TIC-TAC MEN** *who — until the arrival of walkie-talkies — were employed by bookmakers to place bets and communicate odds across long distances using the hand signs of* **TIC-TAC**.

*Standing on boxes or ladders, wearing white cotton gloves, these* **ARM-SWINGERS** *(or* **RACECOURSE TELEGRAPHISTS**) *would windmill their messages over the heads of the punters — literally and metaphorically. And because tic-tac is a universal code, each* **TICCY** *sold his own coloured* **TWIST CARD** *on which that day's race numbers were jumbled; this ensured that only paying subscribers could decode the messages.*

*Below is the bookie* **BARRY "BISMARCK" DENNIS** *(1941–2024) who, for almost 50 years, was an unmistakable presence at betting rings across the United Kingdom.*

**1/1**
EVENS
*Flap hands up and down*

**11/10**
TIPS
*Bring fingertips together*

**5/4**
WRIST
*Place hand on wrist*

**11/8**
UP THE ARM
*Move hand from wrist to elbow*

**6/4**
EAR'OLE
*Back of hand to ear*

**13/8**
BITS ON THE EAR'OLE
*6/4 followed by 11/10*

**7/4**
SHOULDER
*Hand touches shoulder*

**15/8**
DOUBLE TAP
*Hand taps shoulder twice*

**2/1**
BOTTLE
*Hand touches nose*

*Tic-Tac men at a British racecourse*

**9/4**
TOP OF THE HEAD
*Both hands to head*

**5/2**
FACE
*Both hands to face*

**11/4**
ELEF A VIER
*5/2, then touch fingertips together*

**3/1**
CARPET
*Touch chest below chin*

**100/30**
BURLINGTON BERTIE
*3/1, then touch fingertips together*

**7/2**
CARPET AND HALF
*Both hands touch chest*

**4/1**
ROUF
*Draw L-shape in front of chest*

**9/2**
(ON THE) SHOULDERS
*Hands to shoulders*

**5/1**
HAND(FUL)
*Right hand to shoulder*

**6/1**
EXES
*Right hand to shoulder, then head*

**7/1**
NEVES
*Right hand to shoulder, then nose*

**8/1**
T.H.
*Right hand to shoulder, then chest*

**9/1**
ENIN
*Like a teapot*

**10/1 · 20/1**
COCKLE · DOUBLE TAP
*Punch fists together ... Twice*

**25/1**
PONY
*Punch fists together twice, touch shoulder*

**33/1**
DOUBLE CARPET
*Cross arms over chest*

**50/1**
BULLSEYE
*Stack fists together*

**100/1**
CENTURY
*Cross hands in front of body*

Other tic-tac signs communicated horse and race numbers or identified individual bookmakers; e.g., Ladbrokes was signalled with a halo, and William Hill with a hill-shaped undulation.

## THE (GOLDEN-AGE) ARGOT OF ON-COURSE BOOKIES

**MAN ON THE STOOL** · Bookmaker. *A.k.a.*, **BOOKIE / LAYER / SATCHEL SWINGER.**

The adage "*It's not the prices, but the man on the stool*" may be an exaggeration, but if every **FIRM** in a **RING** has the same odds, **PUNTERS** tend to gravitate to charismatic characters.

**JOINT** · The **TOOLS** of the trade. Historically, this involved little more than an **APRIL** [fool = **STOOL**]; **MUSH** [umbrella]; painted **SIGN**; **CHALKBOARD**; and **HOD** [cash bag] hung from a **TRIPOD**. Now joints include laptops, printers, and L.E.D. displays.

**TICKETS AND CHALK** · An allusion to the halcyon days of bookmaking. As Barry Dennis once said, with tongue firmly in cheek:

> It's an easy game, bookmaking — all you need is tickets and chalk. Change the prices, take the money, and win.[1]

**TISSUE** · A bookie's race card annotated with notes and prices; now essentially obsolete.

**TRAVELLING CIRCUS** · The coterie of bookies who traipse to races across the country.

**FIRM** · A bookie and his **CREW**, including:

› **CLERK** · Who records every bet taken in the **CAPTAIN**, i.e., the betting ledger.

› **BAG MAN** · Who takes in and pays out cash.

› **FLOOR MAN** · Who tracks rival prices and market moves (now all but obsolete).

**CARD MARKER** · An expert on **FORM** (i.e., a horse's racing record) who sells his wisdom.

**ODDS COMPILER** *or* **SETTER** · One who calculates the (**CHOC**) **ICES** (i.e., prices) for bookies, balancing a knowledge of form with movements in the market.

**CHALK & WATER MAN** · A chap (often an ex lightweight boxer) who once sold sticks of chalk and water-soaked rags to clean the boards.

**TIPSTER** · A (professional) forecaster who sells, or gives away, betting recommendations. (In Australia, a tipster who demands a share of the winnings is a **COAT TUGGER**.)

**PITCH** · The specific location on a course where a bookmaker is permitted to **ANCHOR** his **JOINT**, and take bets from the public.

Until 1998, pitches were allocated on the basis of inherited seniority (hence the gallows humour, "*Any good deaths in the ring lately?*").

Nowadays, bookies pick the most lucrative (i.e., visible and well-trafficked) pitches based on their number on the **PICK LIST** — positions on which can change hands for small fortunes.

Most courses locate pitches in **BETTING RINGS**, which are positioned to serve the various course **ENCLOSURES**, for example:

› **RAILS** · Pitches along the fence that divides the **MEMBERS' ENCLOSURE** from **TATTS**. The best pitch is usually **№ 1 ON THE RAIL**.

› **TATTS / TATTERSALLS** · Often the busiest betting ring, where punters have access to the paddock. Named after the legendary horse auctioneer Richard Tattersall (1724–95).

› **SILVER RING / COURSE ENCLOSURE** · The most informal enclosure with the lowest admission price, usually located outside / inside the actual course, respectively. Sometimes *A.k.a.*, **FAMILY ENCLOSURE**.

## ODDS SLANG

| | |
|---|---|
| 1/1 | **EVS / MAJOR STEVENS** [= **EVENS**] **LEVELS** (**YOU DEVILS**) / **STRAIGHT UP** |
| 2/1 | **BOTTLE** [of glue *or* beer = ear] / **BICE** |
| 3/1 | **CARPET** [a] / **GIMMEL** / **TRES** |
| 4/1 | **ROUF** † |
| 5/1 | **CHING / HAND**(**FUL**) / **MONKEY** |
| 5/2 | **FACE** ‡ / **BICE N'ALF** |
| 5/4 | **WRIST** ‡ |
| 6/1 | **EXES** † / **XIS** † / **TOM MIX** |
| 6/4 | **EXES TO ROUF** † / **EAR'OLE** ‡ |
| 6/5 | **SAIS A CHING** |
| 7/1 | **NEVES** † / **NEVIS** † |
| 7/2 | **CARPET N'ALF** [a] |
| 7/4 | **NEVES TO ROUF** † / **SHOULDER** ‡ |
| 8/1 | **T.H.** ("*tee 'aitch*") † |
| 9/1 | **ENIN** † |
| 9/2 | (**ON THE**) **SHOULDERS** ‡ |
| 9/4 | **TOP OF THE HEAD / HORNS** ‡ |
| 10/1 | **COCKLE** [and hen = ten] / **NET** † |
| 11/1 | **ELEF** † |
| 11/4 | **ELEF A VIER** † [b] |
| 11/8 | **UP THE ARM** ‡ |
| 11/10 | **TIPS** ‡ |
| 12/1 | **NET AND BICE** † |
| 13/8 | **UNLUCKY / BITS ON THE EAR'OLE** ‡ |
| 14/1 | **NET AND ROUF** † |
| 15/8 | **DOUBLE TAP** † |
| 16/1 | **NET AND EX** † |
| 20/1 | **DOUBLE NET** † |
| 25/1 | **PONY / MACA**(**RONI**) [c] |
| 33/1 | **DOUBLE CARPET** [a] |
| 50/1 | **BULLSEYE** [d] |
| 100/1 | **CENTURY** |
| 100/30 | **BURLINGTON BERTIE** [e] / **SCRUFFY AND DIRTY** |

† Backslang. ‡ Based upon the tic-tac gesture. [a] Often said to be derived from British prison slang, where a three-month (or year) sentence was a drag, which was then rhymified into carpet[-bag]. [b] Four in German is *vier*. [c] Cockney rhyming slang for pony. [d] The points for an inner bullseye in darts. [e] The character of two (oft confused) music hall songs: "Burlington Bertie"(1900) was a paean to aristocratic idling; "Burlington Bertie from Bow" (1915) was its parody.

**DECIMAL ODDS** · The fractional odds listed above — used universally by on-course bookmakers — represent the *profit* (e.g., 5/1 means you win £5 win for each £1 staked). The decimal odds used by online exchanges represent the *return* (e.g., 2.5 means you win £2.50 for every £1 staked).

## PUNTERS

**PUNTER / BILLY** [Bunter] · One who bets.

**MUG PUNTER** · One who bets **LAZY MONEY** e.g., on lucky names, random tips, complex systems, famous jockeys, patriotic horses, &c. *Also*, **STEAM** [tug = mug] / **DONOR**.

**NOTED** *or* **SMART** *or* **SHREWD MONEY** · Bets by **FACES / SHREWDIES / SHARPOS** (i.e., professional punters) whose **ACTION** (if identified) will be **NOTED** by bookies and may influence the odds offered. Such **SHARP MONEY** sometimes prompts *"half the staff to jump off the pitch and place their own bets."*

**BEARDS** · Accomplices who place bets on behalf of FACES (or banned punters) to avoid alerting bookies. {☞ CLEANSKINS p.120}

**SIGHTSEERS / LOOKERS** · Those who hover around a PITCH but never place a bet.

## BETTING

**LUMPY / CHUNKY / THICK 'UN / BIG 'UN** · A hefty bet, or sometimes a hefty loss. (*"He's* **DOING CHUNKS** *after that* BOGEY *came in!"*)

**CUTTING** · To accept only part of a bet. (*"He wanted £1,000 at 6/4, but I* **CUT** *him to £400."*)

(**GIVE 'EM**) **THE BLUFF** · To avoid taking a bet without actually **KNOCKING IT BACK** (i.e., refusing it). In the maelstrom of the ring, bookies **BLUFF** punters by pretending not to hear them; looking over their heads or in the wrong direction; or claiming another punter has taken the bet before changing the price.

**DUCKING** · When bookies discourage punters by offering deliberately unattractive odds, to reduce their liability to a race and help balance their books.

**TOP OF THE BOOK** · When LUMPY bets placed by a FACE are recorded separately, and do not influence the calculation of other odds in the book. Bookies will **STAND** such top of the book action (i.e., lay without HEDGING) hoping to win off the FACE in the long term.

**IN-RUNNING** · Bets taken during a race.

**COMMISSION AGENT** · One who places bets (e.g., for celebrities), in return for a **TASTE**.

**NAP** · A tipster's best bet of the day, possibly derived from the card game Napoleon. (The nap is not necessarily the JOLLY.)

**N.B.** · The **NEXT BEST** tip, after the NAP.

**ARBING / ARBITRAGE** · Attempting to guarantee a profit by placing bets at different odds (with different bookies) to cover every outcome of an event. *A.k.a.*, **SUREBETTING**.

**SLEEPERS** · Stakes and winnings that remain unclaimed by punters.

**HEDGING / LAYING OFF / COVERING / BACKING IT BACK** · When bookmakers reduce their exposure to a race (e.g., after an especially LUMPY bet) by placing balancing bets with rival firms. Not all bookies agree with the strategy: *"Hedging is for gardeners!"*

**THE AMBULANCE WON** · A race where not even the horses came out on top.

**OPEN YOUR SHOULDERS** · To bet with confidence. (*"Bravado backed up with cash."*)

**SIMPLE** · A straightforward bet — usually one horse to win in a single race. *Conversely*, **EXOTIC** · A bet on multiple outcomes.

**ACCA / ACCUMULATOR** · A bet combining multiple selections, all of which must win.

**ON THE THUMB** · When odds are shortening across the RING. Named after a thumb-wagging TIC-TAC signal.

**RICK** · A bookmaker's error.

**CHALK PLAYER** *or* **EATER** · One who **BETS THE CHALK**, i.e., backs only JOLLIES.

## GEE-GEES

**JOLLY** · *"The jolly old favourite!" A.k.a.*, **THE CHALK** (because of a profusion of odds erased by its name on the board), or **THE SPLONK**.

**BANKER** · A bet on a **LOCK**, **CERT**, *or* **SHOO-IN** — i.e., a nag whose win is **NAILED ON**.

*A bookie's* **HOD**

**BISMARCK** · A **JOLLY** that bookies predict (i.e., hope) will sink; named after the doomed German battleship scuttled in 1941.

**BOGEY** · The worst possible horse (or result) from a bookie's perspective. When a bogey wins, bookies suffer a **NOSEBLEED**.

**RAG** · An outsider with no chance.

**SKINNER** · An unbacked horse that, should it win, allows bookies to **SKIN THE LAMB**, i.e., keep all the stakes and pay nothing out.

**HYPE HORSE** / **BUZZER** · A favourite that dominates pre-race coverage, which (**MUG**) punters enthusiastically **OVERBET**.

**DRIFTER** · A horse whose odds lengthen as the market cools. ("*Drifters can't win.*")

**STEAMER** / **SPRINGER** · A horse whose odds shorten in the face of market support.

## BEES & HONEY [MONEY]

**TANK** · [Tommy **TANK** = bank] · A bookie's cash reserve — ideally deep enough to sustain a **BAD RUN**. If a bookie is **POTLESS** (skint) he might look for an **ARTHUR** (money lender) to **BANKROLL** his operation until fortunes change. [J. **ARTHUR** Rank = bank (among other things).]

(**FLY A**) **KITE** · (To pay by) cheque.

Loose change.......................... **SHRAPNEL**
Cash ............... **NELSON** [Eddies = reddies]
£1 ......................... **QUID** / **BAR** / **NICKER**
£2 ................................ **BOTTLE** [of glue]
£5 ............. **LADY** [Godiva] / **JACKS** [alive]
£10............. **COCKLE** [and hen] / **BIG BEN**
£20 ................... **SCORE** / **BOBBY** [Moore]
**APPLE** (**CORE**) / **HORN** [of plenty]
£25.......................... **PONY** / **MACA**[roni]
£50 ........................................ **BULLSEYE**
£100............... **TON** / **CENTURY** / **ONE-ER**
£500 ......................................... **MONKEY**
£1,000.............. **GRAND** / **BAG** (**OF SAND**)

**FIDDLER** · A bookie who takes only **ROCK CAKES** (i.e., **SMALL MONEY** bets).

**SMALL BUT BRISK** · A flurry of **ROCK CAKES**, e.g., from the **HOLIDAY CROWD**. *Conversely*, **SERIOUS PUNTING ACTION**.

**RING BET** · One made on credit; so-called because the punter's name is circled in the book. (The ring is erased once the debt is paid.)

**KNOCKING** · When a punter fails to pay the stake on a lost **RING BET**. ("*A cardinal sin.*")

**FLIMPING** · Ripping punters off, e.g., paying less than they've won. ("*Very naughty.*")

**DOING YOUR COBBLERS** · Suffering a disastrous race, day, or season. ("*Doing his cobblers? He's* **JUMPING OFF THE GRANDSTAND**!")

**BEESWAX** / **AJAX** · Betting tax.

# Gymspiration at the Glorious House of Gainz

*The lore and language of the* **GYM.**

## GYM GOERS

**GYM RAT** · One whose free time is gym time.

**CLASS JUNKIE** · One who signs up for every class (and aspires to be the **CLASS STAR**).

**LIBRARIAN** · One who finds, reads, brandishes, and argues about articles (of varying reliability) on training, nutrition, and fitness.

**LIVE STREAMERS** · Those who (have abandoned the gym to) take online classes at home; a trend accelerated by Covid.

**MASCOT** · An omnipresent gym regular who takes it upon themselves to befriend everyone and/or complain about everything.

**JUICER / JUICE HE(A)D / STED HE(A)D** · Those who (ab)use anabolic steroids (*A.k.a.*, **GEAR / VITAMIN S**) to **GET RIPPED**.

**NATTY** · A "natural" athlete who eschews artificial aids and relies on training and diet to achieve a **NATTY PHYSIQUE**. *Hence*, **FAKE NATTY** · A secret JUICER.

**SUPPS** · Nutritional supplements.

**HURLER** · A vomiter.

**MEATHEAD / LUNK** · Obnoxious, muscle-bound (wo)men who are loud, inconsiderate, and simply drop their weights when done.

**JANUARY JOINER / RESOLUTIONARY** · One who joins or frequents gyms in the new year, to turn over a leaf or atone for festive excess. ("*New year, new me!*") Gyms also see spikes when summer looms, from those seeking a **SUMMER** or **BIKINI BOD(Y)**.

**STRETCHIBITIONIST** · A gym poseur.

**CARDIO BUNNY** *or* **QUEEN** · One who obsesses on cardio (e.g., treadmills) but shuns weights. *A.k.a.*, **ELLIPTICAL ADDICT**.

**WEEKEND WARRIOR** · One who works out (only) on Saturdays and Sundays.

**MACHINE STALKER** · One who lurks around an occupied machine, guilting its user to quit.

**MACHINE HOG** · One who monopolizes a piece of equipment, refusing to **ALTERNATE**.

**NON-WIPER** · One who leaves a trail of sweat.

## BROS

**GYM BRO** · An obnoxiously macho GYM RAT usually fixated on (shirtless or tank-topped) body-building. Seldom seen without a plastic **GALLON JUG** of water and a **TRIPOD** to take selfies for Insta. The kind of **CHAD** who:

› Eats only **C.R.B.** (chicken, rice, broccoli)
› Worships at the **IRON TEMPLE** or the **GLORIOUS HOUSE OF GAINZ**
› Hashtags **#SHRED_FLEX_REPEAT**
› Wears a **PUMP COVER** (oversized t-shirt)
› Rallies to the cry of **WE GO JIM!**

**FIGHTING DEMONS** · When **GYMCELS** (incel GYM BROs) **GO UNDER THE BAR** (lift weights) to turn rejection and heartache into **GYMSPIRATION**. {☞ INCELS, p.263}

**GYMSHARK** · Female-focused gym apparel; and a term for a predatory GYM BRO.

**BRO SCIENCE** · The urban myths and anecdotal **FIT-SPLAINING** of **BROFESSORS**.

**GYM, TAN, LAUNDRY (G.T.L.)** · The holy trinity (and daily prayer) of the **BROSEPH**.

*"Perspire to Greatness" at Crunch in Chelsea, Manhattan*

## WORKOUTS

It's no accident that so many gyms claim (or aspire) to be **JUDGEMENT-FREE**, since many body-conscious people fear the scrutiny of others and the reality of their reflection. (Gyms often remove mirrors for this reason.)

**PRE-WORKOUT** · **SUPPS** taken to enhance athletic performance. *Also*, **PRE** *or* **POST TRAIN** · Eating before *or* after working out.

**NON** *or* **HIGH-STIM** · **SUPPS** devoid of *or* packed with stimulants (e.g., caffeine, methylhexanamine). **STIMS** may improve endurance and alertness, at a cost of side effects like skin **TINGLES**, jitteriness, and insomnia.

**PROTEIN SLUDGE** · Low-calorie, high-protein (homemade) foods, usually containing protein powders (e.g., whey). *Also*, **PROATMEAL**, oats and whey; and **PROTEIN FLUFF**, **SLUDGE** in the form of a (frozen) dessert.

**REP(ETITION)** · A single performance of any exercise. E.g., one squat or biceps curl.

**SET** · A group of **REPS** performed without rest. E.g., one **SET** of push-ups = 12 **REPS**.

**SUPER SET** · Performing a **SET** of two different exercises, back to back, with no (or little) rest. Endless variations exist, such as **PUSH-PULL SUPERSETS** (e.g., *bench press + barbell row*) and **UPPER-LOWER SUPERSETS** (e.g., *back squat + chin-up*).

**ONE REP MAX** · The maximum liftable weight for one **REP** of a given exercise.

**TABATA** · A variation of **H.I.I.T.** (High-Intensity Interval Training) that involves 20 seconds of exercise and 10 seconds of rest, for eight rounds (i.e., four minutes). Named after the protocol's inventor, Dr. Izumi Tabata.

**PRIME-TIME** · The most popular gym hours, usually 05:00–08:30, 12:00–13:00, 16:30–20:30. Certain groups favour specific hours, e.g., city traders who exercise 16:00–18:30, after the markets have closed.

**NOOB(IE) GAINS** · The rapid muscle growth **NEWBIES** enjoy during training's first flush.

**BRO SPLIT / BODY PART SPLIT** · A regimen that dedicates a day to specific muscle groups, and incorporates **REST DAYS**. E.g.:

| | |
|---|---|
| Monday | CHEST |
| Tuesday | BACK |
| Wednesday | SHOULDERS |
| Thursday | LEGS |
| Friday | ARMS |
| Saturday & Sunday | REST |

**INTERNATIONAL CHEST DAY** · It's unclear how or why Monday became established as **I.C.D.** — some credit Arnold Schwarzenegger's daily routine, others claim it's simply an inspiring way to kick off the week.

**STRIDE OF PRIDE** · One effect of **LEG DAY**.

**NIGHT RIDERS** · *Those who work out into the small hours at* **BIG BOX** *gyms*

**BEAST MODE** · Pushing yourself to (or way beyond) your physical limit, i.e., (**GOING TO**) **TOTAL FAILURE**. *Also*, entering a high-performance flow state known as **THE ZONE**.

**D.O.M.S.** · Delayed Onset Muscle Soreness, e.g., caused by doing **A.M.R.A.P.** (As Many Reps As Possible). *A.k.a.*, **THE SORENESS**.

**LABOUR PAINS** · Excessive workout grunts. *A.k.a.*, **GYMGASMS**.

**SPOT** · To assist a lifter in using free weights safely. **SPOTTERS** will indicate that they are not assisting a lift with **IT'S ALL YOU!** Some assert that if a spotter even touches the bar, the **REP** has been **STOLEN** and does not count.

**WORK IN** / **JUMP IN** · To take turns with a piece of equipment (i.e., **ALTERNATING**) by **TRADING SETS** and **RESTS** with other users.

**CHEATING** · Deploying **IMPROPER FORM** (*A.k.a.*, **BODY ENGLISH**) to make an exercise easier or to overcome a training hurdle.

**EGO LIFTING** · Lifting more than you can (safely) handle (often with **POOR FORM**) for bragging rights or to look cool.

**FORM POLICING** · Offering unsolicited, unwanted, and often erroneous "advice" on technique — increasingly common in online comments. ("*Hey man, quick tip* ... ")

**CURL MONKEY** · One fixated on their biceps.

**'MIRIN'** · Admiring your own **FORM**, or the **EYE CANDY** of others (e.g., a **GYM CRUSH**). *Hence*, **WORKING ON THE FACE** · 'Mirin' in the mirror.

**WAIST-UP** *or* **MIRROR MUSCLES** · Those that can easily be **'MIRED** in the mirror and posted to Insta (e.g., biceps, triceps, chest, lats, shoulders). Working only **WAIST-UP** risks muscle imbalances and postural problems.

**DO YOU EVEN LIFT?** · Trademark **GYM BRO** sneer made to provoke (or amuse) by challenging someone's expertise, prowess, or strength.

## WEIGHT NICKNAMES

| *lb* | *nickname* |
|---|---|
| 100 | **C NOTES** / **HUNNIES** / **HUNDOS** |
| 45 | **45S** / **PIES** / **PLATES** / **BIG WHEELS** / **DOGS** / **CADILLACS** / **COLTS** / **DONUTS** / **COOKIES** |
| 35 | **FAKE 45S** |
| 25 | **QUARTERS** / **HALVES** |
| 10 | **DIMES** |
| 5 | **NICKELS** / **5S** |
| 2.5 | **SILVERS** / **PENNIES** / **BAGELS** / **WASHERS** / **FRISBEES** / **FAKE 5S** |

## BODIES & BODY TYPES

| | |
|---|---|
| **RIPPED** | large and lean |
| **B.F.** | Body Fat |
| **SKELETOR** | ripped but skinny |

**PEELED** .................... lean and thin-skinned
**CUT** ............ body with well-defined muscles
**JACKED** ......................... larger but less lean
**SWOLE / SWOL** ... so **JACKED**, you're swollen
**YOLKED** ... to have well-developed shoulders
**HENCH** ........... muscular and well-developed
**HUGE** ........ big muscles and a little extra **B.F.**
**FREAK** ................................ beyond **HUGE**

**THIN-SKINNED / SINEWY** · When every muscle and tendon is visible and defined; the desired **STAGE READY** state for competitors.

**TONED** · Synonym for **MUSCLE DEFINITION**, often used by **CARDIO QUEENS** when they (finally) start strength training: "*I don't want to* **GET BIG**, *I just want to* **TONE UP**."

**SKINNY FAT** · A person who appears skinny and wears smaller-size clothing but has a high percentage of body fat. The opposite is **BUILTFAT** *or* **BUSCULAR** · Fat but muscular.

**UNBIG YOUR BACK (FOR THE SUMMER)** · (Obnoxious) injunction to lose weight.

**BULKING** · Gaining muscle mass with heavy weights and a high-calorie diet. *Conversely*, **CUTTING**: Going into **CALORIE DEFICIT** to **LEAN OUT** and show off what you've built. (Winter is **BULKING SEASON**; in summer we **CUT FOR THE BEACH**.)

**WHEELS** .................................. quadriceps
**BIS** ................................................. biceps
**TRIS** ............................................... triceps
**HAMMIES** ................................ hamstrings
**LATS** ................................. *latissimus dorsi*
**BOULDERS** .................. (bulging) shoulders
**GUNS** ........................ arms / biceps / triceps
**PINS / WHEELS / TOOTHPICKS / CHOPSTICKS / POLES / DOGS** ............ legs

**BIRD LEGS** · A result of (over)working the arms and upper-body and neglecting the **PINS**.

**PUKIE THE CLOWN** · An unofficial CrossFit "mascot" celebrating the unpleasant, emetic consequences of **GOING TO TOTAL FAILURE**.

**UNCLE RHABDO** · A cartoon clown who warns of rhabdomyolysis — a potentially fatal consequence of over-exertion, associated with CrossFit. Depicted vomiting and/or bleeding and hooked up to a kidney dialysis machine.

**GROWTH GUT** · A muscular **POTBELLY**; one side-effect of human growth hormone (**H.G.H.**), which is taken (illegally) by those seeking rapid muscle development.

**H.G.H.** abusers risk becoming **ALL GUT NO BUTT** and can develop a bulging, muscular jaw, known as **WATERMELON FACE**.

## TRAINERS

In addition to creating bespoke and efficient exercise **ROUTINES**, trainers provide their clients with a range of services, e.g.: ensuring good **FORM**, **TECHNIQUE**, and the safe use of equipment; setting **GOALS** and tracking **PROGRESS**; adapting to a client's **MEDICAL LIMITATIONS** or concerns; offering (basic) **NUTRITIONAL ADVICE**; providing **ACCOUNTABILITY** (keeping clients honest); and offering **ENTERTAINMENT** (keeping clients engaged, not least with **VARIETY**).

**VERBAL QUEUING** · The careful use of encouraging language to coax clients to do exercises they would otherwise shirk.

**ROLE MODELS** · Like hairdressers, trainers are asked if they can help their clients achieve a certain **LOOK**. Some of the most popular current looks include buttocks like Lauralie Chapados, abdominals like Ryan Reynolds or Jessica Biel, and arms like Gemma Atkinson.

**REP-COUNTERS** · Trainers who pay clients scant attention, and simply count their **REPS**.

**BIG BOX GYM** · Branded chains (e.g., Planet Fitness, Equinox, LA Fitness, and Crunch). In contrast to **BOUTIQUES**, **INDIES**, and **PERSONAL TRAINING STUDIOS**.

**PROSPECTING / NEW BUSINESS** · Generating new client leads and/or enrolling a newbie into a training program.

**K.O.** · Conducting a fitness assessment and providing a timeline for achieving goals.

**FUNCTIONAL TRAINING** · Designing exercise routines that mimic real-life activities, to avoid injury and develop strength and form.

**RE-RACK** · To walk the floor and pick up after **MEATHEADS** who don't replace weights. ⊙

D316 KJT

# Hosing It Down with the Nikon Choir

*The dark arts of the flash-gun* **PAPARAZZI.**

The roguish celebrity photographer has been part of pop-culture ever since Walter Santesso depicted Paparazzo in Federico Fellini's *La Dolce Vita* (1960). This character was based on Tazio Secchiaroli (1925–98), who evolved from humble *scattini* [street photographer] to hungry *volpe* [fox], Vespa-ing down Rome's Via Veneto to snap some of the earliest candid press photos of stars like Sophia Loren, Anita Ekberg, and Ava Gardner.

Although early paps staged *paparazzati* — deliberate irritations (e.g., flash guns in the face) designed to provoke a sellable shot — the stars they targeted soon saw there was an upside to such "spontaneous" press coverage.

But, down the decades, the uncomfortable symbiosis between **PAPS** and stars devolved into something darker, punctuated by two tragedies and a technology.

First, the fatal pursuit of Princess Diana and the public breakdown of Britney Spears proved the human cost of tabloid froth. And then, the explosion of social media allowed celebrities to control, curate, and monetize their own images. (It's deeply ironic that the most intimate photos of the youngest British royals are now taken and published by their mother, Catherine, Princess of Wales.)

All this leaves the paparazzi in a tricky position: swamped by competition, constrained by regulation, crushed by deflation, crowded by Instagram, and scorned by a public that continues to lap up ever more set-up shots.

## TECHNIQUE

Although many paparazzi will also cover set-piece **RED CARPET** events, **PRESS AVAILS**, and other **STEP & REPEATS** (where stars pose against a backdrop of interlocking sponsor logos), **PAPPING** "proper" can be divided into two main types, which are defined by the choice of camera lens:

1. **LONG LENS** · Snapping unaware celebrities from a distance (200–300 yards) using 300–800 mm telephoto lenses. (*"Like photographing wildlife — the trick is not to disturb them."*)

**GOING LONG** to **STEAL** a picture in this way takes planning, patience, **TIP OFFS**, and technique — and, when successful, can be rewarded with a lucrative exclusive.

2. **SHORT & FLASH** · Shooting **UP CLOSE AND PERSONAL** with a wide (16–~50 mm) lens and flash gun. *A.ka.*, **WIDE & FLASH.**

The technique most associated with the ...

**GANG BANG** · An undignified (and unsafe) paparazzi **SWARM** / **SCRUM** / **PILE ON** / **WOLF-PACK**, e.g., between a celebrity exiting a restaurant and hustling into their car.

Although gang-bangs are a relatively good way to secure a shot (*"Stars have to leave the club at some point"*), the presence of other paps inevitably diminishes a **SET**'s value, and risks (further) antagonizing the subject.

**BURNING** · Abandoning a **LONG-LENS STAKEOUT** and going for a **SHORT & FLASH.**

**DOORSTEPPING** · Lurking near a celebrity's house, waiting for them to emerge {☞ p.261}. Sometimes necessitating the presence of a **PISS BOTTLE.**

**THE FOLLOW** · When paps **CHASE** a star's vehicle, often with scant regard to traffic laws or basic safety. (Some paps simply abandon their cars in the road to get a shot.) More than five cars **ON A FOLLOW** is known as a **TRAIN.**

Sometimes paps pursue in teams, borrowing the tactics of counter-intelligence officers, e.g., a **HEAD AND TAIL FOLLOW** where a star's car is **BOXED IN** front and rear {☞ p.126}.

In response, stars take evasive action, e.g., having their security detail drive a **STICK CAR** tight behind them, to fend off the paps.

☞ *Paps erect scaffolding to shoot Prince Harry's sports day, 1994*

**(JOB) JUMPING** · To hijack another pap's job — after a lucky street **PICKUP** or **TIP-OFF**. Jumping is considered a serious infraction of the "code" (unless you are the **JUMPER**).

Paps working on profitable exclusives may hire (luxury) cars to avoid being jumped (and to blend into high-class neighbourhoods).

**PICKUP** · A chance sighting of a celebrity — or a fellow pap who is on a **STAKE OUT**.

**PING-PONG** · Pap Matthew Suárez explains the term in relation to snapping Pete Wentz and Ashlee Simpson's baby, Bronx Mowgli:

> Ping-ponging is when you work with someone and take different angles so they can't escape. I was the distraction. They thought they were hiding the baby from me. And BAM! From the other side. Master of photography sneakily getting perfect pictures of the baby. [1]

**CAR SHOT** · Snapping stars inside their cars without getting run over, or garrotted by your camera-strap as it's hooked by a wing-mirror. Pap king Darryn Lyons explains the technique:

> Set your aperture at *f*.8 to *f*.11, full manual power on the Quantum flash unit, 250th of a second on the shutter speed, run at a car, and crash-bang-wallop with a wide-angle lens. [2]

**THROUGH TINTS** · Snapping covertly from a vehicle fitted with blackout windows.

**HOSE (IT DOWN)** · Firing off the motor-drive in the hope of securing a usable frame.

**HAIL MARY** · Holding a camera above your head and shooting blind (more miss than hit).

**TAPE UP** · Securing the focus ring of a wide-angle lens with thick tape, to ensure a sharp shot in the middle of a GANG BANG.

**DOUBLER** · A teleconverter that extends the magnification of a lens: A 2× doubler turns a 400mm lens into an 800mm. ("*Stick a doubler on it — she's miles away!*")

**SPOTTING** · The ability to spot celebs (and their cars) is a key skill. Paps will **TRAWL** likely locations, hoping to stumble on a **PICKUP**.

**TIP-OFF** · Many **GETS** come from an army of informers (club bouncers, restaurant workers, valet parkers, hospital staff, limo dispatchers, &c.) who are paid for their information or, in rare cases, given a cut of the **SET**'s earnings.

P.R.s secretly inform on clients who need a boost, and the location of reality-T.V. "stars" is regularly tipped by a show's production team.

**GREETERS** · Airport handlers (e.g., at L.A.X.) who expedite stars through the terminal. Paps are tipped off by the presence of **GREETERS** — who are sometimes tipped for their help.

**STALKERAZZI** · Regarded in the industry as a misnomer since, while many celebs *feel* that the paps are stalking them, there is a significant distinction between annoying photographers and (dangerously) obsessional fans.

One exception is the "paparazzo extraordinaire," Ron Galella, who so hounded Jacqueline Kennedy Onassis that she sued him for harassment, infliction of emotional distress, assault and battery, and invasion of privacy. Galella later admitted: "I had no girlfriend ... she was my girlfriend, in a way." [3]

**MELTING** · Blasting a subject with flashes (as a punishment for not **GIVING IT UP**).

**NIKON CHOIR** · The unmistakable sound of dozens of motor-drives firing in unison.

## SHOTS

**DOWN THE BARREL** · When a celebrity looks into the lens and connects directly with the viewer. ("*They're smiling just for us!*")

The value of such shots leads paps to yell to get a celebrity's focus. ("*To your left, Brad!*") Some paps are not above swearing at celebs to get them to stare down *their* barrel.

**CLEAN FULL-LENGTH** · An unobstructed, head-to-toe shot is the most sellable frame. *Conversely, "Only a* **HEAD SHOT**."

**THE PEOPLE FRAME** · A clean, sharp, smiling, down-the-barrel **MONEY SHOT** that is guaranteed to sell. Named after *People*, one of the last celebrity magazines still standing.

In Britain, a wining frame used to be called a **BOTTICELLI**, and many paps still pray for the legendary **RETIREMENT SHOT**.

*Britney Spears* vs *the Los Angeles paps, 2007*

**STARS – THEY'RE JUST LIKE US!** · In 2002, *Us Weekly* introduced a new feature that dramatically increased the options for paparazzi. In addition to looking poised and glamorous, celebrities can now also be snapped performing quotidian activities (*shopping! laundry! getting coffee!*) and suffering from quotidian afflictions (*cellulite! acne! bad hair!*).

**MUZ / MUZZY** · Soft focus, but still sellable. As paparazzo Phil Ramey said: "Quality is never an issue if the content is there." [4]

(**BIG**) **GET** · A sellable subject. The biggest gets are currently Taylor Swift, Tom Cruise, Brad Pitt, Beyoncé, and Meghan (and Harry).

## INTERACTIONS

**GIVE IT UP** · Said of celebs who **PLAY THE GAME** and allow themselves to be papped, sometimes in exchange for then being left alone. In theory, "*those who give it up don't get followed*" ... the reality is often very different.

**SET-UP** · When stars (and their P.R.s) work with the paparazzi to create authentic-looking shots in the hope of boosting a flagging profile, controlling their image, or painting a happy (post-scandal) family picture.

Historically set-ups were relatively rare, and would often be framed (e.g., through foliage) to look candid. More recently the "shame" of set-ups has evaporated, and openly **PLANDID** [planned + candid] shots are commonplace. Ironically, this trend has ended up making *truly* candid shots more valuable.

Of course, not all set-ups are negotiated, and savvy stars know how to play the paps to their advantage. Paris Hilton turns most press encounters into a runway, e.g., by carrying a Bible, or flaunting her own line of handbags. And in 1994, Diana responded to Prince Charles's televised admission of adultery by wearing a black silk "revenge dress" that she knew would hit front pages across the globe.

**COVERING** · When celebrities shield their faces (with hands, bags, pet dogs, &c.) to deny a clean shot. ("*Never run from a pap — cover!*")

If creative, covering can become the story. In 2014, Emma Stone and Andrew Garfield covered their faces with handwritten signs promoting charities: "*We don't need the attention, but these wonderful organizations do.*"

**BLOCKING** · When celebrity flacks or security details obscure their clients bodily, or with props (e.g., clipboards, umbrellas). Drivers use underground parking lots wherever possible and reverse into locations where the passenger doors can obscure their client's entry and exit.

Paps who accidentally (or deliberately) block their colleagues will earn the ire of the pack and risk having the leads yanked from their flashgun battery-packs (a traditional punishment / prank of the trade).

**SAVAGING** · Pestering a celeb to the point of destroying whatever goodwill existed. Even in **GANG BANGS**, some paps call for restraint.

*Emma Stone and Andrew Garfield charitably* COVER, *2014*

**PEDORAZZI** · A term coined in 2014 by Kristen Bell and Dax Shepard to publicize their **#NOKIDSPOLICY** boycott of publications using paparazzi shots of celebrities' children.

**COUNTERMEASURES** · Stars attempt to vex the paps in many ways, including **WALKING BACKWARD** or **SIDEWAYS**, and sending out **BODY DOUBLES** or **DECOY CARS**.

In the early 1990s, Princess Diana denied the paps sellable shots by wearing the same Virgin Atlantic sweatshirt every time she visited her Chelsea gym, a ruse copied by Daniel Radcliffe who, in 2007, wore the same hat and jacket when leaving the Gielgud Theatre where he was starring in Peter Shaffer's *Equus*.

Other less effective countermeasures include firing flash guns at the paps, shining torches into their lenses, or wearing "anti-paparazzi" reflective clothing of dubious effect.

## SELLING

**SET** · How photos are sold, from a single frame (**SET OF ONE**) to however many a story requires. In the days of film and scanners, sets were pared down to the essential images; now, websites publish "celeb-scroll" **GALLERIES**. Recently, the *Daily Mail Online* published 15 near identical (and frankly dull) frames of Prince Andrew leaving a London restaurant.

**PITCHING** · The process of haggling with photo agencies and media outlets in the hope of creating a **BIDDING WAR**.

**EXCLUSIVE** · A **SET** that no-one else has, offered for higher fees to a single agency or publication. *Conversely*, **NON-EX** · A **SET** of photos where other paps were present.

**ALL ROUND / A.R.** · When no-one bites at an exclusive, and the **SET** is offered (at a lower rate) to everyone. *A.k.a.*, **BLANKETING**.

**DOUBLE DIPPING** · To sell different frames of a **SET** to more than one agency or outlet.

**SYNDICATION** · Additional income from (global) sales made after the **EXCLUSIVE PERIOD** (usually 24 hours) has lapsed.

**RAG-OUT** · When publishers (or broadcasters) who don't want to pay for a **SET** simply run an image of the publication that did.

**MEMO** · A document required by an increasing number of agencies and publications to satisfy their legal and compliance obligations, and get photos **OVER THE LINE**.

Memos ask for a range of details, e.g., how a location was found and whether it was public or private; where all parties were standing; what lenses were used; whether the subject asked them to stop or said anything else; &c.

Paps will sometimes video celebrity interactions for their own protection, and even run tricky assignments past their own lawyers.

While public interest defences exist to taking even very controversial shots, paps who place publications at risk of litigation risk being **BLACKBALLED** by the industry. ⊙

# Wen Lambo, Crypto Bro?

*Since Bitcoin's launch in 2009, global* **CRYPTOCURRENCY** *has grown to a market cap of ~$3 trillion, and created a entire culture of* **CRYPTONAUGHTS, CRYPTO BROS,** *and* **NOOB** *investors suffering from* **CRYPTOSIS.** *This is their* **CRYPTOBABBLE** *...*

## MINDSET

**HODL** · In 2013, "GameKyuubi" posted to the Bitcointalk forum a confession of being a bad trader titled, "I am hodling." This typo swiftly became a meme and then the rallying cry of PERMABEARS who **BUY-AND-HOLD** indefinitely (i.e., **NEVER** SELL). The term was later backronymed as **HOLD ON FOR DEAR LIFE.**

**HOPIUM** · Blind optimism in one's positions. *Also,* **COPIUM** · (Ir)rationalizations deployed to cushion setbacks — or getting REKT.

**FOMO** · Fear Of Missing Out · A force driving NORMIE **NOOBS** into crypto, and triggering DEGENS to double down. *Conversely,* **JOMO** · Joy Of Missing Out (on a poor investment).

**YOLO** · You Only Live Once · The justification for any intemperate (or DEGEN) investment.

**TO THE MOON!** · An (irrational) conviction that a particular coin (or crypto in general) is set for galactic gains. (Represented online by strings of rocket emojis.) *Hence,* **MOON BOY / MOONBOI / MOONING / MOON SOON!**

**NUMBER GO UP!** · A meme expressing (or mocking) unwavering confidence, and the conviction that, despite all previous **TULIPS** (i.e., bubbles), **THIS TIME IT'S DIFFERENT.**

(**BIG**) **GREEN** *or* **RED DILDO** · The coloured bars of (high, low, open, close) **CANDLESTICK CHARTS** showing gains or losses, respectively.

**WE RICH!** · If **BIG GREEN DILDO GO UP!**

**MONEY PRINTER GO BRRR!** · The sound of crypto's unstoppable rise; a **HOPIUM** meme.

(**WA**)**GMI** · (We All) Gonna Make It · The community-rallying (and hype-pumping) cry. *Conversely,* **NGMI** · Not Gonna Make It.

## PEOPLE

(**PERMA**)**BULL** .... (dogged) market optimist
(**PERMA**)**BEAR** ... (dogged) market pessimist
**BULLTARD** ......... a stupid, obnoxious BULL
**BEARTARD** ......... a stupid, obnoxious BEAR

**WHALE** · A person who holds market-moving **BAGS** of one or more cryptocurrencies. Lesser sea creatures are sometimes used to rank more minor investors, e.g., **CRYPTO MINNOWS.** **CRABS** are those who trade **SIDEWAYS**, i.e., cautiously, during periods of low volatility.

**BAGHOLDER** · One who HODLS a position, even as it (rapidly) collapses to DUST.

**DIAMOND HANDS** · Bulls who HODL. *Conversely,* **PAPER** *or* **WEAK HANDS** · Bears who fold under pressure and **PANIC SELL.**

**DEGEN** · A **DEGENERATE** cryptoholic who makes speculative, high-risk trades fuelled by fashion, FOMO, bravado, and HOPIUM.

**MAXIMALIST / MAXI** · One with a fervent faith in a specific currency (usually Bitcoin).

**CRYPTO BROS** · Like GYM BROS {☞ p.92} they never stop boasting about their **GAINZ.**

**JEET** · One who sells at the first hint of a RED DILDO that might imperil their trifling profit. Possibly an acronym for Just Exit Early Trader.

**BANKSTER** · A cryptosceptic proponent of centralized **TRAD-FI** [traditional finance] and all of its associated (archaic) regulations.

**NO COINER** · A (sceptical) **NORMIE** with no (interest in) cryptocurrency.

**FUDDER** · One who feeds upon and spreads **FUD** (Fear, Uncertainty, Doubt) caused by a market downturn, or existential pessimism.

TO THE MOON (*in a pair of* HEAT *Onitsuka Tiger Mexico 66* KICKS {☞ p.22})

## TRADING

**ALTCOIN** … alternative coin that isn't Bitcoin
**SHITCOIN** … one with low or no value
**MEMECOIN** … one based on an online joke
**STABLECOIN** … one pegged to "stable" assets e.g., commodities (gold) or fiat currencies ($)

**BT(F)D** · Buy The (Fucking) Dip · War cry to invest in a falling market. ("*Go full buy mode!*")

**TINA RIF** · There Is No Alternative [to crypto or a specific coin] Resistance Is Futile.

**BUYD!** … Buy Until You Die!
**LFG!** … Let's Fucking Go!
**DYOR** … Do Your Own Research
**DD** … Due Diligence
**NFA** … Not Financial Advice
**BHSL** … Buy High Sell Low [sic]
**ATH / ATL** … All Time High / Low
**HSBAF** … Holy Shit Bulls *or* Bears Are Fucked

**COPY TRADING** · Cloning another's investment strategy. *A.k.a.*, **WHALE WATCHING**.

**INVERSE CRAMER** · A trading strategy that adopts the opposite position to the louder-than-life T.V. market pundit Jim Cramer.

Other **INVERSE INDICATORS** mirror the myth that Joe Kennedy (or John D. Rockefeller) liquidated his investments prior to the 1929 crash when a shoeshine boy offered him stock tips. **PAPER HANDS** are similarly spooked by sudden crypto interest from Uber drivers, hairdressers, parents, or grandparents.

**NOT YOUR KEYS, NOT YOUR COINS** · A reminder that whoever controls the encrypted **KEYS** controls the crypto assets. *Similarly*, **NOT YOUR KEYS, NOT YOUR PIANO / NACHO** (**NACHO KEYS, NACHO COIN**).

**APEING** · Blindly investing in a new cryptocurrency (without sufficient DD), e.g., to avoid FOMO. ("*Only degens* **APE IN** *on memecoins.*")

**SHILLING** · (Aggressively) hawking a cryptocurrency — usually without disclosing your financial interest (or any risks). In 2023, U.S. authorities charged eight celebrities with "illegally touting" crypto assets on social media.

**DUST** · Tiny sums of cryptocurrency left over from transactions; often too small to trade. *Hence*, **GOING TO DUST** (**GTD**) · When a coin is **CIRCLING THE DRAIN / DUMPING**.

(**GETTING**) **REKT** · Suffering severe losses.

**IYKYK** · If You Know You Know · A cryptic teaser that hints at inside crypto knowledge.

**PND / PUMP & DUMP / PAMP 'N' DAMP** · The age-old finance scam of artificially inflating prices before bailing out; tailor-made for a new generation of crypto **RUGS** (scams).

**RUG PULL** · An **EXIT SCAM** where the **DEVS** (developers) of a new venture steal the funds. *Hence the question*, **ARE DEVS DOXXED**? i.e., is the core team publicly known and therefore (marginally more) trustworthy.

## N.F.T.

**N.F.T. (NON-FUNGIBLE TOKEN)** · A unique digital asset stored on a BLOCKCHAIN.

**BLOCKCHAIN** · A decentralized digital ledger that records transactions transparently, securely, and immutability across a network.

**MINTING** · Converting a digital asset into an N.F.T. by publishing it on the BLOCKCHAIN.

**1:1 / 1 OF 1** · A unique (edition of one) N.F.T. *Conversely*, **OPEN EDITION** · N.F.T.s that can be minted an unlimited number of times.

**SWEEPING (THE FLOOR)** · Acquiring N.F.T.s at their lowest **FLOOR PRICE**.

**UTILITY** · N.F.T.s that bestow **I.R.L.** (In Real Life) benefits, e.g., entry to a music festival.

**WEARABLE** · N.F.T. that bestows clothes or accessories to **AVATARS** (virtual characters).

**TRAITS** · The design details of each unique N.F.T. in a collection, used to establish rarity.

**SOULBOUND TOKEN** · A non-transferable N.F.T., locked to an individual, used, e.g., to validate identity, qualifications, vaccines, &c.

**PFP** · Picture For Profile *or* Proof · Using an N.F.T. avatar as a social media profile picture.

**ROYALTY** · The fee paid to an N.F.T.'s creator each time that N.F.T. is resold.

**VALHALLA** · A state of N.F.T. success, named after the Hall of the Slain in Norse mythology.

**BURNING** · To remove an N.F.T. from circulation (by adding it to an inaccessible wallet) e.g., to reduce supply and increase value.

**SEEMS RARE** *or* **LEGIT** · The snarky response to anyone asking for feedback on their N.F.T.

**RIGHT CLICK SAVE AS** · A meme mocking N.F.T.s as copyable image files and rejecting the BLOCKCHAIN's role in validating ownership.

**IT'S MONEY LAUNDERING!** · The allegation that (high-value) N.F.T. trading is (simply) a novel way of washing illicitly obtained cash.

## CRYPTO CULTURE

**GM (FRENS)** · Good Morning (Friends) · An online greeting swapped by crypto enthusiasts.

**WEN LAMBO?** · A plea for life-changing (and Lamborghini-buying) crypto opulence. *Also*, **WEN ROCKET? / WEN MOON?**

**WEN MARKETING?** · When those who have APED IN to a new project pressure its DEVS to start SHILLING the damn thing.

**SATOSHI IS WATCHING!** · A joking meme that posits **SATOSHI NAKAMOTO** (Bitcoin's presumed, pseudonymous creator) observes from the shadows and judges your trades.

**I'M IN IT FOR THE TECH** · Proclaiming an interest in decentralization, transparency, and innovation only when the market is dumping.

**PROBABLY NOTHING** · A sarcastic suffix appended to any item of dramatic news, e.g.: "*China banned Bitcoin ... probably nothing.*"

**LOST IN A TRAGIC BOATING ACCIDENT** · A joke meme explaining how you mislaid your crypto keys and therefore owe no tax.

**420 / 69** · Numbers that CRYPTO BROS find hysterically funny, especially in combination.

**HFSP** · Have Fun Staying Poor · How CRYPTO BROS taunt NO COINERS.

**LOSS** *or* **GAIN PORN** · Posting screenshots of your REKT *or* MOONING investments; a form of COPIUM *or* HOPIUM, respectively.

**GOING TO THE FIAT MINES** · Toiling away in an I.R.L. job ... until **WE GO MOON!**

**MCDONALD'S** · The FIAT MINE job of last resort (after **LAMBO DREAMS** are REKT).

**THIS IS THE WAY** · Expression of approval: "*Buy red and sell green ... This is the way!*"

**NKSAF** · Nobody Knows Shit About Fuck.

**GN (SER)** · Good Night (Sir).

[The abbreviations above are written without interstitial full stops, as is the custom of the cryptonaught people.] ⊙

# Hunting / Sabbing

*The hunting of foxes in their natural state with (horses and) hounds has been an iconic element of Britain's countryside tradition for centuries. In addition to its role in flock protection and pest control, the "Sport of Kings" has inspired art, poetry, literature, and song; underpinned artisan trades and rural economies; and contributed deeply to the texture of country life and the text of the English language.*

*Although fox hunting has always provoked passionate opposition in Britain, organized direct action dates to the late 1950s when the League Against Cruel Sports began disrupting hunts, inspiring the creation of the Hunt Saboteurs Association in 1963. Seven decades on, "sabs" still regularly face off with huntsmen, pledging not to cease "sabbing" until a practice they consider barbaric is consigned to the archives.*

## THE HUNT

While a few hunts are owned by individuals (e.g., the Duke of Beaufort), the majority belong to a **HUNT COMMITTEE** that oversees the hunt's policies, management, and fundraising, and hires (or appoints) its staff and officials, including:

**MASTER (OF FOXHOUNDS) (M.F.H.)** · Responsible for all of the hunt's sporting operations, including directing the **HUNT STAFF** (traditionally, **SERVANTS**) and obtaining **PERMISSION** from landowners and farmers to ride across their property. Hunts may have several **JOINT-MASTERS**.

**HUNTSMAN** · Responsible for directing the hounds during a hunt, and therefore the only person to use a HORN. A paid huntsman is termed a **PROFESSIONAL**; a MASTER who also hunts hounds is an **AMATEUR** even if paid.

**WHIPPERS-IN** · Assist the HUNTSMAN generally in the field and kennels, and specifically in controlling the PACK and collecting strays. (Artless whippers-in are sometimes derided as **DOG WALLOPERS**.)

**FIELD MASTER** · Directs the FIELD in following the hounds (not the fox), and prevents riders from OVER-RIDING or otherwise hindering the pack; damaging fences or crops; or trespassing onto neighbouring land.

**NON-JUMPING FIELD MASTER** · Guides the **GATE CROWD**, i.e., riders who do not wish, or are unable, to jump.

**SECOND HORSEMAN** · Traditionally rode **RELIEF MOUNTS** for HUNT STAFF during arduous days. Nowadays, **SECOND HORSES** are usually met at pre-arranged locations.

**THE FIELD** · All other mounted participants. The size of fields varies greatly; smaller hunts can attract 5–10 on a weekday, and 20 at the weekends. Grander hunts on HIGH DAYS can attract 100–200. Some hunts deputize members of the field to be **GATE SHUTTERS**.

**FOOT FOLLOWERS** · Unmounted participants who track the hunt on foot or by bicycle, car, or quad bike. Sabs sometimes attempt to **INFILTRATE** this group to glean intelligence. Famously, Mike Huskisson went undercover between 1981 and 1983 to document the activities of stag, mink, and fox hunts.

**KENNEL HUNTSMAN** · One responsible for feeding, exercising, and caring for the hounds, often with the assistance of **KENNELMEN**.

Although the roles above are commonly unisex, the traditional male titles are maintained.

## SABS & ANTIS

Compared with the feudal stratification of traditional hunting, the anti-hunt community is not just egalitarian but anti-hierarchical.

The clearest division in this community is between **ANTIS** who oppose hunting generally and **SABS** who deploy **DIRECT ACTION**.

While a few sab groups **ROAM** across the country, most are tied to the hunts in their

*A* MONITORING *photo of two black-clad* SABS *accompany a member of the hunt*

region, which they **HIT** regularly, deploying the local knowledge collected over decades.

On occasion, sab groups congregate for regional or national **MASS HITS**, offering **MUTUAL REINFORCEMENT** in response to an egregious act of intimidation or violence.

**SABBING** · Deterring hunts from setting off, and sabotaging hunts in progress — often by redeploying the hunt's techniques against it.

**MONITORING** · Following a hunt to document (and deter) illegal activity; naturally. monitoring became relevant only after recent changes in the law. Sabs sometimes have to decide in the heat of a moment whether to protect a fox by sabbing, or collect evidence of criminality by monitoring a kill.

(**BIG**) **SAB IN THE SKY** · Drones are increasingly used to deter (and record evidence of) illegal hunting. (Sab drones have been shot out of the sky by hunt supporters.)

**HIDDEN CAMERAS** · Located in COVERTS to capture footage of illegal hunting and TERRIERWORK.

**EVIDENCE GATHERING TEAM (E.G.T.)** · Some hunts collect counter-surveillance evidence to prove (or falsely claim) that a fox was killed accidentally — sometimes because the hounds were distracted by the actions of sabs.

**INTIMIDATION** · A charge levelled by both sides. Sabs have been accused of targeting businesses that support hunts, or pubs that host MEETS, with negative online reviews or other forms of harassment, e.g., false bomb threats against hunt balls. Hunt participants have been accused of harassing and attacking antis and of filing false police complaints.

Both parties regularly film confrontations with cellphones and body cams to collect legal evidence and social-media propaganda.

## THE LAW

Recent legislation has upended centuries of British fox-hunting tradition. At its simplest: In England and Wales, the **HUNTING ACT 2004** banned hunting mammals with dogs, subject to certain exemptions. And in Scotland, the **HUNTING WITH DOGS (SCOTLAND) ACT 2023** banned hunting mammals above ground with more than two dogs.

Fox hunting with dogs remains legal in Northern Ireland as well as the Republic of Ireland, the U.S.A., Canada, France, Italy, &c.

Most commentators agree that while the 2023 act effectively ended hunting with hounds north of the border, the loose wording of the 2004 Act has enabled hunting, if not to flourish, then to persist in the margins in England and Wales.

The most significant "loophole" in the 2004 Act involves **TRAIL HUNTING**. Here human **LAYERS** set cross-country trails that simulate the jinks and zig-zags of fleeing foxes. Layers use rags, socks, sponges, and spray bottles filled with artificial scent, purchased fox urine, or

*Exercising the Percy Hunt foxhounds, 2014*

homemade **BROTH / JUICE** extracted from mulched fox carcass and road-kill, mixed with oil, water, and paraffin to create a lasting trail.

As a consequence of the 2004 act, many English and Welsh hunts transitioned to legal trail hunting to maintain their pastime and preserve its traditions. However, opponents claim that a small group of unscrupulous huntsmen have used trail hunting as a "smoke-screen" to subvert the law, relying on the defence that their hounds "accidentally" pursued (and killed) a fox, despite their "best efforts." Such huntsmen usually do enough to satisfy the letter of the law (e.g., videoing trails being laid) with no intent to respect its spirit.

Other hunts have adopted two of the other forms of legal hunting with hounds that rarely result in "inadvertent" kills.

First, **DRAG HUNTING**, where an artificial, non-animal scent (e.g., aniseed) is laid along predetermined routes that avoid livestock, roads, fragile habitats, and areas known to house foxes.

And second, **HUNTING THE CLEAN BOOT**, where bloodhounds pursue the scent of human runners, in the expectation of treats and affection. In both activities, because the hounds are not trained on animal scents, they are less likely to pursue animal lines.

The legality of fox hunting across the island of Ireland, and the uneasy status quo of trail hunting in England and Wales, means that while many of the terms explored here are *de jure* obsolete, they are still in *de facto* use.

(The more truly archaic terms are indicated in the text with a dotted underline, **THUS**.)

## THE CALENDAR

The **HUNTING YEAR** starts on 1 May, and the **SEASON** is divided into two:

› AUG–OCT · **AUTUMN HUNTING** · When horses and packs are exercised, and new hounds are **ENTERED**, i.e., trained to follow a scent, work in a pack, and obey calls. Where legal, this period is known by its traditional name, **CUB-HUNTING**, and is used to disperse the cub population and encourage foxes to run at the sound of the hunt.

› NOV–MAR · **TRAIL** (or **FOX**) **HUNTING** · The **SEASON PROPER** draws larger fields, more followers, and is attended by greater ritual and formality. It begins with the **OPENING MEET**.

**MEET** · Where PACK and FIELD gather before **SETTING OFF**. Meets tend to be distributed across a hunt's **COUNTRY** (i.e., the strict and exclusive boundaries of land owned by each U.K. hunt, or land they are permitted to use).

Most meets start ~11 A.M., both to maximize the hours of daylight and take advantage of fresh SCENTS.

Hunts meet between two and four times a week. Midweek hunts are less likely to be sabbed, because most antis have jobs. (To ride on horseback to a meet is to **HACK**.)

Once the MEET has assembled, the MASTER signals to the HUNTSMAN who takes the hounds off to the first COVERT to DRAW for a fox, and FLUSH it out into the open.

**MEET CARD** · The season's schedule of MEETS and other social events (which historically were published in *Horse & Hound* magazine). Cards are sought by sabs to plan hits, and occasionally supplied (anonymously) by "*disgruntled members of the rural population.*"

**HIGH DAYS** · Special days on the calendar: usually the OPENING MEET, Boxing Day, New Year's Day, and days meaningful to each individual hunt.

**LAWN MEET** · One hosted at a private house, rather than, say, a pub or village green.

**KENNEL WATCHING** · Obtaining the location of a MEET by surveilling the kennels, and following the **HOUND VANS**.

Regularly sabbed hunts may move their hounds to a friendly farm the night before a meet, or send out empty **DECOY VANS**. (Sabs blow horns close to these vans to check for hidden hounds.)

**ROAD WATCHING** · Staking out major junctions to spot hunt traffic (e.g., hunt vehicles, horse boxes, and uniformed riders) and follow it to the meet. (Sabs have been accused of attaching electronic **TRACKERS** to hunt vehicles and follower cars.)

**THE CIRCUIT** · The road access around the location of a meet. A significant part of sabbing involves driving in circles around this circuit to track the hounds and locate the fox.

**SUBSCRIBERS** · Members of a hunt, who pay an annual fee.

**CAP** · The fee non-subscribers pay for a day's hunting. *Hence*, **CAPPING** · Collecting fees.

## ATTIRE

There are endless local variations on "correct" hunting attire. Below is an elementary guide:

**RATCATCHER** · The uniform for informal or AUTUMN HUNTING, i.e., tweed jacket; buff or fawn breeches; neck tie or non-white hunting stock; brown (or black boots) without tops; and a hard hat or (traditionally) a bowler.

The golden rule is that well-presented RATCATCHER is "never wrong."

From the OPENING MEET on, the dress code becomes more formal:

**COAT** · The most iconic (and provocative) element of hunting's **FULL FIG** uniform is the red hunt coat worn by MASTERS, HUNTSMEN, WHIPPERS-IN, and those bestowed the HUNT BUTTON.

To call this red coat (**HUNTING**) **PINK** is an error. Similarly, one either "wears scarlet" or a "red coat"; one never "wears a scarlet red coat."

(Romantic infatuation with senior huntgoers is known as **SCARLET FEVER**.)

Not all hunts sport scarlet. E.g., the Duke of Beaufort's and the Heythrop wear green; the Hampshire Hunt, blue; and the Kimblewick, a tawny yellow. Many hunts have contrasting collars on their coats as part of the uniform.

SUBSCRIBERS and others members of the FIELD wear black or (if women) blue coats, with dark buttons. Hunting farmers traditionally wear black coats, or RATCATCHER.

**STOCK / HUNTING TIE** · Usually worn in white or cream, with a gold **STOCK PIN** secured vertically (MASTERS and STAFF) or horizontally (FIELD). Safety pins are used to hold down the ends of the stock.

**BREECHES / JODHPURS** · Usually worn in buff, white, or canary; white is worn with red.

**BOOTS** · Brown during autumn hunting; black thereafter, with optional spurs.

**HEAD GEAR** · Once a common sight, the **TOP HAT** has all but faded from the field, for reasons of safety and cost. Nowadays, riding hats and safety helmets (covered in black or blue silks) with chin straps are standard, though some riders still sport **BOWLER HATS**.

**BUTTONS** · There is a significant distinction between plain buttons, worn by members of the FIELD, and **HUNT BUTTONS** (unique to each hunt) worn by MASTERS, HUNTSMEN, WHIPPERS-IN, and those personally honoured by a MASTER for services to the hunt or a conspicuous act of bravery. (Some hunts award buttons to all SUBSCRIBERS.)

SUBSCRIBERS wear three buttons on the front of their coats; MASTERS wear four; and HUNTSMEN and WHIPPERS-IN wear five (or six in the case of hunts with specific aristocratic links, like the North Cotswold).

**WHIPS** · Hunting whips are carried to guide hounds away from horses, and assist when opening and holding gates.

**CAMOUFLAGE** · In decades past, the sab look tended toward "*dreadlocks and field camo.*" Now the fashion is for **BLACK BLOC** — an anonymizing monochrome uniform popularized in the 1970s by German leftists and anarchists ("*Euro-rioting strip*").

Some **MONITORS** advertise their pacific intent by wearing high-viz jackets emblazoned with the words **HUNT INVESTIGATOR**.

## HORSES & RIDERS

Mounts are expected to be clean and well-groomed, and tack to be neat and modest. Many riders do not plait their horse's manes (or tails) until the OPENING MEET.

**TAIL RIBBONS** · A young or inexperienced horse should have a **GREEN TAIL RIBBON**; one liable to kick, **RED**. If a mount kicks when crowded (e.g., at a gate), its rider should put one hand behind their back to warn others.

All horses should be turned to face passing hounds, to avoid any being kicked.

**EYE TO HOUNDS** · A hunt-goer's skill in reacting to movement of the leading hound(s).

**FOX SENSE** · The ability of HUNTSMEN (and hounds) to "think like the fox."

**BRUISER** · A reckless or inconsiderate rider; one who **OVER-PUNISHES** a horse.

**LARKING** · Jumping fences other than during a chase; a frowned-upon tomfoolery.

**OVER-RIDING** · To ride **ON TOP OF**, or ahead of, the hounds; a serious error.

**THRUSTER** · A member of the FIELD who rides tight behind the FIELD MASTER, and seeks out the biggest jumps.

## HOUNDS

**DOG** · Male hound.

(**HOT**) **BITCH** · Female hound (in heat).

**STERN** · A hound's tail, which is not "wagged" but **FEATHERED**.

**PACK** · All of the hounds in a **KENNEL**. *Also*, those hounds selected to hunt for the day.

**DRAFTING** · Rejecting unsuitable hounds, which are given to other hunts. (By tradition, hounds are never sold.)

**COUPLES** · Hounds are counted in pairs, so 21 hounds would be "*ten-and-a-half couple.*" (Single hounds are never referred to as "*half a couple*" but "*one hound.*")

By tradition, most packs on hunting days contain an odd number of hounds. "*Why include the half-couple?*" — the old joke goes — "*Because that's the hound that catches the fox!*"

**MIXED PACK** · One with DOGS and BITCHES; most packs are mixed.

**LEVEL** · A pack of hounds matching in size and speed — ideally you should "*be able to throw a tablecloth over the whole pack whilst they're running.*"

**ENTERED HOUNDS** · Those that have started hunting. *Conversely*, **UNENTERED**.

**TRENCHER FED** · A hound kept by an individual and added to the PACK at a MEET. *Hence*, **TRENCHER-FED PACK**. Most common nowadays in the Lake District.

**BIDDABLE** · Said of a responsive hound.

**SPEAK** · The cry of a hound when following a scent. (Hounds *never* "bark.")

**LOW SCENTING** / **COLD NOSE** · A hound able to detect the faintest of scents.

**MUTE** · A hound that does not SPEAK ("*an unpardonable fault*"). *Also*, when a hound runs too fast to SPEAK. *Similarly*, **TIGHT IN THE TONGUE** · Almost MUTE.

**BABBLER** / **NOISY** · A hound that SPEAKS in the absence of a scent.

**SINGING** · The melodic noise hounds spontaneously make (when in kennel).

**CUR DOG** · Any dog other than a hound.

*Sabs on* THE CIRCUIT *scanning for* CHARLIE

## FOXES

*Vulpes vulpes* have a number of traditional hunt-bestowed nicknames:

- **CHARLIE** · After the Whig politician Charles James Fox (1749–1806).
- **TODD** · A Middle English term for fox.
- **REYNARD** · After the fabulous Middle Ages character Reynard the Fox.

**BRACE** · Two foxes; three is a **LEASH**.

**PAD** · A fox's foot. *Hence*, **PADDING** · Finding or following a fox's prints.

**MASK** / **PATE** · A fox's head.

**BRUSH** / **DRAG** · A fox's tail.

**BILLET** / **SCAT** · A fox's excrement.

**SINKING** / **STIFF** · A fox run to exhaustion.

## THE HUNT

The traditional **RUNNING ORDER** of a (fox) hunt is as follows:

| | |
|---|---|
| 1 | TRAIL / FOX |
| 2 | HOUNDS |
| 3 | HUNTSMAN (& SABS) |
| 4 | FIELD MASTER |
| 5 | THE FIELD |
| 6 | FOOT FOLLOWERS |

**THE LINE** · The scented trail a quarry leaves.

**SCENT** · The odour of a fox (or TRAIL) and therefore a hunt's *sine qua non*.

Scent tends to hang in layers, and its strength will be influenced by a range of factors including humidity, air pressure, and temperature. The demeanour of hounds at a **MEET** can often indicate how good a day's scent will be: Lolling hounds suggest poor conditions; eager and **BURSTING** hounds invite optimism.

There are a range of traditional terms for scent strengths:

| | |
|---|---|
| **BURNING** / **SCREAMING** | strong |
| **BREAST-HIGH** | so strong that the hounds don't STOOP |
| **MOVING** | fresh |
| **FLIGHTY** / **CATCHY** / **TICKLISH** | variable |
| **HOLDING** | faint but followable |
| **THROWN OUT** | **LOST** |
| **RECOVERED** | lost, then found |

**DRAWING** · When the **HUNTSMAN** sends the pack into a COVERT to **FLUSH** a fox; how all hunting days begin. If no quarry is found, you have **DRAWN A BLANK**.

**FEATHERING** · When a hound hesitates over a LINE, usually without SPEAKING.

**COVERT** · Thick brush, coppice, or woodland where foxes shelter. [Pronounced "*cover*."]

Sabs near a covert when a fox breaks will often kneel or lie down to avoid **PUSHING** the fox back in toward the hounds.

*Members of the Grove and Rufford Hunt, Boxing Day 2018*

**CASTING** · Searching for a scent in a specific area, or direction. **HUNTSMEN** cast hounds, and hounds cast themselves.

**STOOPING** · When hounds lower their heads to search for, or follow, a scent. Not necessary when the scent is **BREAST-HIGH**.

**STRIKE** · When a hound **HITS THE LINE**; the first hound to do so **OPENS** or **CHALLENGES** the line.

**OWNING** · Hounds **OWN A LINE** when they **PICK UP** its scent and **SPEAK ON IT**.

**SPEAKING** · The noise a hound makes on locating a scent for certain. *A.k.a.*, **GIVING** *or* **THROWING TONGUE**.

**HONOURING** · When hounds run to assist a hound that has found a **LINE**, or a fox.

(**IN**) **FULL CRY** · When hounds **SPEAK** in unison. *A.k.a.*, **HOUND MUSIC**.

**DON'T POINT AT THE FOX!** · The iron rule of sabbing is never to indicate you've seen a fox, thereby (literally) giving the game away.

(**CARRY A**) **GOOD HEAD** · When hounds run up together. *Conversely*, **STRUNG OUT**.

**SKIRTING** · When a hound runs wide of a **LINE**, cutting corners; a fault.

**BURST** · The initial part of a run.

**QUICK THING** · A fast run.

**COURSE** · Pursuing a quarry in view.

**RUN** / **HUNT** / **CHASE** · The active pursuit of a fox. Runs can last for hours and cover 6–7 miles, but the average run in 2000 lasted 15–20 minutes, and many are shorter still.[1]

**POINT** · A **RUN**'s crow-fly distance, as distinct from the distance travelled by the hounds. ("*It was a 4-mile point, 6 miles as the hounds ran.*")

**WIND IN THEIR TEETH** · When hounds run into a strong wind.

**OVER-RUNNING** / **FLASHING** · When hounds run past the **TRAIL**.

**CHECK** · When the hounds lose a scent. After a check, the **HUNTSMAN** will **CAST** the hounds to recover the **LINE**.

**THROW UP** (**THEIR HEADS**) · When hounds **LIFT** their heads, because they have lost a scent or been distracted (by sabs).

**DWELLING** · When a hound is unresponsive to a **CALL**, or lingers on a stale scent. (*Also*, a disparaging term for a slow **HUNTSMAN**, *A.k.a.*, "Steady Eddie" or "Tarmac Tim.")

**ALL ON** · Indication from **WHIPPER-IN** to **HUNTSMAN** that all hounds are present.

**VIEW** · A fox is viewed, not "spotted" or "seen."

**RIOT** · When hounds chase forbidden quarry, e.g., deer.

**FOIL** · Anything that disturbs the SCENT — from other animals to car exhaust. **CLEAN GROUND** is that which is free from foil.

Sabs will deliberately foil lines by spraying odoriferous substances such as citronella or eucalyptus oil.

**RINGING** · When a fox runs in circles.

**RUNNING FOR FOIL** · A fox's evasive actions, e.g., running through water or packs of sheep, or across roads.

**RUNNING HIS FOIL** · When a fox doubles back on its own track.

**HEADED** · When a fox is diverted from its intended line of escape by a human, vehicle, CUR, or (unforgivably) member of the FIELD.

**CURRANT JELLY** · When foxes accidentally latch onto the scent of a hare.

**JINKING** · When a fox makes sudden turns to evade its pursuers.

(**RUNNING THE**) **HEEL LINE** · (Following) the right line, but in the wrong direction.

## VOICE & HORN

Huntsmen communicate with their hounds, and therefore the FIELD, by **VOICE** (when close) and **HORN** (at a distance), though there is a wide variation in the style of blowing and pronunciation.

### A SELECTION OF HORN CALLS

**MOVING OFF** ........ *a short call that informs the* MEET *that the hounds are leaving for the first draw*
**DOUBLING THE HORN** .... *an excited call that returns the pack to the* HUNTSMAN *and onto a line*
**STOPPING THE HOUNDS** .................. *a long, steady, unbroken note that halts both pack and field*
**GONE AWAY** ..................... *a long, drawn out, pulsating call that encourages a pack to follow its line*
**THE KILL** ................................ *a long wavering note sounded when the hounds catch their quarry*
**GOING HOME** ..................... *a long, ululating call signalling the end of a day's (or season's) hunting*

Some dedicated hunting folk request at their funerals the blowing of GOING HOME, followed by GONE AWAY.

### A SELECTION OF VOICE CALLS

**LIEU IN!** ...................................... *encourages the hounds into a* COVERT *or other specific location*
**HOLLOA!** ("*holler*") ..................... *draws attention to a quarry that has left cover and is in the open*
**HUIC HOLLOA!** ("*hike holler*") .................. *directs the hounds toward the location of the* HOLLOA
**TALLY HO!** ............................................................. *called when a quarry has been sighted*
**TALLY HO BACK!** ................... *called when a quarry has briefly emerged from cover, and returned*
**FORRARD ON!** ...................................... HUNTSMAN*'s imprecation to the hounds to go forward*
**WHO-WHOOP!** .................. *high-pitched call, deployed at a kill to praise and encourage the hounds*

### GENERAL HUNTING EXPRESSIONS

**HUNTSMAN** *or* **WHIP, PLEASE!** .................. *warning that* HUNT STAFF *are riding past the field*
**FIELD, PLEASE!** ................................................. FIELD MASTER*'s instruction to follow him*
**HOLD HARD!** .................................................................... *order to stop immediately*
**GATE, PLEASE!** ............................... *essential reminder to close a gate; passed back down the field*
**KEEP IN, PLEASE!** ....................................... *reminder to stay close to a verge or away from crops*
**KICK ON!** .......................................... *instruction not to give way (say, at a gate), but to move on*
**WARE WIRE!** *or* **'OLE!** *or* **GLASS!** .................. *warning shouted to beware wire, or a hole, or glass*
**LOOSE HORSE!** ..................................... *warning of a rider-less horse, and an invitation to assist*
**HOUNDS, PLEASE!** ..................... *warning to give way to a pack, and turn horses to face the hounds*
**CAR, PLEASE!** .......................................................................... *warning to let a vehicle pass*
**GOOD NIGHT!** ............................................ *the polite post-hunt farewell, regardless of the hour*

**RATE** · To reprimand a hound vocally (or with the crack of a whip) for **RIOTING**, straying, or otherwise misbehaving.

Ratings are used to call hounds off (e.g., **LEAVE IT!**, **HAVE A CARE!**, **GET ON!**); to guide them from an erroneous line (**WARE HEEL!**); or ward them off specific animals, e.g., **WARE HAUNCH!** (deer); **WARE HARE!** (hares or rabbits); **WARE WING!** (birds). Short for "beware," **WARE** is pronounced "*war.*"

**SAB CALLS** · Sabs subvert hunting's traditional lingo to distract hounds from finding a line (**HEADS UP!**); divert them when in full cry (**LEAVE IT!**); and warn them off a kill (**GET BACK-TO-'IM!**). Similarly, talented sabs blow hunting horns to confuse the pack or TAKE HOUNDS OFF.

**SAB WHIP** · A makeshift version of the hunting whip (broom handle, climbing rope, and bootlace) that is cracked to **RATE** hounds off a kill, or push them back from danger.

On occasion, sabs and hunt staff will use their whips together, e.g., if a pack is heading toward a dangerous road.

**TAKING *or* BRINGING HOUNDS (OFF)** · When sabs **SPLIT THE PACK** — i.e., lure hounds away from the huntsman, who must waste time **GATHERING THEM UP**. (*A.k.a.*, **DOGNAPPING**.)

**TAKING THE WHOLE PACK** is a rare and cherished sab victory.

**GIZMO** · An audio device used to broadcast HOUND MUSIC and draw a pack to the sabs. Traditional gizmos were bulky loudspeakers powered by car batteries; modern versions amplify M.P.3.s — ideally, a recording of the specific pack of hounds being sabbed.

**MARKING (TO GROUND)** · When hounds SPEAK round an earth where a fox has GONE TO GROUND.

**POINT RIDER** · One who does not follow the hounds, but (under instruction from the FIELD MASTER) **RIDES WIDE** to look for the fox, or to head hounds away from a specific direction (e.g., a road, railway line, or crop).

**HOLDING UP** · Driving foxes in a specific direction, e.g., away from a road or land where the hunt has no permission.

**LIFTING** · When a **HUNTSMAN PICKS UP** the **PACK** and takes it to a new location where he hopes a scent may be found.

**GIVEN BEST** · When CHARLIE has outwitted a hunt and is left for another day.

**BLANK DAY** · A day with no foxes.

**JIBBING** · When either side retreats in the face of overwhelming odds. ("*Two landies* [Land Rovers] *pulled up, but they took one look at the Manchester lot and jibbed it!*")

**PACK UP** · Sabs declare victory when a hunt gives up and goes home. If one hunt quits especially prematurely, sabs may hit other locations ("*The Chid's* **PACKED EARLY**, *but the Grove's* **STILL OUT**.")

**TIME** · Wasting a hunt's time is a key sab tactic, since every inconvenience eats away at the remaining hours of daylight, and every intervention gives Charlie more time to escape. More generally, sabs aim to demoralize hunt communities to the point that they disband.

**HUNT REPORT** · An account of a day's hunting. The sab equivalent is a **HIT REPORT**. Prior to the various bans, hit reports were filed away to be used as intelligence when planning future actions. Now, the reports are a vital weapon in the social-media propaganda war, and will often be written in the van and posted online on the drive home.

## TERRIER WORK

**TERRIER WORK** in fox hunting involves the highly controversial practice of deploying dogs to continue the pursuit underground.

**STOPPING (UP)** · Using soil, rocks, &c. to seal earths, setts, drains, and other bolt holes to prevent foxes from **GOING TO GROUND**. Usually undertaken the night before a meet.

**PRE-BEATING** · Back when MEET details were printed in *Horse & Hound*, sabs attempted to stymie hunts before they had set off by spraying citronella over well-used routes and rousing foxes from known COVERTS by setting off **ROOKIES** (i.e., fire crackers used by farmers to scare off rooks).

*Fox (Vulpes vulpes) killing a pheasant (Phasianus colchicus)*

**DIGGING OUT** · Using spades to expose a subterranean fox, or free a trapped terrier.

**BOLTING** · When terriers were sent in to underground holes to **FLUSH OUT** a fox so the hunt can continue. Frowned upon, even traditionally.

**GIVEN LAW** · A "sporting" head start granted to a BOLTED fox before the pack is **LAID ON**.

**COUNTRYMEN** · Those who assist the hunt by laying trails, mending fences, closing gates, &c. According to sabs, often a re-branding of **TERRIER MEN** to cover their illegal actions.

**HARD / SOFT TERRIERS** · Dogs that habitually fight their quarry / **STAND OFF** and **BAY** (i.e., speak).

**BAGGING** · When a **BAG MAN** would catch and hold a **BAGGED FOX** to be hunted at a later date, or thrown to hounds to keep them IN BLOOD. Deprecated, even historically.

**ARTIFICIAL EARTHS** · The (archaic) practice of building man-made earths to encourage the fox population for hunting and/or locate foxes in specific places (e.g., away from farms). Sabs argue that artificial earths contradict claims that hunting is merely for pest control.

**TERRIER BOX** · A dog carrier (often attached to a quad bike). Sabs question why "countrymen" would require such boxes if they were not actually terrier men.

## THE KILL

**DISPATCHED** · One of many euphemisms for killing a fox; others include **ROLLED OVER** and **ACCOUNTED FOR**.

**CHOPPING** · When hounds suddenly encounter a fox and kill it.

**WORRYING / MOBBING** · When hounds tear at a fox, **BREAKING** or **SPLITTING** it up.

**A NIP TO THE BACK OF THE NECK** · The euphemistic cliché for how hounds neatly and quickly dispatch a fox; much mocked by sabs and antis.

**TROPHIES** · By tradition, a freshly killed fox would be held aloft in celebration before its BRUSH, PADS, and MASK were cut away and presented as trophies to honoured guests or especially proficient (or young) members of the FIELD.

**(WELL) IN BLOOD** · Hounds enthused by a recent kill. Some MASTERS kept their hounds in blood by throwing them the fox carcass to BREAK UP. *Conversely*, **OUT OF BLOOD**.

**BLOODING** · Initiating (young) hunt neophytes by daubing their faces with the blood of a freshly killed fox, and letting it dry. In his 2023 memoir, *Spare*, Prince Harry describes how he was **BLOODED** with a red deer carcass.

**TALLY** · A count of foxes DISPATCHED. ⊙

# Wall Street Consensus

*The 2011* **OCCUPY WALL STREET** *protests in Lower Manhattan's Zuccotti Park drew public attention to a taxonomy of hand-signals designed to facilitate consensus-based decision making.*

*These audience gesticulations have a long, progressive history, learning and borrowing from Quakers, anarchists, occupationists, Greens, feminists, and anti-austerity activists — indeed, the* **UP TWINKLE** *sign comes from the deaf community, where it is used to signal applause and approval.*

*The goal of non-verbal signals is to encourage mass participation without the aural disruption of applause, shouts, heckles, or boos. However, one novel verbal feature of such assemblies is the* **HUMAN MICROPHONE**, *where every phrase a speaker utters is repeated by the crowd. This (somewhat laborious) process encourages active listening and facilitates communication without amplification. To announce a new speaker, or dampen extraneous conversation, a call is made of* **MIC CHECK!**

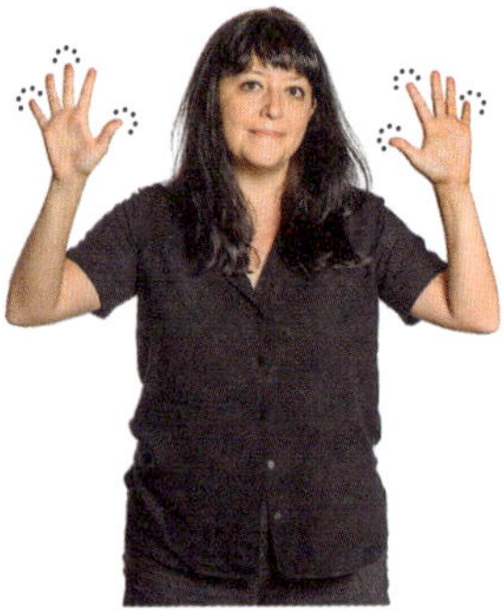

**AGREE**
*A.k.a.,* **UP TWINKLES**
Signals assent, approval, and enthusiasm.

**NEUTRAL**
Signals mixed feelings, or being on the fence; may also sign a request for further information.

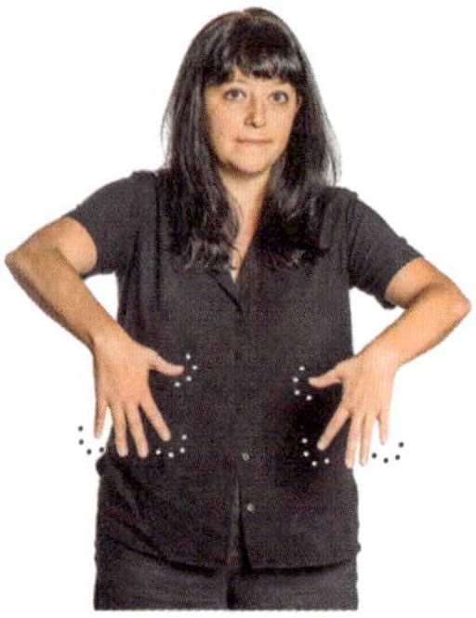

**DISAGREE**
*A.k.a.,* **DOWN TWINKLES**
Signals dissent, disagreement, or disapproval.

**BLOCK**
Signals vehement dissent from something that threatens the ethics or safety of the group; to be used sparingly.

**WRAP IT UP**
Urges a speaker to cut to the chase.

**GET ON STACK**
Alerts the **STACK TAKER** that you wish to **JOIN THE STACK** — i.e., add your name to the list to speak or raise an issue.

**CLARIFYING QUESTION**

**POINT OF INFORMATION**

**SPEAK MORE LOUDLY**

**POINT OF PROCESS**
Used to raise specific issue of procedure.

**RESPECT THE HOUSE**
Calls for an end to overspeaking, or other chaotic dissent.

**DIRECT RESPONSE**
Indicates critical information is missing from something said.

*In addition to the consensus processes, signals are used to communicate actions:*

**DISPERSE**
Signals activists to blend into the crowd and act like civilians.

**GATHER**
Signals activists to congregate; the opposite of disperse.

**FULL BODY MELT**
Signals activists to fall to the ground in passive resistance.

The hand signals are demonstrated by **Marisa Holmes**, organizer, filmmaker, and author of *Organizing Occupy Wall Street: This Is Just Practice* (2023).

# The Mice, Moles, & Chicken Feed of Spycraft

*Even as* **ESPIONAGE** *explodes into cyberspace, states still rely on human intelligence — where case officers run agents to subvert, sabotage, and steal from countries, corporations, criminals, and terrorists. From detonating a network of pagers to infiltrating Buckingham Palace, such operations demand not just nerve, but the dark arts of* **TRADECRAFT**, *of which this is a partial glossary.*

## JOHN LE CARRÉ

No lexicon of espionage could fail to acknowledge the influence of David Cornwell (1931–2020), who, under the *nom de plume* John le Carré [J.L.C.], did more than any novelist to popularize the lore and language of espionage while simultaneously devalorizing its motives and methods.

Indeed, a few of J.L.C.'s terms of art came to be adopted by the real-life spies he fictionalized, as he told the B.B.C. in 1979:

> I have since met a number of intelligence officers and ex-intelligence officers — mainly American — and I'm gratified to learn that some of my jargon has gone into their language. [1]

Most notably, although J.L.C. did not *coin* the spy term **MOLE** — which was first used in 1622 by Sir Francis Bacon — he unquestionably established it as part of spying's vernacular.

> Ivlov's task was to **SERVICE** a **MOLE**. A **MOLE** is a **DEEP PENETRATION AGENT**, so called because he burrows deep into the fabric of Western imperialism. [2]

Below are other fragments of tradecraft jargon that J.LC. neologized or popularized, though most see active service only within his novels:

**THE CIRCUS** · J.L.C.'s darkly ironic nickname for M.I.6., geographically based on its (fictional) location on Cambridge Circus, London.

**LAMPLIGHTERS** · "Their job was to provide the support services for **MAINLINE OPERATIONS**: watching, listening, transport, and safe houses." [2]

**SCALP-HUNTERS** · "A small outfit, about a dozen men, and they were there to handle the hit-and-run jobs that were too dirty or too risky for the residents abroad." [2]

**SWEAT** · To interrogate.

**PAVEMENT ARTIST** · Expert in street-level surveillance and pursuit.

**SOUND THIEF** · Expert in bugging.

**WATCHER / LISTENER** · Expert in visual / audio surveillance.

**TRADESMAN** · A civilian professional who undertakes tasks for **CIRCUS** personnel.

**BABYSITTER** · One who guards an **OFFICER** or **AGENT**, for protection or control. (Russia uses the term **NYANKI** [nursemaid].)

(**TAKING**) **BACK-BEARINGS** · Retracing an enemy's (in)actions to establish the limits of their knowledge and their lines of reasoning.

(An approximate actual U.S. equivalent is **WALKING BACK THE CAT**, i.e., reassessing past events in the light of new information.)

**ROLL UP** · "He had made a mistake in Berlin, and ... his network had been rolled up." [3]

**SUBCONSCIOUS** · J.L.C.'s most quoted contribution to the language of espionage concerns not the gritty tricks of tradecraft but the underlying philosophy of spy-backed statecraft:

> Haydon also took it for granted that secret services were the only real measure of a nation's political health, the only real expression of its subconscious. [2]



*The remnants of John le Carré's tin pavilion off Lime Walk, Hampstead Heath* ☞

"There's a tin pavilion on Hampstead Heath, ten minutes' walk from East Heath Road, overlooking a games field on the south side of the avenue, sir. The safety signal was one new drawing-pin shoved high in the first wood support on the left as you entered."

"And the counter-signal?" Smiley asked. But he knew the answer already.

"A yellow chalk line," said Mostyn. "I gather yellow was the sort of Group trade mark from the old days."

JOHN LE CARRÉ, *Smiley's People* (1979)

*Fiction aside, tradecraft's true lexicon continues:*

## INFO & INTEL

**INFORMATION** · Unevaluated **RAW PRODUCT** from any source — which may contain **INTELLIGENCE INFORMATION**, i.e., information with (potential) intelligence relevance that is not in the public domain.

**FINISHED INTELLIGENCE** · The (**END**) **PRODUCT** supplied to **CUSTOMERS** (e.g., politicians, policymakers, planners, &c.).

The C.I.A. defines an **INTELLIGENCE CYCLE** by which information becomes intelligence:

**PLANNING & DIRECTION** → **COLLECTION** → **PROCESSING** → **PRODUCTION** → **DISSEMINATION**

There exists a vast array of intelligence types (**COLLECTION DISCIPLINES**), including:

› **HUMINT** · Human Intelligence; e.g., from agents, diplomats, prisoners, journalists, aid workers, refugees.

› **MASINT** · Measurement and Signature Intelligence; e.g., radiation detection, weapon recognition, seismic sensing.

› **IMINT** · Imagery Intelligence; e.g., aerial photography, satellite imagery, lasers, radar.

› **FININT** · Financial Intelligence; e.g., financial transactions, bank records, reporting obligations, suspicious activity reports.

› **OSINT** · Open-Source Intelligence; e.g., news reports, social media, academic papers, commercial imagery. **OSINT** has recently become quasi-democratic, with the rise of collaborative groups like Bellingcat.

Practitioners are often known by their discipline, e.g., **HUMINTERS**, **IMINTERS**, &c.

**RUMINT** · Jocular term for unproven gossip.

**CX** · A code for **INTELLIGENCE REPORTS**, popularized by Mansfield Smith-Cumming, the first chief of Britain's Secret Intelligence Service, who signed himself "C" in green ink.

**COUNTERINTELLIGENCE** · Any espionage effort designed to detect, deter, study, or disrupt hostile intelligence threats.

**AUNT MINNIES** · (Amateur) photographs that inadvertently contain intelligence. As the former C.I.A. director William Colby said:

> Even such a trivial thing as a photo of somebody's Aunt Minnie on a beach in a bathing suit [is put to use]. If experts noted she was standing by a truck, for example, they would know that the beach was firm enough for military or espionage vehicles. 4

Aunt Minnies are newly relevant in the age of social media. After the 2013 Boston Marathon bombing, U.S. security services "rewound the internet" to see every post, image, and video uploaded in a **GEOFENCED** area around the explosions during the hours before the attack.

**CHATTER** / **TRAFFIC** · Communications (either clandestine or **IN CLEAR**) that contain intelligence information.

**TRIPLEX** (**XXX**) · British term for intelligence material obtained from a diplomatic pouch.

**BLACK JUMBO** · British term for intercepted (and decrypted) diplomatic communications.

**S.C.I.F.** ["*skif*"] · U.S. term for a Sensitive Compartmented Information Facility, which allows classified information to be viewed and discussed. (A British equivalent is the **TANK**.)

**EYES ONLY** · Material so sensitive it can be read only in a highly secure environment, by a named individual. *Similarly*, **EARS ONLY**.

**SANITIZE** · To render classified materials safe for wider dissemination via **REDACTION** or revision. *Or*, to remove personal items from an **AGENT** that might compromise a **COVER**.

**EVALUATION** · The Americans evaluate intelligence using a system of letters and digits, where **A-1** is the best, and **F-6** the worst.

**TECHNICAL INTERVIEW** · Euphemism for a polygraph test. A **LIFESTYLE POLY** is one that explores (blackmailable) foibles, like drug abuse and sexual indiscretion. To be subjected to a **POLY** is to be **FLUTTERED** or **BOXED**.

*British police caught* **TOMBSTONING**

## PERSONNEL

**INTELLIGENCE** *or* **CASE OFFICER** · An employee of a service who **RUNS** a (**NETWORK** of) agents. *A.k.a.*, **HANDLER**.

(**INTELLIGENCE COLLECTING**) **AGENT** · One who clandestinely acts for an intelligence service and generates **PRODUCT**, but is not an **OFFICER** or employee. *A.k.a.*, **SPY** / **SPOOK** / **JOE** / **C.X. PRODUCER** / **ASSET**.

**HEAD AGENT** · An **AGENT** who is trusted to run their own (network of) **SUB-SOURCES**.

**ASSET** · Any human, technical, organizational, &c. resource that is available to an intelligence operation.

Human **ASSETS** are not (usually) full **AGENTS**, though the two terms are commonly used interchangeably.

**FACILITIES ASSET** · One who gives technical assistance to foreign-based agents (e.g., with mobile phones, bank accounts, &c.).

**ACCESS AGENT** · One who provides access to organizations, networks, or secure locations; *or* who facilitates introductions so officers can **GET ALONGSIDE** potential recruits. ("*Someone who throws dinner parties with the great and the good can be used as an access agent.*")

**LEGAL** · An agent **CREDENTIALLED** with **OFFICIAL COVER** of varying depth, e.g., cultural or defence attaché. *A.k.a.*, **OPEN SPY**.

**ILLEGAL** · An **UNDECLARED** agent under **DEEP** *or* **NATURAL** *or* **NON-OFFICIAL COVER** (**N.O.C.**) usually in a hostile country.

**AGENT OF INFLUENCE** · One who uses their prominent position to sway policymaking and/or public opinion on behalf of a foreign power (though rarely engages directly in intelligence collection).

One Chinese term for the cultivation of influence agents is **EXQUISITE SEEDING**.

**AGENT IN PLACE** · One who provides help, or discloses intelligence, from an established position of insight or power. *A.k.a.*, **HIGH-LEVEL CONTACT**.

**SLEEPER** · A dormant but ready **MOLE**.

**DEFECTOR** · One who openly disavows their country to assist a foreign (hostile) power.

**CONFUSION AGENT** · A sower of discord rather than a source of accurate intelligence.

**AGENT PROVOCATEUR** · One who incites others to incriminate themselves, or to commit actions useful to an intelligence agency.

**DOUBLE AGENT** · An agent working for two competing services, one of which is given real intel while the other is fed **CHICKEN FEED**. *Hence*, **DOUBLE CROSS** (**XX**).

**NOTIONAL AGENT** · A fictional asset created as part of a deception operation.

*Although always welcome,* WALK-INS *will be suspected as* DANGLES

**PEDDLER / TRADER** · One who sells (purported) intelligence (to the highest bidder). *A.k.a.*, (**INTELLIGENCE**) **TART**.

**FABRICATOR / PAPER-MILL** · A creator and PEDDLER of counterfeit intelligence; often motivated more by profit than politics.

**FELLOW TRAVELLER** · One who assists a political cause (historically, the Communist Party) without being a formal member.

**USEFUL IDIOT** · Historically, the K.G.B. term for a western Communist sympathizer who could be manipulated into helping its cause. Nowadays, any **DUPE** who unwittingly (or ignorantly) supports a hostile power.

**VIKINGS** · Russian term for intelligence officers; operationally supported by **BORZOIS**.

**CO-OPTEES** · Diplomats, civilians, and other human assets who are asked, ordered, or coerced to aid an intelligence agency.

**DIRECTED TRAVELLER** · A co-opted businessman or tourist employed to undertake a specific mission in a DENIED territory.

**CUT-OUT** · An intermediary used to minimize officer–agent contact. *Also*, an organization used to obscure clandestine activity, e.g., the source of funding or useful materiel.

**CLEAN(SKIN)** · One unknown to the intelligence services, recruited as a deniable asset.

**DECOYS** · CLEANSKINS or CO-OPTEES who (act suspiciously to) draw enemy attention.

**STAY-BEHIND** · An agent (or network) embedded domestically to resist an enemy invasion and sabotage their occupation.

**FLOATERS** · OCCASIONALS or civilians used for low-level (one-off) tasks.

**SNITCH JACKET(ING)** · False accusations or fake evidence of collaboration designed to destroy an individual's credibility and/or draw scrutiny away from a genuine asset.

Similar to the Russian **PROVOKATSIYA** [provocation], which describes both agit-prop stunts and personal smear campaigns.

**TARGET / HARE / PIGEON** · The object of an intelligence operation.

## RECRUITMENT

Because security services are endlessly contending with novel threats, their recruitment goals and methods must ceaselessly evolve to find agents and assets with expertise in newly relevant or suddenly urgent spheres, e.g.: regions (Gaza), languages (Ukrainian), cultures (Houthi), and technologies (A.I.).

The **RECRUITMENT CYCLE** is usually thus:

SPOTTING → ASSESSING → DEVELOPING → RECRUITING → TRAINING → HANDLING → TRANSFERRING → TERMINATING

**MICE** · A C.I.A. acronym used to categorize the motive(s) of agents and defectors:

MONEY · IDEOLOGY · COMPROMISE
*or* COERCION (i.e., threats or blackmail)
EGO *or* EXCITEMENT

**MONEY** is often key to **LOCKING IN** even ideologically motivated agents, and agencies wait for the moment a long-cultivated contact takes the bait which may be disguised as, e.g., a finder's fee or help with medical expenses. Many agents are still paid in cash (to avoid a banking TRAIL), and in person (to ensure they turn up to meetings). The sums are calculated to be attractive, but commensurate with the agent's lifestyle (£2,000–£5,000 a month is standard in the U.K.), and officers may wrap banknotes up like a gift. Some agents merge the cash into their daily spending, others convert it into portable assets like gold.

While money establishes reciprocity, and bonuses keep agents motivated, cash creates **DEPENDENCY** ("*They get used to the wealth*"). This makes TERMINATION more complex (and costly), and risks agents **FABRICATING** information to stay **ON THE PAYROLL**.

**CARLA F. BAD** · An (F.B.I.) mnemonic of (exploitable) weaknesses: Character; Associates; Reputation; Loyalty; Ability; Finances; Bias; Alcohol *or* Addictions; and Drugs.

**TALENT SPOTTER** · One who identifies **POTCONS** (potential contacts) but does not necessarily participate overtly in recruitment. *Also*, **NIGHTCRAWLER** · One who trawls for talent in the underworld.

**BUMP** · The actual introduction of the target agent to a recruiter.

**CULTIVATION** · The painstaking process of befriending a potential recruit and winning their confidence, in preparation for the ...

**PITCH** · The actual moment of attempted recruitment; either **HOT** (via a known source) or **COLD** (an approach by a stranger).

Not all agents are pitched; agencies also recruit and run assets at arm's length, either through think-tanks, academic institutions, &c., or via **CYBER-RECRUITMENT** (e.g., on LinkedIn). Such **UNCONSCIOUS AGENTS** may never know they are being exploited.

**GANGPLANK PITCH** · A Hail Mary approach to an intelligence officer from a hostile country as they leave at the end of their tour. *Similarly*, **CRASH PITCH** · Approaching a low-level POTCON (e.g., a foreign student from a trouble spot) without CULTIVATION.

**MOSQUE CRAWL** · Seeking informers inside Islamic **COMMUNITIES OF INTEREST**.

**BADGE UP** · The ability of domestic agencies simply to approach a citizen, flash an I.D., and ask them to help their country. ("*It's easy for* M.I.5. *to recruit, they just badge up.*")

**ELICITATION** · The art of acquiring information without raising suspicion. E.g., asset journalists may use a **PRETEXT INTERVIEW** with targets to slip in relevant questions.

Agents with good access but poor social skills are given **ELICITATION TRAINING**.

**VALIDATION** · Cross-referencing an agent's story with independent data (e.g., passenger manifests, phone records, bank transactions).

Handlers may regularly inspect their agent's cellphones, both to check for (or install) spyware and to assess their activity and contacts.

**TIME ON TARGET** · Actual in-person interaction with a (potential) agent.

**WALK-** *or* **WRITE-IN** · An aspiring agent or defector who **SELF-RECRUITS** by offering their services to a hostile power — sometimes by simply walking into a foreign embassy. (A **TALK-IN** makes the approach by telephone.)

Agencies are naturally sceptical of such **VOLUNTEERS** (fearing DISINFORMATION or a DANGLE), yet a successful **TURNAROUND** of a well-placed WALK-IN can prove invaluable. The Russian term for a walk-in is **DOBROZHELATEL** [well-wisher].

**DANGLING / COAT-TRAILING** · Tempting the enemy to approach one of your own agents or officers, thereby recruiting themselves a DOUBLE. A successful **DANGLE** involves BACKSTOPPING a convincing LEGEND.

Various signs alert agencies to potential dangles, e.g.: information that is **TOO GOOD TO BE TRUE**; individuals who know what they are doing ("*It's not normal to be too confident*"); and those who are overly keen to meet ("*It's like dating ... eagerness is off-putting.*")

**FALSE FLAG RECRUITMENT** · Pretending to represent a country appealing to a **POTCON**. E.g., if pitching a Greek citizen, Turkey's spy agency, Milli İstihbarat Teşkilatı, might claim to represent America, Italy … or even Greece.

**TURN AND BURN** · (Briefly) recruiting an agent to access a higher-value target.

**BURN NOTICE** · The C.I.A. term for disavowing a previously trusted **AGENT** or **ASSET**, and warning friendly agencies to do the same.

**NUGGET** · An inducement (money, asylum, sex, &c.) offered to a potential **DEFECTOR**.

**INTERNAL TELEPHONE DIRECTORY** · The clichéd example of non-public but low-level, and readily procurable secret material used to test the nerve and capability of new agents.

**AGENTSUMPF** · German term [agent swamp] for a location (e.g., Berlin, Vienna, Beirut) awash with intelligence assets of many nations.

**CIRCULAR REPORTING** · When information repeated in various assessments is shown to come from a single source; sometimes a sign that the agent involved is **CONFLICTED** (i.e., working for more than one allied service).

**DECONFLICTION** · Checking with a friendly security service whether an agent is also working for them. Since "*declaring an asset is the last thing you want to do*," this can be a delicate dance — even to the point where both parties simultaneously slide names across a table.

**HANDOVER** · The sensitive process of transferring an agent to a new case officer, before **BACKSTEPPING** (i.e., withdrawing). When possible, executed slowly over many months to **SOCIALIZE** the agent to change.

In an ideal world, agents would be "*loyal to the institution and not to individuals*," though most retain a strong bond with their recruiter: "*The first handover is always the hardest.*"

**ON ICE** · When an agent's activity is **FROZEN** (temporarily) in response to a security breach, a personal crisis, a change in service priorities, or an infraction that requires **COOLING OFF**.

**AGENT AUDIT** · A purge of sources based on an assessment of their productivity.

**DISCARD** · A **BLOWN** or **DOOMED** (low-level and expendable) agent; often sacrificed to protect or acquire an agent of greater value.

**TERMINATION** · When an agent who is no longer relevant, required, or reliable is **DISCONTINUED**; ideally amicably, via a gradual process of **CONDITIONING**.

## STATECRAFT

**DISINFORMATION** · A general term for **PROPAGANDA** used to promote a cause and/or undermine an enemy.

The C.I.A. reportedly recognizes three grades of propaganda: **WHITE**, issued openly by a government source; **GREY**, issued without attribution by a third-party **CUT-OUT**; **BLACK**, issued under a false or misleading name, or without attribution.

Russia uses the terms **DEZINFORMATSIYA** (*or* **DEZA**) and **AKTIVNIYYE MEROPRIYATIYA**, *A.k.a.*, **ACTIVE MEASURES**.

**EYEWASH** · *Internal* disinformation planted in the files to protect sources or **COMPARTMENT** material. Eyewash risks undermining trust and poisoning the well of intelligence.

**SUBVERSION** · Undermining the economic strength, political structure, social fabric, industrial capacity, military capability, or morale of a hostile state.

Modern subversion seeks less to invent new threats than to "*pick the scab*" of existing tensions, e.g., racial unrest, vaccine denial, election fraud, culture wars, &c.

**COMPARTMENTATION** · Segregating intelligence on a **NEED TO KNOW** basis (e.g., by department, source, region, operation, &c.).

**BIGOT LIST** · Those with **CLEARANCE** on a **COMPARTMENTED BIGOT CASE**. Someone suitably **INDOCTRINATED** is **BIGOTED**.

**STRATEGIC DECEPTION** · A sophisticated, long-term intelligence operation that manipulates an adversary's cognitive biases.

E.g., in 1998, India stunned the world with five underground nuclear tests, in part because it had learned from America's earlier interventions how best to dupe foreign inspectors and defeat their satellite detection.

*Waiting for a* BRUSH PASS

**GAVRILOV CHANNEL** · A (deniable) back-channel between hostile agencies (e.g., India and Pakistan), based on the C.I.A.–K.G.B. hotline established in 1983.

**MIRROR-IMAGING** · A cognitive bias whereby an intelligence agency attributes its own knowledge and worldview to its adversaries.

**SICK THINK** · When intelligence operatives develop a paranoid and overly conspiratorial **DREAM WORLD SPOOKOLOGY.**

**SHEEP DIPPING / DE-BADGING** · Spuriously "discharging" military personnel before transferring them into clandestine roles.

E.g., in 1968, U.S. airmen were "hired" as "civilians" by Lockheed to obscure America's involvement in Laos.

The number of former F.B.I. and C.I.A. employees now working in Big Tech has led some to suggest the technique has evolved.

**TAKING IN WASHING** · When a British intelligence agency supports domestic law enforcement (e.g., M.I.5. assisting the police).

**COUNTERFIRE** · Denigrating the character and qualifications of a **DEFECTOR** to cast doubt on their value to the enemy, and *pour encourager les autres* domestically.

**COUNTERTHREAT FINANCE** · Halting or disrupting the funding of hostile espionage, and threats like drug trafficking, people smuggling, terrorism, W.M.D., and organized crime.

**HONEY TRAP** *or* **POT** · A sex snare designed to collect **PILLOW TALK** intelligence and **KOMPROMAT**. (Female lures are **SWALLOWS**; males are **RAVENS** *or* **ROMEOS**. The **K.G.B.** term for gay ravens was **QUIET ONES**.)

As the *W.S.J.* reported in December 2024:

> Months before Putin invaded Ukraine, America's Moscow embassy sent a memo to Washington warning that the number of Russian women requesting K-1 fiancée visas to marry American men with security clearances was statistically improbable.[5]

**KOMPROMAT** · Russian term for compromising (sexual, financial, criminal) material collected (or forged) for immediate blackmail or long-term leverage. The Damoclesian sword of threatened but unused *kompromat* has been likened to "*walking with a stone in your shoe*."

Agencies have recently begun weaponizing **DATING APPS** (e.g., Tinder, Grindr) to find (or fabricate) deployable incrimination.

**CHICKEN FEED** · (Relatively) accurate and expendable intelligence disclosed to an enemy to engender trust in a **DOUBLE AGENT**. *A.k.a.*, **PLAY MATERIAL / FOODSTUFF.**

**BARIUM MEAL (TEST) / LITMUS TEST** · Releasing false information (or **CHICKEN FEED**) to see where and by whom it is leaked. *Similarly*, **CANARY TEST** · Releasing individually doctored versions of a document to trap specific leaker(s). Apparently coined by Tom Clancy in his 1987 novel, *Patriot Games*.

**BLOWBACK** · When disinformation gains currency in its originating country. *Or*, more generally, the undesirable (domestic) repercussions of a covert action.

**PROPRIETARIES / DELAWARES** · Front companies covertly operated by intelligence agencies. E.g., Air America (1946–76), which the C.I.A. used to support American operations in Southeast Asia. When proprietaries exist only on paper, they are **NOTIONALS**.

**MR. BIG** · A compliant executive who will use their legitimate business to **BACKSTOP** agents with genuine cover, e.g., a friendly newspaper proprietor might credential a "journalist" and send them to a useful hotspot.

**PERSONA NON GRATA** · Declaring a "diplomat" suspected of espionage (or other crime) an unwelcome person, and expelling them from the country. *A.k.a.*, **P.N.G.-ING**.

The 2018 poisoning of Sergei and Yulia Skripal in Salisbury, England, prompted >20 countries to P.N.G. Russian diplomats; the U.K. expelled 23, and the U.S. 60.

A **SILENT P.N.G.** is when an expulsion is executed without denunciation or fanfare.

**NON-STATE THREAT ACTORS** · Ranging from **INSIDER THREATS** and (foreign or domestic) **LONE WOLVES** to **FOREIGN TERRORIST GROUPS** (e.g., Boko Haram, Al-Shabaab, al-Qaeda) and **TRANSNATIONAL ORGANIZED CRIME** (e.g., human trafficking, drug running).

**FALSE FLAG OPERATION** · Misrepresenting a hostile action to implicate another party.

Originally a naval term (warships hoisted misleading flags to sail within striking distance), its abuse by conspiracy theorists to deny even school mass-shootings has rendered the accusation threadbare.

**SHAKING THE TREE** · Provoking the opposition into (precipitous) action, e.g., by arresting a known agent.

**FERRET FLIGHT** · An airborne incursion designed to **TURN ON THE LIGHTS** — i.e., expose an enemy's countermeasures.

**EXFILTRATION** · Smuggling a (**BLOWN**) agent out of a hostile location.

## SELECTED NICKNAMES

**THE COMPANY / LANGLEY / THE AGENCY** · The Central Intelligence Agency.

**COUSINS** · British term for U.S. intelligence folk generally, or the C.I.A. specifically.

**THE FARM** · A C.I.A. training facility at Camp Peary, Virginia.

**PIPELINER** · The C.I.A.'s counter-surveillance course for Clandestine Service personnel destined for operations in **DENIED** territory.

**THE FORT** · An M.I.6. training facility at Fort Monckton, near Gosport, Hampshire.

**S.I.S.** · Britain's **SECRET INTELLIGENCE SERVICE**, *A.k.a.*, M.I.6.

**SKIRTS** · What M.I.6. called (calls?) M.I.5.

**TWATS** · What M.I.5. calls M.I.6. (seemingly an acronym for The Wankers Across the Thames).

**FRIENDS** · (M.I.5.) nickname for M.I.6.

**THE DOUGHNUT** · Britain's Government Communications Headquarters (G.C.H.Q.); those who work there are **CONEHEADS**.

**NEIGHBOURS** · "Sister" (i.e., sympathetic) intelligence agencies.

**FIVE EYES (FVEY)** · An intelligence alliance between Australia, Canada, New Zealand, the United Kingdom, and the United States.

**LA BOÎTE** · Nickname [*the firm*] for France's *Direction Générale de la Sécurité Extérieure* (**D.G.S.E.**) the Paris H.Q. of which is called **LA PISCINE** due to its proximity to La Piscine des Tourelles, which hosted the 1924 Olympics.

## TRADECRAFT

**MEETINGS** · Establishing safe meetings with **AGENTS IN THE FIELD** is no simple task. ("*Getting a meeting to actually run is quite an achievement.*") Timings must fit inconspicuously into an agent's routine, **VENUES** have to be **SURVEYED** for security, and even the smallest doubt will lead to cancellation.

*The* S.I.S. *building on the Thames, at Vauxhall Cross; home of the* TWATS

**FALLBACK** · A pre-planned backup meeting. *Also*, **RESERVE** · A fall back to the fallback.

**SAFE HOUSE** · A secure and inconspicuous location, free from (hostile) surveillance.

**MOSCOW RULES** · Protocols of attitude and action used by the Americans when operating inside Russia, to counter the bear-hug of counter-surveillance. E.g., "*Do not look back; you are never completely alone*" and "*Do not harass the opposition.*"

This usage likely borrows from J.L.C., who used **MOSCOW RULES** to define a set of strict tradecraft techniques, e.g., "If you physically *carry* a message, you must also carry the means to discard it." [6]

**DENIED AREA** · An aggressively hostile location where agents must contend with **UBIQUITOUS SURVEILLANCE**, e.g., North Korea.

**COVER / LEGEND** · A false identity devised to protect an asset. Some covers are (semi-)official (e.g., diplomatic); others are non-official (e.g., journalist, businessman, aid worker).

In addition to being **AUTHENTICATED** with forged documents and other convincing **WALLET LITTER**, covers can be **BACKSTOPPED** with **WINDOW DRESSING**, e.g., phones answered by professionals, or front companies with websites and staffed offices.

Agents may also need cover stories for their own family, e.g., to explain an absence, or an influx of extra cash. ("*I'm helping the embassy with some translation.*")

**SEASONING** · Validating a COVER by **WEARING** it over time. When a COVER becomes so **WORN** as to be compromised, it is **BLOWN**.

**SNAP COVER** · An instant, low-tech disguise.

**IMPERSONATION** · Acquiring authentic COVER documentation by **TOMBSTONING**, i.e., adopting the identity of a **DEAD DOUBLE** (deceased person).

**SMOKE** · Deploying deliberate distractions to obscure one's actions and confuse the enemy, e.g., hiding one's true destination by booking train tickets to multiple locations.

**TREFF** · A meeting between a case officer and an agent, often in a neutral country. Likely derived from the German *treffen* [to meet with].

**(DEAD) (LETTER) DROP (D.L.D.)** · An inconspicuous location where material can be left for collection: from station lockers to rat carcasses (doused in hot sauce to deter scavengers). Russia uses the term *dubok* [little oak].

To indicate a drop has been **LOADED**, a unobtrusive **LOAD SIGNAL** (e.g., a chalk mark on a nearby postbox) may be **PUT UP**.

**LIVE DROP** · Where material is transferred in person (e.g., swapping identical briefcases).

**DIGITAL DROP** · Inconspicuously downloading data from a cellphone, or other device, to a hidden collection unit (e.g., using near-field communication technology).

*Quotidian, yet characteristic: an iconic* RECOGNITION SIGNAL

**POST OFFICE** *or* **MAN** · A (co-opted) intermediary trusted to deliver messages. *A.k.a.*, **CLEARING HOUSE / LIVE LETTERBOX.**

**RECOGNITION SIGNAL** · A sequence of actions by which agents and officers identify one another. E.g., in 1985, the **EXFILTRATION** of K.G.B. Colonel Oleg Gordievsky was initiated by him holding a Safeway bag outside a Moscow bakery, and an M.I.6. officer countersignalling by carrying a Harrods bag and eating a Mars bar. (If a party has any doubts, they will deploy a **GO AWAY** signal, and move off.) *Similarly*, **PAROLE** · A verbal **RECOGNITION SIGNAL.**

**SIGN OF LIFE** · A signal **PUT UP** (intermittently) simply to indicate that an agent is safe.

**DANGER** *or* **DURESS** *or* **CONTROL SIGNAL** · A subtle, prearranged signal that indicates an agent is in danger, or under coercion. E.g., using the wrong name, or misspelling a word.

**HELLO NUMBER** · A **CUT-OUT** phone line used for (emergency) agent contact; answered with an innocuous greeting, e.g., "*Hello?*"

**SURVEILLANCE DETECTION ROUTE / CLEANING RUN** · The (laborious) process of ensuring you are not being followed, or of **SHAKING A TAIL.** E.g., by **STAIR STEPPING** (taking zig-zag routes to expose a tail) or **CHANNELLING** (exposing followers at a narrow **CHOKE POINT**). **WASHING THE ROUTE** in this way takes many hours and will often involve multiple modes of transport.

**DETERRENT TAIL** · Heavy-handed surveillance designed to intimidate hostile agents.

Other harassment techniques (often aimed at scaring a wife) include vandalizing cars; killing pets; letting down tyres; and breaking into homes before stealing or rearranging objects, or leaving faeces in the toilet (or the fridge).

**RATLINE** · A clandestine (escape or supply) route across a border or **DENIED AREA.**

**(SPY) DUST** · Substances invisible to the naked eye (e.g., nitrophenyl pentadienal) used to surreptitiously tag and track enemy assets.

**PAPER** *or* **DIGITAL TRAIL** · Records left by clandestine activity that must be **BRUSHED OVER** or **SANITIZED** with a **COVER STORY.**

Digital footprints are increasingly pervasive. E.g., when in 2017 the fitness app Strava published a global heat-map of exercise routes, it accidentally identified various secret **BLACK SITES**, because soldiers and intelligence officers love jogging around a camp's perimeter.

Since even turning a cellphone off leaves a digital trace, when handlers and agents meet, phones are kept in **FARADAY POUCHES**, or held at a safe distance by a third party.

**ACTIVE CONCEALMENT** · A concealment device that works as intended (e.g., a U.S.B.-drive lighter that still produces a flame).

**BRUSH PASS** *or* **CONTACT** · Transferring material (in silence) with the subtlest of physical interactions. *A.k.a.*, **BRIEF ENCOUNTER.**

**LIGHTNING CONTACT** · A moments-long meeting between officer and agent, during which a few words can be exchanged.

**HAND** *or* **CAR TOSS** · Transferring material by throwing it (from or into a moving car).

**ROLLING CAR PICKUP** · Entering a moving (or fleetingly stationary) vehicle.

**JACK-IN-THE-BOX** · An (inflatable) dummy deployed to resemble a car passenger.

**STAR-BURST MANOEUVRE** · When multiple moving targets suddenly split up, forcing any followers to pick which subject to trail.

**WAGON TRAIN / TAILGATING** · Entering a secure area simply by following closely behind someone with access.

The codes to (alpha-)numeric locks can sometimes be obtained by **SHOULDER SURFING** (i.e., close observation) or noting which keypad numbers are **WORN BY USE**.

(**WORKING IN**) **THE GAP** · Exploiting fleeting lapses in hostile surveillance, e.g., a BRUSH PASS made instantly after turning a corner.

**DRY CLEANING** · Detecting and evading hostile surveillance.

**BEFORE AND AFTER** · Taking (cellphone) photographs of a location (e.g., hotel room) to see if anything has been disturbed in your absence (or by your clandestine activities).

**FIST** · The unique pattern of a Morse code transmitter, detectable by those in the know. *Similar to* J.L.C.'s concept of **HANDWRITING** · An agent's identifiable tradecraft style.

**FLAPS & SEALS** · Covertly opening, inspecting, and resealing mail. *Similarly*, **MAIL COVER** · Examining only the exterior of mail.

**GARBOLOGY / GARBINT / DUMPSTER DIVING** · Looking for intelligence in rubbish bins. *A.ka.*, running a **TRASH COVER**.

Often undertaken with genuine (or fake) garbage trucks, or by posing as a scrap dealer and scavenging through every bin in a street.

**BLACK BAG OPS** · Illegal acts to collect intel, plant evidence, install spyware, &c. *A.k.a.*, **SURREPTITIOUS ENTRY**.

The F.B.I. term for a burglarious entry is **SECOND STOREY JOB**, undertaken by a **SECOND STOREY MAN**.

**BANG & BURN** · C.I.A. term for demolition and sabotage operations.

**WET WORK** · Assassination; seemingly from the Russian **MOKROYE DELO** [*wet business*] alluding to the spilling of blood.

**LIVING IN (THE) GREY** · Living under (deep) COVER in a hostile environment. *A.ka.*, **GOING GREY**.

(**IN**) **BLACK / IN OBSCURA** · Being free from surveillance. ⊙

*Narrowing down access codes by identifying* **WORN KEYPAD** *numbers*

# Double Decanting the Tattle of the Somm

*SOMMELIERS are on the front line of customer service and profit generation in first-class restaurants — where the price of a bottle of wine can easily dwarf any sum spent on food. But despite headline-grabbing horror stories of gratuitous UPSELLING, any SOMM worth their TASTEVIN will be eager to share their oenological passion and hard-won expertise.*

## TYPES OF DINER

**(DEEP) WHALE / PLAYER / BALLER / DEEP OCEAN** · A **SERIOUS DRINKER** who will regularly **DROP** more than $1,000 on a single bottle.

**BIG WHALES / EXTRA BIG BALLERS (E.B.B.)** · Those who spend, say, more than $100,000 [sic] on wine during a single meal.

**DROPPING THE HAMMER** · When an E.B.B. or WHALE is on a spending spree.

**ENTHUSIAST / WINE HI$TORY / WINE PX** · Diners given V.I.P. treatment because of what they spend on wine. ("*We've got a* **LIVE ONE**.")

Naturally, some **BIG SPENDERS** are less profligate at meals they can't expense.

**NEEDY / HIGH TOUCH** *or* **MAINTENANCE** · One who requires a lot of **SOMM LOVE**.

**CORK DORK / (WINE) GEEK** · One who delights in the weirdest and most unusual wines on (or off) the list.

**POINT GRABBER / PARKER GUY / POINT** *or* **LABEL CHASER / VINTAGE CHART HOLDER** · A diner who selects wine based on scores from wine magazines, experts, or charts.

(An **iPARKER** checks out the critic scores on their phone.)

## SERVICE TOUCHES

**STYLE THEM OUT / MAKE IT RAIN / PIMP 'EM / BLOW 'EM UP / KNOCK 'EM OUT** · To take exceptional care of an **ÜBER-V.I.P.**

**DECANTING** · Wine is decanted for many reasons, e.g., to **WARM** it; to let it **BREATHE** (i.e., **AERATION**); to enhance its **AROMA**; to separate **SEDIMENT**; and for **THEATRE**.

Wines are also **DOUBLE DECANTED** — to speed up **AERATION** or so that bottles with sediment can be cleaned and refilled.

**AUDOUZE** · To prepare a (fine, ancient) wine in the style of François Audouze, i.e., by very gently uncorking the bottle, before leaving it upright and untouched for 4–10 hours. (Less romantically called **SLOW OXYGENATION**.)

**CHARGE / AVVINARE / PRIME / SEASON** · To remove extraneous odours and flavours from glassware by swirling it with wine.

**SPEED BUMP / PRE-WINE / PRE-GAME** · Wine drunk while a second bottle **OPENS UP**. The "*tragedy of restaurants*" is that fine wines can require a long time to develop — thus, for diners, "*the last glass is often the best.*" Some WINE PX's plan ahead, so that a special bottle will be opened well before their arrival.

**LOW POUR (L.P.)** *or* **NO POUR (N.P.)** · One who likes only a small amount of wine to be poured or to **POUR THEIR OWN** wine. (Some somms write **L.P.** or **N.P.** on bottles to warn other waitstaff.)

**DROP / MARK / MISE** · To lay glasses, e.g.:

**BURG(S) (BOWLS)**....large Burgundy glasses
**A.P. (WHITE** *or* **RED)**......all-purpose glasses
**CHARDS**......................Chardonnay glasses
**BORDEAUX**............................claret glasses
**CORDIALS**.........for dessert wines, port, &c.
**SOMM SERIES**..................the finest glasses

*A* **LOW POUR** *into a* **BURG BOWL**

## BEHIND THE SCENES

**FRONT LINE PRICE** ......cost of a single case
**CASE BREAK** ....... discounts for bulk orders
**3/5/10 CASE DROP** .. a 3-, 5-, or 10-case order
**BIG DROP** ............... any large order of wine
**BIN** .................... to unpack and cellar wines
**BUFFING** ..........polishing glassware by hand
**BUFFING PIT** ....where the buffing gets done
**BLIND IT** ...attempt to identify an unmarked wine (to **NAIL IT BLIND** is to succeed)
**DO THE PULL** ............ restock a service area
**INVENTORY** ......(regular) cellar stock check
**BOTTLE TO THE HEAD** *or* **FROM THE NECK** ............ to drink directly from the bottle
**HAND SELLING** .... finding the perfect diner for a curious or unique bottle
**REVISIT / CHECK IN** ....... re-tasting a wine to assess how it has developed over time

## WINE TERMS

**AUTOMATIC ORDER / GRANDMA WINES / EASY / FILLER / GIMME / WORKHORSE / MUST HAVE** · The chicken or salmon of the *carte des vins*: wines that are widely accepted, if not especially interesting (e.g., sauvignon or pinot grigio).

**CULT WINES** · Über-fashionable wines with a dedicated following; often hard to acquire.

**STORY WINES** · Those with a curious history or production or a tale personal to a somm.

**WINES BY THE GLASS** (**B.T.G.**) · Served at the bar and table, **B.T.G.** wines are chosen to complement menu items, cover popular styles, and cater to various budgets. (Some **B.T.G.** wines are used for **TASTING MENU WINE PAIRINGS**, though most somms are keen not to use only **B.T.G.** wines for such **FLIGHTS**. Somms **AMP UP** their wine pairing selection for **WINE PX**'s.) **DISTRIBUTORS** are eager to have their products served **B.T.G.**, since it makes a wine highly visible, adds prestige, and results in larger orders.

**KIDS / BABIES / GEMS / UNICORNS / SPECIAL INTEREST** · Rare, unique, or idiosyncratic wines. Certain somms try to ensure their cherished children (on or off the list) are drunk only by those who will appreciate them, even by pretending to be **86**'d (i.e., out of stock). Some somms will refuse to sell a supernacular **GEM** to an ignorant big spender, directing their attention to a similarly profitable but less historically significant bottle.

Discovering a **KID** has been sold, a somm might ask, "*Who drank it, and did they deserve it?*" — before checking whether it **DRANK WELL**. Squandering a gem on a coked-up fool is considered "*a waste of history*" — though somms can also be guilty of **HOARDING**.

**GLOU-GLOU** · Onomatopoeic French term for light, easy to drink, crowd-pleasing (**GLUG-GLUG**) wines. *Also*, **VIN DE SOIF** · Thirst quencher. *Similarly*, **PORCH POUNDER**.

**A.B.C.** · Anything. But. Chardonnay.

*Aldo Sohm's* TASTEVIN

**COUGAR JUICE** · California chard or Malbec — especially those with **OAK BOMB** qualities.

**BOJO** ........................................ Beaujolais
**NATTY** .................................... natural wine

**PÉT-NAT** · *Pétillant-naturel* · Naturally sparkling wines made using the **ANCESTRAL METHOD** of spontaneous fermentation without additional yeast or sugar.

**PARKER WINE** · Wine produced to match the perceived taste of the renowned wine critic Robert M. Parker Jr. (i.e., big, bold, rich).

**BIRTH-YEAR VINTAGE** · Wine to match the birth year of a diner. Ideal for claret drinkers born in 1961; not so great if born in 1974.

**LARGE FORMAT** · (In vogue) big bottles, like the **MAG**[num] and the **JERO**[boam].

**SPOOFULATED** · Wine manipulated (e.g., with oak chips) for a bigger flavour. Such wines are sometimes said to be **WEARING TOO MUCH LIPSTICK**.

## FAULTS

Wines can be spoiled by many faults, e.g.: being **CORKED** (by various compounds); **OXIDIZED** (exposed to air); **MADERIZED** (cooked by heat); or **BRETT(Y)** (infected by the yeast *Brettanomyces*, though not always ruinously so).

Some somms sample every bottle (a few use the traditional **TASTEVIN** bowl), but all should replace wine not **SHOWING** properly.

Diners don't taste wine to see if they *like* it but to confirm it's not **FAULTY** (or **FLAWED**). However, somms regularly replace bottles diners simply dislike (especially if they themselves have recommended them), before offering the unwanted bottle **B.T.G.** to other customers.

## BUYING

Although somms buy wine at auction and (in certain circumstances) directly from winemakers or other suppliers, the bulk of stock is purchased via distributors — who usually represent a portfolio of labels.

In addition to maximizing profits, distributors are eager to place their wines into high-profile restaurants. To secure key **ALLOCATIONS** of high-profile or hard-to-find bottles, somms have to form bonds with distributors. However, these relationships tend to be more symbiotic and educative than the standard seller-buyer dynamic — especially as many distributors are themselves former somms.

The best distributors understand and respect the unique needs of each restaurant and specific tastes of each somm. Most somms cherish the friendships they forge with their distributors, unless they prove to be **BAR WEASELS** — wine reps who **HAUNT** a restaurant's bar in an attempt to **TASTE** a somm on their **PORTFOLIO** and hustle a sale.

**ALLOCATION** · The controversial practice of rationing in-demand wines and controlling where they are sold.

**CULT WINES** and wines with a very limited production (e.g., premier cru Burgundy) are **HIGHLY ALLOCATED**, and somms need to develop good relationships with distributors and producers to ensure a decent supply.

Some producers go to great lengths to track their wines: to deter forgery and resale, and to ensure they are served only in the best restaurants, and under the correct conditions.

**DOLPHIN / PORPOISE / JUNK / THROW OFF** · Lesser wines that restaurants are obliged to buy in order to get an allocation of a wine they *actually* want (named after accidentally netted marine life). Such wines often end up being served **B.T.G.** or kept for inclusion on **BANQUETING** menus.

**CONSIGNMENT WINES** · Fine wines listed on behalf of a private collector or connoisseur, who receives a pre-agreed cut of the price if/when their bottles are sold. (More common in the U.S.) Consignments allow restaurants to offer rare and expensive bottles without vast capital investment — and they often explain voluminous and absurdly expensive wine lists.

## SELLING — UP & DOWN

Sommeliers have two interconnecting roles: guiding diners to wines that suit their order and maximizing restaurant revenue. Despite horror stories of gratuitous **UPSELLING** (**BANGING**), serious somms are keen to foster trust and generate repeat business.

Often, "upselling" is no more than offering choice. For example, rather than assuming "a glass of Champagne" is the house brand, a somm will present the range of **B.T.G.** sparkling wines. Equally, a somm may guide a diner toward a bottle that better matches the food while respecting a general price range.

Somms will typically enumerate the positives of wines rather than denigrate a cheaper bottle. (That said, **OVER-HYPED** or **TROPHY** wines may be **TAXED** or **PUNISHED** by higher-than-usual mark-ups.)

Somms also **DOWNSELL** by discounting wines about which they are especially evangelical, or by recommending less expensive bottles as a show of good faith.

## PRICING

The **MARKUP** on bottles is usually 300–500% — depending on the level and location of the restaurant. (The markup is generally higher in hotel restaurants.)

However, markups decline at the very top end: Thus, cheaper wines carry the highest profit margin, and the most expensive offer the best relative value (to the very wealthy).

**B.T.G.** pricing is usually based on selling a single glass for the price of the entire bottle (based on a four-glass bottle to account for spillage, spoilage, sampling, and labour).

**CONSIGNMENT** wines, though the more expensive bottles, carry a lower markup.

Many wine lists recognize **SWEET SPOTS** — price brackets that suit the financial comfort zones of different diners, e.g.:

Restaurants with **WINE ACTION**
£35–£50 | £55–£70 | £70–£90

**FINE-DINING** restaurants
£75–£140 | £190–£270 | £350+

Bargains can be discovered in the gaps outside these brackets. Indeed, sales of a wine can be improved by lowering or even raising it into a sweet spot. The **SWEETEST SPOT** is £45–£75, which represents the greatest jump in quality proportionate to cost — though prices are quickly inflating and wine is now progressively taxed based on its Alcohol By Volume (A.B.V.).

Although the cheapest wines **ANCHOR** prices on a list, many somms are keen to offer good and interesting wines at every price point and take pride in finding excellent and characteristic wines for drinkers at the **SHALLOW END**. (More cynically, somms also know that modest diners are more likely to order a second bottle of a cheaper wine.)

That said, many diners are embarrassed to order the cheapest wine on the list, and believe there is some magic inherent in the **SECOND CHEAPEST BOTTLE**. There usually isn't.

The golden rule is this: If a restaurant has a sommelier, you should think twice about ordering wine without first consulting them. For even if you are a qualified somm (and what are the chances?), you will not know what pairs well with a menu you have not eaten, nor will you know what newly acquired **OFF LIST** gems might be lurking in the cellar. ⊙

# White Elects & Black Rejects in London's Clubland

*From 400 clubs in 1900 to some 55 clubs today,* **LONDON'S CLUBLAND** *has shrunk dramatically. Yet the code, character, and quirks of these august establishments remain timelessly idiosyncratic.*

## MEMBERSHIP

*"It would be better that ten unobjectionable men should be excluded than one terrible bore should be admitted."* — THE GARRICK CLUB

**PROPOSING** or **SECONDING** a new member is not a decision to be taken lightly; indeed some clubs prohibit new entrants from nominating candidates until they themselves have been members for a specified number of years.

Most clubs have a **CANDIDATES' BOOK** in which each prospective member has a **PAGE** that details their name, age, address, and profession, along with the names of their proposer and seconder(s). Existing members indicate their support by **SIGNING THE PAGE**; some clubs ask those who know the candidate personally to sign the page's front, while others sign the reverse. (Comments are prohibited.)

**ACTIVE CAMPAIGNING** (e.g., pestering members; bribing with drinks; horse-trading candidate support; handing out names on slips of paper, &c.) is considered bad form and can, *in extremis*, delay or defeat an election. Instead, proposers **BRING IN** candidates as guests, and introduce them to existing members at the bar or around the CLUB TABLE.

Most clubs require a minimum number of supporting signatures (~10–30), and especially famous candidates are sometimes required to demonstrate greater than usual support, to counter any sense of "passive opposition."

Because clubs are defined by their members, membership is carefully calibrated to match a club's character — be it social, political, aristocratic, artistic, journalistic, theatrical, or sporting. At least, that's the theory.

The reality is often a clash of cliques where professional groups (most infamously lawyers, medics, and bankers) nominate their friends and colleagues and, in so doing, skew a club's character to the pin-stripe mainstream.

Given the average age of club members, it's not uncommon for a proposer or seconder to die while their candidate is still in the book. In such circumstances, the membership committee will usually canvass for a replacement.

Once a candidate has demonstrated sufficient support, their name goes forward to the **MEMBERSHIP COMMITTEE**. The procedure for (and formality of) considering candidates varies widely; many clubs ask for letters of recommendation, others require an interview.

Yet even a PAGE crammed with signatures does not guarantee admission if the committee judges a candidate incompatible or unacceptable, e.g., because of previous actions, statements, or posts on social media.

(Clubs have been known to make informal checks with the security services, if an existing member has discreet access to the files.)

Once elected, new members are asked to pay a (more or less eye-watering) **JOINING FEE**.

**REJECTION** · Much is made of **BLACKBALLING**, whereby a controversial candidate is rejected by a single antagonist or a tiny cabal of opponents. (The term derives from the traditional wooden **VOTING BOX**, into which members would clandestinely deposit a white ball to elect, or a black ball to reject.) 📷

In reality, committees endeavour to balance the demand for quality candidates with the pressure from nominating members — ensuring that vetoes are wielded judiciously.

Some clubs, fearful of direct rejection, let unpopular or undesirable candidates wither on the vine, hoping that — after many months or years languishing **IN THE BOOK** — they or their nominees will take the hint and bow out.

In years past, any member whose nominee failed to be elected would resign on principle — the rejection being considered transitive. Nowadays, whatever ignominy results from a defeated nomination is shrugged off at the bar.

*A porter's welcome at the Reform Club, Pall Mall, London*

## WOMEN

For centuries, the concept of single-sex clubs was not just uncontroversial but ineluctable. And, although an assortment of female-only clubs came and went, the dominant majority (in number and influence) excluded women completely, or tolerated them as guests only in certain rooms and on specified staircases.

Things changed slowly and sporadically — after all, the House of Lords only admitted women in 1958. But a combination of financial need, social pressure, and potential equal-rights legal liability has encouraged all but a handful of "male bastion" holdouts to admit women as full members.

## RECIPROCITY

Most clubs develop reciprocal relationships with like-minded establishments, so that their members can drink port in a storm if travelling (abroad) or when their own club is closed for the holidays.

Some clubs have just a dozen or so **RECIPS**, others take pride in a sprawling network. For example, the City University Club in London has 602 reciprocal clubs across 59 countries.

Visiting a recip usually involves presenting a **CARD** *or* **LETTER OF INTRODUCTION**, after which you are treated as a member. That said, *paying* for any food or drink consumed sometimes involves venturing deep into a club's backstairs bureaucracy or engaging in complex international correspondence.

## CLUBBABILITY

Much is made of this personality type, which, like *simpatico*, is easier to spot than define — though the O.E.D. defines **CLUBBABLE** as:

> ... well-suited to being a member of a club; that is skilled at or particularly enjoys social interaction; agreeable, friendly, sociable.

Of course, aggressively clubbable members can quickly slide into becoming a ...

**CLUB BORE** · Bores are loud when the mood demands quiet, and silent when it calls for ebullience; they whisper halitotically or boom histrionically; and they repeat the same dull stories *ad infinitum* and *nauseam*.

To re-appropriate the diversely attributed definition of a fanatic: A bore is one who can't change his mind and won't change the subject.

The heart sinks when a bore bears down on you at the CLUB TABLE.

## DRESS CODE

Despite the precipitous collapse of formal business attire, most clubs prohibit jeans and trainers, and require men to wear a **JACKET** and **TIE** — the latter, at least for dining.

(There is usually a box of **LOANER TIES** to be rummaged through by under-dressed members or guests. And the requirement for jackets is often waived during heat waves.)

Circa 15 clubs have ties of varying garishness.

*A* **YES/NO BALLOT BOX**: *Electors secretly drop their* **PILL** *(i.e., ball) into the appropriate drawer*

Some members sport the **CLUB TIE** whenever they visit; others wear it only at formal events; and a few would not be seen dead in the rag.

(It is considered ostentatious to wear one's club tie when appearing on television.)

## FOOD & DRINK

The cliché that club dining is no better than **NURSERY FOOD** is (more or less) a joke of the past — though savvy diners will err on the side of club-classic caution (steak and kidney pud) over *nouvelle* novelty (squid-ink risotto).

Clubs often feature a daily roast, carved by the chef from the **TROLLEY**, and themed food events are common (e.g., **CURRY LUNCH**, **PIE WEEK**, **FINE WINE DINNERS**, &c.). The Glorious Twelfth is commonly marked by gluttonous **GROUSE DINNERS**.

It's a golden rule that half a club's members will declare the food is "*much better than it used to be*" while the other half will swear it has "*gone downhill terribly.*"

**MENUS** · Since only members are legally allowed to pay (and to prevent money from raising its vulgar head), clubs will often present **MENUS WITHOUT PRICES** to any guests — allowing the shameless ordering of the *Lobster à La Riseholme*.

In the early 1900s, the female-only Lyceum Club had two different menus with identical covers — *à la carte* and *table d'hôte* — designed to cater for "many a woman who hides a slender purse under a brave aspect."[1]

**ORDERING** · In some clubs, waiters take food orders, as at a restaurant; in others, members pen their order (and that of their guests) on a slip of paper, which is then handed to a waiter (who rather diminishes the democratic effect by painstakingly re-confirming every dish).

**NAPKINS** · Many clubs maintain the practical (if rather unprepossessing) tradition of sewing **BUTTONHOLES** into the corner of their napkins, so a cloth barrier to the mulligatawny may be firmly secured to the shirt.

**CLUB TABLE** · Most clubs have some form of communal table that allows for convivial dining on an (unreservable) first-sat-first-served basis.

Members (accompanied, in some clubs, by one or two guests) sit in the order of their arrival, encouraging serendipitous encounters.

In less-convivial establishments, the club table is a social Siberia, avoided by all but the most forsaken. In others, it is the pulsating heart of the place, where members, guests, and candidates meet, dine, gossip, and plot.

A few of the most *intime* clubs offer only a club table.

**PRICES** · The tradition that clubs should be "expensive to join, and cheap to use" is harder to maintain in an era of decent living-wages and ever-rising costs.

Nevertheless, it is invariably cheaper to eat and drink at a club than at a restaurant of equivalent rank, which explains why clubs often counter-cyclically boom during recessions.

**WINE** · While smaller clubs offer a limited selection of wines (sometimes placed on the **CLUB TABLE** for self-service), larger establishments have extensive cellars and impressive lists — often selected by a **WINE COMMITTEE** of (highly) expert oenophilic members.

Because of lower mark-ups, large cellars, and longer storage time-frames, many clubs offer remarkable wines at reasonable prices.

Some clubs allow members to store wine from their own collections (or vineyards), charging a corkage fee for each bottle drunk.

## STAFF

It's hard to overstate the importance of a club's **STAFF** (historically called **SERVANTS**), since while bumping into fellow members is often serendipitous, the staff are always there.

Like Oxbridge porters, club staff are (reputed to be) possessed of elephantine memories, which are occasionally jogged by mugshot annotated member lists. It is something of a rite of passage when, as the months of membership roll by, a newbie is welcomed by name.

Certain clubs tolerate(d) staff-related curiosities. For example, the stewards at the Beefsteak were once all called **CHARLES**, and the waiters at Pratt's are called **GEORGE** or **GEORGINA**. (Presumably this is based on the theory that it is unreasonable to be expected to learn the name of each new butler.)

## PAYMENT

Only members may pay for food, drink, and other services. Some clubs require payment to be made at the time of purchase; others allow members to pay **ON ACCOUNT**, billing them every month.

A few clubs still offer the archaic service of cashing personal cheques (for a limited sum). But long-gone are the days when clubs such as Boodle's and Brooks's would boil-wash silver coins before handing them back to members in change.

**TIPS** · While it is generally forbidden to give staff individual **GRATUITIES**, clubs usually have an annual (Christmas) **STAFF FUND** to which members may donate. (Some clubs display an alphabetical list of contributing members, to shame the miserly.)

## BUSINESS

It is usually against the rules (and bad form) to **CONDUCT BUSINESS** in a club — though a deal-clinching cheese-course chat will fly well below the radar. This prohibition means that members may not **SHOW PAPERS**, nor may they take calls, or whip out their laptops.

## ERSATZ CLUBS

A *true* club is owned by and operated in the interests of its members — who adjudicate everything from the make-up of the membership to the mark-up of the wine list.

This definition places it in opposition to a growing group of *ersatz* establishments that walk and talk like clubs but — being privately owned and run — are not really clubs at all.

Perhaps the most successful *ersatz* club is Soho House, which currently has 260,000 global members and a waiting list of 99,000. Of course, after Soho Houses went public in 2021, its *real* members are not its dues-paying peons, but shareholders like Goldman Sachs.

## EXPULSION

It's not easy to get kicked out of a club; nor should it be. However, clubs will expel members who *consistently* fail to pay their bills (after an alphabet of apology has been exhausted) or who are **DECLARED BANKRUPT**.

(In the event of war, some club rulebooks have special provisions to expel members who are the citizens of antagonist nations.)

Members guilty of **GROSS MISCONDUCT**, or convicted of a **HEINOUS CRIME**, will be expected to **RESIGN**. Sadly not all do, and so many institutions have a catch-all provision whereby those who **BRING THE CLUB INTO DISREPUTE** or exhibit **UNGENTLEMANLY BEHAVIOUR** may be shown the door.

In 1824, London's Stratford Club (the home of whist and bridge) was so unnerved by the disreputable antics of the "noted duellist" and "inveterate gambler" Major General Thomas Charretie that they feared society scandal. Unable to expel him under any existing rule, the members voted to dissolve the Stratford entirely and establish a new venture — the Portland Club — which had an identical membership, bar one.[2] ⊙

# The Omnibore's Dilemma

*Semi-serious authorial neologisms for first-world* **DIETARY FADS AND FOIBLES.**

**MICROBIOTIC** · Consuming an absurdly large portion by painstakingly dividing it into seemingly insignificant nano-bites.

**DETOXYMORON** · One who compensates for unhealthy overindulgence with unhealthy abstemiousness.

**BACONATARIANS** · Vegetarians who make an exception for crispy rashers.

**EAT CUTES** · One for whom sandwiches are *sandos*, nuggets are *nugs*, pizzas are *zas*, &c.

**E.W.F.** · Eating While Famous · When emaciated celebrities pose with gluttonous foods in an attempt to portray themselves as normal.

**BESTETARIAN** · One who eats only the purest (or most costly) meat, fish, eggs, or dairy.

**HIPSTER VEGAN** · An urbanite who bravely (if vocally) subsists on limited-edition kale burgers and vegetarian chicharrones.

**SOUTH-BEACHED WHALE** · One who is doggedly loyal to diets of the dim and distant past (e.g., Atkins, Cabbage Soup, Scarsdale, Blood Type, Beverly Hills, Zone, &c.).

**OMNIBORE** · One who is so proud of eating absolutely everything, they become as insufferable as those who eat absolutely nothing.

**GLUTENAUGHT** · One who disdains gluten — not for any medical reason, but because it's considered to be A Bad Thing In General.

**F.O.M.O.VARIAN** · One who simply has to fork a bite of everyone else's dish.

**MENUNOMICS** · Tactical ordering to obtain a subtle advantage when splitting the cheque.

**TEETOTOLL** · The penalty paid by non-drinkers when splitting the bill with booze-hounds.

**GREENBACK JUICER** · One for whom the success of a cleanse is correlated with the price of the juice.

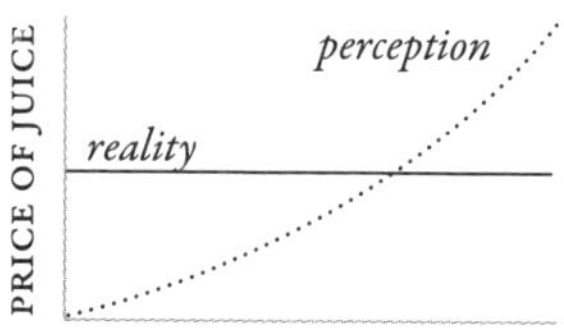


**BLEAKEND** · The dismal "off days" of a 2:5 "intermittent fast" (where you eat like a beast for five days before starving yourself for two).

**INSTAVORE** · One unable to eat anything without photographing and sharing it online.

**DESSERT PRATS** · Those who queue for the faddiest **FRANKENFOOD** pastries (crookies, cretzels, brookies, cronuts, cruffins, &c.).

**DR. NO-MA** · One who dined at Noma once ... and Never Fails To Remind You.

**BONE BROTHER** · One who imagines he is the very first to discover stock.

**GYMATHTICS** · The complex calorie calculus that uses exercise to justify eating, for example:

| *Activity* | *justifies* |
|---|---|
| Thinking about going to the gym | croissant |
| 5-minute warm-up with a yoga ball | chocolate croissant |
| 15 minutes on a recumbent bike | the third beer |
| Elaborate posing with free weights | cheeseburger and fries |
| 20-minute jog in the park | tasting menu with wine pairing |

**À LA CART** · *Declaring that truly authentic dishes can only be eaten at food trucks*

**VENTRILOQUISINE** · The art of deploying incessant banter about food to distract from the fact that you never actually eat anything.

**ANAFAUXLAXIS** · Misrepresenting a mild dietary preference as a life-threatening allergy.

**CLAFOUTISTOCRAT** · One who insists "the pastries are far superior in France." *Similarly*, **STOUTLAW** · One who insists that Guinness is *only* worth drinking in (rural) Ireland.

**PAC-MANGEUR** · One who ostentatiously orders an indulgent dish "for the table," only to consume the lion's share themselves:

**K.W.F.** · Kosher While Flying · Non-Jews who request the in-flight kosher option because the food is better. *Similarly*, **K.W.I.** · Prisoners who order Kosher While Incarcerated. *Also*, **H.H.K.** · High Holiday Kosher · Jews who keep Kosher only during Rosh Hashanah and Yom Kippur. *Similarly*, **O.D.R.** · Observant During Ramadan · Muslims who up their food restriction game during the holy month.

**S'MORALIZING** · Serenely declining dessert before taking a spoon to the group pavlova.

**SPIRALIZER** · One who carves carb-free vegetable noodles (if zucchini, a **ZOODLIST**).

**SIDEOPHILE** · One who thinks dressings contain fewer calories when ordered and eaten "on the side." *Also*, **SIDEOPHOBE** · One whose diet involves substituting fries with salad. *Also*, **PATTYVORE** · One who orders the burger but leaves the bun.

**BLISTICLES** · Those who select restaurants (and dishes) based on internet listicle ranking.

**BIKINILIMIA** · Crash dieting before a holiday. *Similarly*, **WEDDINGREXIA**.

**BREATHOPHOBE** · One who shuns garlic, onions, and other plants of the genus *Allium* for fear of their halitotic consequences.

**TERROIRIST** · One who seizes the wine list before imposing a bankrupting bottle. *Also*, **FANATTYQUE** · One who picks funky and barnyardy "natty wines" that only they enjoy.

**PLATE-OH?** · Getting food served on wooden boards, slate sheets, and fabric scraps, or inside tin cans, Mason jars, and tiny wire trolleys.

**WASTING MENU** · When one person insists on a tasting menu that no one else can manage.

**NOSE TO FAIL** · When chefs who think they are Fergus Henderson prove they are not.

**BOREDAINS** · "Foodie" influencers and T.V. personalities who fancy themselves as the heir to Anthony Bourdain (despite the disdain he would rightly have shown them). ⊙

# Boffo Slanguage & Supercurt Styles

*Every major newspaper and magazine has a* HOUSE STYLE *— defining, say, the use of em-dashes. But a few publications go far further, developing an idiosyncratic tone or private lexicon that first reflects and then defines their editorial persona.*

## VARIETY

1905—

For well over a century, the **H'WOOD** bible *Variety* has coined a rich currency of industry terms, including: **JAILBAIT** (1914), **FLASHBACK** (1916), **CLIFFHANGER** (1931), **STRIPTEASE** (1936), **ZINGINESS** (1938), **DISC JOCKEY** (1941), **SHOOT-'EM-UP** (1953), **SITCOM** (1956), and **BLOOPER REEL** (1971). These fizzy neologisms evolved into a distinctive **SLANGUAGE** that has come to define the jaded optimism of Tinseltown, where the MITTING of CRIX at a PREEM indicates whether the B.O. will be WHAMMO or FLOPPOLA. Below are some of the most beloved examples of **VARIETYESE:** [1]

**ANKLE** .......... to walk out, or be sacked †
(**AUTO**)**BIOPIC** .......... (auto)biographical film †
**B.O.** .......... box office (receipts)
**BOFF / BOFFO / BOFFOLA** .......... outstanding
**BORSCHT BELT** .......... Catskills resorts †
**CHANTOOSIE / THRUSH** .......... female singer
**CHOPSOCKY** .......... martial arts film
**CLEFFER / TUNESMITH** .......... songwriter
**CRIX** .......... critics
**DEEP THROATER** .......... husky singer †
**DISKERY** .......... record company
**DUCATS** .......... tickets
**FEEVEE** .......... pay TV
**FLOP / FLOPPOLA** .......... a B.O. failure
**GRIND HOUSE** .......... low-rent cinema †
**HARDTOP** .......... indoor movie theatre
**HELM / HELMER** .......... to direct / a director †
**HORSE OPERA / OATER** .......... Western movie
**HOTSY** .......... strong B.O. performance
**ICER** .......... show on ice
**INFOPIKE** .......... the internet
**INK** ... "to sign on the line which is dotted" †‡
**KIDVID** .......... children's television
**KUDOCAST** .......... awards ceremony
**LEGS** .......... box-office longevity
**LENSE** .......... to film †
**MELLER** .......... melodrama
**MITTING** .......... applause
**MOUSE** (**HOUSE**) .......... Walt Disney Co.
**NABE** .......... local, neighbourhood cinema †
**N.S.G.** .......... not so good
**NITERY** .......... nightclub †
**NIX** .......... to reject or decline
**OZONER / PASSION PIT** .......... drive-in theatre
**PLUGOLA** ... surreptitiously paid-for promo †
(**TEN**)**PERCENTER**(**-Y**) .......... agent / agency
**POUR** .......... cocktail party
**PRAISER**(**-Y**) .......... publicist / P.R. firm
**PREEM** .......... première †
**PROSTIE** .......... prostitute †
**SCRIBBLER** .......... writer
**SCRIPTER** .......... screenwriter
**SKEIN** .......... a T.V. series
**SOCK**(**O**) .......... excellent
**SPROCKET OPERA** .......... film festival
**SUDSER** .......... soap opera
**SUSPENSER** .......... suspense film
**TERPER** .......... a dancer (after Terpsichore)
**WHAMMO** .......... sensational — super-BOFFO
**YAWNER** .......... a boring show or event
**ZITCOM** .......... teen-focused comedy

† Indicates a "first cited usage" in the O.E.D.
‡ David Mamet, *Glengarry Glen Ross* (1992)

## TIME

1923—

Central to the creation of *TIME* magazine was the belief of its co-founders — Henry R. Luce and Briton Hadden — that a staccato form of Homeric telegraphese would attract middlebrow "strap-hangers" bogged down by the worthy prose of *The New York Times* and its ilk. As Luce himself decreed:

> Everything in *TIME* should be either titillating or epic or supercurtly factual.

Quickly, **TIMESTYLE** (*or* **TIMESESE**) was defined by a frenzy of textural tics, including:

| | |
|---|---|
| Compound adjectives | *sour-visaged* |
| Verbified nouns | *to eyewitness* |
| Titular prefixes | *Demagog Hitler* |
| Punchy variations | *potent* (for powerful) |
| Foreign loanwords | *tycoon*; *pundit* |
| Euphemisms | *great and good friend* |
| Alliterations | *shuffling and shivering* |
| Portmanteaux | *cinemansion*; *motormaker* |
| Inverted syntax | *in time's nick* |

In 1936, the many tics of Timestyle ("a nervous disease of the typewriter," according to the journalist Westbrook Pegler) were given a gloriously vicious kicking by Wolcott Gibbs, who penned for *The New Yorker* a 4,000-word pastiche that contained the immortal line, "Backward ran sentences until reeled the mind," and concluded "Where it all will end, knows God!" [2]

In fact, it all ended in March 2007 when, after 84 years, *TIME* was given a new look and a less eccentric tone of voice.

## THE NEW YORKER

1925—

The singular and eccentric tone of *The New Yorker* owes less to top-down editorial dicta than bottom-up proofreading dogma. As E. B. White told *The Paris Review* in 1969:

> If sometimes there seems to be a sort of sameness of sound in *The New Yorker*, it probably can be traced to the magazine's copy desk, which is a marvellous fortress of grammatical exactitude and stylish convention. Commas in *The New Yorker* fall with the precision of knives in a circus act, outlining the victim. This may sometimes have a slight tendency to make one writer sound a bit like another. [3]

In addition to "close" punctuation — where commas safely fence-off even the remotest ambiguity — the magazine is famed for its ...

| | |
|---|---|
| Double consonants | *focussed*; *carrousel* |
| Hyphenation | *e-mail*; *teen-ager* |
| Number spelling | *twenty-two-year-old* |
| Diaereses | *coöperate*; *naïve*; *reëlect* |

## JENNIFER'S DIARY

1945–1991

If not quite a house style, Mrs. Betty Kenward M.B.E. invented an idiosyncratic approach to writing about British Society in her much-loved (and mocked) column, *Jennifer's Diary*, first for *Tatler* and finally in *Harpers & Queen*.

Covering dinners, dances, weddings, and polo, much of Kenward's reporting consisted of (comically) banal lists of minor aristocrats, and the jewels they wore. However aficionados of the diary knew that, while she was never *directly* critical, Kenward's copy was littered with a code of bitchy euphemisms.

Successful hostesses were **GENEROUS** or **EXTREMELY PRETTY**, whereas **ACTIVE** or **TIRELESS** signified that a party had flopped. Brides were inevitably **RADIANT**, but when Kenward called a woman **GOOD LOOKING** she was damning with faint praise. In 1965, a 17-year-old Camilla Shand (now Queen Camilla) was dismissed as **ATTRACTIVE** — only one rung kinder than **SPIRITED**.

If a woman was especially unprepossessing, Kenward would simply omit her, as she *always* omitted her nemesis, Margaret, Duchess of Argyll. Similarly, she refused to acknowledge the Earl of Snowdon who, prior to marrying Princess Margaret, had made the unpardonable error of being one of her photographers.

Even the punctuation was pompous, as one of her editors, Nicholas Coleridge, recalled:

> Untitled guests were followed by a comma ("Mr. and Mrs. John Smith, Mr. and Mrs. Philip Jones," et cetera). Titled guests got a semi-colon ("The Earl of Margadale; The Marquess and Marchioness of Pershore;") — the semi-colon signalling superior status, and allowing the reader to draw breath in wonder. Members of the royal family merited a full stop ("Her Majesty the Queen. The Prince of Wales."). [4]

# PRIVATE EYE

1961—

Although *Private Eye* launched on the anti-establishment wave of the 1960s, the **ORGAN** (as it proudly calls itself) gradually merged into the mainstream, and is currently Britain's best-selling current affairs magazine.

As a result, British media and politics are studded with what were once in-house in-jokes, including parenthetical editorial asides (*That's enough, Ed.*); evergreen catchphrases (*New technology baffles pissed old hack*); a sprawling cast of bizarre contributors (teenage poet E. J. Thribb; royal correspondent Sylvie Krin); and a host of regular features, such as:

**PSEUD'S CORNER**
A rogue's gallery of purple-prose journalese (Will Self holds the record for appearances).

**ORDER OF THE BROWN NOSE (O.B.N.)**
Awarded for services to sycophancy.

There is also a lengthy lexicon of euphemisms, nicknames, and characters — many of which have entered the British (media) vocabulary:

**UGANDAN DISCUSSIONS** (i.e., sex)
After a female journalist was "disturbed in the arms of a former cabinet minister of President Obote of Uganda during a party" in 1973.

**TIRED AND EMOTIONAL** (i.e., drunk)
Used to describe the inebriated antics of the Labour politician George Brown (1914–85).

**THE CURSE OF GNOME**
When those who sue the *Eye* suffer disaster.

| | |
|---|---|
| **LORD GNOME** | the *Eye*'s proprietor |
| **EMMANUEL STROBES** | Gnome's lackey |
| **INSPECTOR KNACKER** | the police |
| **ST CAKE'S** | stock public school |
| **DAVE** *or* **DIEDRE SPART** | stock Trots |
| **PHIL SPACE** | stock male hack |
| **POLLY FILLER** | stock female **HACKETTE** |
| **MIKE GIGGLER** | "hilarious" letter-writer |
| **SIR BUFTON TUFTON** | stock Tory M.P. |
| **SIR HERBERT GUSSETT** | stock old buffer |
| **SUE, GRABBITT, & RUNNE** | stock solicitors |
| **SPIGGY TOPES** | stock pop/rock star |
| **THE TURDS** | **SPIGGY**'s stock band |
| **DIRTY DIGGER** | Rupert Murdoch |
| **CAP'N BOB / THE BOUNCING CZECH** | Robert Maxwell |
| **BRILLO PAD** | Andrew Neil |
| **PIERS MORON** | Piers Morgan |
| **PETER CARTER-FUCK** | Peter Carter-Ruck |
| **BRENDA** | Elizabeth II |
| **BRIAN / BAT EARS** | Charles III |
| **CHERYL** | Princess Diana |
| **THE GRAUNIAD** | *The Guardian* |
| **THE TORYGRAPH** | *The Daily Telegraph* |
| **THE INDESCRIBABLYBORING** | *The Independent* |
| **THE DAILY GETSWORSE** | *The Daily Express* |
| **EXOTIC CHEROOT** | cannabis |
| **TREBLES ALL ROUND** | journo celebration |
| **LUNCHTIME O'BOOZE** | stock pissed hack |
| **ER ...** | **THAT'S IT (CONT. PAGE 94)** |

# SMASH HITS

1978–2006

As well as borrowing *Private Eye*'s parenthetical snark, and sarcastic "scare" quotes, the **POPTASTIC** teen 'zine *Smash Hits* created its own absurdist lingo. For example, "the" was often substituted with **VER** (ver kidz, ver Zep, ver Smiths, and even ver *Hits*), and stars were frequently given madcap monikers:

**FAB MACCA WACKY THUMBS ALOFT**
**LORD FREDERICK LUCAN OF MERCURY**
**SIR BILLIAM OF IDOL · BYRON FERRARI**
**CHRIS DE BLEEURGH · ALAN ANT**
**"SNORTEN FORTEN HORTEN" HARKET**
**DAME DAVID** (Bowie) · **PAUL WELDER**
**PINT-SIZED PURPLE PERV** (Prince)

Ver *Hits* also created a **SWINGORILLIANT** lexicon of neologisms, both for linguistic laffs and to elide the chasm between its tender readers and the "adult" "antics" of its subjects:

| | |
|---|---|
| **FOXTRESS** | "appealing" female "singer" |
| **SPEWGUSTING** | disgusting |
| **UNCLE DISGUSTING** | pervy womanizer |
| **ACKCHERLOI** | actually |
| **FRIGHTWIG** | absurdly overdone hairdos |
| **PERVBREEKS** | inappropriate trousers |
| **SONGWORDS** | lyrics |

**('MAZIN') RUMPO** ....... sex
**ROCK 'N' ROLL MOUTHWASH** ....... booze
**RAWKNROLL** ....... rock 'n' roll
**DOWN THE DUMPER** ....... (predicted) failure
**BLEEE / GROOO** ....... onomatopoeic disgust
**PUR-LEASE!** ....... camp disbelief / disdain
***BACK! BACK!! BACK!!*** ....... any comeback

## SPY

1986–1998

Although *Spy* magazine owed much of its personality to *Private Eye*, it adapted from *TIME* its gleefully poly-adjectival celebrity insults:

*Self-loathing homosexual thug* ....... Roy Cohn
*Forgetful Nazi* ....... Kurt Waldheim
*Overproductive novelist* ....... Joyce Carol Oates
*Almost-English-speaking* ....... Ivana Trump
*Mummified boulevardier* ....... Oleg Cassini
*Churlish dwarf billionaire* ....... Laurence Tisch
*Litigious widow* ....... Joan Rivers
*Former child-star* ....... Michael Jackson
*Hobbity celebrity profiler* ....... Norman Mailer
*Socialite-war-criminal* ....... Henry Kissinger

*Spy*'s perpetual nemesis was Donald Trump, whom it called: *Queens-born casino operator*; *Ugly cuff-link buff; Joyless punk millionaire*; *Shuttle-owning dilettante megalomaniac*; *Well-fed condo hustler*; *Stinky*; and *The Donald*. One sobriquet hit hard: Trump still rails against being called a *Short-fingered vulgarian*.

## the ONION

1988—

Whereas other satirical publications seek to hone a distinct house style, *The Onion* subverts the form (and gravitas) of traditional journalism to mock global news and human frailty:

New President Feels Nation's Pain, Breasts

Winner Didn't Even Know It
Was Pie-Eating Contest

Holy Shit, Man Walks on Fucking Moon

Man Brings Lunch from Home to
Cut Down on Small Joys

Drugs Win Drug War

U.S. Continues Quagmire-Building
Effort in Afghanistan

New, Delicious Species Discovered

The website also lampoons the clichés of local journalism, based on the acts of "Area Man":

Area Man Knows all the Shortcut Keys

Area Man Unsure if He's
Male-Bonding or Being Bullied

*The Onion*'s most famous feature first appeared in May 2014, following a killing spree in Isla Vista, California {☞ p.263}. Since then, it has run (with only minor revisions) after >38 mass-shootings, under the evergreen headline:

"No Way to Prevent This," Says Only
Nation Where This Regularly Happens

## UP WOR THY

2012—

Despite pledging "positive stories that inspire and uplift," the website *Upworthy* will long be remembered as ground zero for **CURIOSITY GAP** headlines — cynically worded baits that coerce grudging (and quickly regretted) clicks.

His First 4 Sentences are Interesting. The 5th
Blew my Mind. And Made me a Little Sick

Watch The First 54 Seconds. That's All I Ask.
You'll Be Hooked After That, I Swear

9 out of 10 Americans are Completely
Wrong About this Mind-Blowing Fact

## AXIOS

2016—

The news website *Axios* pioneered **SMART BREVITY** (*or* **AXIOS-ESE**) featuring short (often <300-word) stories structured with hand-holding bullets and boldface subheads:

**WHY IT MATTERS**
**WHAT THEY'RE SAYING**
**ZOOM IN · THE OTHER SIDE**
**BETWEEN THE LINES · WHAT'S NEXT**

# Up, and Apparently Unharmed!

*Deep in the heart of Switzerland's Engadin Valley, in the town of St Moritz, lies the* **CRESTA RUN** *— a private, ¾-mile, natural-ice skeleton track that, since the winter of 1884–85, has crossed death-defying amateur sport with the eccentricities of boarding school, barracks, and society ball.*

Cresta riders descend 514 ft in around a minute, down gradients ranging from 1:2.8–1:8.7, at speeds reaching 80 M.P.H. According to the writer Clement Freud, it is "the most reliable laxative imaginable."

More curiously, the Cresta may well be the last great amateur sport, both because it is self-funded and regulated — by the St Moritz Tobogganing Club (S.M.T.C.) — and because the location-specific course melts every spring and must be hand-carved anew each year.

Consequently, while the Cresta's structure remains consistent, no two years are identical, and riders must adapt each winter to subtle changes in the length and height of its curves.

Operating December–March, the Cresta has three unofficial seasons: first, pre-Christmas and new year, which tends to be a family affair; second, January, which is colder and tougher, suiting serious racers and teams from the armed forces; and finally February, which is the most important season, featuring two of the major races from TOP.

(There are no runs on Christmas Day.)

## CANNON FODDER

Notwithstanding its militaristic manner and aristocratic air, the Cresta is open to anyone with 700 Swiss francs and sufficient gumption.

After confirming they have insurance, and signing a liability disclaimer, **BEGINNERS** attend the **DEATH TALK**, where the risks of riding are graphically illustrated by a **LIFE-SIZE X-RAY SKELETON** constructed from some of the injuries previously suffered. ◎

Those undissuaded by this blunt warning enter **BEGINNERS' SCHOOL**, where **GURUS** (experienced old hands) equip the **CANNON FODDER** with safety kit, and teach them the rudiments of riding.

New riders are only ever **BEGINNERS** on their first day, after which they become **SUPPLEMENTARY LIST** (**S.L.**) riders entitled to ride on **PRACTICE DAYS** and in designated races (at the secretary's discretion).

In contrast to the majority of sports, the Cresta is no respecter of youth, and riders of all ages compete on equal terms. Moreover, while fierce competition exists during races, the club's tone is one of ice-forged camaraderie.

## ARMOUR & TOBOGGAN

The basic Cresta **ARMOUR** consists of a compulsory crash helmet, elbow and knee pads, steel-sheathed hand-guards, and **GO FAST** boots fitted with jagged metal **RAKES** — which are the only means of braking. Some riders augment this kit with motorcycle body armour and Kevlar — *"not that it helps very much."*

Riders vary in what they wear: many sport looks that are quintessentially English (plus fours, cricket jumpers), or Alpine (Lederhosen); the speed-focused favour aerodynamic Lycra **SPEED** *or* **CONDOM SUITS**.

The Cresta uses many types of **TOBOGGAN**, and the tinkering quest to find an ever-faster **WAGON** is endless. The basic models are:

› **AMERICAN** · The original, long design with a soft and unsliding soft "mattress" seat.

› **TRADITIONAL** · The first to have a sliding seat allowing riders to move back for better steering and forward for additional speed. The wagon on which all beginners start.

› **FLAT TOP** · Features a solid, sleek, aerodynamic frame with no sliding seat — favoured by the fastest riders.

› **CUT-AWAY** · A TRADITIONAL / FLAT TOP hybrid with sliding seat and cut-away back.

› **BONSAI** · A toboggan $1/16^{th}$ the normal size — a novelty, though still used for some races.



*A rider negotiates* STREAM *on a* FLAT TOP ☞

## THE RUN

The Cresta has two starting points: **TOP** and, slightly lower, **JUNCTION**. Beginners and S.L. riders are only permitted to start from Junction (hence its nickname, **THE FOUNTAIN OF YOUTH**). Experienced riders may ride from TOP, once the **UPPER BANKS** are ready for racing in mid-January.

The open-curved Cresta is emphatically *not* a bobsled run, which has closed curves to keep riders inside the course. As the S.M.T.C. notes:

> A curling stone sent down a bob run will arrive at the finish. A curling stone sent down the Cresta Run, whether from Top or Junction, will come out at the first such opportunity.

Such opportunities tend to arrive at one of the Run's nine most dramatic corners:

**CURZON → BRABAZON → THOMA → RISE → BATTLEDORE → SHUTTLECOCK → BULPETTS → SCYLLA → CHARYBDIS**

The most notorious of which is **SHUTTLECOCK** — "*a long, low, raking, left-hand bank*" — which claims around one in every 12 riders, and is diligently prepared for accidents with fresh snow, straw, and crash pads.

Despite being overlooked by a spectator's platform — the **VULTURES' PIT** — Shuttlecock is considered a "safety valve," ejecting out-of-control riders before they reach the faster and more hazardous corners to come.

All riders who fall here join the **SHUTTLECOCK CLUB** and are entitled to wear its club tie. An annual Shuttlecock dinner has been held since 1934; one early menu offered:

*Potage à la Piste · Sole de Stream Corner*
*Filet de Bouef Shuttlecock, Sauce Benzoni*
*Straw Choux Bulpetts · Pêche Scylla*

While the Shuttlecock Club has amassed thousands of members over the decades, the more recent and exclusive **THOMA CLUB** — for those who have fallen from the **UPPER BANKS** above Junction — currently has 82.

Runs are usually completed in 50–70 seconds; the **FIVE-O CLUB** consists of riders who have broken 51 seconds from Top. Only one rider has ridden in 49: Lord Wrottesley.

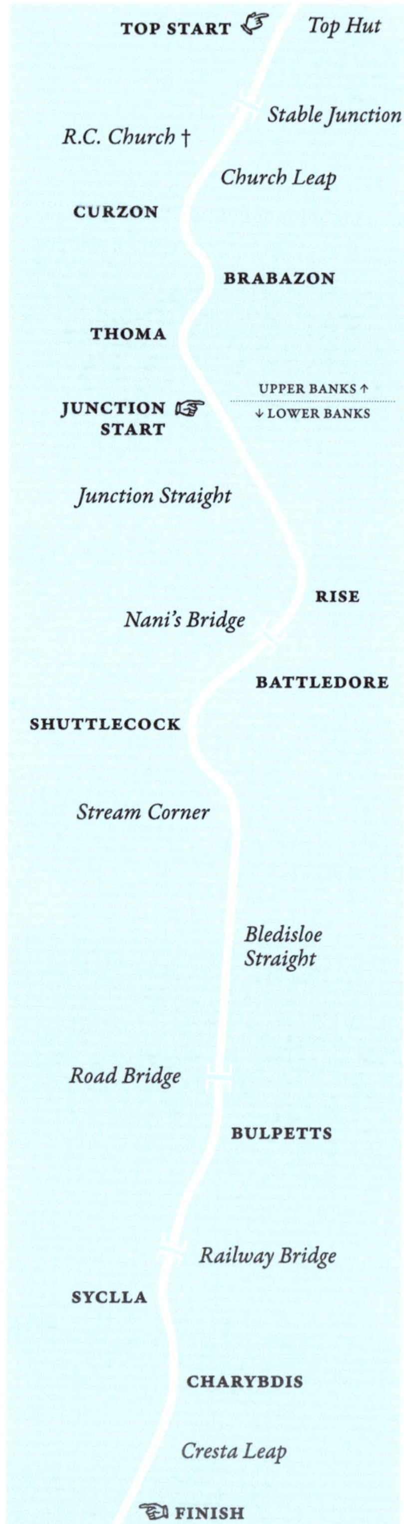

## AND THE NEXT RIDER IS …

Riders descend the Run based on the **ORDER OF RIDING** broadcast by Tower and acknowledged in turn with a raised hand. (To prevent any advantage from warm metal runners, riders must acclimatize their wagon outdoors 15 minutes before their time.)

Tower summons each new rider **TO THE BOX!**, where they hand their toboggan to an **ARBEITER** [worker], who halts its premature descent down the Run with his foot (at Junction) or the wooden barrier (at TOP).

Once Tower has announced **RUN CLEAR!** it declares **AND THE NEXT RIDER IS**, using full names for members and surnames for others (notwithstanding any royal rank).

Riders **ADDRESS** their toboggan (placing it to their satisfaction on the ice) and, once they hear a single toll of the Tower **BELL**, propel themselves down the Run.

Riders adjust their speed and direction by shifting their weight on the wagon and **RAKING** their feet on the ice. They adopt the bullet-like **KAMIKAZE POSITION** down the straights to maximize speed.

Assuming they reach **FINISH**, toboggans are slowed by foam matting, and bodies are arrested by large, padded **WOOLLY BAGS**. Riders clear the Run quickly — helping the **ARBEITER** carry their wagon to the minibus **CAMION** that drives them back to Junction.

## TOWER

The Cresta is directed from **TOWER**, which sits above the Art Deco-ish club house, and overlooks much of the Run (all of which is now covered by cameras). Operated by the **SECRETARY**, two assistant secretaries, the membership secretary, and three teenage **TOWER KINDER**, Tower is responsible for the safety of the riders and administration of the Run. It also helps set the Club's tone — not least through how each secretary wields the **TANNOY** that echoes out across the valley.

The most famous secretary of modern times was Lt Col Digby Willoughby M.C. (1934–2007), who, for 24 years, was famous for his brusque charm, his dedication to the club, his secret parties (*A.k.a.*, **UNMENTIONABLES**), and his habit of blasting incongruous music —Bobby McFerrin's *Don't Worry Be Happy* has serenaded many a fallen rider.

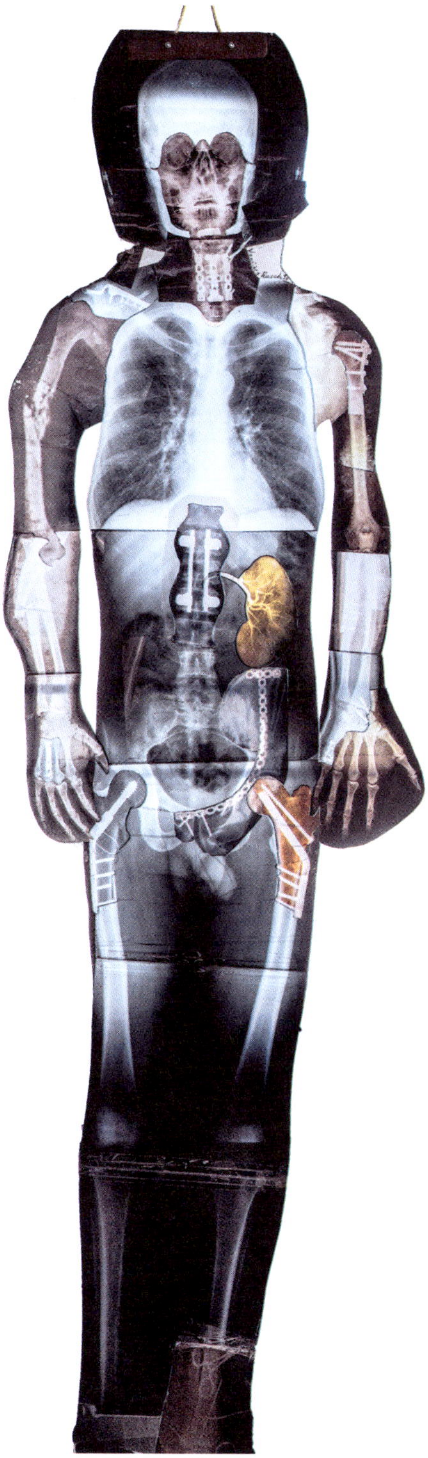

*A composite X-ray skeleton illustrating a selection of injuries sustained by riders on the Cresta Run*

*A rider joins the* SHUTTLECOCK CLUB

Digby was also noted for his turn of phrase: classic **DIGBYISMS** included national stereotypes ("*Ze Chermans!*"); nicknames (Heavy Metal, The Pink Panther, &c.); and beloved catchphrases, e.g., "*Get that child off my Run — he might hurt one of my riders!*" and "*He's up, and apparently unharmed!*" — announced when a fallen rider had signalled all was well.

Other Tower announcements include:

**PREPARE THE BURNING OIL! / UP DRAWBRIDGE!** · A warning that dubious-looking non-members are approaching the club-house.

**HUND AN DIE LEINE, BITTE!** · A serious warning to *keep dogs on leads*, and off the Run.

**ACHTUNG SCHLITTEN!** · Warning that a toboggan is hurtling riderless down the Run, posing a serious risk to those below.

**TIMES** · The Tower broadcasts the finish time of every rider, sometimes with comments on the performance. A rider's fastest time of the season receives a "**WELL DONE!**," and their fastest time ever earns a "**HELLO! HELLO!**"

**THE POWER OF THE TOWER** · The belief that riders who break the rules are likely to meet misfortune. *A.k.a.*, **CRESTA KARMA**.

Those who incur the Tower's wrath (e.g., by **FAILING** to turn up) are likely to receive that most damning of things: a **HANDWRITTEN LETTER**. (**FAILING** is considered profoundly unsporting, as it propels other riders **TO THE BOX** before they are psychologically ready.)

**UNPUNCTUALITY WILL DISQUALIFY** · The strict enforcement of this rule reflects the reality that the Cresta is a precious and wasting asset — limited by days in the season and hours in the day. As the temperature rises with the sun, so the melting ice becomes more hazardous. Hence the adage: "*Beware of south banks on a sunny day.*"

**TERMINATO! TERMINATO!** · Announced at the end of each day. Seasons end with a rider descending from Top with fireworks attached to his back and smoke grenades strapped to his feet ... to the strains of "Rule Britannia".

## RACES

Racing is central to the Cresta spirit, ensuring the Run remains a competitive sport and does not "*degenerate into a fairground attraction.*"

Held every Saturday, Sunday, and Wednesday, races vary in character and composition. The most important are the four **CLASSICS** (**CURZON CUP**; **MORGAN CUP**; **BRABAZON TROPHY**; and **GRAND NATIONAL**), but there are also races for the military, brothers, fathers and sons, **BONSAI** toboggans, &c. Perhaps the most spectacular are the **NIGHT RIDING** races down a flaming torch-lit Run.

**COOKING / SANDBAGGING** · Attempting to obtain a better handicap by going slow during practice runs, or swapping to a faster type of toboggan when racing. More or less obsolete now that all ride times are computerized.

## THE RAKE'S PROGRESS

"All attempts at short-cuts
lead to the hospital."
— *Hints to Beginners on the Cresta* (1933)

Signalled by a triple tolling of the Tower bell, **FALLS** are an inescapable feature of regular Cresta riding — the only variable is severity.

Riders who come a cropper are instructed first to push their skeleton away from them (to prevent a catastrophic collision) and then to demonstrate the severity of their injuries by standing and waving both arms above their head, thereby illustrating both their orthopaedic and neurological capability. (The Cresta has three degrees of medical response: **WAGON → AMBULANCE → HELICOPTER**.)

Once TOWER has established the extent of a rider's injury, and the whereabouts of the skeleton, it reopens the Run with the words:

**THE FALLING AREA IS CLEAR, THE RUN IS CLEAR, THE NEXT RIDER IS ...**

Despite its manifest perils, the Cresta has claimed surprisingly few lives. In 2017, 72-year-old Ralph Hubbard became only the fifth rider to die on the Run, after he broke his neck at Shuttlecock. Of course, injuries are commonplace, from bumps and bruises to broken ribs and fractured collarbones — not to mention the digits that have been pinched, crushed, or severed by the toboggan or the ice. (When Lord Bledisloe removed his glove to find a partially severed digit, he observed wryly, "at least it's not my trigger finger.")

A few characteristically Cresta injuries have earned specific nicknames:

**BARKING** · The consequence of skin contact with ice, at speed.

**CRESTA ELBOW** · Pain caused by the unusual wear and banging to a rider's arms and elbows.

**CRESTA KISS** · When a rider comes into contact with the Run, with varying degrees of severity depending on their speed.

**SHIPTON-STOKER** · When a rider's legs go over the top of Shuttlecock while their torso is still on the toboggan. (Named after two riders who were so-injured back to back.)

## LADIES

In common with ships, trains, and nation states the Cresta is female — perhaps out of respect, perhaps because of her curves. (As Lord Brabazon of Tara wrote: "the Cresta is like a woman, but with this cynical difference: to love her once is to love her always.")

For the first 44 years of the Cresta, women rode the Run on the same basis as men. But in 1929, citing medical concerns linking "chest-down" skeleton riding with breast cancer, women were restricted to riding on an annual Ladies' Day. (It has been suggested that female participation actually ended after Mrs. Bott beat Lord Curzon, the then President.)

In 2018, sensing both a societal shift and pressure from the British armed forces (which could no longer participate in a men-only sport), the S.M.T.C. voted by a two-thirds majority to allow women equal access.

Various initiatives now encourage female participation, including the women-only Lorna Robertson Challenge Cup, which was inaugurated in 2019.

And, at some stage, an unknown hand removed from the changing-room door the notorious sign:

"Where women cease from troubling
and the wicked are at rest."

## SOCIAL

Although passionately committed to skeleton racing, the Cresta is nothing if not also a social club — after all, the first Run was built by five guests of the Kulm Hotel who had established an "outdoor amusements committee."

This esprit de corps finds its expression in a whirl of parties, balls, and dinners — to say nothing of the **PRIZE GIVING** ceremonies in the **SUNNY BAR** of the Kulm Hotel that follow every race

Here the top 6th, 5th, and 4th riders receive a kiss from a specially nominated **KISSER**, and the 3rd, 2nd, and 1st riders are awarded **CUPS** (kept by the club) and **TAKEAWAYS** (trophies that may be taken home).

Finally, one of those who fell in the race leads their fellow fallers (and other spectators) in the **CRESTA FIREWORK** — a spirited vocal impression of spectacular pyrotechnic explosions. ⊙

# Grinding the Siren's Bean Water

*The blarney of* **STARBUCKS** *baristas.*

## PEOPLE

**THE SIREN** · A Starbucks nickname derived from the mythical aquatic muse of its logo which — according to its designer — is a "metaphor for the allure of caffeine, the sirens who drew sailors into the rocks." [1]

**STARBIES / STARBS / THE BUX / SBUX / BUCKS / BARSTUCKS** · Some of the many internal nicknames for **THE SIREN'S DEN**.

**STARBUDDIES** · Co-workers. Many **SBUX** employees are technically **PARTNERS**, since they are granted **BEAN STOCK** (i.e., shares).

**BARISTA** · Although all **PARTNERS** are known as baristas, only those with sufficient training can **PULL SHOTS** at **THE BAR**.

**GREEN BEAN / BABY BARISTA** · A new hire.

**GREEN BEAN ROASTING** · The hazing of newbies. ("*Can you drain the hot water tap?*")

**PHANTOM** · A partner **BORROWED** (i.e., temporarily transferred) to another store.

**CUSTIES / CRUSTIES** · Customers.

**KAREN** · A female (Gen X) **CUSTIE** with entitled "*Can I speak to your manager?*" energy.

**GERTRUDE** · An endlessly dissatisfied female (Boomer) **CUSTIE**. ("*A 'Trude with 'tude.*") The male version is **GERTDUDE** *or* **GERARD**.

**BACK-SEAT BARISTAS** · **CUSTIES** who correct every stage of a drink's creation (only to discover it's not theirs). *A.k.a.*, **HECKLERS**.

**BUT MY REGULAR STARBUCKS DOES IT!** · Inevitable **CRUSTIE** whimper when an unreasonable or impossible demand is declined.

**TOUCHERS** · **CUSTIES** who manhandle *every* cup to see if it's theirs. ("*Don't touch the lid!*")

**GRABBERS** · **CUSTIES** who take (and sip) a drink without checking it's actually theirs.

**REACHERS** · **CUSTIES** who lean over the counter (and round **PLEXI**-glass screens) to take lids, drinks, &c. Some partners discard anything a **CUSTIE** touches, to comply with health regulations and as a "*show of power.*"

**NO** · Appended to orders from customers who (aggressively) decline even to invent a name. ("*It's Marc with a C.*" Writes on cup: Carc.)

## DRINKS

**SECRET MENU** · There. Is. No. Secret. Menu.

There are "*fan created*" **ZOMBIE DRINKS** that get aggregated in clickbait listicles, shared on social media, and demanded from baristas, often with only a random name or screen-grab image to go by.

According to a 2023 Bloomberg analysis, there are 383,201,280,000 ways to order a straightforward Starbucks latte. [2] And the recent explosion of fictional **TIKTOK BEVERAGES** has added to the workload.

E.g., in January 2022, stores were swamped with orders for the **UNDER THE SEA REFRESHER**, which turned out to be a viral TikTok hoax, seemingly concocted from blue cleaning fluid and gummy worms. Other times **CUSTIES** simply demand "*the TikTok drink*" with no further explanation.

That said, social-media pressure does sometimes work. In 2017, after the "secret menu" **PINK DRINK** went viral, **CORPORATE** added the Strawberry Açaí Refresher made with coconut milk to the year-round menu.

In January 2025, **CORPORATE** announced it would eliminate ~30% of its "overly complex" menu to streamline service.

**HACKS** · Social media propagate endless ways to "game" Starbucks, e.g., by deliberately going to the **WRONG STORE** to collect a mobile order, to blag two drinks for the price of one.

ON BAR *at the Starbucks Reserve Roastery in Manhattan*

**ORDER ORDER** · The most efficient (barista-friendly) sequence to order a drink is one that matches the corporate computer system: *size* → *temp* (hot/cold) → *beverage* → *milk* → MODS.

**MODS** · Modifications to a drink.

**MEDICINE BALL / SICK TEA** · Supposedly SECRET MENU terms for the standard "honey citrus mint tea." **H.C.M.T.** became popular during the pandemic (hence the nickname, **COVID BUSTER**), which did little to endear it to baristas who had to face the public all day.

**DEAD SHOTS** · The belief that espresso shots "die" if they are not served (or mixed) within (ten) seconds. Some dispute this (claiming it's a CORPORATE tactic to hustle partners), and reassure STARBUDDIES that, though the flavour may change, **SHOTS DON'T DIE!**

**UM, I ORDERED A VENTI, NOT A TALL** · A common customer scam to get a larger drink; recently popularized as a TIKTOK HACK.

*Similarly*, **UM, I WANTED THAT ICED** · Refusing a hot drink, not because the barista made a mistake, but to scam a second beverage free. *A.k.a.*, **ICE FISHING**.

In both circumstances the CUSTIE will get a **REMAKE**, but if FISHING is suspected, they likely won't also get to keep the original drink.

**SURPRISE ME!** · A not-uncommon customer request. Some baristas will ask for guidance (hot/ice, coffee/non-coffee, allergies, &c.), and most will warn, "*There's no* REMAKE!"

**UNDERTOW / BREVE BOMB / JOHN WAYNE** · Espresso shot(s) pulled over a chilled spoon on top of cold cream. Sometimes made as a **TEAM DRINK**. {☞ BARTENDER'S HANDSHAKE p.76}

## DAILY GRIND

**SHIFTS** · Hours of operation vary by location, but shifts are generally 6–8 hours long, and are divided, e.g., into OPENING / MORNING → MIDS → EVENING / CLOSING.

**PLAYBOOK** · Shifts are divided into (2-hour) **PLAYS** by the **PLAYCALLER** (a manager or shift supervisor), using the **PLAYBUILDER** app on the store's iPad. Each play assigns a partner to a specific **STATION / POSITION**:

› **ON BAR / BARISTA** · Making beverages. Larger stores split this play into **HOT BAR** (espresso, steamed milk, &c.) and **COLD BAR** (blenders, ingredients, &c.).

› **REGISTER / P.O.S.** · Taking and **RINGING IN** orders into the point of sale machine.

› **WARMING** · Heating hot food and getting (i.e., **PULLING**) other items, e.g., pastries.

› **CUSTOMER SUPPORT (C.S.)** · Assisting partners who are **PLANTED** (i.e., unable to move from their PLAY), and **CYCLING** through a **CUSTOMER SUPPORT CYCLE**, (e.g., checking ice and cups, cleaning dishes).

*The* FORBIDDEN BROWNIE

› **DRIVE-THROUGH** stores have extra **PLAYS**: **DRIVE-THROUGH ORDER (D.T.O.)** takes orders from the **BOX**; **WINDOW** takes payment and **HANDS OFF** orders.

› **CLEAN PLAY** · (Deep) cleaning a specific station or area (e.g., mopping under the fridges). Some partners hate clean play; others relish the time away from customers (listening to their music on headphones).

**(PLAY) ADJUSTMENT** · Switching partners mid-play to **SUPPORT** a busy station. ("*I'm* **PULLING YOU OFF** C.S. *to help* WARMING.") *A.k.a.*, **FLEXING (THE PLAY)**.

***x*-PERSON PLAY** · The number of partners in a play; the lower the number, the tougher the shift. ("*Two-person play during rush hour?!*")

**LOBBY SLIDE** · To clean a customer area.

**CLOPENING** · When a **CLOPENER** closes the store one night and opens it the next day.

**PRINCESS SHIFT** · A short (4–5-hour) shift.

**BREAK YOURSELF!** · Instruction to **TAKE YOUR 10** (or, in some cases, **15**) minute break; or your **30**-minute lunch break. ("*I'm breaking you.*"; "*I'm going to lunch you now.*")

**TARBUCKS** ........*a Starbucks inside a* Target
**KROGERBUCKS** ........................... Kroger
**AIRPORTBUCKS** .......................... airport
**BOOKBUCKS** ...................Barnes & Noble

**SEQUENCING** · Streamlining multiple drink orders for speed and efficiency. E.g., prepping a Refresha while a Frappuccino is blending.

**PARTNER DRINK** · A free drink that partners **MARK OUT** for themselves while at work.

**B.O.G.O.** · A promo where Rewards members **BUY ONE GET ONE** [free]; often on Thursdays. *Hence*, **THURS-YAY** (for **CUSTIES**) and **THURS-NAY** (for **PARTNERS**). Increasingly a generic term for any special-offer deal.

**STICKER** *vs* **SHARPIE** · Whereas once all orders were written on cups, the majority of stores transitioned to **STICKER MACHINES** (until the machines break down). In 2024, **CORPORATE** declared a return to "writing little notes on the cups" (which leads some **CUSTIES** to imagine their barista is flirting).

**LONG TICKET** · A comically elaborate drink, which can become a **2-** or even **3-STICKER ORDER** — especially via the mobile app.

**MOBILE ORDERING** · In Q1 2024, 30% of U.S. Starbucks sales came via the mobile app.

The upside for customers is that they can order precisely what they like, without holding up a line or enduring the stress of human interaction (which apparently terrifies Gen-Z).

The downside for staff is that they can be overwhelmed with (highly complex) orders that **CUSTIES** often expect to be ready the moment the order is placed. (Some even place mobile orders *at* the drive-through window.)

**THIRD PLACE FEEL** · The aspiration that **SBUX** stores should be relaxed, welcoming, free-wheeling social spaces between home (first place) and work (second place).

In January 2025, **CORPORATE** reversed the **OPEN DOOR POLICY** that allowed anyone to hang out in its stores or use its restrooms, and introduced a code of conduct designed to prioritize (and safeguard) paying customers.

**PAY-IT-FORWARD (P.I.F.)** · The charitable, Good Samaritan origins of this trend — where **CUSTIES** buy extra drinks to be claimed by the less fortunate — was inevitably hijacked by social media. Now the "game" is to create long (and viral) pay-it-forward **CHAINS** at drive-through stores. (In 2014, 378 people paid it forward during an 11-hour chain in St. Petersburg, Florida.)

**P.I.F. CHAINS** are generally disliked by **PARTNERS** already juggling complex orders; indeed, some call a halt to the madness with various ruses, e.g.: *"Sorry for your wait! Your order is on us today!"*

Additionally, some **PARTNERS** feel that **CUSTIES** with money to burn on strangers in the drive-through might instead consider tipping their hardworking baristas. (*"Have no shame. Break the chain!"*)

## MISCELLANEOUS

**CRUSHTOMER** · A **CUSTIE** on whom a **PARTNER** has a crush.

**FORBIDDEN BROWNIE** 📷 · A "hockey puck" of used espresso grounds rescued from the **GROUNDS BIN** (and topped with cream and caramel drizzle) before being served as a prank to **GREEN BEANS**.

**DECAFFING / DECAF SURPRISE** · The controversial (and probably overstated) practice of **PUNISHING** obnoxious **CUSTIES** with decaf (or half-caf) drinks. *A.k.a.*, **CODE BLUE / BLUE BUTTON SPECIAL**, after a button that released decaf beans on older machines.

Other punishments include watering down drinks; finding and serving the smallest possible slice of loaf; or placing a lemon loaf slice in the paper bag icing-side down.

**VENTI** · To vent, and therefore a rant (online). *Consequently*, **TRENTA** · A big rant.

**MOBILE ORDER STARE** · The look certain **CUSTIES** give when mobile orders placed just seconds earlier are not instantly ready.

**THE (DEATH) STARE / (MEAN) MUGGING** · The (unpopular) tendency of **CUSTIES** to hover at the **HAND-OFF PLANE** and glare at busy baristas as if they were *"zoo animals"* or *"performing monkeys."* Obnoxious hoverers who ignore warnings may find themselves "accidentally" caught in the **SPLASH ZONE**.

**WE'RE NOT A BANK** · When **CUSTIES** try to pay for $5 drinks with $100 notes.

| APRON | SIGNIFICANCE |
|---|---|
| Green | *standard uniform* |
| Red | *holiday season* |
| Black | *Coffee Master* |
| Purple | *Barista Champion* |
| Tan | *Via latte taste challenge* |
| Yellow | *Vivanno Nourishing Blend promo* |
| Orange | *King's Day (Netherlands)* |
| Light blue | *Frappuccino promo* |
| Sickly yellow | *Oleato promo* |
| Tan & leather | *Starbucks Reserve & Roastery* |

**COFFEE BREAK** · Starbucks offers partners who have completed ten consecutive years of service a 12-month unpaid sabbatical, during which they keep their benefits, &c.

**MATCHATHELIOMA / MATCHA LUNG** · Gallows humour for choking clouds of green matcha powder (*"Cremated Shrek!"*). *Also*, **MOCHATHELIOMA** (mocha powder).

**(DOOR)DASHERS** · A generic term for the delivery drivers who collect app orders.

**BAR DOUBT** · A nagging (3 A.M.) panic that you accidentally served a customer the wrong order. ("... *Did* I use soy milk?")

**BLUE LIGHT SPECIAL** · A light that glows (in some stores) to warn that a toilet has been occupied for more than ~8 minutes; not good.

**PROMOTED TO CUSTOMER** · Getting fired.

**SELF-PROMOTED TO CUSTOMER** · Quitting and becoming an **EX-BEAN**.

[The majority of these terms are sourced from U.S. and U.K. store workers, and may not be universal.] ⊙

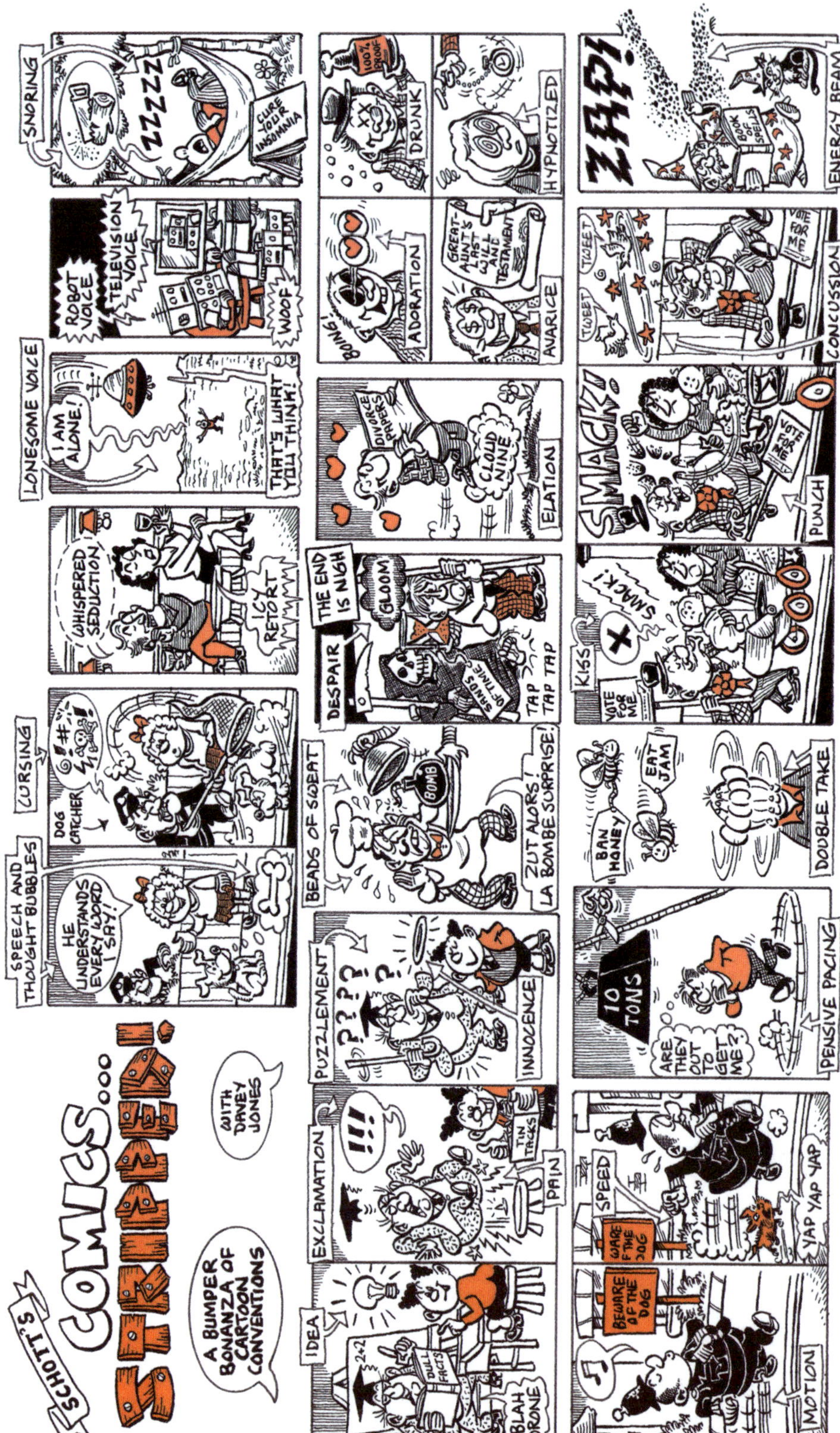
SCHOTT'S
COMICS...
STRIPPED!
A BUMPER BONANZA OF CARTOON CONVENTIONS
WITH DAVEY JONES
SPEECH AND THOUGHT BUBBLES
HE UNDERSTANDS EVERY WORD I SAY!
CURSING
DOG CATCHER
WHISPERED SEDUCTION
ICY RETORT
LONESOME VOICE
I AM ALONE!
THAT'S WHAT YOU THINK!
ROBOT VOICE
TELEVISION VOICE
WOOF
SNORING
ZZZZZ
CURE YOUR INSOMNIA
IDEA
2+2
DULL FACTS
BLAH DRONE
EXCLAMATION
!!!
TIN TACKS
PAIN
PUZZLEMENT
???
?
INNOCENCE
BEADS OF SWEAT
BOMB
ZUT ALORS! LA BOMBE SURPRISE!
DESPAIR
THE END IS NIGH
GLOOM
SANDS OF TIME
TAP TAP TAP
DIVORCE PAPERS
CLOUD NINE
ELATION
BOING!
ADORATION
GREAT-AUNT'S LAST WILL AND TESTAMENT
AVARICE
100% PROOF
DRUNK
HYPNOTIZED
BEWARE OF THE DOG
MOTION
WARE F THE DOG
SPEED
YAP YAP YAP
10 TONS
ARE THEY OUT TO GET ME?
PENSIVE PACING
BAN HONEY
EAT JAM
DOUBLE TAKE
KISS
VOTE FOR ME
SMACK!
SMACK!
VOTE FOR ME
PUNCH
TWEET
TWEET
VOTE FOR ME
CONCUSSION
ZAP!
BOOK OF SPELLS
ENERGY BEAM

FLIES = STENCH
FLOWERS = AROMA
PARFUM
HAIR STANDING ON END
DADDY?
JUMPING OUT OF BOOTS
EXPLOSION
KA-BOOM!
DOUG'S DISCOUNT DYNAMITE
EVERYTHING MUST GO!
HUNGRY VULTURE
SLURP!
MIRAGE
SAUCEPAN STUCK ON HEAD
DOCTOR'S SURGERY
TOOTH ACHE
GOUT
"EMPTY WALLET" MOTH
Fancy Jewellery
ENORMOUS DIAMOND
CLONK!
DESERT ISLAND
ST CAKES
SKOOL'S OUT
STINK BOMBS
"SCAMP"
RACING
BALL AND CHAIN
"MARRIAGE"
FART GAG
TRUMP!
MORE TEA
"VICAR"
LOTTERY TICKET
"TRAMP"
LOTTERY PAYOUTS HERE
£100
SOLID GOLD
"TOFF"
SPECTACLES
DUNCE'S CAP
D
HARD SUMS
EASY SUMS
?
"SWOT AND CLOT"
SHOVE!
"TOUGH"
KNOCKOUT POTION
"CRACKPOT INVENTOR"
BUTCHER
CUSTARD PIE
DOG STEALING SAUSAGES
"SLAP-UP FEED"
CAFE
menu
BANGERS AND MASH
SNOOTY WAITER
POSH
CAT STUCK UP TREE
PUSS
GRAND OPENING
MAYOR CUTTING RIBBON
ANVILS R US
FALLING SAFE
SAWING HOLE UNDERFOOT
EXPLODING CIGAR
OPEN MANHOLE
BUMP ON HEAD
GONE FISHING
PIE COOLING ON WINDOWSILL
SWAG
WET PAINT
NEWS
RAIN INSIDE UMBRELLA

# Chandelier Bids at the Tournament of Value

*The world of* **FINE ART AUCTIONS** *may seem sedate, but this decorous veneer conceals a highly complex, expert, and competitive underbelly.*

## PRE-SALE ACTIVITY

It took Sotheby's a mere 43 seconds to **KNOCK DOWN** Basquiat's *Portrait of the Artist as a Young Derelict* for £15m, in June 2024. But the process of making that near-instant sale likely involved many of these preliminary steps:

› Wooing potential CONSIGNORS to sell
› Assessing the **PROVENANCE**, **AUTHENTICITY**, and **EXHIBITION HISTORY** of every lot, along with how it has been recorded in the relevant literature (e.g., in the CATALOGUE RAISONÉE)
› Writing CONDITION REPORTS
› Assessing value, setting ESTIMATES, and negotiating RESERVES and GUARANTEES
› Cleaning or restoring, where needed
› Taking high-resolution photographs, and/or making promotional videos
› Researching and writing promotional **CATALOGUE NOTES**
› Arranging pre-sale exhibitions, and creating marketing campaigns (for **MARQUEE** sales)
› Enticing bidders, e.g., with a **TRAVEX** (travelling exhibition) around global sale rooms, or by taking lots to the homes of key buyers to show how they might adorn a collection

**BIG THREE** · The triad of top auction houses, i.e., Sotheby's, Christie's, Phillips. (Some prefer the **BIG TWO** designation and, according to the age-old joke, "Christie's are gentlemen pretending to be businessmen; Sotheby's are businessmen pretending to be gentlemen.")

**CONSIGNOR** · The individual, institution, organization, or other entity that gives a lot to an auction **HOUSE** to sell on its behalf.

**DESIGNATION** · Consignors are designated by name or by elliptical description: "*Property of a distinguished Spanish collector.*"

**HILLING** · The weekly assessment of newly consigned art at Christie's; named after a ramp that runs from salesrooms to storage racks.

**CONDITION REPORT** · Compiled for guidance by the house (or a third-party conservator). Notwithstanding such reports — which often have to be requested — lots are usually sold **AS IS**, without any warranty.

**SEQUENCING LOTS** · Traditionally, auctions were structured by the chronology or thematic unity of the lots; now **LOT PLACEMENT** is more calculatingly commercial.

Houses **FRONT LOAD** sales with a flourish, offering lots they hope will outstrip the **HIGH ESTIMATE**. (Nothing is more depressing than opening with pieces that are **BOUGHT IN**.)

High value lots are often sequenced around № 7–10, to allow buyers time to settle in, and some Asian sellers are keen that their lot is "lucky" № 8 in the catalogue.

Sequencing may also consider relevant time zones (e.g., placing American artists after ~2 P.M. G.M.T. in a major London sale).

**LOW–HIGH ESTIMATE** · The range within which a lot is expected to sell. Houses consider the low estimate (**L.E.**) very carefully, because:

› L.E. that are too high risk dissuading bidders (even attending) — "*Not in my price range*" — resulting in lower interest, and increasing the chance of the lot being BOUGHT IN.
› L.E. that are too low risk damaging the reputation of a lot, and dissuading sellers.
› Because the RESERVE cannot be higher than the L.E., houses that propose aggressive L.E. may beat more conservative competitors in obtaining significant consignments.
› Auctions are often judged on the aggregate price achieved *vs* the sum total of the L.E. ("*The sale made triple the low estimate.*")

**ROSTRUM LEAN** *as Sotheby's takes bids for Lucian Freud's* Portrait on a White Cover, *2018*

The sweet spot is a "*come and get you*" L.E. that satisfies (and flatters) sellers while luring buyers into bidding (ideally way above the **H.E.**).

Estimates refer only to the HAMMER PRICE, and do not include BUYER'S PREMIUM.

**RESERVE PRICE** · A confidential sum, negotiated between house and seller, below which a lot will not be sold; often a percentage of the LOW ESTIMATE.

Auctioneers will start the bidding below the reserve (both to keep the reserve sum secret, and to build momentum), unless two or more COMMISSION BIDS exist at or above the reserve, when the auctioneer will begin at that price: "*And I can start immediately at ...*"

If a lot fails to meet its reserve, it is said to be BOUGHT IN (*A.k.a.*, **PASSED**), and returned to the seller. Lots sold without a reserve are sometimes described as having **NO FLOOR**.

**POST-SALE OFFER** · One made on a piece that PASSED at auction; sellers must accept the offer if the sum exceeds the RESERVE.

**MISSED RESERVE** · Houses may sell *below* a RESERVE if they make up the difference to the seller. (Transacted, e.g., if it would cost the House more in return shipping fees were the lot to be BOUGHT IN.)

**STAR** *or* **TOP LOT** · One predicted to prompt bidding fireworks and **ANCHOR** an auction.

**TROPHY LOTS** · (Press term for) pieces with an (estimated) sale price >$10m.

## GUARANTEES & INCENTIVES

Houses will seek to entice sellers with a:

› **HOUSE GUARANTEE / GUARANTEED MINIMUM PRICE** · When the house agrees to pay the seller a (confidential) sum for one or more lots, even if the piece HAMMERS below its LOW ESTIMATE, or is BOUGHT IN. (Offered to secure the consignment.)

› **THIRD-PARTY GUARANTEE / IRREVOCABLE BID (I.B.)** · When, prior to the auction, a third party secretly undertakes to purchase a lot. If, during the live sale, another buyer tops this agreed sum, the third party may be paid a percentage of the **OVERAGE**, i.e., the upside difference between their bid and the winning sum. If the third-party bid wins, it will usually be given a **FINANCING FEE** discount for shouldering the risk.

Such guarantees are indicated in the catalogue (with little icons) — though not the parties nor the sums involved.

At a major evening sale, it's not uncommon for >50% of lots to have a guarantee.

Pieces put up without a guarantee are sometimes said to be **NAKED**.

**REBATE COMMISSION / ENHANCED HAMMER** · When the house agrees to pay the seller a percentage of the BUYER'S PREMIUM.

**ADVANCES** · Houses may incentivize sellers by offering advances, in the form of loans.

**IN THE BOX** *at the Sotheby's sale of Hospices de Beaune wines, 2024*

**COVER LOT** · Houses will sometimes attempt to entice consignors (away from competitors) by offering to promote one of their pieces on the cover of the sale catalogue.

## AUCTIONEERS

Before each sale, auctioneers will familiarize themselves with the provenance, history, and pronunciation of every lot — along with its **ESTIMATE**, **RESERVE**, and **GUARANTEE** — and will assess the names of registered bidders and interested collectors. (Such data is annotated in an in-house **AUCTIONEER'S BOOK**.)

When **ON THE ROSTRUM** (*A.k.a.*, **IN THE BOX**), auctioneers combine the skills of actor (engaging an audience), academic (reassuring waverers), and conductor (cueing bids in the room, on the phones, and across cyberspace).

The best auctioneers blend warmth, formality, and command — keeping the bids flowing with subtle admonitions ...

"*It's* **AGAINST YOU**, *sir.*"
"*Don't let this* **GET AWAY**, *madam.*"

... and cajoling encouragements ...

"*Can you give me 20?*"
"*Will you try* **ONE MORE**?"

... orchestrated with a beguiling symphony of gesticulations: encompassing sweeps of the arm; pointed fingers of identification; and engaging **ROSTRUM LEANS** ◎.

**RHYTHM** · Fine art auctions average 30–120 lots per hour (with 60 as a sweet spot).

Auctioneers are keen to maintain a rhythm within and between lots — deploying pauses to coax vacillators, without losing momentum or antagonizing those with a winning bid.

**SUPERSTITIONS** · Like all performers, auctioneers are comforted by personal routines, lucky charms and clothing, or a nip of liquor.

## BIDDING

**REGISTERING** · Houses will require bidders (individuals, companies, organizations, trusts, &c.) to pre-register with documentary proof of identity, address, &c. Bidders may also be asked to provide financial references or put down a refundable deposit.

Most auctions start with a **HOUSEKEEPING** recitation of rules and commissions; a **SALE ROOM NOTICE** of any guarantees that do not appear in the catalogue; and a list of any lots that have been **WITHDRAWN**.

**WITHDRAWAL** · Lots are **PULLED** from sales (at the last minute) for reasons *technical* ...

- Doubts concerning authenticity, condition, provenance, or **TITLE** (i.e., ownership)
- Allegations of theft or looting
- Death or divorce of the seller
- Import, export, or tax complications
- An auction contract that remains unsigned

… and *financial* …

- Doubts a lot will make its LOW ESTIMATE, (because of insufficient pre-auction interest)
- External events that dampen demand (terror attack, financial crash, natural disaster, &c.)
- Objections to DEACCESSIONING, e.g., from a consigning museum's significant donors
- Changes of personal circumstances, or heart

Depending on the context, consignors may be charged a **WITHDRAWAL** *or* **KILL FEE** (e.g., 25% of the LOW ESTIMATE, plus any costs).

Historically, withdrawing lots was generally frowned upon as a bait-and-switch dilution of the sale. Nowadays it is commonplace — not least because the "stigma" of withdrawal is usually less consequential than the impact of the piece being BURNED, both for the seller (in terms of future value) and the auction house (in terms of SELL-THROUGH RATE).

**LOT HAS BEEN REQUESTED** · Warning that a piece has been pledged, e.g., to an exhibition.

**CONSECUTIVE BIDDING** · An auctioneer may kick off the bidding on behalf of the seller by taking a **PHANTOM BID** from a non-existent buyer, and then taking further fake **WALL** *or* **CHANDELIER BIDS** ("*depending on the grandeur of the house*") up to (i.e., not matching or exceeding) the value of the RESERVE.

This (controversial) tactic of **BOUNCING** *or* **TAKING BIDS OFF THE WALL** is designed to encourage real bids, build momentum, and camouflage the RESERVE price.

**(GETTING ON) THE RIGHT FOOT** · The art of establishing the correct bidding sequence for a piece with a RESERVE, so that the auctioneer can set up a winning bid by taking a WALL BID one increment below the RESERVE.

E.g., if a lot has a RESERVE of 20,000, an auctioneer may start the bidding at 18,000 and, if there are no bids, take a WALL BID of 19,000 so the next *real* bid will meet the RESERVE.

Were the bidding to start on the **WRONG FOOT** at 17,000, and a WALL BID taken for 18,000, a genuine bidder at 19,000 would fail to meet the RESERVE and, since the auctioneer could not legally WALL BID 20,000, the lot would have to be BOUGHT IN. In this situation, an auctioneer might get back on the right foot by taking a (RESERVE-revealing) PHANTOM SPLIT BID of 19,500.

**COMMISSION** *or* **ABSENTEE** *or* **WRITTEN BID** · One deposited with the house before an auction, giving the buyer's maximum bid. When two or more commission bids are for the same sum (i.e., **CONFLICTING BIDS**), the auctioneer will favour the first bid deposited.

**MAIDEN BID** · The opening bid; usually of interest only when also the **WINNING BID**.

**DEALER BIDDING** · Galleries will bid on pieces by artists they represent both to acquire the work, and to elevate the artist's AUCTION RECORD and inflate the value of their stock.

**BIDDING INCREMENTS** · Bidding usually starts below the LOW ESTIMATE, and rises in increments to ensure order and build momentum. Most houses use **10% INCREMENTS**:

| £, $, € | *rise* |
|---|---|
| 50–1,000 | 50s |
| 1,000–2,000 | 100s |
| 2,000–3,000 | 200s |
| 3,000–5,000 | 200s/500s/800s |
| 5,000–10,000 | 500s |
| 10,000–20,000 | 1,000s |
| 20,000–30,000 | 2,000s |
| 30,000–50,000 | 2,000s/5,000s/8,000s |
| 50,000–100,000 | 5,000s |
| 100,000–200,000 | 10,000s |

**SPLITTING BIDS** · To coax more cash (when prices hit a level worth haggling over) auctioneers may accept a bid below the next increment: "*I have £1.2 million,* **I'LL TAKE** *£1.25.*"

Once the bidding has been split, the increments remain **RE-SET** at the lower level until the next (or a natural) plateau is reached.

Split bids proposed by buyers may be taken or declined ("*I'm sorry, my next bid is…*"). But in accepting a split bid, the auctioneer risks changing the pace and dynamic of the entire sale, encouraging other buyers to try their luck.

**JUMP BID** · When a bidder breaks ranks and offers a sum *higher* than the next increment.

In 2017, the record-shattering bidding at Christie's for Leonardo da Vinci's *Salvator Mundi* concluded thus: … $328m → $332m → $350m → $352m → $355m → $370m → $400m.

Two motives are usually given for **JUMPING** — impatience and intimidation — and there is evidence that the tactic works best when deployed at the earlier stages of bidding.[1]

(**TAKING A BID**) **ON THE HAMMER** · When an auctioneer accepts a bid made at the precise moment the hammer falls.

**HAMMER PRICE** · The winning bid, without BUYER'S PREMIUM or any other fees. *Conversely*, **PRICE REALIZED** · The HAMMER PRICE, plus the BUYER'S PREMIUM.

**DECLINING PRICE ANOMALY** · When the value of bids declines over the course of a long auction. (*A.k.a.*, **AFTERNOON EFFECT**).[2]

**PHONES** ◎ · The popularity of phone bidding has soared thanks to the globalization of the market, the mobility of wealth, the lingering impact of Covid, and the lure of anonymity.

Telephone operators (usually house experts and other staff) are positioned in the room so they can relay the atmosphere of the sale and signal to the auctioneer. (A raised hand means, "*I have a bid*"; a horizontal hand means, "*I'm waiting to hear*"; a throat-cut means, "*I'm out.*")

Landlines are used whenever possible to avoid the risk of dying batteries and dropped connections ("*I'm going into a tunnel!*"). If a line is lost, the handler may signal to the auctioneer for a short pause so they can redial, or try a backup number.

The popularity of phone (and online) bidding leads houses to deploy **SEAT FILLERS** so that the sale room does not appear too empty. (Though shy buyers will occasionally bid by phone while in the room.)

To ensure no-one can hear (or lip-read) their communications with the bidder, telephone operators often hold a hand over their mouths. So ingrained is this habit, it continued even when masks were worn during Covid.

**PADDLE** · Anything that shows the buyer's **BIDDER NUMBER** — from a wooden "ping-pong" bat to an iPhone. *Hence*, **PADDLE SPOTTING** · Scanning to identify buyers. *And*, **BID SPOTTERS** · Employees who ensure that a PADDLE is not missed: "*Bid here, sir.*"

When famous bidders are **IN THE ROOM**, the auctioneer may joke, "*Of course, we don't need to see* your *paddle, madam!*"

**FAIR WARNING / THE HAMMER IS UP** · Some of the terms auctioneers use to indicate the end of bidding. (The movie cliché of **GOING ONCE, GOING TWICE** is not unheard of, but considered somewhat déclassé.)

**LIVE-STREAMING** · For generations auction houses battled against what the Germans call *Schwellenangst* [threshold anxiety] — the fear of entering new and intimidating places.

And then suddenly, enabled by the internet and catalysed by Covid, houses discovered a global audience of buyers (and gawkers). Now auctions are broadcast live on YouTube, and especially juicy bidding wars or record prices are clipped for Twitter, TikTok, Weibo, &c.

As a result, auction houses have been kitted out like T.V. studios, and auctioneers are more than ever expected to play to the audience.

**BOUGHT IN** (**B.I.**) · When a lot fails to hit its RESERVE (or has no bidders) and is **TAKEN TO HOUSE**, i.e., returned to the seller.

Houses dislike B.I. lots because they chill the mood and momentum of a sale, negatively impact the SELL-THROUGH RATE, and risk discouraging future sellers. Sellers dislike them because they may still have to pay a SELLER'S FEE, and because the piece may end up ...

**BURNED** · When a lot (unexpectedly) fails to sell at auction, denting the reputation of the piece (and sometimes the house).

Owners of burned lots may attempt to sell through a different house and/or in a different location; or they may hold the piece (for several years) before **REINTRODUCING** it.

Pieces can also be burned in the private market if they are **SHOPPED** around to too many potential buyers: It's a small art world.

**SELL-THROUGH RATE** · The ratio of sold to unsold lots — used to judge the success of an auction and, over time, the strength of a house. A DAY SALE **S.T.R.** of 80% or higher is usually considered **STRONG**.

As a result, some houses seek to boost their S.T.R. — e.g., by WITHDRAWING lots unlikely to meet their RESERVES, or seeking THIRD PARTY GUARANTEES to underwrite a sale.

**WHITE GLOVE SALE** · An auction at which every lot is sold (i.e., a S.T.R. of 100%). Some houses celebrate the occurrence by presenting the auctioneer with a pair of white gloves. *A.k.a.*, **GOLDEN GAVEL SALE**.

To secure a white glove sale, houses sometimes engage in "sleight of hand" — e.g., by strategically WITHDRAWING lots, selling below a RESERVE, or **RE-OPENING** at the end of an auction any lots that failed to sell.[3]

## ATTRIBUTION QUALIFIERS

A lexicon of qualifying terms used to associate work by unknown hands with famous artists, e.g.:

| *Catalogue description* | *meaning* |
|---|---|
| *X* [artist's name] | by *X* |
| **ATTRIBUTED TO *X*** | likely by *X*, in whole or in part |
| **STUDIO *or* WORKSHOP OF *X*** | by an artist likely in *X*'s studio or workshop and working under their supervision or in collaboration |
| **FOLLOWER OF *X*** | likely by an (approximate) contemporary of *X*, not a pupil |
| **CIRCLE OF *X*** | likely by an unknown associate of *X*, possibly a pupil |
| **SCHOOL OF *X*** | likely by an artist close to, and in the style of, *X*; not (necessarily) a pupil |
| **STYLE *or* MANNER OF *X*** | likely by an artist aping *X*, and created at a later date |
| **AFTER *or* FROM *X*** | a copy of a work known to be by *X* |

## COMMISSIONS, FEES, &c.

The actual HAMMER PRICE is only part of the financial story. *Buyers* may additionally face:

› **BUYER'S PREMIUM** · A percentage of the HAMMER PRICE charged by the house; tiered by lot value (e.g., 20% > $6m > 10%).

› **SALES TAX / V.A.T.** · Based on the (Byzantine) rules of each jurisdiction, and often levied on HAMMER PRICE and BUYER'S PREMIUM. *Similarly*, **IMPORT TAXES**.

› **RESALE ROYALTY** · {See below.}

*Sellers* must contend with:

› **SELLER'S *or* VENDOR'S COMMISSION (V.C.)** · A percentage of the HAMMER PRICE that is paid to the house.

› **OVERHEAD PREMIUM** · An additional percentage (e.g., 1–2%) levied by the house for administration, &c.

› **FIXED GUARANTEE COMMITMENT FEE** · Where works are sold with a GUARANTEE houses may charge the sellers an additional percentage to defray their costs.

› **SUCCESS FEE / PERFORMANCE COMMISSION** · An extra percentage fee levied if the HAMMER PRICE is greater than expected, e.g., over the agreed HIGH ESTIMATE.

› **ADDITIONAL EXPENSES** · Charged, e.g., for restoration, advertising, framing, shipping, &c.

**CAPITAL GAINS TAX** · Levied by some tax authorities on any differential between sale price and original purchase price; varies by jurisdiction, lot, &c.

**RESALE ROYALTY / DROIT DE SUITE / ARTIST RESALE RIGHT** · In certain jurisdictions (e.g., Australia and the E.U.), artists (and sometimes, for a fixed time period, their heirs) are entitled to royalties whenever one of their original works (or a limited-edition copy) is resold.

The U.K. resale royalty rates vary from 4% (≤£50,000) to 0.25% (>£500,000), though the maximum payment is capped at £12,500.

Various attempts to establish a similar resale royalty right in the U.S. have failed.

## AUCTION TYPES

**EVENING SALE** · Usually reserved for high-profile, **MARQUEE** events. *Conversely*, **DAY SALE** · For more run-of-the-mill lots.

**SINGLE-OWNER (S.O.) SALE** · When all of the lots come from a single (and notable) collector, collection, or estate. *Conversely*, **VARIOUS OWNER (V.O.) SALE**.

**SINGLE-LOT AUCTION** · Hosted to demonstrate the significance of a specific lot or artist. E.g., in 2023, Christie's sold Japanese pop-art pioneer Yoshitomo Nara's *Can't Wait 'til the Night Comes* at a **STAND-ALONE SALE** for HK$92.8m.

**HYBRID AUCTION** · One that adds online participation to physical and telephone bids.

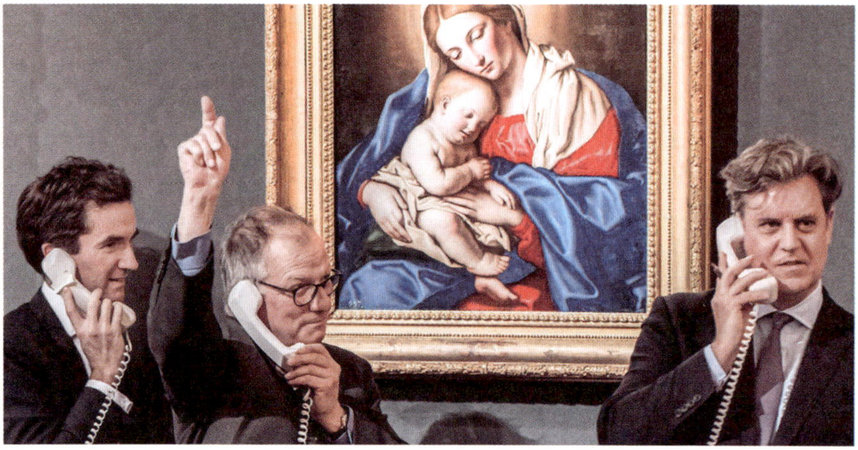

**TELEPHONE BIDDING** *at the Sotheby's Old Masters Evening Sale, 2016*

**ATTIC SALE** · A genteel euphemism for flogging off the odds and ends of a notable estate.

In 2010, Sotheby's Chatsworth House attic sale (instigated by the Duke of Devonshire to "make some space") raised ~£6.5m.

**SELLING IN SITU** · An auction held in a location relevant to its content. Most famously, the 1977 auction at Mentmore Towers, Buckinghamshire, which raised £6m (~£47m in today's money) over nine days of selling.

**RELAY AUCTION** · An auction held simultaneously in multiple locations, to maximize participation. In July 2020, during the pandemic, Christie's held a four-hour sale of 78 lots across the house's H.Q.s in Hong Kong, New York, Paris, and London, which raised $362m (with a S.T.R. of 94%) and attracted an online audience of over 20,000.

**SEALED / SECRET / BEST BID** · Auctions that require (**BEST AND FINAL**) written or online bids. Since the sale price is not disclosed, sealed auctions shield sellers and buyers from scrutiny, and protect lots from being BURNED if the bidding is disappointingly low.

**CHARITY** *or* **BENEFIT AUCTION** · Auction houses (and auctioneers) often offer their services **PRO** *or* **LOW BONO**. In addition to a more relaxed (and cajoling) tone, charity auction SEQUENCING tends to crescendo to a finale of STAR LOTS. And, where services or experiences are auctioned (e.g., a meal cooked by a famous chef; a week in a villa) the auctioneer may **DOUBLE UP** the lot and allow the underbidder(s) to match the winning sum. (This is not always popular with the winner.)

## MISCELLANEOUS

**THREE DS** · The driving forces behind most auctions: Debt, Divorce, Death — to which some add Downsizing, Diversification, and ...

**DEACCESSIONING** · When museums sell pieces from their collections, e.g., to raise money (for infrastructure projects or new staff); pay unexpected (tax) liabilities; free up funds to purchase new works; execute a change in editorial direction (e.g., acquiring works from under-represented groups); &c.

**DROIT DE PRÉEMPTION** [Pre-emption right] · At the **HAMMER FALL** of French auctions, a (previously silent) representative of the government may stand up and declare its interest in acquiring the lot at the winning price — *"Préemption pour les musées de France au profit de* [xxx] *musée!"* — after which, the state has 15 days to confirm the purchase.

This right of first refusal allows works of cultural significance to be saved for France, at the cost of dissuading some private sellers and buyers.

**SLEEPER** · A work that is more than it seems; one than has been **UNDERVALUED** and/or **UNDER-CATALOGUED**. *Hence,* **SLEEPER SPOTTERS**. {☞ M&Ms p.199}

**AVAILABLE MONEY** · A theoretical sum that helps indicate the **MARKET INTEREST** in a given piece; calculated by adding a lot's final bids. E.g., a lot that sold for $900 with two unsuccessful **UNDERBIDDERS** — offering $800 and $850 respectively — showed available money of $2,550.

**PRIVATE SALES** · Those facilitated by a house outside of the auction room.

**N.S.V.** · No Sale Value, i.e., a piece below the financial viability (and dignity) of a house.

**C.O.I.N.** · Collector Only In Name · Those who prize assets over aesthetics.

**COLLUSION** · Though in theory auctions are public demonstrations of **PRICE DISCOVERY**, they can (like all markets) be prey to illegal activity, when, for example:

› Sellers **BUMP-UP** the price by using **SHILLS / BY-BIDDERS / POTTED PLANTS / PUFFERS** to keep the bidding going
› A **RING** of buyers drives down prices by agreeing not to bid against each other — after which they divide the savings accrued, or arrange for a second, private **KNOCK OUT** auction among themselves
› Auctioneers misrepresent lots; secretly place bids; or fix commissions between houses

**AUCTION HISTORY** · Describes pieces that have previously **COME TO THE BLOCK** and therefore have a documented market reputation. *Conversely*, pieces that are **UNSEEN** *or* **FRESH (TO MARKET)**.

Because public auctions are considered **TOURNAMENTS OF (FAIR** *or* **OPEN MARKET) VALUE**, they help establish **REFERENCE VALUES** for pieces and artists.

**EXHIBITION HISTORY** · A chronology of a piece's appearances in (major) exhibitions — which may help raise its value.

**CATALOGUE RAISONNÉ** [reasoned catalogue] · A detailed (and exhaustive) academic compendium of an individual artist's work, used to research the history, provenance, attribution, location, (and potential value) of specific pieces. Houses may decline to sell works of major artists not included in the relevant *catalogue raisonné* or authenticated by …

**ARTIST'S COMMITTEE** · A group of experts (and heirs) that acts as a *de facto* guarantor of a deceased artist's work. E.g., the *Association pour la Défense de l'œuvre de Joan Miró*, whose terms and conditions allow it to attach "for confiscation or destruction" works attributed to Miró "which are considered after examination to be fakes or artistic frauds."

In recent years many of these **AUTHENTICATION BOARDS** have disbanded in the face of legal challenges from collectors outraged that their unearthed masterpiece was rejected and stamped (sometimes literally) as a fake.

**COLLECTOR CLASS** · The cohort with the interest and income to acquire art and, by extension, bid at auction. The class has been expanded by the accessibility of art fairs, auction **LIVE STREAMING**, and **RED-CHIP** art.

**BLUE** *vs* **RED CHIP** · **BLUE CHIP** art is that by renowned artists with established followings and long records of value appreciation (e.g., Picasso, Agnes Martin, Michel Basquiat).

**RED CHIP** art is by **EMERGING** artists who develop explosive followings often via non-traditional channels, like social media (e.g., Flora Yukhnovich and Jadé Fadojutimi).

Some classify A.I., generative, and other digital art as red chip, e.g., Beeple's N.F.T. collage, *Everydays: The First 5000 Days*, which in March 2021 sold at Christie's for $69,346,250.

For some, red chip's popularity is an indication of market **FROTH**; when liquidity dries up, buyers flee to the safety of classic blue chip.

**AUCTION FEVER** · An emotional response to the excitement and pressure of a live sale, based on "competitive arousal" and the "psychological inability to ignore sunk (irrecoverable) costs." [4] Or, as Bertie Wooster put it:

> The bidding had acquired an inexorable momentum, like a toddler's first headlong lurches towards an unattended stove. If you've ever been to an auction you'll know this is a sure sign that some poor devil is about to lose their shirt. [5]

**SPENT OUT** · When a recent run of blockbuster sales depletes the coffers of potential buyers (and third-party guarantors).

**AUCTION EXHAUSTION** · The sale-room cousin of **ART FAIR-TIGUE**. ⊙

# Cue Camera Three!

*In addition to overseeing studio operations — equipment, set, crew, audience, guests, talent, &c. —* **TELEVISION FLOOR MANAGERS** *(A.k.a., floor directors) provide a vital link between the gallery and the studio floor. Although many presenters now wear earpieces — through which they can hear* **SWITCH TALKBACK** *(dedicated messages to individual presenters) or* **OMNIBUS** *(open mic from the gallery and the floor) — hand signals are still used as a backup, especially on live shows.*

*Demonstrated by* Nick Ross.

STAND BY

30 SECONDS

15 SECONDS

10 SECONDS

5 SECONDS

4 SECONDS

3 SECONDS

2 SECONDS

1 SECOND

COME CLOSER

MOVE BACK

STOP / DON'T MOVE

SPEAK MORE SOFTLY

SPEAK MORE LOUDLY

KEEP TALKING

SPEED UP

SLOW DOWN / STRETCH

WRAP UP

ON TIME

INDICATES NEXT CAMERA

CUT

# As Far as the Arm Can Reach

*A glossary of* **GRAFFITI WRITING.**

## GRAFF *vs* STREET ART

Graffiti has two defining attributes: First, it is criminal vandalism. Second, it is (primarily) letter-based. And so **GRAFF** is not **STREET ART**, and its practitioners are not "artists" but **WRITERS.**

Of course, the two forms share equipment and expertise, and some graff writers go on to paint legal murals and sell commercial pieces. Indeed the gentrification of graff by corporate advertising and social media is muddying the waters of what was once a simple distinction.

Genuine graffiti may best be understood as a private conversation on which passersby eavesdrop without understanding. For while street art is painted to charm the public, graff is written first and foremost for fellow writers.

This tension is encapsulated by two Brits: the graff writer King Robbo (real name, John Robertson) and the anonymous street-artist Banksy (whose style owes much to the French stencillist Blek Le Rat).

In 2009, Banksy reportedly painted over one of King Robbo's earliest works — a 1985 piece that had been **RUNNING** for decades on a canalside wall in Camden Town, London. This unsubtle **DISS** provoked a tit-for-tat feud of over-painting that still rumbles on, despite King Robbo's accidental death in 2014.

To this day, members of Team Robbo will deface Banksy's street art whenever it appears — to protect the memory of a British graff pioneer and protest Capitalism's annexation of vandalistic expression. {📷 1}

## GETTING UP

A second tension within the world of graff exists between quality and quantity.

While complex, colourful, and expertly executed (**MASTER**)**PIECES** are rightly respected, so is lasting notoriety — achieved by the unending pursuit of **GETTING UP.**

Like a dog marking its territory, getting up is about dominant omnipresence, as Cat said:

> Everything belongs to me — anything I write on, anything I touch is mine. It's like everything is one big piece of paper for me to write on. And every neighbourhood I go to is like tuning a page on a book to write my name again.[1]

**ALL LINES** · To be **UP** across a transit system.

**ALL CITY** {📷 2} · To be **UP** across an entire cityscape. *Hence*, the insult: **SMALL CITY.**

**BOMBING** · Saturating a location with **TAGS** and **THROWIES.** Bombing is the quickest way to **GET UP** and develop a **REP**(utation).

Serious bombers are **HEAVY HITTERS**, and to **BOMB BIG** is to **NUKE.**

Cope 2 defined the mentality:

> When you wanna go bombing, you go *bombing*. You go out there, and you fucking destroy everything. I'm talking about highways, rooftops, buildings, trains, anything — police cars — anything you wanna slam you slam. No better feeling than bombing, especially if you're dedicated, and you know what it is to destroy ... Let's say you go bombing in one night, you can get maybe 100 throwups, all city ... all city, just destroying shit.[2]

Bombing is both a learning curve and a rite of passage. As Claw said: "If you don't **BOMB** then you can't **PIECE.**"[3]

**RIDING / RUNNING / BURNING** {📷 3} · Said of any work that **STAYS UP** for months (or years) without getting **BUFFED** or **DISSED.**

Graff **RIDES** because of its inaccessibility or quality, or because it is the work of an **ANGEL.**

It is a source of some discontent that, while graff **PIECES** are swiftly **BUFFED**, Banksy's street art **RIDES** with official protection and press approbation. In 2024, a headline in *The Independent* encapsulated the double standard: "Anger after latest Banksy vandalized with white paint overnight."

1. *Team Robbo's defacement of Banksy's "fisher boy" stencil, London, 2010*

## WRITER TYPES

**TOY** {📷 4} · A beginner: one whose technique needs work; *Or*, one who does not respect the unwritten codes of graff. Often wielded as an insult ("*Straight toy, go back to the* BLACKBOOK") especially by toys themselves {📷 5}.

That said: "*No kings without toys.*"

**KING / QUEEN** {📷 6} · A (self-proclaimed) monarch, whose TAG may feature a **CROWN**.

> To be a king you've got to really apply yourself and put the work in and go out there and hit as many walls, alleys, roofs, tunnels, as you possibly can including buses and trains et cetera. — M.B. [4]

**LEGEND** · A KING whose dominion has been recognized beyond his ego and crew.

**ANGELS** · Dead LEGENDS. As a mark of respect, angelic work that posthumously RIDES is (usually) considered untouchable.

Writers pay homage to angels by tagging their names in remembrance, adding a halo, and writing **R.I.P.** (**REST IN PAINT**). {📷 7}

**CREWS** · A group of writers who GET UP together, collaborate on large PIECES, and offer mutual support and validation. Crew names are often represented by two- or three-letter codes, notably: IUP, MSK, TKO, &c.

**SNITCHES** · (TOY) writers who, motivated by envy or enmity, shop their rivals to the cops.

## FORMATS

**TAGGING / HANDSTYLE** {📷 8} · Graff's elemental form, which every TOY must learn.

Mastering the art involves devising an original **TAG** (**NAME, IUP, SIG**) and perfecting the technique to **CATCH IT** (i.e., repeat it) quickly, crisply, confidently, and consistently.

TOYS will practice their tags in page after page of BLACKBOOK **REPS** (repetitions) before venturing onto the streets to **DO LOOPS**.

Over time, writers may evolve or **CHANGE UP** their tag, and some deploy multiple tags.

Although tagging's aggressively solipsistic character makes it the most controversial form of graff, it is foundational to more "popular" work. As TOOMER of the TKO crew explained:

> Some people come up to me when I'm doing a mural, and be like, '*Wow this is beautiful! I like the colours, and I like these animals you put on there, and incorporate it in this whole thing, I just hate that damn tagging shit, though.*' And I tell 'em: It's the same thing! I mean, it starts with a little tag and from the little tag it gets a little throw up, and the little throw up gets a little burn, a little burn turns into a piece, and the piece turns into a mural — and if I didn't do that tag, I wouldn't be able to do your building. [5]

**HIT UP** · Tagging another writer's name as a sign of respect, or remembrance.

**ROLL CALL** {📷 9} · Where multiple (CREW) names are written together as a list.

**ONE LINER / BUS FLOW** · A TAG or THROWIE executed in a single stroke.

**THROW-UP / THROWIE** · A simple and casual rendering (usually of a writer's name) intended to get maximum coverage in minimal time, i.e., when BOMBING to GET UP.

A **HOLLO(W) / HOLLER** {◎ 10} is a throwie with no fill (or shadow); a **FILL IN** {◎ 11} has a fill.

Some writers abbreviate their name (even to one or two letters) for additional speed, to save paint, or when in a HOT SPOT.

Although **THROWIES** can be highly stylized, most use simple, curved **BUBBLE LETTERS** with clean lines, minimal NEGATIVE SPACE, and a **TWO-CAN FILL** colour scheme — classically chrome/silver fills outlined in black (*A.k.a.*, **CHROMIES / DUBS** {◎ 12}).

**FAMILIES** of throw-ups written consecutively are said to be **BACK TO BACK** {◎ 13}.

**SCRUB** *or* **DUSTY** *or* **GHOST FILL** {◎ 14} · A quick and dirty FILL IN sprayed with semi-opaque **TIGER STRIPES** for speed, effect, and /or paint economy.

**STRAIGHT LETTER** {◎ 15} · A more elegant, skilful, and time-consuming style — usually a stylistic step-up from BUBBLE LETTERS.

**STOMPER** · A large-scale STRAIGHT LETTER (e.g., E.2.E. on a wall) usually with little embellishment. A **BLOCKBUSTER / BLOCKIE** is a stomper with squared-off, angular lettering.

**ROLLER** {◎ 16} · A piece written with a roller brush, using **BUCKET PAINT** and (long) extension **POLES**. Used primarily with large-scale STRAIGHT LETTERS, FLOATERS, and HANGDOWNS, or to **TOP** (i.e., write above) existing pieces without SIDEBUSTING.

**(MASTER)PIECE** {◎ 17} · Sophisticated graff with clean fills, crisp outlines, elegant backgrounds, and a host of stylistic details.

**BURN(ER)** · An especially impressive PIECE; one that **BURNS** the competition.

**MURAL** · A large-scale masterpieces: **DOPE** if illegal; DISSED if (corporate) street art.

**WILD STYLE** {◎ 18} · Hyper-ornate lettering that is deliberately tricky to decipher.

**CALLIGRAFFITI** {◎ 19} · Pieces that borrow from the formality of calligraphy.

**ETCHING / SCRIBING** {◎ 20} · Scratching TAGS or HOLLOWS onto metal, glass, plastic, &c. (Dubbed **SCRATCHITTI** by the media.)

**ACID TAGGING** {◎ 21, 42} · Using caustic chemicals (e.g., hydrofluoric acid) to create milky-white tags on glass, plastic, &c.

**DUST TAGGING** · Fingering away grime. *Similarly*, **FINGER TAGGING** the cooling fins of air-conditioning units {◎ 22}.

**STENCILLING** {◎ 23} · Spraying through cut-outs; usually dissed as STREET ART.

**SLAPS** {◎ 24} · Stickers that are TAGGED, or marked with a THROWIE, and stuck onto public surfaces. *Hence*, **STICKER SLAPPING**, **SLAP BOMBING**, **SLAP TAGGING**, &c.

Slapping tags on private property is usually a less serious crime than tagging; consequently slapping is generally less respected. That said, the fêted street-art activist Shepard Fairey started with "Andre the Giant Has a Posse" slaps that evolved into "Obey Giant."

Though blank slaps are widely sold, writers repurpose courier waybills, **HELLO MY NAME IS** stickers, and, notoriously, the U.S. Postal Service's **LABEL 228** {◎ 25}.

**EGGSHELLS** · Tamper-evident security stickers that peel away in irksome fragments.

**STICKER TRADING** · Writers swap slaps (by post) both to add to their collections and to get their tags stuck on walls around the world. {☞ BOOMERANG p.77}

## SPOTS

"All surfaces are good if you can get to them.
I'm an equal opportunity offender."
— Sento TFP [6]

**CHILL** {◎ 26} · A **LOW KEY** spot where detection is unlikely, or inconsequential, e.g.: **BANDOS** (abandoned buildings); sites set for demolition; tunnels; drains; dead malls; &c.

When not kept secret, chill spots are shared by word of mouth and Instagram, or scouted using Google Maps.

2. **SLAP** *claiming to be* **ALL CITY**

3. **THROWIE** *that has been* **RIDING**

4. *The work of a* **TOY**

5. *Graff* **DISSED** *as the work of a* **TOY**

6. *A self-proclaimed* **KING**

7. **TRIBUTE** *to an* **ANGEL**

8. **TAG**

9. **ROLL CALL**

10. (**DAYTIME**) **HOLLER THROWIE**

11. **FILL IN THROWIE**

12. **CHROMIE**

13. **BACK TO BACK THROWIES**

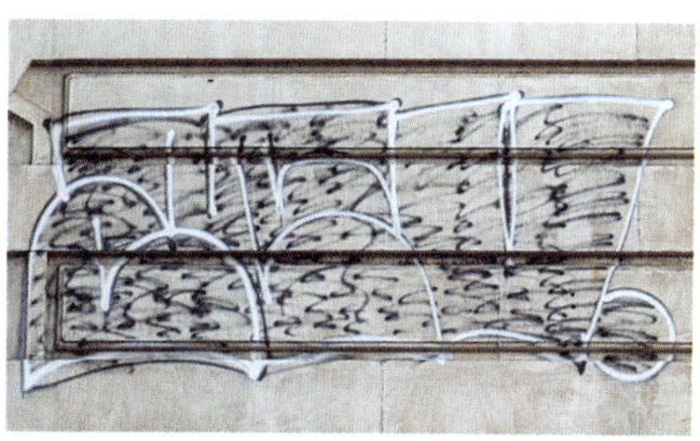

14. **GHOST FILL**

15. **STRAIGHT LETTER**

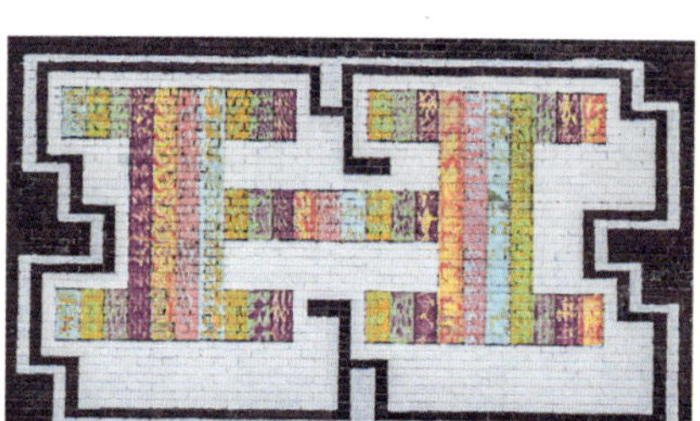

16. **ROLLER**

17. **PIECE**

18. **WILD STYLE**

19. **CALLIGRAFFITI**

20. **ETCHING / SCRIBING**

21. **ACID TAG**

**CUTTY** · An inconspicuous or out-of-the-way spot, i.e., one *"in the cutts."*

(**BIG**) **STOMPER** · An in-your-face spot.

**LEGAL** · A spot where graff is sanctioned (to promote tourism); tolerated by landlords (to add "edge" to a commercial investment); or otherwise encouraged (e.g., Wynwood Walls in Miami, Florida).

Various websites list legal spots around the world, and writers share locations on social.

It's sometimes claimed that **LEGAL WALLS** reduce illegal graff, though likely not tagging.

**RED HOT** · A spot with high traffic or surveillance, and a concomitant risk of detection.

**HANGOVER** / **HANGDOWN** {◎27} · When writers lean over a ledge at the top of a building and paint upside down with cans or rollers. (*"Hitting the* **GARGOYLE SPOT**.")

**FLOATER** {◎28} · Work that hangs in the middle of a (very tall) space.

*Also*, work written above an existing piece which, if too close, risks being perceived as SIDEBUSTING.

**HEAVEN** {◎29} · A spot so high or hazardous that access risks serious injury or death. THROWIES are more common than PIECES in such **SUICIDE SPOTS**, and quality is sometimes sacrificed to audacity.

When asked online how heavens are hit, the usual response is **TRAMPOLINE**, **DRONE**, or **JET PACK**. In fact, such spots are accessed via temporary scaffolding, retractable ladders, rappelling with ropes, and heart-stopping bravado.

**ROOFTOPS** · Writing directly onto a roof to be seen from above; *Or*, using rooftop access to hit high walls, water towers, &c.

**KILLING** / **MOBBING** · When multiple writers tag-swarm a location, bus, subway car, &c.

**DON'T BURN THE SPOT!** · Encouragement not to draw attention to CUTTY SPOTS (especially YARDS or LAY UPS), e.g., by CATCHING TAGS around an entrance; discarding used cans and trash; leaving cut fences gaping open; or otherwise behaving conspicuously or antisocially.

## TRANSPORT

"Being a train bomber ...
that's what graff's all about" — JISOE [7]

It's not hard to see the lure of public transport for graff writers: an unending supply of vast, "victimless" canvases that carry your name across a city or, indeed, a country — to say nothing of the adrenaline of writing in train **YARDS** and bus **DEPOTS**, and the links to the glory days of New York **TRANSIT GRAFF**.

**STEEL** / **PAINTED FREIGHT** / **FR8** · Writing on train or subway cars — for which there is a generally accepted hierarchy of **COVERAGE**:

**WINDOW DOWN** →
**TOP TO BOTTOM** (**T.2.B.**) →
**END TO END** (**E.2.E.**) →
**WHOLE CAR** → **WHOLE TRAIN**

**STAMPING** · If graff obscures a train car's identification or safety markings, it risks being **STAMPED OVER** with an ugly block of new data — and increases the chances of the entire car being BUFFED.

Writers who want their work to RIDE (especially E.2.E. PIECES) may **TAPE OFF** this area before getting to work.

**ROLLING ALLEY** · A heavily graffed train.

**LAY UP** · Any spot where trains or buses are parked long enough for writers to work.

**TRACKSIDE** · Writing on surfaces visible to train passengers, e.g., walls and sound barriers.

**INSIDES** · Writing inside trains and buses.

**BACKJUMP** · A speedily executed TAG or THROWIE — usually on a bus or train that is briefly stationary (at a stop). Writing on moving vehicles is called **MOTION TAGGING**.

## STYLE / TECHNIQUE

There is an endless and evolving lexicon of graff style, of which this is merely a sample:

**CAN CONTROL** · The essential skill of hand-can coordination. Good can control is key to writing **CLEAN**, and at speed.

**DRIPS** {📷30} · When paint trickles down: cool if intentional and elegant; **TOY** if not.

**DOODADS** {📷31} · Ornamental additions to a piece, e.g., arrows, quote marks, underlines, asterisks, drips, clouds, and halos. The term was seemingly neologized on the fly by Seen in *Style Wars* (1983). *A.k.a.*, **BITS**.

**NEGATIVE SPACE** {📷32} · The gaps between letters: too much space and the piece falls apart; too little and it becomes hard to read.

**FLARES** {📷33} · Wrist-flicking a can fitted with a **FLARE** or **FAT CAP** to create angled gradations of spray intensity.

**CHARACTERS** {📷34} · Although graff is definitionally text-based, writers sometimes turn their tags into characters, and often incorporate cartoon characters, graff legends, or notable people into their pieces. (After his murder in 2020, George Floyd was commemorated in pieces across the world.)

**SKETCH (UP)** · Making preliminary guides for a complex piece; the opposite is **FREESTYLE**.

**BUBBLE BACKGROUND** · A soft, cloud-like backdrop against which a piece stands out. *Similarly*, **FORCEFIELD** · A final **KEYLINE** around a piece, added to help it **POP**.

**CUTBACK** · Spraying over errors (drips, overlaps, over-spray) to create clean, crisp lines.

**STINGER / SOAKER** {📷35} · Certain types of fire extinguisher can be emptied, filled with paint, and re-pressurized for use as high-impact, long-reach, low-accuracy sprays.

Soakers are mainly used for quick and dirty **TAGS** and **THROWIES** and, more recently, as part of high-profile activism like Just Stop Oil.

> It's like messy, it drips out the bottom: this is for graffiti, it isn't for anybody else ... it's a performance work in itself, good old fucking vandalism — ANON [8]

**ANTI STYLE / TRASH GRAFF** {📷36} · Deliberately naive, convention-defying, and opinion-dividing pieces. *A.k.a.*, (and sometimes confused with) **TOY STYLE**.

**CURING** · Waiting for paint to dry.

## EQUIPMENT

**RACKING** · Shoplifting.

Writers habitually **RACK** because paints and markers are hella expensive; to circumvent legal age-restrictions; and since graffiti is already a crime, why not add theft to vandalism?

As Relm admitted in the 1989 documentary, *Bombing L.A.*:

> Now you can buy a whole mess of paint, and you probably won't feel as good as if you walk out with your money *and* the paint. What I usually like to do is buy a few cans and like rack more than I buy, so I'll probably, like, rack three buy one. [9]

**ROLLING** · Stealing paint from other writers.

**BLACK BOOK / GRAFF PAD** · A sketchbook that (TOY) writers use to practice their tags and plan more significant pieces. To work on your graff is **TO BOOK**.

**MARKERS** · The primary tool for tagging, markers come in a vast array of shapes, sizes, colours, and types of ink and paint.

› **FELT TIPPED** · Used to create sharp, crisp tags; chisel tipped (for a calligraphic edge) or bullet tipped (for a rounded finish). Either **GRAVITY FED** or **PUMP ACTION** — which requires **JUICING**, i.e., drawing ink to the nib by pressing it down on a hard surface.

› **MOPS** · Wide, sponge-tipped, and squeezable markers used to create **DRIPPY**, round-edged tags on smooth (metal, glass, plastic) surfaces — brought commercially or D.I.Y.-constructed from shoe-polish bottles, bingo markers, deodorant rollers, &c.

› **DAUBER** · A woollen ball on a stick, dipped in runny ink and used to create drippy tags.

› **STEEL TIPS** · Metal-point markers, ideal for rough surfaces, like concrete and brick.

› **STREAKERS / PAINT STICKS** {📷37} · Solidified paint "crayons" that leave lasting lines on a wide range of surfaces.

› **WHITE OUT** *or* **CORRECTION PENS** {📷38} · Easily pocket-able (and deniable) tools for small tags on smooth surfaces.

22. **A/C UNIT FINGER TAGGING**

23. **STENCIL**

24. **SLAPS**

25. **LABEL 228**

26. **CHILL SPOT / BANDO**

27. **HANGDOWN**

28. **FLOATER**

29. **HEAVEN SPOT**

30. **DRIPS**

31. **DOODADS / BITS**

32. *Two versions of* **NEGATIVE SPACE**

33. **FLARE TAG**

34. **CHARACTER**

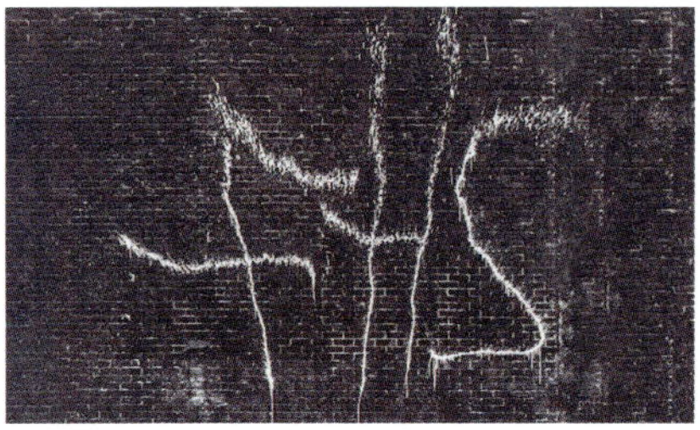

35. **STINGER / SOAKER**

36. **ANTI STYLE**

37. *Multicoloured* **PAINT STICK**

38. **WHITE OUT**

39. **BUFFING A HIT MONUMENT**

40. **DISSING / LINING**

41. **GHOST** *visible after* **BUFFING**

**SPRAY PAINT** · The primary tool for PIECES and THROWIES. Historically, writers would repurpose sprays from industrial brands like Krylon and Rust-Oleum (*A.k.a.*, **RUSTO**); now they are spoiled for choice by "graff-positive" brands like MTN, Molotow, and Loop ("THE Spray Paint of Graffiti Culture!!").

Some writers have affection for specific cans (e.g., because of their pressurization or flow) and many develop Proustian associations with unique colours, famously Krylon's discontinued icy grape, jungle green, and pennant blue.

**CAPS** · Writers use interchangeable spray-can caps to get the coverage or style of line they need, e.g., narrow **NEEDLES**, wide **FAT CAPS**, or calligraphic **TRANSVERSALS**.

**PRESSURE** · As spray cans lose pressure when cold, writers working in chilly conditions will sometimes pack **HOT WATER BOTTLES**.

**SAFETY GEAR** · Many writers wear **GLOVES** to protect their hands from paint (and cold) and to conceal their fingerprints.

As the hazards of paint inhalation become better-known (and after the cultural shift of Covid) more writers are wearing **MASKS** and **RESPIRATORS**, especially for large PIECES.

**HIGH VIZ** · Some writers, especially those working in YARDS, adopt the reflective safety gear of authorized workers to blend in.

## ETIQUETTE & CULTURE

While some claim that graff has no rules, a loose **CODE** of conduct does exist, specifically about SPOTS that should never be HIT, e.g.:

Graveyards · Memorials · Places of worship
Ancient or historic monuments {📷39}
Nature (e.g., trees) · Animals (e.g., cows)
Private houses and vehicles
Small businesses (*Also*: don't RACK from)
Schools (especially your own) · Hospitals

Public transit, infrastructure, and big business are considered "*victimless*" fair game; indeed writers regularly argue that they are "*providing work*" for the cleaning crews.

**BITING** · Copying another writer's style, name, colours, &c. — a serious transgression.

**BEEF** · Antagonism between writers (or entire crews) provoked by GOING OVER, BITING, turf-encroachment, personality clashes, &c.

Bad behaviour risks **CATCHING BEEF**; beefs that are settled are **SQUASHED**; online enmity is **E-BEEF**.

**GOING OVER** · To paint over existing work. It's generally considered a DISS to **COVER** a **CLEAN PIECE**, but fair game if the piece is in a poor condition or has already been DISSED, TAGGED, or otherwise defaced.

(Some writers take photos of a site before GOING OVER, to pre-empt potential BEEF.)

There is even a (disputed) hierarchy of **COVER UP** acceptability — which mirrors the skill each piece involves:

HOLLOWS *over* TAGS
THROWIES *over* HOLLOWS
STRAIGHT LETTERS *over* THROWIES
PIECES *over* STRAIGHT LETTERS
(legit) MURALS *over* PIECES
and, to many,
ANYTHING *over* STREET ART
(especially if corporate)

The ultimate DISS is to go over an ANGEL, and the riskiest is to go over **GANG TAGS**. Yet it's not always easy (for a TOY) to know which (faded) pieces are LEGACY ... or lethal.

Some writers gleefully **STAMP OVER** everything — a practice known as **CAPPING**. This appears to be an eponym derived from the writer Cap who, in late 1970s New York, threw his name up across even the freshest burners — as he explained in the 1983 documentary *Style Wars*:

> Anybody tries to screw around with me and my friends, I go over everything they got forever. Everybody, from Brooklyn to Manhattan. *Everybody*. And that's the way it is. Especially with me. The object is *more*. Not the biggest and the beautifullest, but *more*. It's like a little piece on every car, is what counts. Not one whole car on every 30 cars that goes by. Once you start going over someone, you can't stop.[10]

**DISSING** {📷40} · Crossing out (**LINING**), or otherwise defacing, another writer's work in retaliation for a slight, or as part of a BEEF.

Those who **DISS** are generally expected to sign their name: "*Anonymous diss is toy.*"

**SIDEBUSTING / SPOT JOCKING** · Painting obnoxiously close to another writer's piece, thereby diminishing its impact, stealing its credibility, or falsely implying a collaboration. (*"The graff equivalent of photobombing."*)

Sidebusting graff that has been RIDING increases the risk of the SPOT being BUFFED. *Also*, **CROWDING** · Not as close as SIDEBUSTING, but still considered TOY, or even a DISS. *Also*, **CLIPPING** · Overlapping the edge of an existing piece, by accident (e.g., underestimating the space required) or as part of a BEEF.

**DAYTIME** {📷 10} · Added to indicate graff was executed during the day (in a HOT SPOT).

**ONE / 1 / SOLO** · Indicates a writer worked alone (i.e., not in a CREW). Also used to preempt BEEF about collaboration when painting near another piece. Sometimes tagged to assert the №1 spot, or rights to a name.

**BENCHING** · Old-school term for sitting on **THE BENCH** at transit hubs and watching the PIECES roll by. Named after the original **WRITER'S BENCH** at 149th St.–Grand Concourse station in New York City.

## REMOVAL

**BUFFING** {📷 42} · When local government, transit crews, private contractors, or business owners (attempt to) remove or obscure graff with **CHEMICAL BUFFS**, high-pressure spray, or simple **OVER-PAINTING**.

Writers tend to be phlegmatic about buffing (*"Tag more and the buff don't matter"*), and some note that *"painting over is just cleaning the canvas."* (That said, areas **ROLLED OVER** with ugly boxes of non-matching paint may get *"extra love"* from the graff community.)

Indeed, writers may buff a wall themselves before beginning a PIECE. And the threat of buffing encourages writers to hit HEAVEN SPOTS where contractors fear to tread.

The goal of relentless buffing is to engender a sense of futility, ensuring writers know that their work will RIDE for just days (or hours) before being erased. It was by this technique (alongside increased security and a change in car design) that in May 1989, New York's subway system declared its trains "graffiti free."

Of course, the impact of social media means that whereas graff once risked a mayfly existence, it now RIDES online forever.

**VIGILANTES** · Private citizens who aim to rid their streets of graffiti, sometimes to the point of causing near-equal visual disfigurement.

(The 2011 documentary *Vigilante Vigilante* follows the anti-graff crusades of the Silver Buff, the Silver Circle, the Graffiti Guerrilla, and the Gray Ghost.)

**GHOST / SCAR / STAINER** {📷 41} · The echo of a piece still visible after BUFFING.

**PATROLLING (YOUR WALLS)** · To check if your pieces have been DISSED, COVERED, or BUFFED before over-painting any damage or RECLAIMING the spot with fresh work. ⊙

42. *A shopkeeper failing to* BUFF *his window from an* ACID TAG

# Shelf-Cocked, Else Fine

*The bibliopolic babble of* **ANTIQUARIAN BOOK DEALERS.**

## EDITIONS

The traditional goal of most bibliophiles is to locate a rare, perfect, first edition — i.e., a copy of a book as it would have existed on its very first day of release. Yet defining what a FIRST EDITION *is*, is not necessarily simple.

**EDITION** · Every copy of a book printed from the same set of plates (or typesetting) forms part of an edition. In theory, a book printed from the original plates even decades after initial publication could still be described as a **FIRST EDITION.**

Editions subsequent to the first (i.e., second, third, &c.) usually contain substantive changes beyond typos: e.g., a major revision, new front or back matter, reordered chapters, &c.

**PRINTING / IMPRESSION** · A print run, of which each EDITION may have many (of varying sizes), depending on sales, e.g., "*First edition, fourth impression.*" A book's printing is traditionally shown on its NUMBER LINE.

**ISSUE** · Groups of books from the same PRINTING run that vary in some way (e.g., with different publishers' adverts TIPPED IN) and enter the market at different times.

| | | |
|---|---|---|
| 1st EDITION | | |
| 1st PRINTING | | 2nd PRINTING |
| 1st ISSUE | 2nd ISSUE | |

**STATE** · If changes are made *during* a PRINTING (e.g., to correct a typo or change binding), each new variant represents a new state. (The term is often used synonymously with ISSUE.)

**TRUE FIRST** · Sometimes used to describe a copy from the FIRST PRINTING of the FIRST EDITION (and also the first ISSUE or STATE).

**POINTS (OF ISSUE)** · (Often tiny) physical or textual variations that help identify an exact EDITION, PRINTING, ISSUE, or STATE. E.g., the back panel of the FIRST EDITION of *The Great Gatsby* has Jay Gatsby's name spelled with a lowercase *j*, and corrected by hand.

**NUMBER LINE** *or* **ROW / PRINTER'S KEY** · Digits that indicate a book's PRINTING, traditionally found on the copyright page. The lowest visible number indicates the printing (and sometimes also the date). E.g., all the number lines below are for a SECOND PRINTING; the last also shows the year (1954):

10 9 8 7 6 5 4 3 2 · 3 5 7 9 10 8 6 4 2
2 3 4 5 6 7 8 9 10 57 56 55 54

This curious format dates to the days when plucking a letterpress block, or erasing a digit from a plate, was significantly easier and cheaper than adding new text. (The layout of the second example is designed so that the number block remains roughly centred on the line as each digit is removed.)

Some books have **LETTER ROWS**, e.g., where a second printing would be labelled B.

**FIRST THUS** · The FIRST EDITION of any new version, e.g., the first paperback edition released subsequent to a hardback.

**LIMITED EDITION** · One with a **DECLARED** print run, often in the hundreds; copies will usually be signed and (hand) numbered.

*Similarly*, **LETTERED EDITION** · Those limited to — and marked with — letters of the alphabet, e.g., A–Z (26 copies) or Aa–Zz (52).

**LIMITATION PAGE** · A page on which the number of a LIMITED EDITION is marked mechanically or by hand (and confirmed by a signature, often the author's). {📷 1}

**OUT OF SERIES** · Unnumbered and unsigned "extra" copies of a LIMITED EDITION, printed for review, or as an insurance against damage.

**IDEAL COPY** · The (personal) paradigm of the "perfect" edition and condition of a book, against which other copies are judged.

*Bronze interpretation of* The Bookworm *by Carl Spitzweg, at The Grolier Club, Manhattan*

## PROVENANCE

As the antiquarian market matures, and the modern market becomes ever-more saturated, so many collectors and academic institutions are less fixated on **TRUE FIRSTS** than with copies that have a **STORY** to tell.

**DEDICATEE'S COPY** · A copy owned by the person to whom it was dedicated (and **INSCRIBED** to them by the author). E.g., A copy of *Madame Bovary* that Gustave Flaubert signed to the dedicatee, Maitre Sénard.

**PRESENTATION COPY** · One given by the author / editor / &c. *Also*, **JOINT PRESENTATION COPY**, e.g., from author and illustrator.

**ASSOCIATION COPY** · One owned by: the author (**PERSONAL COPY**); someone related or connected to the author; someone involved with the book's production (e.g., illustrator, editor, printer); or someone associated with the book's content (e.g., Alice Liddell's copy of *Alice's Adventures in Wonderland*).

It is debated whether copies merely *owned* by famous people (with no connection to the author or content) should be so described, or simply labelled: **FROM THE LIBRARY OF**.

**EX-LIBRIS** · A copy from a private library — the bookplate of which may also add interest.

*Not to be confused with*, **EX-LIBRARY** · An (uncollectible) copy **WITHDRAWN** from a public library, often with ink stamps, record checkout pockets, barcodes, &c.

(**AUTHOR'S**) **FAVOURITE EDITION** · Often little more than marketing blurb for a new offering, e.g., an edition with notable cover art, binding, illustrations, foreword, &c.

**PREPUBLICATION COPY** · A **GALLEY**, **PROOF**, or **A.R.C.** (Advanced Reading Copy) used for production, promotion, or review.

## INSCRIPTIONS &C.

**SIGNED** · A copy signed by the author, with or without other **INSCRIPTIONS**. (Cue the joke: "*The unsigned copies are more valuable!*")

**FLAT SIGNED** · A copy simply signed by the author, without an inscription (or date).

**INSCRIBED** · A copy where the author has added text in addition to a signature — which can turn a book into an **ASSOCIATION COPY**.

**SECRETARIAL INSCRIPTION** · A signature or inscription added on behalf of an author, and with their consent. (E.g., "*With the compliments of the author.*") Common in **PRESENTATION COPIES** of books by politicians.

**MARGINALIA** · Notes, doodles, corrections, &c. written in the margins (or across the body) of a text, which may add to (or detract from) a book's value, depending on the hand. E.g., a copy of Nat Hentoff's 1992 book, *Free Speech For Me — But Not For Thee*, extensively annotated by *Playboy* founder Hugh Heffner.

## RARITY

Though wags contrast books that are **SCARCE** (i.e., hard to find) and **RARE** (i.e., worth looking for), the words are often used synonymously, and in terms like **VERY SCARCE / SCARCE TO SEE / RARELY ENCOUNTERED** / &c.

**SCARCE THUS** · *See*, FIRST THUS. *Similarly*, **RARE IN THIS CONDITION.**

**SCARCE IN COMMERCE** · Books that seldom appear on the **OPEN MARKET**, i.e., at auction or in (online) shops. Of course, such books may be **WIDELY HELD IN LIBRARIES** *or* **INSTITUTIONAL COLLECTIONS.**

**NO OTHER COPIES LOCATED** · Usually given with a qualifying description, e.g., **IN COMMERCE** *or* **ACADEMIA** *or* **ONLINE.**

## CONDITION

Condition description is subjective, unstandardized, and frequently optimistic — even though "all defects should be noted."

Below is one interpretation of the most commonly used condition terms:

**AS NEW / VERY FINE / MINT**
*As it would have left the printers*

**FINE (F/FN)**
*Unused and undamaged, but showing the expected effects of time's passage*

**NEAR FINE**
*Possibly opened and read, but without any damage or defects*

**VERY GOOD (VG)**
*Showing signs of wear, but not tear*

**GOOD (G)**
*A well-used book, with all pages intact, but generally* **NOT COLLECTIBLE**

**FAIR**
*Where the main text is intact, but worn and possibly missing endpapers, title page, &c.*

**POOR**
*With significant wear and damage*

**READING COPY / ACCEPTABLE**
*The text is complete and legible*

**BINDING COPY**
*Where the* BOOK BLOCK *is in good condition, but the binding is missing or needs replacement*

**WORKING COPY**
*One in need of significant repair*

If two descriptors are used, the first relates to the book, and the second to the dust-jacket: e.g., **F/VG** or, if the jacket is missing, **F/–**.

Some dealers modify their descriptors as schoolteachers modify essay grades, e.g., **NEAR FINE, FINE +, V.G. PLUS.** Others deploy informal terms ranging from **EXCEEDINGLY FRESH** to **UNHAPPY STATE.**

**TIGHT** · A book that does not easily open, or stay open. *Conversely*, **LOOSE.**

**UNOPENED** {📷2} · Where the folded sheets have not been cut at the top and fore-edge, and must be paper-knifed before reading.

**UNCUT** {📷3} · Where the edges of a book have not been **TRIMMED** level (and smooth).

**A.E.G** ........ All Edges Gilt
**T.E.G.** ........ Top Edges Gilt

## DAMAGE

Many damage descriptors need no elucidation (e.g., **SCRATCHED, RUBBED, HANDLED, CHIPPED, SHELFWORN, CREASED, DOG-EARED,** &c.); others are more rococo ...

**FOXING** {📷4} · Yellow, rust-coloured, or brown paper spots, likely caused by oxidation or fungal growth and exacerbated by heat and humidity. The term may derive from the paw pattern of foxes or the colour of their pelt; the Japanese use the word **HOSHI** [stars].

**SUNNING** · Fading, darkening, or other **DISCOLOURATION** caused by exposure to (U.V.) light — often on a spine of a book exposed to sunshine. *A.k.a.*, **BROWNING / TONING.**

**DETATCHED** · When a BOOK BLOCK is no longer joined to its hardbacked binding.

(**SHELF**) **COCKED** · A book that is warped out of its true alignment in various ways (due to poor stacking on a shelf).

**CLOSED TEAR** · A clean tear, the edges of which neatly align. *Conversely*, **OPEN TEAR** {📷5} where paper is missing.

**WORMING** {📷6} · Damage caused by (the larvae) of various book-feeding beetles, &c.

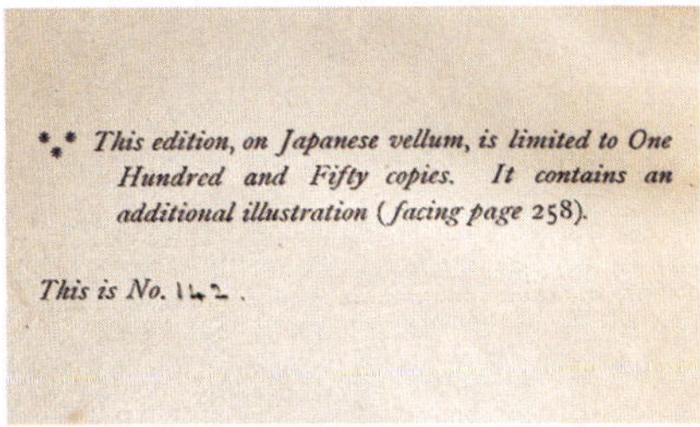


1. **LIMITATION PAGE**

2. **UNOPENED**

3. **UNCUT**

4. **FOXING**

5. **OPEN TEAR**

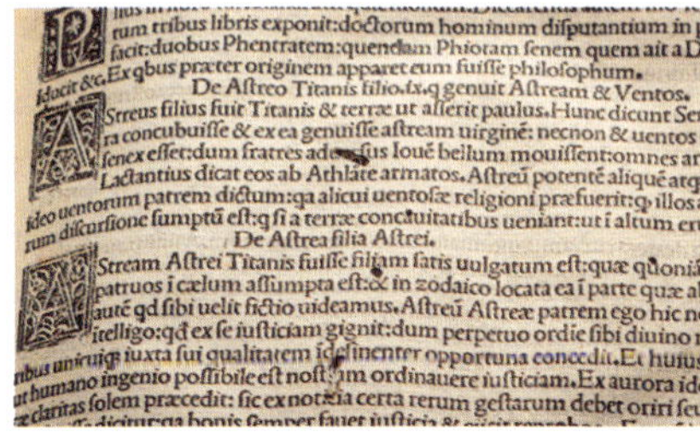

6. **WORMING**

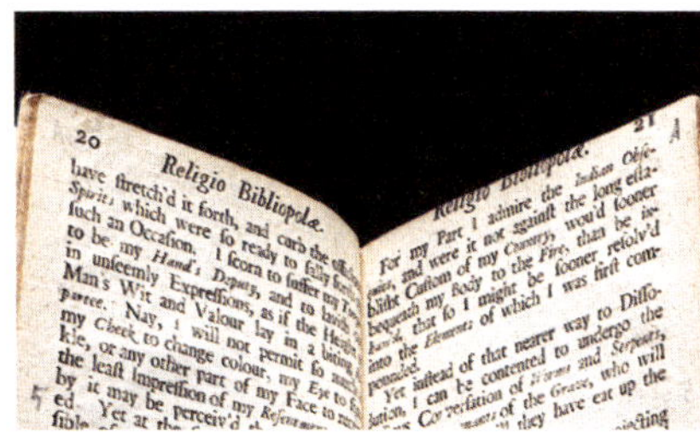


7. **SHAVED**

8. **RED ROT**

9. **STAIN**

10. **TIDE MARKS**

**SHAVED** {📷 7} · When slivers of text have been cut away by inexpert trimming. ("*Touched by the binder's knife.*") *Worse still,* **CROPPED** · When entire words have been hacked off.

**RED ROT** {📷 8} · Where old leather bindings crumble into a reddish-brown powder.

**SPRUNG** · Where the pages fan-out or bow — usually due to water damage or humidity.

**BUMPING** · An indentation caused by impact.

(**SLIGHT**) **MUSTY** (**SMELL**) · May indicate the presence of mould or mildew. *Also,* **FUSTY**.

**STAINED** {📷 9} · Often described in (comic) detail, e.g., "*Tea-ring stains and coffee splashes.*" Water stains sometimes leave (a shoreline of) **TIDE MARKS** across the paper. {📷 10}

**AS USUAL** · Explains that a curiosity (that might be perceived as a defect) is actually commonplace, e.g., "*Missing jacket, as usual.*"

**ELSE FINE** · A supposedly reassuring suffix appended to a (long) list of faults: "*Heavily soiled, damaged cover, spine cocked, else fine.*"

**W.A.F.** · With All Faults · When an imperfect book is **SOLD AS SEEN** *or* **AS IS** (at auction).

## MISCELLANEOUS

**GATHERING / SIGNATURE / QUIRE** · A group of leaves formed by folding the printed sheet to size for sewing or gluing into the binding.

**BOOK BLOCK** · A set of sewn or glued signatures (not yet attached to the binding).

**FOLLOWING THE FLAG** · E.g., collecting only Australian editions of Australian authors.

**HYPERMODERN** · Collectable editions of newly published "future classics" (e.g., by J. K. Rowling), especially by authors who eschew signings (e.g., Cormac McCarthy). Usually purchased in the speculative hope of profit.

**YAPP EDGES** · When a book's soft covers extend protectively beyond the text block, even to the point of wrapping the book entirely.

**ERRORS** · In contrast to other forms of collecting (e.g., philately), bibliophiles are seldom especially interested in printing or typographical mistakes. One key exception being the field of **BIBLE ERRATA**, which delights in texts like the 1612 *Printers Bible*, where Psalm 119:161 reads, "Printers [instead of Princes] have persecuted me without a cause."

**ERRATA** · A list of discovered textual errors and/or misprints that is **TIPPED IN** after binding, or added to later **ISSUES/EDITIONS**.

**COLLATION** · Manually checking that a book's pages, illustrations, &c. are true to the published edition. Those that are may be labelled **COLLATED, COMPLETE** *or* **COLLATED & PERFECT**.

**HONEST SET** · An original set of books (e.g., *The Oxford Sherlock Holmes*) that has remained together since publication.

**MADE-UP** *or* **SOPHISTICATED COPY** · One that has been assembled using parts of other (defective) copies. The Folger First Folio 36 contains leaves from five other Shakespeare first folios. *Also,* **MADE UP SET**. *Conversely,* **UNSOPHISTICATED** · Not **FAKED UP**.

**MARRIED** · When the dust-jacket from one copy is placed on another; usually uncontroversial if both come from the same issue.

**BOOK BREAKER** · One who disassembles books to sell their valuable elements, e.g., maps and illustrations. *A.k.a.,* **LEAF REMOVAL**.

**TIPPED IN** · A separately printed illustration or page that is glued or stapled into a book.

**INCUNABULUM** · An early book; usually one printed before (the arbitrary year of) 1501.

**F.O.N.** ..................... Former Owner's Name
**F.O.I.** ..................... Former Owner's Initials
**P.O.I.** .............. Previous Owner's Inscription

**FIRST APPEARANCE IN PRINT** · The initial printed version of, e.g., a short story, essay, or speech. E.g., T. S. Eliot's *The Waste Land* first appeared in the October 1922 edition of *The Criterion* magazine, two months before it was published in book form by Boni & Liveright in a **LIMITED EDITION** of 1,000. ⊙

# "Where To, Guv?"

*The transporting world of the* **LONDON BLACK TAXI.**

## THE KNOWLEDGE

*"The longest job interview in the world."*

There are two types of licensed London cabbie: those with a **YELLOW BADGE**, who can **PLY FOR HIRE** in one of Greater London's nine suburban sectors; and those with a **GREEN BADGE**, who can ply anywhere. The following applies predominantly to the latter.

**STAGE 1** · After passing medical and vision tests, and attending an introduction talk, candidates sit a **SELF-ASSESSMENT**, which quizzes them on the first 80 **RUNS** in the **BLUE BOOKS** — four official publications that list the 320 routes that every **KNOWLEDGE BOY** and **GIRL** must be able to **CALL** out loud, fluently, from memory, and *in both directions.*

Perhaps the most famous RUN (traditionally the first and last asked of every student) is **MANOR HOUSE STATION** (N4) **TO GIBSON SQUARE** (N1), which might be CALLED thus:

*Leave on left* Green Lanes → *right* Highbury New Park → *comply* Roundabout → *leave by* Highbury New Park → *right* Highbury New Park → *left* Highbury Grove → *right* Saint Paul's Road → *left & right* Highbury Corner → *left* Upper Street → *right* Barnsbury Street → *left* Milner Square → *forward* Milner Place → *forward* Gibson Square

Although (online) map study is useful, candidates master their runs by **BIKE WORK** *or* **PUPIL RUNS**: driving the streets on scooters fitted with Perspex **KNOWLEDGE BOARDS** on which they affix paper maps, or iPads.

Along each RUN, candidates must learn **POINTS (OF INTEREST)** — a daunting list that includes places of worship, sporting stadiums, museums, courts, housing estates, hotels, clubs, restaurants, galleries, prisons, parks, town halls, hospitals, theatres, schools, government offices, cinemas, police stations, &c.

Additionally, at either end of each RUN, some candidates attempt to augment their knowledge by **SATELLITING** — studying quarter- or half-mile radius **DUMBBELLS**.

**STAGE 2** · Within two years of an initial application, candidates must sit a multiple-choice **WRITTEN EXAMINATION** that poses five questions on BLUE BOOK RUNS and 25 on POINTS along the way. The pass mark is 60%, after which the hard work really begins.

**STAGES 3–5** · These involve nerve-shredding one-on-one oral **APPEARANCES**, each lasting around 20 minutes, during which examiners ask four questions on the shortest route between *any* two POINTS in London — e.g., "*B.B.C. rehearsal studios to The Ritz.*"

To become fluent in this **POINT TO POINT** process, candidates will practice with a **CALL-OVER PARTNER**, and some still use the traditional technique of **COTTONING THE RUN** ◎ i.e., using a length of string to illustrate the tightest, crow-fly route. Many also attend **KNOWLEDGE SCHOOLS**, which offer expertise, structure, and camaraderie.

The goal is to become an accurate and speedy **WHOOSHER**, the fastest of whom can call 80 RUNS in 30 minutes.

(Some KNOWLEDGE BOYS and GIRLS describe **SEEING IT** — an epiphany when the entire map of London becomes theirs; for many, though, this is a poetic aspiration.)

The frequency of appearances starts at ~**56** days (STAGE 3), and the **INTERVALS** tighten as candidates are **DROPPED** (i.e., promoted) first to ~**28** days (STAGE 4), and then to ~**21** (STAGE 5). As candidates progress through stages 4 and 5, examiners ask trickier RUNS, e.g., those avoiding traffic lights or one-way streets; roadworks lasting more than 26 weeks; or specific **TURNAROUNDS**, i.e., sets of roads used to change direction, so drivers can SET DOWN on the correct side of the street.

Each appearance is scored **A**, **B**, **C** [pass] or **D** [fail], with marks deducted for inaccuracy, illegality, inefficiency, or hesitation. (While As and Bs are possible, Cs and Ds are common.)

Until recently, anyone failing a stage would be **REDLINED** back to the earlier stage; nowadays redlining requires candidates to restart from scratch only their current stage.

COTTONING THE RUN

**STAGE 6** · The final exam tests whether candidates have a good working knowledge of suburban London, specifically 27 suburban routes listed in Annex C of the Blue Book.

Once every knowledge-based hurdle has been cleared, candidates submit to a criminal record check before attending a pre-licensing briefing and a badge presentation, after which they are immediately free to **PLY FOR HIRE**.

The shortest time it can take to obtain the Knowledge (*"with luck, skill, and hard work"*) is ~18 months; most spend several years acquiring a badge; and some take more than a decade. But, as the age-old adage goes:

*"You can't fail the Knowledge, you can only quit."*

## CABOLOGY

Below is an exploration of cabbing's unique culture, language, and tradition.

However, as the trade evolves and drivers from diverse backgrounds are welcomed into the fold — many of these archetypal London terms are becoming ever rarer to encounter.

**SHERBET** (**DAB**) / **FLOUNDER** (**& DAB**) / **SANDY** (**MCNAB**) · Cockney rhyming slang terms for a cab, or **JOE** (**BAXI** = taxi).

Other nicknames include **BEGGING BOX** and, archaically, the Polish term **DROSHKY**.

At the other end of the linguistic spectrum is the old Society term, **FAST BLACK**.

Contrary to popular belief, London taxis have never been restricted to black; pre-war cabs were sold in a variety of colours, though black became the standard for many decades after WWII. (Rental garages used to spray the hubcaps of their cabs in a signature hue.)

**JOURNEYMAN** · A driver who rents a cab.

**MUSHER** · A driver who owns their cab. A **STARVING MUSHER** is one still paying for their cab. Rain is called **MUSHER'S LOTION** *or* **MIXTURE**, because it brings forth trade.

**FRARNY** · Archaic cabbie term for rain (from the rhyming slang "France and Spain").

**BUTTERBOY** · What newly licensed drivers are called for their first three years; possibly derived from the term "but a boy."

**FIVE MINUTE JERK** · A **LOCAL** journey.

**ON A ROLL**(**ER**) · Instantly consecutive fares.

**IN & OUT** · A fare that returns to its origin.

**P.O.B.** · Passenger on board. *Hence*, **POBBING** · When the streets are bobbing with trade.

**THE MAP LINE** / **KEEPING IT BIG** · A direct route using **ORANGES & LEMONS**.

**ORANGES & LEMONS** · Main (**BIG**) roads; based on the respective colours of A- and B-Roads in the Geographers' A-Z Map. *A.k.a.*, **MACARONI**.

*Inside a* FLOUNDER *as it approaches the Museum of London*

**GOING WIDE** · Taking a less direct route, to avoid a known delay (or to **BUMP** a fare).

**BACK DOUBLES** · Shortcuts through little-used side streets; now increasingly rare due to London's extensive "traffic calming" measures.

**CUTTING** *or* **CARVING IT UP / DUCKING AND DIVING** · Deploying the KNOWLEDGE and its BACK DOUBLES to evade the traffic.

**CHURCHILL** · A meal (break), so called because Winston Churchill, when Home Secretary (1910–11), allowed cabbies to refuse fares while eating. More controversially, Winnie permitted drivers to smoke in their cabs.

**KIPPER SEASON** · The opening months of the new year (traditionally January and February), when business can be painfully slow.

**COPPERBOTTOM / LEATHER ARSE** · The consequence of driving long hours to make a wage; common during KIPPER SEASON.

**BUTTERFLY** · A summertime (only) driver.

**STRING VEST** · A (stereotypical) old-fashioned and unreconstructed cabbie.

**LIVE SIDE** · The driver's side of a cab that is exposed to traffic, and hazardous to use.

**SUICIDE DOOR** · The rear-hinged doors on some cabs; so-called because an overtaking collision could crush an exiting passenger.

**FLIP** *or* **CRICKET** *or* **JUMP SEATS** · The **TIP-UP** seats behind the driver's partition. *A.k.a.*, **THE CONFESSIONAL**, because (late at night) punters sit with their back to the cabbie and pour out their troubles, as to a priest.

**NICKNAMES** · Cabbies delight in descriptive names, from *Bring 'em Back Jack* (who always secured a return booking from passengers he dropped at the airport) to *Claude the Bastard* (who would shamelessly nick fares).

**THE OTHER MOB / THE DARK SIDE / SCABS** · Uber, Bolt, Lyft, &c.

**APPS** · Many cabbies have embraced messaging apps and social media to swap real-time intel on traffic incidents, road closures, gossip, and rank availability (*"Loo needs cabs"*). According to some, it has made a traditionally solitary lifestyle significantly more sociable.

Black cab hailing apps (e.g., Gett, FreeNow) have replaced the old **RADIO CIRCUIT** as a way to find fares.

Old-timers who were once mocked for **BUNGING** hotel commissionaires a **DRINK** (i.e., bribe) to secure lucrative FLYERS are now amused by apps that leech a percentage of every single journey.

## AUTHORITY

**BLUE TREES / KOJAK WITH A KODAK** (**KWAK**) · A policeman with a **HAIR-DRIER** (i.e., speed gun).

**TOES UP!** · To reduce speed when you spot a **JOHNDARM** (policeman), or speed trap.

**C.O. BLOKE** · Traditionally an inspector from the **CARRIAGE OFFICE**; now a TfL **COMPLIANCE OFFICER** who enforces everything from a cab's road-worthiness to a driver's badge and **BILL** (i.e., Hackney Carriage licence).

Cabbies are subject to a range of other rules, e.g., they cannot smoke in their cabs even if no passengers are aboard.

## RANKS

London has more than 700 taxi **RANKS** (i.e., stands), of which several dozen are designated to give drivers 45 minutes for **REFRESHMENT**, or 60 minutes for **REST**.

The larger ranks are sometimes divided into multi-part **FEEDERS**, each portion of which is effectively a **MINI-RANK** allowing passengers to hire a cab at the break of each section without walking to the front of the rank proper. Cabs **ON POINT** at a **FEEDER** must promptly **MOVE UP** to the next portion when a space opens up.

The first two drivers on any rank, or portion, must be with their cabs and available for hire.

Some ranks (e.g., **PADDERS**) have an interleaving shuffle system to maximize capacity and minimize passenger waits; others (e.g., Euston) remain pretty chaotic.

A few ranks have earned nicknames, including **THE SCENT BOX** at King's Cross (after its characteristic odour), and **THE RAT HOLE** at Embankment Station (after its dimensions).

**RANKING UP** · Joining a rank.

**ON** *or* **THE POINT** · The first cab on a rank.

**ON AND OFF** · Driving onto a rank and immediately getting a fare. ("*Touch!*")

**THE (OLD) MARK** · A driver's favourite rank. ("*Where's Brian? He's on his mark.*")

**(COLD) BLOW** · A (windswept) rank.

**LEAD CAB** · The front cabbie (on the streets or at a rank) who has the right of way.

**BANGED OUT / OVER RANKED / LOADED / RANKED OUT** · A rank at its capacity.

**PUTTING ON FOUL** · Joining a **LOADED** rank (hoping you won't be caught).

**TO BE LEFT SUCKING THE MOP** · Arriving at the front of a rank (**POLE POSITION**) just as business has **DRIED UP**.

**BROOMING (DOWN)** · When the **POINT** cab **BRUSHES** a passenger off to the next cab in line because the journey is too short, too irksome, or in the "wrong" direction.

By law, cabbies may only decline a job if it is longer than 12 miles, would take over an hour, or if the passenger is disorderly or drunk.

**KNOCK BACK** · To refuse a legitimate job.

**HANGING (IT UP)** · Loitering around a likely area (waiting for a **BURST**). It is unlawful for taxis to **PARK UP** with their light on.

**FAKE** *or* **GHOST RANK** · Any area where taxis queue up that is not an official rank, and need not be respected as such by other cabbies, e.g., Praed Street, Paddington.

**PUT ON THE LONG RANK / PLYING / CRUISING / MOOCHING / LOOKING FOR GOLD / COASTING / HUNTING** · Driving the streets looking for a fare.

**ROASTING / DOING SOME BIRD** · A long wait on a rank.

## HEATHROW

**T.F.P.** · The Feeder Park at London's Heathrow Airport; cabbies enter the **NORTH PARK**, progress to the **SOUTH PARK**, and exit past **THE BARRIER**, where they are directed to the rank at one of L.H.R.'s four terminals.

If the airport is **RUNNING** (i.e., busy), it can take as little as an hour to get a fare; the average wait is 2–3 hours, or 4–5 if L.H.R. is **DEAD**.

When taxis are urgently needed (e.g., during a train strike) a **CODE RED** allows drivers to drive directly to any terminal's rank.

**LOCAL** · A job in the immediate vicinity of Heathrow. If drivers can drop off at any location on the **LOCAL LIST** and return to the airport within an hour, they can skip T.F.P. and drive directly to any terminal's rank.

A302

**SLEEPER** · A driver who arrives at **T.F.P.** after the last flight and sleeps in the back of his cab, so as to be first in the queue in the morning.

**FACES** · A closed shop of cabbies who, back in the day, controlled the Heathrow rank and allocated the best jobs to their mates.

**WALL OF DEATH** · Framed obituaries in the Heathrow cabbies' canteen.

## FARES

**CLOCK / TICKBOX / TICKER / HICKORY DICKORY DOCK** [= clock] / **BLUE PETER** [= meter] / **HARMONICA** · The electronic taximeter that calculates the fare, after which the taxi is named. Cabbies rent their meters, which are checked and calibrated regularly.

**TARIFFS** · Notwithstanding regular headlines accusing cabbies of "hiking" fares, the cost of a taxi journey is set by the independent regulator, Transport for London. (Indeed, some cabbies despair that "tariff inflation" is pricing them out of the market.) There are three time- and day-specific tariffs:

› **TARIFF 1** · Monday to Friday 5 A.M.–8 P.M., other than on a public holiday.
› **TARIFF 2** · Monday to Friday 8 P.M.–10 P.M. or Saturday & Sunday 5 A.M.–10 P.M., other than on a public holiday.
› **TARIFF 3** · Any day 10 P.M.–5 A.M, or at any time on a public holiday.

**EXTRAS** · Cabbies used to charge for a range of additional services (passengers, luggage, &c.), but now the only extras are for picking up (£2) and dropping off (£5.20) at Heathrow; for fares over Christmas and New Year's Eve (£4); and for app or online bookings (£2).

**FLAG FALL** · The fixed price of hailing a cab (currently £3.80), which includes the first 170.4 metres, or 36.6 seconds, on **TARIFF 1**.

**LEGAL AMOUNT** *or* **SUM** · The metered fare, with no gratuity. To be **LEGALLED OFF** is to be given no tip.

**DRINK** · Tip. ("*He gave me a nice drink.*")

**DROP (HEAVY)** · To tip (well).

**YOU SURE YOU CAN SPARE IT, GUV?** · The iconic, sardonic response to a **LIGHT DROP**, alongside "*I'll have half a cup of tea!*" / "*Don't leave yourself short!*" / "*Mind how you go!*"

**CLOCK AND A HALF?** · (Usually humorous) attempt to con unsuspecting (foreign) passengers into paying 50% more than the meter.
Before fares from Heathrow were regulated, cabbies would charge "clock and a half" to help pay for their **DEAD MILES** back.

**DEAD MILES** · A long, empty slog back to civilization after a **ROADER** or **FLYER**.

**ROADER** · A long job out of central London; sometimes negotiated for a fixed price.

**FLYER** · An airport job (usually Heathrow).

**HURRY UP JOB** · When a customer demands a cabbie **STEP ON IT**.

**THIS THE QUICKEST WAY?** · Contrary to cliché, cabbies don't often take the **SCENIC ROUTE** or go **AROUND THE HOUSES** since **GETTING OFF** a job and **CATCHING** a new fare is the most efficient way to maximize **FLAG FALLS**, earnings, and tips. (Moreover, the shortest route isn't always the fastest.)
That said, obnoxious punters may notice their driver conscientiously stopping at every single amber light. {☞ BANGING p.131}

**STALKING** · When cabbies cruise with their light out, hunting for the most desirable (i.e., well-dressed, sober, opulent) passengers. This game has three-steps:
› Explanation: *Sorry, I'm on my way home.*
› Question: *But, where are you going?*
› Decision: *Heathrow? Okay! Hop in.*
In decades past, when cabbies worked **ON THE CLOCK** (for 60% of the fare) stalking meant driving passengers **OFF THE METER** to evade paying a 40% cut to the rental garage; sometimes the passengers would sit on the floor so as to remain out of sight. (The **STALK** is old slang for the flag.)

**BURST / POP** · A surge of eager punters when theatres, clubs, and other venues turn out.
**BERTIE'S POPPED** indicates that the show at the Royal Albert Hall is over.

**LAST KNOCK(ING)** · The final fare of shift.

*The* IRON LUNG *on Horseferry Road*

## PASSENGERS

**BILLY / PAX / PX / PUNTER**......a customer
**BILKER** ............one who **DOES A RUNNER**
**SINGLE PIN** .......................a lone passenger
**BOTTLE OF GLUE** .............. two passengers
**FOUR HANDER** .................four in the back
**COCK AND HEN**....... a male and female fare
**SUIT / BOWLER** ...............city businessman
**PENGUIN**.....................a punter in black tie
**DARLINGS / BRASSES**.............. prostitutes
(especially those working Kings X or Sussex Gardens)

**PUKER** · One who may be charged the official £60 **SOILING FEE** to compensate the driver for the cost of cleaning and loss of earnings.

**HANDS** · Passengers in search of a yellow light. ("*Loads of hands around the Dilly.*")

## PLACE (NICK)NAMES

**THE MAGIC CIRCLE** ........Pica(dilly) Circus
**THE GAS WORKS** ...... Houses of Parliament
**TRIPE SHOP** ............... Broadcasting House
**THIEVES' KITCHEN**.......... Stock Exchange
**AMERICAN WORKHOUSE** ... Park Lane Htl
**SPARROW CORNER**.........Tower of London
**KANGAROO VALLEY**...............Earls Court
**THE ADMIRALS**................Dolphin Square
**INSIDE OUT** ..................Lloyd's of London
**DOL**.................(Dear Old) Langham Hotel
**MANDY**................Mandarin Oriental Hotel
**LINK** .................... Limehouse Link Tunnel
**PIPE** ........................... Rotherhithe Tunnel
**BERTIE**........................... Royal Albert Hall
**B.M.W.**........................ Belgrave Mews West
**DOYS** ..........................Duke of York Square
**FLOWER POT**.................... Covent Garden
(The former flower market site; now in Nine Elms)
**DEAD ZOO**...........Natural History Museum
**WEDDING CAKE**........... Victoria Memorial
**P.G. TIPS** ................. Palace Garden Terrace
**LOO**................................ Waterloo Station
**PADDERS**.....................Paddington Station
**BONE**.......................... Marylebone Station
("Meat on the bone" means "busy at Marylebone")
**ST PANCAKES /**
**BOX OF BRICKS**.............St Pancras Station
**ROYAL LOBSTER**. King's Cross (**KX**) Station
(*Possibly* because it sounds like "King's crustacean")
**HEX**...............................Heathrow Express
**SEX / STEX**......................Stanstead Express
**GEX / GATEX** ..................Gatwick Express
**THE RAFT** ...... **GEX** rank at Victoria Station
**RATTLER**........... any railway station or train

**HOT & COLD CORNER** · The intersection of Exhibition Road and Kensington Gore; so called because the edifice of the nearby Royal Geographical Society houses two statues: the Africa explorer David Livingstone [hot]; and the Polar explorer Ernest Shackleton [cold].

**IRON LUNG** 📷 · A less-than-salubrious public convenience on Horseferry Road. So called because of its curious shape and/or its mephitic odour makes breathing difficult.

**THE HUMP** · A route to and from the City via Pentonville Road and City Road.

*The* NURSERY END *on Wellington Place*

**PILL AVENUE / PILL ISLAND** · The home of private medicine: Harley Street. *A.k.a.*, **THE RESISTANCE**, because of the antipathy of many doctors to the founding of the N.H.S.

**TIARA TRIANGLE** · The bougie shopping district demarcated by Harrods, Harvey Nichols, and Sloane Square.

**ZOMBIE TRIANGLE** · The boho hipster district demarcated by Old Street, Great Eastern Street, and Shoreditch High Street.

**PALACE ROADS** · Those near **BUCK HOUSE**, i.e., St James Street, St James's Palace, The Mall, Victoria Memorial, Buckingham Gate.

**GAFF STREET** · Theatreland in general, or Shaftesbury Avenue specifically. ("*The gaff's burst!*" means the theatres are out.)

**THE BATCAVE** · Lower Robert Street · An eerie tunnel between York Buildings and Savoy Place.

A useful **RAT RUN** to cut from the Strand to Victoria Embankment and access the Savoy Hotel's river entrance.

**DIRTY DOZEN / TERRIBLE TEN** · A sequence of roads that (prior to "traffic calming") cabbies used to drive from Regent Street to Charing Cross Road without using Oxford Street, including: Great Marlborough Street, Noel Street, Berwick Street, D'Arblay Street, Wardour Street, Hollen Street, Great Chapel Street, Fareham Street, Dean Street, Carlisle Street, Soho Square, Sutton Row.

**FRANCE** · Anywhere south of the Thames. The reluctance of cabbies to **GO SOUTH** ("*At this time of night!?*") has largely faded into folklore, not least because of the gentrification of Battersea, Clapham, Balham, and Tooting (*A.k.a.*, **THE NORTHERN LINE EFFECT**).

## SHELTERS &C.

Of the ~61 iconic green cabmen's shelters built between 1875 and 1914, only 13 remain.

Yet most of these now-listed wooden huts still offer refuge and sustenance to licensed cabbies, and take-away snacks to the public. A handful of shelters have location-based nicknames:

- **BELL AND HORNS** (Thurloe Place) · After a now-defunct pub.
- **NURSERY END** (Wellington Place) 📷 · Due to its proximity to the Nursery End of Lord's Cricket Ground. *A.k.a.*, **THE CHAPEL**.
- **ALL NATIONS** (Kensington Road) · Possibly because of its proximity to a dozen or so embassies and high commissions.
- **THE PIER** (Chelsea Embankment) · Because of its adjacency to Cadogan Pier.

**SERVICE TOILETS** · A small number of enlightened establishments (e.g., Claridge's and the Connaught Hotel) have lavatories that cabbies are suffered to use.

## AIDES-MÉMOIRE

**CAT EATS WELL THEN SHARES HER BEEF GRAVY** · A path of one-way streets north from the Aldwych: Catherine, Exeter, Wellington, Tavistock, Southampton, Henrietta, Bedford, Garrick.

**GOOD FOR DIRTY WOMEN** · The streets running north to south through Soho: Greek, Frith, Dean, Wardour.

**LITTLE APPLES GROW QUICKLY PLEASE** · The order of Shaftesbury Avenue's theatres: Lyric, Apollo, Gielgud, Queen's, Palace.

**C.A.B. & C.O.B.** · The bridges going west along the Embankment (Chelsea, Albert, Battersea) and the roads that feed them (Chelsea Bridge Road, Oakley Road, Beaufort Road).

**THE WASP** · Walpole Street, Anderson Street, Sloane Avenue, and Pelham Street — used to travel between Old Brompton Road and King's Road.

**EAST TO WEST — EMBANKMENT'S BEST** · The best Thames crossing for a westward fare.

## TRADITION & ETIQUETTE

**SAVOY COURT** ◎ · One of the few British roads where cars drive on the right — in this case so that taxis can safely drop passengers at the door of the Savoy Hotel (and Theatre).

**GRATIS** · By tradition (and for luck) cabbies don't charge for their first and last fare. (Of course, "*You don't always know when your last fare will be.*")

Many drivers refuse to accept payment from Chelsea Pensioners, or families taking children to and from the paediatric hospital in Great Ormond Street. And, scores of **POPPY CABS** queue across Westminster Bridge each year to give free rides to veterans attending the Remembrance Sunday Cenotaph ceremony.

**GIVING WAY** · The LEAD CAB has the right of way, and the right to the first fare.

**CHOPPING UP / DOING OVER** · Various contraventions of the cabbie code, including: poaching a fare from a LEAD CAB; taking a fare close to a rank on which cabs are waiting; refusing to give way to a cab with a fare; &c.

**LEADING** · If more than one cab is needed for a large group, the LEAD CAB sets the route which is (generally) followed by the rest, so as not to create a differential in timing or fare.

**THE GAME'S DEAD** · The undying complaint that "*trade ain't what it used to be.*"

Cabbing's last rites have been read after any number of innovations, including: mini cabs; night buses; the Gatwick Express; credit card machines; suitcases with wheels; and Covid. That said, Uber might yet prove the final nail in the BEGGING BOX.

**BE LUCKY!** · The classic cabbie farewell. ⊙

*Cabs driving on the right in Savoy Court*

# The Body Politic

*A field guide to* **POLITICAL HAND GESTURES.**

**PRECISION GRIP**
*A.k.a.*, **SAND PINCH.** Focuses attention to a critical detail.

**CHOP**
Controls debate; emphasizes a point without pointing.

**VERTICAL POINT**
Controls debate (and draws the eye) to a singular detail.

**THIST** [thumb + fist]
Originally the [Bill] **CLINTON THUMB**, now omnipresent.

**VERTICAL THIST**
More emphatic; makes a point forcefully without pointing.

**HORIZONTAL THIST**
More conversational; makes a point firmly but casually.

**INTERLINKED FINGERS**
Projects mastery of complexity; demonstrates integrated thinking.

**STEEPLED FINGERS**
Projects mindfulness, control, consideration, and unity.

**HANDLING A BALL**
Projects mastery of a complex, evolving, or multifaceted issue.

**(TORY) POWER POSE**
An awkward, expansive stance, once said to boost confidence.[1]

**VICTORY SALUTE**
Shameless self-praise, forever associated with Richard Nixon.

**FAKE POINT / WAVE**
Picking out a random audience member, to appear impromptu.

**WIDE PALMS**
Projects openness, honesty, and collegiality; appeals to common sense and the better angels of our nature.

**TRIANGLE OF POWER**
Projects calm mastery; the signature gesture of Angela Merkel — hence its German nickname: **MERKEL-RAUTE** [Merkel rhombus].

**HAND ON HEART**
Projects (patriotic) sincerity; accepts praise with humility.

**OPEN PALMS**
Projects frankness. *Or*, (with eyebrow raised) invites scepticism.

**PUT-DOWN PALM**
Controls the debate; lowers the temperature; forestalls dissent.

**FLAT-FRONTED FIST**
Projects pugnacity and strength; invites solidarity.

**THUMBS UP**
Projects optimism (and gives spare hands something to do).

**FINGER COUNTING**
Carries the audience through a multi-pronged argument.

**DIRECT POINT**
Focuses a point on a specific individual, or the audience.

**BOOKMARK**
Controls the flow of debate; projects ordered thinking.

**CONTAINER**
Narrows the focus of debate; projects controlled thinking.

**PEERING OVER LIGHTS**
Breaks the fourth wall, and implies audience intimacy.

**SCARE QUOTES**
Mocks (and distances the speaker from) a term or concept.

**PRAYER / NAMASTE**
Projects "servant leadership"; accepts praise with humility.

Gestures demonstrated by **William E. Baroni Jr.**, former New Jersey State Senator.

# S.O.G.I.E.S.C. & L.G.B.T.Q.I.A.+

*Given the social, political, legal, medical, religious, and sporting controversies surrounding* ***Sexual Orientation, Gender Identity, Gender Expression, and Sex Characteristics*** *it is hardly surprising that the terms used to frame the debates are hotly contested. Below is an exploration of the fast-evolving vocabulary of* **S.O.G.I.E.S.C.**

**SEX** · The physiological and biological characteristics of men, women, and intersex individuals, e.g., reproductive organs, chromosomes, hormones, &c.

**SEX ASSIGNED AT BIRTH** · An individual's sex as designated (by a medical professional) at the time of birth, based usually on (external, genital) anatomical observation. *Hence*:
**A.F.A.B.** .............. Assigned Female At Birth
**A.M.A.B.** ................ Assigned Male At Birth

**INTERSEX** · Individuals whose genitals, chromosomes, or reproductive organs do not conform to the male/female sex binary.

**GENDER** · The socially constructed characteristics, norms, roles, &c. of women and men, which vary across cultures and over time.

**GENDER IDENTITY** · An individual's personal sense of their gender, which may or may not correlate with their sex (assigned at birth); remain consistent over time; or (be permitted socially or legally to) match their ...

**GENDER EXPRESSION** · How an individual outwardly expresses their gender, e.g., name, pronouns, clothes, hair, voice, behaviour, &c.

**CIS(GENDER)** ["*sis*"] · Those whose **GENDER IDENTITY** aligns to their birth-assigned sex. *A.k.a.*, **NON-TRANS**. **CIS** is a Latin prefix for "on this side of" and is an antonym of **TRANS**, "on the other side of."

**TRANS(GENDER)** · Those whose **GENDER IDENTITY** differs from their birth-assigned sex. *A.k.a.*, **GENDER DIVERSE**. A **TRANS MAN** was **A.F.A.B.**, and may be *A.k.a.*, **F.T.M.** *or* **F.2.M.** [female to male]; a **TRANS WOMAN** was **A.M.A.B.**, and may be *A.k.a.*, **M.T.F.** *or* **M.2.F.** [male to female]. Transgender does not imply any specific **SEXUAL ORIENTATION**.

**GENDER NON-CONFORMING** · Those who do not conform to **CIS** gender stereotypes, without (necessarily) identifying as **TRANS**.

**NON-BINARY** · One who does not identify with the gender binary of male or female.

**AGENDER** · One who does not identify with any gender (or even the concept of gender).

**GENDER DYSPHORIA** · Distress experienced by those whose **GENDER IDENTITY** clashes with their **SEX ASSIGNED AT BIRTH**. (*Previously A.ka.*, **GENDER IDENTITY DISORDER**.)

**GENDER AFFIRMATION** · The process of aligning one's **GENDER IDENTITY** and **GENDER EXPRESSION** — legally, psychologically, socially, medically, &c.

*Hence*, **GENDER-AFFIRMING SURGERY / CONFIRMATION SURGERY / SEX REASSIGNMENT SURGERY**.

The term **SEX CHANGE (SURGERY)** is considered by many to be derogatory, as are the terms **PRE-OP**, **POST-OP**, and **TRANNY**.

**DETRANSITIONING** · A (deprecated) term for halting or reversing a (regretted) process of **GENDER AFFIRMATION**.

**SEXUAL ORIENTATION** · An individual's physical, romantic, and/or emotional attraction to others — or absence thereof.

**STRAIGHT / HETERO** · Being physically, romantically, and/or emotionally attracted to the opposite sex. *Related*, the (transphobic) term **SUPER-STRAIGHT** · Those only attracted to **CIS** members of the opposite sex.

**QUEER** · Though historically considered pejorative, queer has been reclaimed by people who feel constrained by terms like gay, lesbian, bi, &c. *Also*, **GENDERQUEER**.

**QUESTIONING** · Those **CURIOUS** about, or **EXPLORING**, their orientation or identity.

**MEN WHO HAVE SEX WITH MEN (M.S.M.)** · Men who engage in same-sex activity, without (necessarily) identifying as gay or bi.
*Also*, **WOMEN LOVING WOMEN (W.L.W.)**.

**HETERO-** *or* **CISNORMATIVE** · A worldview where being **STRAIGHT** and/or **CIS** is natural, normal, and institutionally entrenched.

**CLOSETED** · A (pejorative) term for one who, for any number of (personal, legal, cultural, religious, &c.) reasons is unwilling or unable to be (publicly) "open" about their orientation.
*Hence*, **COMING OUT (OF THE CLOSET)** · Voluntarily sharing one's sexual orientation with (concentric circles of) friends, family, and society at large. (The term dates to ~1966, and is increasingly considered anachronistic.)
Societies where being **OUT** is uncontroversial are sometimes described as **POST CLOSET**.

**OUT** · Openly sharing one's sexual orientation or gender identity. (The term **OPENLY GAY** is deprecated as patronizing.)
*Hence*, **OUTING** · Unwittingly, accidentally, or maliciously disclosing an individual's **ORIENTATION** or **IDENTITY** without consent.

**L.G.B.T.Q.I.A.+** · Lesbian, Gay, Bisexual, Transgender, Queer, Intersex, Asexual, + all others.
Sometimes prefixed with **2S**, which denotes a third-gender **TWO SPIRIT** identity of some Indigenous North American communities.
A perceived inflation in identity initialisms is ridiculed by the right as **ALPHABET SOUP** / **L.G.B.T.Q.X.Y.Z.** / **L.G.B.T.Q.W.E.R.T.Y.** In response, some in the community proudly call themselves the **ALPHABET MAFIA**.

**HOMOSEXUAL** · Deprecated by some as an outdated clinical term that viewed same-sex attraction as a physical or mental disease. Some style guides suggest the noun be used in quotes.

**TRANSTRENDER** · The accusation that some (high-profile) trans people are merely following the vagaries of (social-media) fashion.

**DEADNAMING** · Unwittingly, accidentally, or maliciously using someone's **BIRTH NAME** after they have changed it. *Similarly*, **MISGENDERING** · **DEADNAMING**, but with **PRONOUNS**, **HONORIFICS**, or gender-specific terms (e.g., son, sister, actress, waiter, &c.).

**PRONOUNS** · The personal pronouns an individual uses to express their gender identity. Asking about someone's **PREFERRED** *or* **CHOSEN PRONOUNS** is deprecated by those who believe it implies identity is a whim.

**HONORIFICS** · Many cultures use titles to show gender and, for women, marital status (*English*: Mr/Mrs/Miss; *German*: Hr/Fr/Frl).
In the '50s, **Ms.** surfaced as a status-neutral alternative, and, more recently, **Mx.** ("*mix*") has emerged as a gender-neutral variant.

**ALLY(SHIP)** · Support, protection, and promotion of L.G.B.T.Q.I.A.+ people and interests.

**TRANS-EXCLUSIONARY RADICAL FEMINIST (T.E.R.F.)** · Those who reject the assertion "**TRANS WOMEN** *are* women" and oppose M.T.F. admission into traditionally female-only spaces and organizations (e.g., sports, toilets, changing rooms, prisons, &c.).
The controversy associated with the term T.E.R.F. has led some to use the alternative, **GENDER-CRITICAL (FEMINISM)**.

## SOME GENDER-NEUTRAL (NEO-)PRONOUNS

| SUBJECT | OBJECT | POSSESSIVE | POSSESSIVE PRONOUN | REFLEXIVE |
|---|---|---|---|---|
| He | Him | His | His | Himself |
| She | Her | Her | Hers | Herself |
| Ey | Em | Eir | Eirs | Eirself |
| Fae | Faer | Faer | Faers | Faerself |
| Per | Per | Pers | Pers | Perself |
| Sie | Sie | Hir | Hirs | Hirself |
| They | Them | Their | Theirs | Themself |
| Ve | Ver | Vis | Vers | Verself |
| Zie | Zim | Zir | Zis | Zieself |

*A* GENDER-NEUTRAL *lavatory sign in Manchester, England, 2019*

**LIFESTYLE** · A term some consider patronizing: as if one's identity or orientation was merely a pose. *Similarly,* **SEXUAL PREFERENCE** · Which implies one's orientation &c. can be swayed, or even "cured."

## GENDER-AFFIRMING SURGERY TERMINOLOGY

**FACIAL FEMINIZATION** · Operations to sculpt, contour, or otherwise "soften" the cheekbones, chin, jaw, brow, hairline, nose, &c. Often combined with non-surgical procedures such as Botox, fillers, hair-removal, &c.

**TRACHEAL SHAVE** (*or* **CHONDROLARYNGOPLASTY**) · Reducing the Adam's apple.

**TOP SURGERY** · Reducing breast tissue for F.T.M. (e.g., via subcutaneous mastectomy and liposuction); *Or,* augmenting breast tissue for M.T.F. (e.g., via silicone or saline implants). May also involve nipple and areola reconstruction or repositioning.

**BOTTOM SURGERY** · Various forms of genital and/or genitourinary reconstruction, e.g.:

**VAGINOPLASTY** · Using the penis, scrotum, and other genital tissue to construct a vaginal canal and vulva (i.e., mons pubis, clitoris, labia, &c.). *Similarly,* **VULVOPLASTY** (*A.k.a.,* **ZERO DEPTH VAGINOPLASTY**) · Creating external female genitalia, with a vaginal canal that is too shallow for penetration.

**PHALLOPLASTY** · Grafting a flap of skin, fat, nerves, and blood vessels (e.g., from the forearm) to construct a **NEOPENIS**. Requires an implanted penile prosthesis for an erection.

**METOIDIOPLASTY** (*A.k.a.,* **META**) · Reconstructing the clitoris to create a **NEOPENIS** 4–6 cm long. This may require **URETHRAL LENGTHENING** to allow standing urination.

**SCROTOPLASTY** · Using tissue from the labia to construct a scrotum (after which **TESTICULAR IMPLANTS** may be added).

**VAGINECTOMY** · Removing (part of) the vaginal canal, labia, and clitoris, and suturing shut the vaginal opening. May also involve a **HYSTERECTOMY** (i.e., removal of uterus).

**PENECTOMY** · Partial or total removal of the penis, and relocation of the urethra. *Similarly,* **ORCHIECTOMY** · Removal of the testicles.

**GENITAL NULLIFICATION / NULLO** · Removing all of the external genitalia to create a "unbroken" transition from the abdomen to the groin. *A.k.a.,* **EUNUCH / SMOOTHIE**.

Many jurisdictions require patients to satisfy various pre-operative preconditions, e.g., two letters of support from mental health professionals; proof of hormonal treatment; a biopsychosocial assessment, &c.

Most of these procedures are also used in general (non-gender-affirming) care, e.g., to treat trauma, birth defects, cancer, &c. ⊙

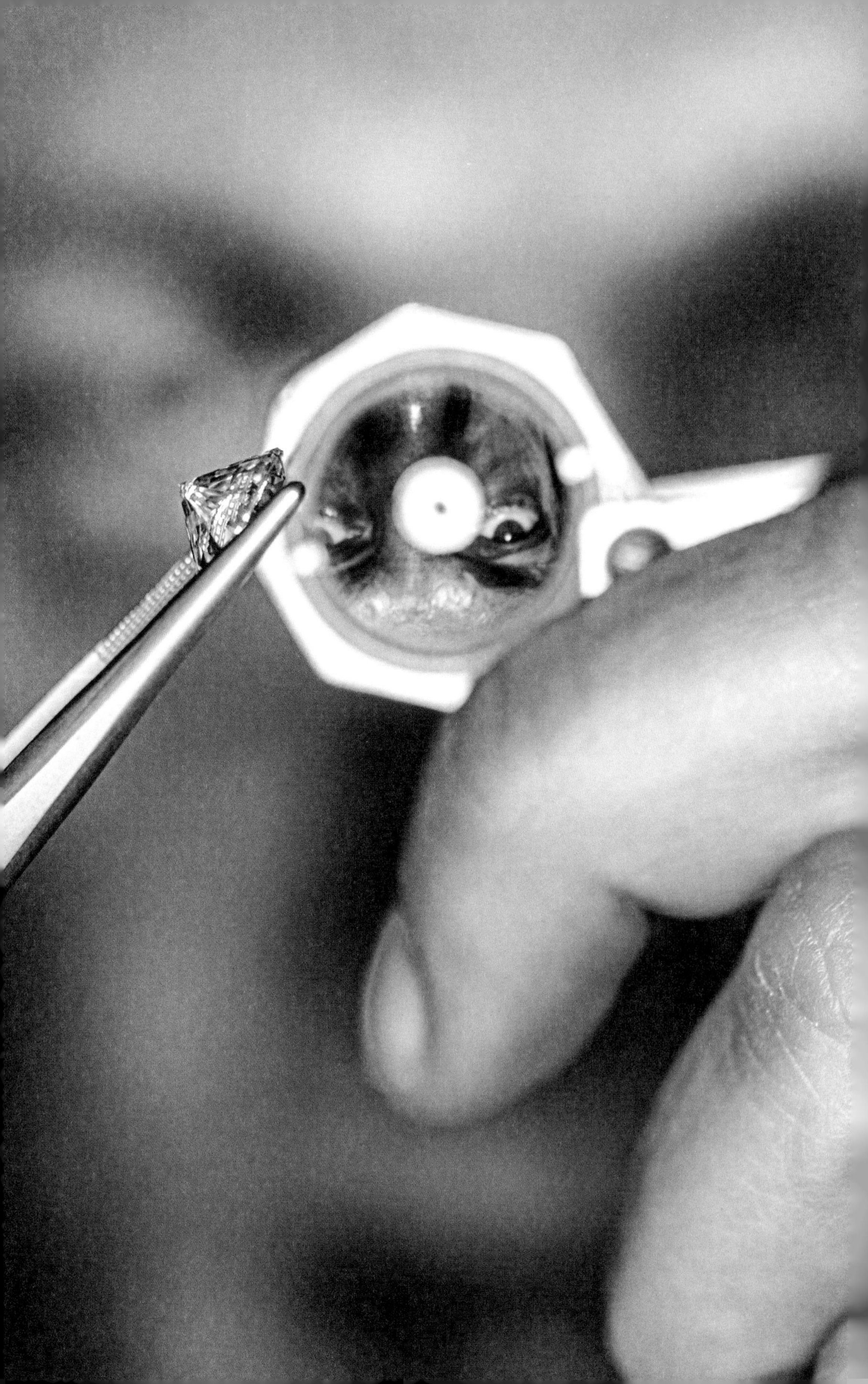

# Making Mazal on Diamond Way

*The public face of* **NEW YORK'S DIAMOND DISTRICT** *is Diamond and Jewelry Way, a block of 47th Street between Fifth and Sixth Avenues lined with dazzlingly lit shops and exchanges and cluttered by hawkers, hustlers, cops, and couriers. But beyond these street-level operations, in back rooms, upper floors, and looming towers, toils an army of cutters, blockers, polishers, sorters, appraisers, graders, designers, and dealers — most of whom the diamond-buying public never sees ...*

*... or hears. The street has its own vocabulary, honed over generations and still used today. The prevalence of Yiddish reflects the historic influence of Jewish craftsmen and dealers. But the diamond business is international, and on Diamond and Jewelry Way it is not uncommon to hear Russian, Indian, Dutch, French, Belgian, Korean, and other accents enunciating the* **MAME-LOSHN** *("mother tongue") of Eastern European Jewry, and a few non-Yiddish phrases as well.*

Diamond sellers, or *diamantaires*, deploy an extensive nomenclature of technical terms to describe their wares — not just the famous **FOUR C**'s of **COLOUR**, **CLARITY**, **CUT**, and **CARAT** weight, but also dimensions, fluorescence, inclusions (flaws), polish, and symmetry. Traders will instantly know what "round G 4.18 $VVS_2$ TRIP X" means, as well as its value. On examination, they can judge if that stone's colour is a "good G" or "low G" and whether its clarity is actually the inferior $VS_1$.

These terms may be tricky to decipher (and trickier still to apply commercially), but they are widely known. In the trade, however, there are many other words used to describe what really matters about a given stone, *steen* (Dutch), *pierre* (French), *almaz* (Russian), *hira* (Hindi), or *shteyn* (Yiddish — the language of many of the words below).

## QUALITY

**CARAT / CT** · One carat (200 milligrams) is divided into both 100 points and four grains. A **20-POINTER** weighs one-fifth of a carat (or 40 milligrams), and a **SIX-GRAINER** weighs 1.5 carats (or 300 milligrams).

Dealers use the term **LIGHT** to indicate weights shy of a common fraction; a **LIGHT-HALF** can weigh from 0.45 to 0.49 carats.

**ROUGH** · Uncut and unpolished stones.

**KHAZERAY** · Junk; trash.

**STROP** · A stone that won't sell; a bad buy.

Some dealers are anxious to unload their strops, even at a loss, to release capital or just to dispose of a dud. Others reckon that strops are not actually costing them anything, so they let them "*sit in the back of the safe*" — literally or metaphorically — for years, or generations.

Forgotten or underrated stones sometimes surge back into fashion, hence the saying, "*People get rich on strops.*"

**LINKS-SHTIVL** [Left-footed boots] · A parcel of **KHAZERAY** in which nothing matches. "*I can't find a pair of stones to make earrings in this links-shtivl.*"

**LINKER** · Left, awry, illegitimate, or illegal.

**SHLOK** · Junk, rubbish, fake, or second-rate merchandise.

**SHVIMERS** [Swimmers] · Very impressive stones that appear to "*swim across the surface*" of loose diamonds, thereby improving the appearance of lesser stones. *A.k.a.*, **FLOATERS**.

**MAME-ZITSER** [Mother sitter] · A very large diamond.

**TAM** [Flavour] · Appeal. When comparing diamonds, an expert will instinctively sense which has the greater **TAM**.

**TRIP(LE) (E)X** · Any stone with an "excellent" grading for cut, polish, and symmetry.

☞ *The diamantaire Yves Ringler examines a* SHVIMER

*Charming the* **WINDOW TRADE** *on 47th Street*

**FISHEYE / PANCAKE** · An unappealingly flat stone.

**ROVAL** · A nearly round, fat oval: ugly, undesirable, and unsaleable.

**MATZO** · A stone made to look larger by cutting it flat at the widest spot.

**FIR-KANTIKE EYER** [Four-cornered eggs] · An impossible request; a stone (or price) that doesn't exist. ("*You're looking for fir-kantike eyer — go down to the Smithsonian!*")

**BLUFF STONE** · An impressive looking (**BLUFFY**) diamond that is not as valuable as it appears.

**MELEE** · From *mêlé* [mixed, in French]; small cut-and-polished diamonds (often ≤0.18 carats) used as **ACCENT STONES** or in dense pavé settings, where many stones cover an area of metal (as cobblestones cover a pavement).

Melee is commonly sold in **PARCELS** or **LOTS**, for which the price rises as the buyer becomes more selective:

**WHOLE** *or* **LOT PRICE** ........... entire parcel
**CUT PRICE** ..................... unsorted division
**SORT** *or* **PICK PRICE** .......... hand-selection

**ESTATE JEWELLERY** · Secondhand. The term **POST-CONSUMER** has recently been adopted to appeal to those concerned about the humanitarian and ecological costs of newly mined stones.

## EQUIPMENT

**BRIVKE** *or* **PARCEL-PAPER** · A folded wrap of paper used to store stones.

**CACHET** · A small, plain (manila) envelope used in deals mediated by a broker. A seller lends a broker a selection of stones to show potential buyers. If a buyer likes a stone (or stones), he wraps it in a **BRIVKE**, seals it in a **CACHET**, and writes his name, offer price, and payment terms along the flap edge. This ensures that the stone can't be **SHOWN** to anyone else. The broker returns the cachet to the seller, who accepts the deal or makes a counteroffer. The broker takes the **CACHET** back to the buyer, who can agree to the sale, strike out the counteroffer and write in a new price, or tear the cachet open — releasing the stone back to the market and ending the negotiation.

Brokers usually take **COMMISH** or **C.O.** (i.e., **COMMISSION**) of around 2% from the seller on any sales they **CLOSE**.

**LOUPE** · A handheld magnifying lens, usually with a magnification 10×. An informal **CLARITY GRADING** rank of diamonds is:

> **LOUPE CLEAN** (no inclusions visible under a loupe) → **EYE CLEAN** (no inclusions visible to the naked eye) → **CENTRE CLEAN** (no inclusions visible in the stone's centre)

**SIEVE SET** · A shaker barrel with graduated sieves, used to sort **MELEE** by size.

**SAFES / VAULTS** · While there is no hard and fast distinction between the two, you can usually walk into a vault.

**SHMATE** · A cloth for cleaning *shmutz* [dirt] from stones.

## BUSINESS

**GESHEFT** · Business.

**LUFT GESHEFT** · Business founded on air; an enterprise without a solid foundation.

**BREN** · Burn, or on fire: "*This holiday season was a bren.*"

**SHTIL** · Quiet. *Similarly*, **SHVAKH** · Weak.

**GORNISHT** [Nothing] · From this comes the phrase **GORNISHT MIT GORNISHT** ("*nothing with nothing*") or **G.M.G.** — which is used to describe inferior goods or times when the trade is depressingly SHVAKH.

**MEKHULE** · Bankrupt.

## MAZL UN BROKHE

The most significant phrase on **THE STREET**, and perhaps across the global diamond trade, is **MAZL UN BROKHE** — "*Good luck and a blessing*" — which is commonly abbreviated to **MAZL**.

It is hard to overstate the power of this verbal handshake, which seals million-dollar deals without lawyers, witnesses, or contracts. In **MAKING MAZL**, *diamantaires* stake their personal honour (and that of their family) and the term garners near-universal respect.

It is said that the **MAZL UN BROKHE** formula has two symbolic elements: The seller has luck in selling (*mazl*), and the buyer has a blessing for future success (*brokhe*).

One interpretation of the Hebrew word *mazl* (מזל) is that it is an acronym encompassing the three elements that determine our good fortune:

מ = מקום = *makom* = PLACE
ז = זמן = *zman* = TIME
ל = לימוד = *limmud* = LEARNING

So, to have *mazl*, one needs to be in the right place, at the right time, with the right wisdom to know how to act.

The overlap of faith, luck, and superstition is evident in several ways. Some Jewish dealers will instinctively deprecate their business fortunes, both out of modesty and to avert any bad luck incited by boasting.

The phrase **KEN EYNE HORE** ("*without the evil eye*") is the Yiddish equivalent of saying "knock on wood" after tempting fate.

Hindu and Sikh dealers may bless loupes, scales, and other tools of the trade during Diwali, the autumn festival of lights. And it is not uncommon to see traditional Hindu swastikas painted on the vaults and safes of Indian dealers, just as many Jewish dealers affix *mezuzot* to their doorjambs.

The widespread use of the pacific Hindu swastika in a heavily Jewish trade is not unproblematic — as one Orthodox dealer said, pointing to a swastika-emblazoned MEMO agreement: "*I know it's lucky for them ... but, you know, it's not so lucky for us.*"

**BASHERT** [Destined] · Something that is "meant to be"; when good fortune drops into your lap.

Some believe that profit is bound to follow if a diamond falls to the floor when a **BRIVKE** is opened (assuming, of course, that it's found). Others will kiss for luck a stone that has fallen or been dropped.

**GOOD HAND** · To have both luck and skill in finding, understanding, and dealing stones. A trader with a good hand is also one with the wisdom and integrity to "*leave a little profit in the deal*" so everyone makes their **PARNOSE** [livelihood].

Dealers will say of a lucrative and lucky trading partnership, "*We have a good hand together.*"

## THE DEAL

**METSIYE** · A great deal; a bargain; a stone bought cheap. Some dealers complain that, because diamonds are increasingly listed online, "*There are no metsiyes anymore.*" Others hunt for **M&Ms** — **MISTAKES** (underpriced stones) and **METSIYES**. {☞ SLEEPER p.160}

**GANEYVE** · A steal; better than a METSIYE.

*A safe marked with a Hindu swastika*

**OYSSHIS** · Rejects or leftovers; hence the saying "*One man's* OYSSHIS *is another man's* METSIYE*!*"

**SHATS** · To price or give an opinion on a diamond. "*Hey,* SHATS *this stone for me.*"

**CHAP LAGNA** · From "to stamp" in Hindi; to value something accurately.

Indian traders also have a range of terms for bargains: **HALWA**, a traditional sweet, but also a good deal; **MUFT**, "free," but also used to describe a great bargain; and **MALAI**, a term for "cream," which describes a deal that will be profitable.

**HONDL** · To bargain, haggle, or trade.

**NEM DI GELT!** [take the money] · An encouragement to stop prevaricating and "*make mazl already!*" The general sense that business must keep moving is evident also in phrases like "*no one died for an offer*" and "*no one went broke taking a profit.*"

**SHLEP** [to drag] · To pay late and make someone carry your debt. ("*You're shlepping — we said 30 days.*")

**SHMIR** · To grease the wheels, or pay a bribe. ("*Sure, I shmired the guy a little.*")

**TOUCH** · Profit. ("*I got a little touch.*")

**KEYSTONE / KEY** · A markup of 100 percent. *Hence,* **DOUBLE** *or* **TRIPLE KEY.**

## ON MEMO

**ON MEMO** is the process by which dealers routinely borrow and lend diamonds in order to match stones with buyers.

The memorandum itself (**JANGAD** in Gujarati) is a slip of paper that itemizes each stone and the **MEMO PRICE** for which it can be sold (usually higher than a **FIRM SALE** price). Technically, the receiver of diamonds on memo has no rights of ownership and no right to sell. It is understood, however, that if a buyer is found at (or, after agreement, near) the memo price, the owner will consent to the transaction.

Even as internet sales rise, the memo business remains central to the trade, because buyers want to assess the stones with their own eyes. That said, the curiously casual nature of trading on memo can result in disputes — for example, when payment becomes long overdue, when already-on-memo stones are sent on memo to a third party, or when stones are returned late, or not at all.

It is not uncommon for dealers to have large stones or important pieces out on memo with big-name stores, which have a wider range of clientele able to afford them.

## REFERENCES

The trust that underpins business on the street is hard won and jealously guarded. Untested dealers who want the privilege of borrowing stones ON MEMO are expected to provide

**REFERENCES** from respected dealers. These dealers are asked how long a prospective client has traded, what credit they have, how much debt is unpaid, and whether they are **SHLEPPING**. ("*It's normal to owe money; it's not normal to be behind.*")

Only once satisfied will a dealer allow their stones out **ON MEMO** — but the value and terms of the memo will be kept in check until a personal bond of trust has been established over time. Time also allows dealers who have erred in some way (even into bankruptcy) to incrementally trade their way back into trust.

A small and curious footnote on trust: The private **DIAMOND DEALERS CLUB** on the 11th floor of 50 West 47th Street has a **LOST-AND-FOUND** board where mislaid stones are listed to be returned to their owners.

## PEOPLE

Several traditional Yiddish terms are used to describe people in the trade:

**MENSCH** ........ good guy
**MEYVN** ........ expert
**GANIF** ........ thief
**HAZER** ........ pig

And, just as every diamond has its **FOUR C**'s, so Yiddish has **THREE S**'s for irksome dealers:

The **SCHNORER** who begs for deals.
The **SHLEPER** who pays late.
The **SHTINKER** who never pays.

**FAYNSHMEKER** [fine sniffer] · A connoisseur with expensive taste, excellent merchandise, or both. *Conversely*, a perfectionist: "*Don't be such a faynshmeker ... nem di gelt!*"

**GOOD EYE** · One who can spot quality.

**HAWKS** · Street-level operatives who coax pedestrians toward a specific retailer in return for **C.O.** on any transaction.

**JALEBI** · An intricately spiralled Indian sweet; used to describe a hustler. ("*He is straight like a jalebi!*")

## RETAIL CODES

Salespeople across 47th Street use a range of codes to speak in front of **PRIVATES** (the public) and secure a diamond's last and most vital journey across **THE LAST 18 INCHES** (the shop's glass counter).

Not all of these terms are widely used, and some are increasingly of only historic interest.

**GEE / G** · A general term for a customer. There are several possible etymologies: It might stand for *gooch* (auction slang for a buyer), *geek* ("grotesque" carnival acts who bit the heads off live animals), or, simply, *guy*. A range of street phrases use the term, including:

› **SHERRY THE GEE** · Get rid of the customer. From "sherry"; to go, sheer off, or run away. "*Hey, your wife Sherry called.*"

*Inside a dealer's safe*

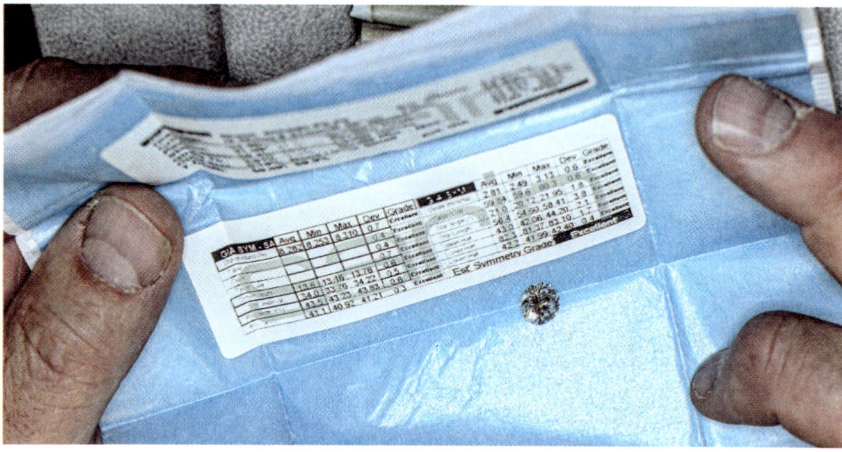

*A* BRIVKE *with a* SHVIMER *and its* CERT

› **KITTY WITH THE GEE** · Keep a customer occupied with small talk.

› **GOOD GEE** · A favourite customer.

› **TEE THE GEE** · Follow the customer once they have left the store. Why? To ensure that a client who has just left a deposit for a piece to be made is not persuaded by a rival HAWK or competitor to transfer his business. [The "tee" may stand for "trail" or "tail."] A hawk will TEE THE GEE until the client is seen safely off 47th Street (into a taxi, onto the subway) — after which the jeweller can build the new piece, confident that the GEE will be back to collect and pay. To avoid alerting a PRIVATE, the hawk might also be asked, e.g., to *"get a cup of tea."*

**SEND THEM TO THE A.P.** · When high-pressure salespeople send wavering clients to a far-from-independent **APPRAISER** (**A.P.**).

To keep the momentum of sale and avoid **B.O.** (backing out), a HAWK (or **A.P. RUNNER**) will physically escort buyer and diamond to get a favourable appraisal — a hustle known as **RING, BOX, GO**.

**2–10** · A warning to keep *"two eyes on ten fingers"* when serving a suspicious customer.

This code (*A.k.a.*, **TWO UPON TEN**) dates to at least the 1860s, and was widely used in retail.

**LOW** *or* **HIGH LINER** · A bad *or* good client, or business prospect.

**COST MARKS** · Many dealers still use traditional **RETAIL CIPHERS**, substituting letters for numbers when writing out price tags or discussing prices in public. Dealers select a ten-letter keyword in which no character is repeated, e.g., **CASHPROFIT**:

| C | A | S | H | P | R | O | F | I | T |
|---|---|---|---|---|---|---|---|---|---|
| 1 | 2 | 3 | 4 | 5 | 6 | 7 | 8 | 9 | 0 |

Here, $150 becomes the unintelligible CPT. To add complexity, additional letters are used as **REPEATERS** ($1,500 might be CPTX) or for additional obfuscation (YYCPTYY).

These ciphers are also used to further encode other codes. E.g., "2–10" would become "ACT" and "56" would communicate "PR" — slang for "profit." (*"Hey, what's the 56 on this?"*)

**D-LINE** · An easy, no-nonsense deal: when a customer sees a ring, buys it, and leaves. (*"I just* D*-lined that* $VS_1$*."*)

## SECURITY

Security on the street is tight. A constant presence by the New York Police Department is augmented by uniformed and undercover guards and armed patrols by retired cops. The area is also surveilled by a network of cameras that, according to the 47th Street Business Improvement District, was partly funded by the Department of Homeland Security.

Inside shops, security is no laxer. Display cases are fitted with burglar-resistant glass; surveillance cameras record audio as well as video; **PANIC BUTTONS** are available to alert the police; and some retailers carry firearms.

Lunch hours, delivery times, and opening and closing procedures are regularly varied to confound anyone **CASING THE JOINT**. And every night, window displays are cleared of merchandise to prevent **SMASH-AND-GRAB** raids.

To foil shoplifters, staff members will show only one or two pieces at a time. And to quickly spot if any merchandise is missing, retailers set out jewellery **SYMMETRICALLY**; keep **DIAGRAMS** or **MAPS** of display case layouts; and insert **PLACEHOLDERS** (e.g., pennies) when removing rings from a tray.

Most businesses off the street are protected by **MAN-TRAPS** — double-door vestibules that allow visitors to be checked before entry and exit, with packages delivered through a hatch.

When dealers **WALK STONES** out of these secure spaces (e.g., for inspection, manufacture, grading, or trade), they usually just wrap them in BRIVKES and slip them into a pocket — though some use money belts, ankle pouches, or underarm cases to foil pickpockets.

Most insurance policies for diamond dealers specify a **CARRY LIMIT** for stones that are **WALKED**. Dealers who need to transport diamonds above this limit first clear it with their insurers, or will divide the stones and make several journeys.

Some take circuitous, zigzag routes and/or hire security guards to accompany them.

## PRICING

Because there are thousands of diamond categories, and the TAM of each stone is subjective, there is no price index for diamonds as there is for fungible commodities like gold.

The most popular pricing benchmark is the Rapaport Price List, established by Martin Rapaport in 1978. Updated each Thursday at midnight, the **RAP** (or **SHEET**) reflects the company's opinion of "high cash asking prices" for a range of "fine-cut, well-shaped" stones, and it is widely used as a basis for quoting and negotiating prices, e.g.:

› **WHAT'S THE RAP?** · What's the list price?

› **I'LL PAY 10 BACK** (*or* **BELOW**) *or* **I WANT 10 OVER** · Indicates a 10% discount or premium on the Rapaport price.

› **ON CONDITION RAP** · Providing that the RAP doesn't change during the course of a negotiation.

**MAGIC SIZES** · Certain **SWEET SPOTS** in weight (0.5, 0.75, 1 carat) at which stones jump in both desirability and price. Diamonds just **LIGHT** of these sizes can be bargains.

**TERMS** · In addition to price, payment terms are central to any deal. Asking for 30, 60, or 90 days in which to pay is often essential to bridge situations of limited liquidity, especially when (much like real estate) sales are predicated on a chain of interdependent transactions.

Untested (or distrusted) buyers will be asked to pay **C.O.D.** (nowadays the "C" usually stands for "cheque," not "cash") or with cleared funds up front.

## CERTIFICATION

As consumers become better informed, the independent analysis of diamonds has become an increasingly crucial part of the trade.

The most respected **CERTS** are those issued by the Gemological Institute of America (G.I.A.), not least because some other organizations have been accused of **BUMPING** (i.e., **OVER-GRADING**).

That said, the G.I.A. notes that it "does not certify or appraise" stones, and offers only "technical information on the dimensions, quality and identifying characteristics of a diamond" from which value may be determined.

Despite a range of security measures (including laser-inscribed serial numbers) the fraudulent mismatching of stones and certs is not unheard of. And so while consumers are often urged never to buy **NAKED** (ungraded) stones, the dealer's golden rule is always:

**BUY THE DIAMOND, NOT THE PAPER.**

⊙

# To Be a Doorkeeper in the House of My God

*Ushers perform a central ministry in churches of all denominations — welcoming, seating, and assisting congregants to create an environment conducive to worship. Often following in the footsteps of their parents, ushers are guided by* Psalm 84:10 — *"I had rather be a doorkeeper in the house of my God, than to dwell in the tents of wickedness."*

*Across America, ushers communicate during services using a sequence of hand signals called the "National Silent Uniform System." Devised by George T. Grier in the 1940s, these signals are still taught to hundreds of volunteers each year by the National United Church Ushers Association of America. Below are the (simplified) central elements of some of these gestures.*

**SERVICE POSITION**

*This "mark of distinction" is adopted by ushers upon entering the sanctuary. It is the default ushering position from which other signals start.*

**GREETING**

*Visitors are welcomed with a warm smile and an open hand.*

**ATTENTION**

*This alerts other ushers that a signal is about to be communicated.*

**PRAYER POSITION**

**USHERS TO TAKE THEIR STATIONS**

**AISLE USHER SIGNS**

*Aisle ushers sign requests to the usher in charge, using one to four fingers held at the chest*

Relief

Programmes

Envelopes

Fans

*The* **COLLECTION PLATE**

## DOORKEEPER SIGNS

*Bending an arm back through the partially closed door, the doorkeeper signals to those outside why they must briefly wait before entering the sanctuary:*

*Prayer*

*Scripture*

*Other*

## AVAILABLE SEATS

*The usher in charge asks all the aisle ushers to signal how many free seats they have:*

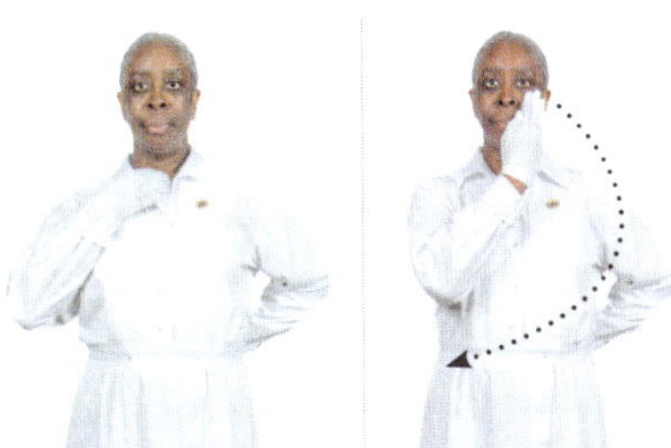

*The aisle ushers respond with the number:*

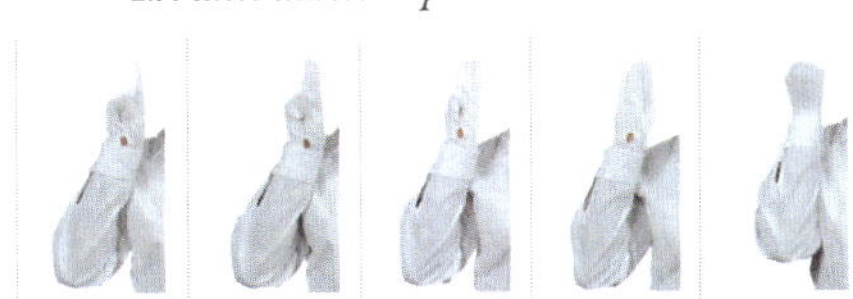

| 1 | 2 | 3 | >3 | 0 |
|---|---|---|---|---|

## DISTRESS SIGNAL

*(as if brushing one's hair)*

## COMMENCE THE OFFERING

With thanks to **Filmore F. Gregory**, President Emeritus of the N.U.C.U.A.A., and **Lillie A. Grant**, National Chairman of the George T. Grier School of Ushering.

# Fans, Stans, Furries, & Shippers

*For decades, being an* **ARDENT FAN** *of a niche pursuit was not merely solitary, it was sneered at by a mainstream for whom eager enthusiasts were* NERDS *at best, and* ANORAKS *at worst. Recently, however, two forces have combined to upend this condescension. First, connected by the internet, disparate fans have established dynamic, creative, and lucrative communities. And second, the ascendency of Gates, Musk, Zuckerberg, et al., suggests the* GEEKS *are busy inheriting the earth. And so, as movies are dominated by superheroes and animation, music is swamped by K-pop and Swifties,* T.V. *is awash with fantasy and sci-fi, and consumption is driven by apps and technology, the time when fans and fandoms could be dismissed or derided is long past.*

## ARCHETYPES

**FAN** · Derived from "fanatic," which the O.E.D. variously defines as one possessed by a deity or demon; one prompted by excessive and mistaken (religious) enthusiasm; or a mad person.

Some **FEN** [sic] are solitary or surreptitious; others embrace sociable **FANDOMS**. For a few, **F.I.A.W.O.L.** — Fandom Is A Way Of Life; for most **F.I.J.A.G.H.** — Fandom Is Just A Goddamn Hobby.

**FANNISH** .............the quality of being a fan
**FAAN**.................. a fan of the fandom itself
**FANOSAUR** ........a long-time, old-school fan
**FANWAR**... an inter- *or* intra-fandom dispute

**FANBOY** *or* **GIRL** · One whose admiration is eager, defensive, unqualified (and immature). E.g., Apple fanboys **SQUEE** (i.e., gush) over *every* new Mac product, no matter how *meh*.

**FAKE GEEK GIRL** · The assertion that (some) women feign geekery for male approbation.

**ANORAK** · British insult for an obsessive (and asocial) fan of anything derided as "uncool" and often based outdoors (buses, planes, &c.) — hence the waterproof garment. *Similarly*, **TRAINSPOTTER** · A train-fixated anorak.

**STAN** · One whose commitment to an idol ranges from seriously devoted (**SOFT STAN**) to psychotically defensive (**HARD STAN**).

Derived from Eminem's 2000 song "Stan," which tells of a rabid fan who, ignored by his singer-hero, commits murder-suicide.

Used also as a verb, e.g., "*I stan Lady Gaga!*"

**OTAKU** · Japanese term [おたく, *home*] for one whose obsessive interest in anime, &c. has a deleterious impact on their social skills / life.

**WEEB / WEEABOO** · A (derogatory) term for (disrespectfully) obsessive Japanophiles.

**BIAS** · Liking only one member of a (K-pop) group. *Hence*, **BIAS WRECKER** · One who attempts to undermine a fan's deep affection.

**GEEKS** *vs* **NERDS** · The difference between these fan-adjacent groups is much disputed, but may not be that dramatic. Both are (obsessively) focused on niche interests, and are often (lazily) bracketed as **NEURODIVERSE** *or* **ON THE SPECTRUM**. Below are the broad-brush media stereotypes:

| GEEKS | | NERDS |
|---|---|---|
| pop culture; tech; FANDOMS | INTERESTS | maths; science; coding |
| first adopters; completionists | PURCHASES | the best; most authentic |
| collectables; gadgets; tech | AMASSES | qualifications; knowledge; skills |
| niche slogan T-shirts; COSPLAY | FASHION | no interest whatsoever |
| practical; problem solving | MINDSET | theoretical; intellectual |
| ± sociable (with like-minded geeks) | PERSONALITY | introvert; un- / anti-social |

In recent years, the **BLERD** [Black + nerd] has become a recognized and distinct trope, catalysed by the likes of Barack Obama, Jordan Peele, Issa Rae, Ryan Coogler, Mica Burton, Ava DuVernay, &c. [1]

*Fans of K-pop band NewJeans park* **PROTEST TRUCKS** *outside the record label Hybe in Seoul, South Korea, 2024. The middle truck says, "Hybe immediately stop malicious manipulating the media that destroys the value of NewJeans."*

**SOLO FAN** · One who **STANS** only one member of a (pop) group. *Similarly*, **AKGAE** · One who denigrates other members of a group (so their idol might have a solo career) — from the Korean term **AKSEONG GAEIN PAEN** [악성개인팬, *malicious individual fans*].

**SASAENG FAN** · A Korean term — 사생팬 — derived from PRIVATE (사, *sa*)+ LIFE (생, *saeng*), and FAN (팬, *paen*) — used to describe obsessive (young, female) South Korean fans.

*Sasaengs* track every detail of their (K-pop) idols' lives (to the point of stalking and trespass), and attempt the closest possible proximity (to the point of physical assault).

*Hence*, **SASAENG TAXIS** · Drivers for hire who enable fans to pursue their idols by car (to the point of reckless, high-speed chases).

*Also*, **PROTEST TRUCKS** 📷 · Sasaeng fans hire billboard vans to drive around Seoul and broadcast their grievances against a band's singers, management, record company, &c.

**LIGHT STICKS** · Every major K-pop band has its own distinctive L.E.D. light stick, which fans illuminate during gigs. *Hence*, **BLACK OCEAN** · When fans turn off their light sticks *en masse* to signal their displeasure.

**FANQUAN** [饭, *meal* + 圈 *circle*] · A Chinese term for cult-like (Gen Z) super-fan groups.

(**I'M**) **TEAM *x*** · When fans pick a side in some (actual or imagined) character **BEEF** (i.e., dispute). E.g., Team Edward (a vampire) *vs* Team Jacob (a werewolf) in *The Twilight Saga*.

**ACTIFANS** *vs* **PASSIFANS** · Those who contribute to a fandom *vs* those who consume it.

**G.A.F.I.A.TING** · Getting Away From It All, i.e., (temporarily) leaving a fandom. *Similarly*, **FANDOM FLOUNCE** · To petulantly quit a fan group over some slight. *Also*. **F.A.F.I.A.** · When life's mundane obligations (e.g., parenthood) mean a fan is Forced Away From It All.

**ANTI-FAN** · One whose antipathy toward a fandom mirrors the adoration of its actual fans. E.g., the subreddit r/travisandtaylor — established to "roast and criticize" Taylor Swift and her Swifties — has 136,000 members.

## FANDOMS

Prior to the internet, **FANDOMS** were limited by mailing lists, handmade **ZINES**, and self-addressed envelopes. Now, linked across cyberspace (and to adapt **RULE 34**) there is no niche too narrow for a fandom not to exist.

Browsing the AO3 website one finds groups devoted to everything from real-life Formula One drivers and *Les Misérables* to Sonic the Hedgehog and *Stranger Things* — not to mention the burgeoning list of celebrity fandoms:

| | |
|---|---|
| **HOOLIGANS** | Bruno Mars |
| **BELIEBERS** | Justin Beiber |
| **BARBZ** | Nicki Minaj |
| **LITTLE MONSTERS** | Lady Gaga |
| **NAVY** | Rihanna |
| **HOTTIES** | Megan Thee Stallion |

FURRIES *at the LondonFurs meet-up in Central London, 2024*

Many fandoms have their own internal lingo, e.g., **WHOVIANS** (fans of *Doctor Who*) use:

› **NOT WE** · Those who are not (devoted) fans.

› **OMNIRUMOUR** · An unsubstantiated belief that a cache of missing episodes from the '60s and '70s is being hoarded (overseas).

› **WIBBLY WOBBLY, TIMEY WIMEY** · A way of shrugging off time-travel plot paradoxes.

**FURRIES** · A fandom in which participants identify as anthropomorphic animals and/or mythical beasts. Furrie terms include:

› **FURSONA / SONA** · An animal avatar that expresses a furrie's persona.

› **FURSUIT** · A (more or less elaborate and engulfing) animal costume.

› **HOMPH** · The act of holding one's fursuit tail (in one's mouth).

› **POODLING** · Showing human skin while in a (partial) fursuit.

› **BOOP** · A nose-tap of greeting or affection.

› **YIFF** · Sexual activity between furries. *Also*, furrie pornography.

**ICEBERG TIERS** · The idea that fandoms encompass mild fans to obsessed fanatics is sometimes illustrated by an iceberg graphic, where the intensity of geekery deepens with depth underwater. E.g., above the surface of a *Breaking Bad* iceberg is Werner Heisenberg, and fathoms below are depictions of Jesse as Jesus, and Walter as both god and the devil.

**ACAFAN** · The academic study of fandoms.

## SHIPPING

**SHIPPING** involves advocating for imagined romantic (relation)**SHIPS** between fictional characters (or real-life celebrities).

The term dates to the late 1990s, when fans of *The X Files* T.V. series fixated on whether Fox Mulder (David Duchovny) and Dana Scully (Gillian Anderson) would get it on.

Since then, shipping has hit every corner of fandom in the form of FANFIC.

**/** · A romantic or sexual SHIP is indicated with a virgule linking the names, e.g., Kirk/Spock from *Star Trek*. The sexual orientation of the SHIP is indicated with tags like: **HET** (M/F); **SLASH** *or* **YAOI** (M/M); **FEMSLASH** *or* **YURI** (F/F), **POLY**(amorous), &c.

**&** · Platonic or familial SHIPS are indicated with an ampersand, e.g., Batman & Robin is a *very* different scenario to Batman/Robin.

**PORTMANTEAUX** · Many SHIPS develop **MASH-UP** shorthand names: e.g., DRARRY = Harry Potter + Draco Malfoy; HANNIGRAM = Hannibal Lecter + Will Graham.

**O.T.P.** · A (formative) **ONE TRUE PAIRING** SHIP to which a fan commits above all others and considers (almost) CANON. *Conversely,* **N.O.T.P.** · **NOT ONE TRUE PAIRING** · A SHIP that prompts **SQUICK** (visceral disgust).

**NOROMO** · One who condones only platonic SHIPPING. *A.k.a.,* **NAXIS** · Not A Kiss In Site.

**MULTISHIPPER** · One who SHIPS multiple pairings (across multiple fandoms).

**JUGGERNAUT SHIP** · A SHIP that achieves widespread support within a fandom. *Conversely,* **SMALL SHIP** · One with little support.

**LAUNCHER OF A THOUSAND SHIPS** · A character SHIPPED with all and sundry. *A.k.a.,* **LITTLE BLACK DRESS SHIP** (looks good on everyone) *or* **FANDOM BICYCLE** (everyone gets a ride). E.g., Steve Harrington in *Stranger Things*, or Hermione in *Harry Potter*.

**CRACK SHIP** · A outlandish SHIP, e.g., SHERIARTY = Sherlock Holmes/James Moriarty. *Similarly,* **RARE PAIR** · SHIPPING minor characters, e.g., Greg Lestrade/Mrs. Hudson.

**CARGO SHIP** · When a character is SHIPPED with an inanimate object, e.g., The Doctor/ Tardis.

**SUNK SHIP** · When a SHIP is doomed, e.g., by a plot revelation unveiled by T.P.T.B. that undermines its premise: "*Canon sinks ships!*"

**PRO-SHIPPER** · One who favours SHIPPING. *Conversely,* **ANTI-SHIPPER** · One who thinks it disrespectful to the CANON (or celebrities) involved, and/or disapproves of certain types of content. *Conversely,* **ANTI-ANTI** · One who opposes censorship, doxxing, and harassment by some activist ANTI-SHIPPERS.

Although the majority of shipping involves fictional characters, fans also engage in **REAL PEOPLE SHIPPING** (**R.P.S.**) — linking their idol(s) with a range of speculative paramours, or rekindling lost loves that live on in the heart of a fandom. {☞ TAYLOR SWIFT, p.32}

Among the most persistent **R.P.S.**-ers are the **LARRIES**, who endlessly speculate about an assumed (and emphatically denied) relationship between Harry Styles and his former One Direction band-mate Louis Tomlinson.

## FANFIC

**FANFIC** (or **FANWORK**) encompasses a vast spectrum of user-generated content inspired by fictional works — from stories and scripts to podcasts (**PODFIC**) and Lego animations.

Given the often personal and private nature of fanfic, it's hard to track the scale of the pursuit. One indicator is **ARCHIVE OF OUR OWN** (**AO3**), a non-commercial, fan-run fanfic repository that, at the time of writing, listed more than 14 million works, covering 68,550 specific fandoms.

**CANON** · The original and inspiring ur-text from which all fanfic derives. Canons can be **OPEN** (still in production) or **CLOSED** (completed), and fanfic works can be more or less **CANON COMPLIANT** *or* **DIVERGENT**.

**T.P.T.B.** · The Powers That Be that create or control the intellectual property of a CANON. *A.k.a.,* **T.I.I.C.** · The Idiots In Charge.

**FANON** · An uncanonical fan creation (that is widely accepted as canon within the fandom).

**HEADCANON** · Uncanonical work (or ideas) that an individual fan considers to be canon.

**R.P.F.** · Real Person Fiction written about celebrities. *Conversely,* **R.W.C.** · Real World Crossover — placing fictional characters I.R.L.

**O/C** · An Original Character added to interact with a **C/C** (Canon Character). *Similarly,* **SELF INSERT** · When authors place (versions of) themselves into their own fanfics.

**MARY-SUE** / **GARY-STU** · A female / male O/C or SELF INSERT who is unrealistically and gratingly attractive, competent, wise, &c.

**O.O.C.** · When a character is depicted acting (radically) Out Of Character from the canon.

**BLANK SLATE** · A character whose limited canonic presence allows for greater fanfic flexibility, e.g., Ellie Bartlet in *The West Wing*.

**FAN LABOUR** · The (unpaid) work of creating FANFIC, running websites, organizing conventions, &c. Often undertaken for **EGOBOO** · The pleasure of being recognized for one's contribution, or seeing one's name in print.

**GEN(FIC)** · General content fanfic that excludes **SEGGS** (and sometimes also romance).

**SEGGS** · A euphemism for sex, used to evade censorship filters. *Similarly,* **PRON** and **P0RN**.

A genre of fanfic adds (more or less graphic) sex to a canon: 16% of stories on AO3 are categorized as **EXPLICIT**, and 3% are tagged as **RAPE / NON CON**. While the intensity of the sexual description is sometimes graded on a **CITRUS SCALE**, where **LEMON** is hardcore and **LIME** softer, **SMUT** and **SPICY** are more common. Other **SEGGS**-related terms include:

› **P.W.P.** · Plot What Plot / Porn Without Plot · A story that gets right down to the **SMUT**.

› **ONLY ONE BED** · A clichéd plot device that helps engineer **CITRUSY** situations.

› **SEX POLLEN** · When a magical substance or supernatural force creates unstoppable erotic desire. Sometimes part of a **FUCK OR DIE** plot, where only fornication can save a life.

**RULE 34** · A meme (popularized by the site 4Chan) that states: "If you can imagine it, it exists as Internet porn."

**WHUMPERFLIES** · The physical discomfort (e.g., butterflies in the stomach) enjoyed by those who like **WHUMP**, **SMUT**, or **DUB CON**.

**PURITY CULTURE** · A move by some to ban (racial, sexual, abusive, age-gap, &c.) fanfic that they deem to be **PROBLEMATIC**.

**DEAD DOVE (DO NOT EAT) / D.D.D.N.E. / D3NE** · A **TRIGGER WARNING (T.W.)** that doubles as an injunction not to complain about (extremely) graphic content. *Similarly,* **DL;DR** · Don't Like; Don't Read · The belief that it's better to abstain from work likely to cause offence, rather than reading it merely to **SPORK**. (*"Don't click the fic!"*)

**SPORKING** · Tearing down (terrible) fanfic.

**!** · An exclamation point is sometimes used to add additional context to a story **TAG**, e.g., **FEMALE!007** tags a gender-swap Bond story.

**BETA READER** · One who volunteers to read fanfic before publication, e.g., proofing for errors of **SPAG** · Spelling, Punctuation, And Grammar. Work that is **UNBETAED** is sometimes tagged, **NO BETA, WE DIE LIKE MEN.**

| *Some fanfic types* | *description* |
|---|---|
| **ORIGINAL FLAVOUR FIC** | so **COMPLIANT** it could be mistaken for canon |
| **ALTERNATE UNIVERSE (A.U.)** | placing **C/C** into a new world (e.g., Jazz Age Bridgerton) |
| **CROSSOVER** | when characters from *Fandom X* are introduced into *Fandom Z* |
| **FUSION** | when *Fandom X* is depicted as if it has always been part of *Fandom Z* |
| **FUSION A.U.** | when *Fandom X* is set in the world of *Fandom Z* — but without *Z*'s characters |
| **FIX IT FIC** | corrects a perceived canonical error or omission; or adds an **H.H.J.J.** ending. |
| **SPITE-FIC** | retaliates against an author or their canon, e.g., writing pro-trans Harry Potter fic |
| **ANGST** | places characters at serious peril or in intense emotional turmoil |
| **WHUMP** | exposes characters to (intense) physical pain and/or mental suffering |
| **HURT/COMFORT** | where one character suffers **WHUMP** or **ANGST**, and is soothed by another |
| **SICK FIC** | revolves around a sick or wounded character (and their care) |
| **DUB CON** | contains dubious (sexual, racial, political) content |
| **DARK FIC** | includes (graphic) sexual abuse, violence, degradation, slavery, torture, &c. |
| **VORE** | depicts a character being (erotically) swallowed whole |
| **DEATH FIC** | depicts a character's demise, sometimes by suicide |
| **CRACK FIC** | outré, outrageous, or comically preposterous |
| **FLUFF** | light-hearted, silly, or good-natured |
| **CURTAIN FIC** | sets characters in scenes of domestic tranquillity, e.g., buying curtains |
| **H.H.J.J.** | Happy Happy Joy Joy; written to inspire **W.A.F.F.** · Warm And Fuzzy Feelings |
| **WOOBIE** | features a beloved character who inspires feeling of protection and nurture |
| **AGED UP** *or* **DOWN** | depicting young characters as older (adults), and vice-versa |
| **BODY SWAP** | when two (or more) characters switch bodies |
| **WHAT IF** | when fanfic meets speculative history |
| **MPREG** | when male characters become pregnant (and give birth) |

*Cosplayers at Chile Comic Con, Santiago, Chile, 2024*

**RECCER** · One who **REC**(ommends) fanfics.

**B.N.F.** · A Big Name Fan, well known in the fandom. *Conversely,* **N.N.F.** · No Name Fan.

**ONE SHOT** · A short, self-contained story.

**DRABBLE** · A story with exactly 100 words.

**LAPSLOCK** · a story entirely in lowercase.

**CONCRIT** · (More or less) Constructive Criticism of fanfic, post publication.

**ORPHANING** · When writers anonymize a story archived online, instead of deleting it.

**BLIND** · (Deliberately) reading fanfic with no prior knowledge of the canon that inspired it.

**SLASH GOGGLES** · When immersion in fanfic mars one's enjoyment of the original canon.

## COSPLAY

A portmanteau of costume + play, **COSPLAY** involves expressing one's fandom (and showcasing one's craft) by dressing as a character or concept, e.g., from a **FICTIONAL REALM** (comic, novel, movie, T.V. show, computer game, &c.); **TEMPORAL PERIOD** (past, future, mythology, &c); or indeed anything else.

For those who struggle to comprehend the concept, or its appeal, consider the observation "*The Met Gala is cosplay for rich people.*"

**CLOSET** *or* **$0 COSPLAY** · A costume created using clothes already in your wardrobe.

**PREMADE / PURCHASED** · A costume that was bought rather than homemade.

**ORIGINAL COSTUME** · One not (directly) inspired by an existing character.

**RULE 63** · A meme (popularized by the site 4Chan) that states: "Every fictional character has a gender-swapped counterpart."

Rule 63 is significant in **FANFIC** and cosplay, as it opens up a world of **GENDER-BENDING**. e.g., male Wonder Women; female Jokers; &c.

**CROSSPLAY** · Cosplaying as a character of a gender other than your own.

**FAN SERVICE** · When cosplayers (are pestered to) pose for photos, quote lines, act scenes, &c., for fellow convention-goers. *Also,* (Sexually explicit) material cynically added by T.P.T.B. (and fanficers) to gratify the audience.

**L.A.R.P.** · Live Action Role Playing; portraying characters and/or re-enacting historical events while dressed in appropriate (period) costume and interacting with other **LARPER**s. Not strictly cosplay to most, but a close cousin.

Although specific **COSPLAY CONVENTIONS** exist — not least Japan's World Cosplay Summit, which, in 2024, featured 36 countries — many cosplayers attend more general comic or anime conventions to see and be seen.

## CONVENTIONS

The structure of fan conventions varies widely, but most will feature many of these activities:

› **PANELS** and **AUTOGRAPH** and **PICTURE SESSIONS** with creators, actors, directors, B.N.F.S, and other **COSPLAY FAMOUS** folk.

› **ARTISTS' ALLEY** · Where vendors sell books, prints, photos, commissions, T-shirts, &c. *A.k.a.*, **TABLING / BOOTHING**.

› **PORTFOLIO REVIEW** · Where aspiring artists can get CONCRIT from professionals.

› **MASQUERADE** · An on-stage competition for handmade costumes, awarding Best in Show, Best Original Design, Best Workmanship, Most Humorous, &c.

› **ZOMBIE WALK** · A parade of living-dead cosplayers; a feature of some conventions.

› **DEAD DOG PANEL** · The final wrap-up panel or event. *Also*, **DEAD DOG PARTY**.

Other attractions include **COSPLAY DATING GAMES; LIP-SYNC COMPETITIONS; LIFE-SIZE COSPLAY CHESS**; &c.

As might be expected, given the myriad fandoms involved, conventions enforce strict rules as to the size, shape, weight, and content of permitted costumes.

Additionally, most will have some form of **PROP-CHECK** area to police such paraphernalia as:

› **SIGNS** · Many conventions restrict or ban the carrying of signs, because they are physically obstructive, politically polarizing, inappropriately sexual, or potentially abusive. The most controversial signs promise **FREE HUGS** or **I'LL SIT ON YOU FOR $5**.

› **PADDLES** · Many conventions ban wooden "spanking paddles" marked **YAOI** or **YURI** — Japanese terms for gay and sapphic attraction, respectively.

› **WEAPONS** · Despite being integral to many costumes, conventions often ban hazardous or hard-edged weapons and replica firearms that risk safety or contravene local laws.

**COSPLAY** *or* **COSTUME IS NOT CONSENT** · The **GOLDEN RULE** of cosplay; intended to curb sexual harassment, abusive touching, intrusive photography, and GLOMPING. Those who ignore this rule are **CREEPERS**, or worse.

**GLOMPING** · An engulfing, hug-like surprise tackle, sometimes preceded by a run-up, and/or celebrated with a victory dance.

Originating in anime cartoons and manga comics, glomping became such an I.R.L. pestilence that the practice is banned at many conventions as dangerous and abusive.

**CREEPSHOTS** · Low-angle, **UP-SKIRT**, or otherwise intrusive or abusive photographs. *Or*, photographs taken without consent.

**FURRCON** · A convention for FURRIES.

**CON CRUNCH** · The last-minute frenzy to complete a costume before a convention.

**LINES** · Queuing is an unavoidable aspect of most conventions; indeed Anime Expo in L.A. is nicknamed LineCon.

The line for Hall H at the San Diego Comic Convention has its own parody X account, with 18,000 followers:

> I am the longest, nerdiest, most demoralizing line at any convention ever made and that's just how you like it. Come get in me.

**L.F.G.** · Looking For Group; a common convention abbreviation. *Also*, Let's Fucking Go!

**REPAIR TABLES** · Designated stations with tools, materials (and staff) to help cosplayers mend their costumes on the fly.

(**STAGE**) **NINJA** · One who helps a cosplayer with their (elaborate) costume, e.g., during a MASQUERADE or other performance.

**FAN** *or* **CON FUNK** · The (overwhelming) aroma of over-dressed and undeoderated fans.

**CON CRUD** · A general term for the spectrum of cold and flu symptoms that sweep through packed conventions. *A.k.a.*, **CON PLAGUE / NERD FLU / COMIC-COUGH**.

**POST-CON SLUMP** *or* **BLUES** · A feeling of depression after a convention has ended. ⊙

# Stunt Shuffles & The Illusion of Danger

*The lingo of* **PROFESSIONAL STUNT PERFORMERS.**

## STUNT COORDINATION

Most film and television stunts originate with a **STUNT COORDINATOR** *or* **ACTION DESIGNER**, who **BREAKS DOWN** a script to assess the type, complexity, and cost of the stunts required — from a simple **SLIP AND FALL** to a mass-casualty oil rig explosion.

This **BREAKDOWN** forms the basis of a **BID** that, if accepted by the producer(s), initiates collaboration with the director, camera crew, and other relevant departments, e.g., costume, make-up, props, **S.F.X** (special effects), &c.

The stunt coordinator is often also responsible for admin tasks like budgeting, devising safety plans, liaising with insurers, &c.

In 2024, Chris O'Hara received the first ever Screen Actors Guild and Directors Guild of America approved **STUNT DESIGNER** credit for his work on *The Fall Guy* {☞ p.16}.

**A.D.J. / ADJ / ADJUSTMENT** · The bonus (**BUMP**) a stunt player receives, over and above the **DAILY** rate. The **A.D.J.** is based on a stunt's complexity and the number of times it is performed.

For example, at current rates, a **FULL-BODY FIRE BURN** might earn a performer an **ADJ** of $5,000–$10,000.

**2ND UNIT** · In many studio movies, the team responsible for the majority of stunt work, which is shot simultaneously but separately from the **1ST UNIT.**

(Where both units film together at the same location, the 2nd is called a **SPLINTER UNIT.** If films require more than one 2nd unit, they are called **ADDITIONAL SECOND UNITS.**)

The 2nd Unit is led by the **SECOND UNIT DIRECTOR** (or **ACTION DIRECTOR**) — sometimes also a stunt coordinator — who works with the cinematographer to ensure the look, feel, and pace of the stunt and action sequences match the rest of the movie.

## REHEARSAL

Stunts are designed and rehearsed in **SLOW MOTION** to plan moves and camera angles:

**WALK THROUGH > HALF SPEED > FULL SPEED**

Players vary their pace based on a **PERCENTAGE** of full-speed. ("*Can you give me 80%?*")

Stunt teams film a **PRE-VIZ(UALIZATION)** (*A.k.a.*, **ACTION-** *or* **STUNT-VIZ**) to show the director, camera crew, &c., how a fight has been **CHOREOG(RAPH)ED.**

Occasionally, with more complex sequences (notably car stunts) these cameras will roll for real in case usable footage is captured.

## GENERAL TERMS

**GAG** · An all-encompassing (and characteristically self-deprecating) term for any stunt — from taking a punch to falling from an exploding helicopter. *Hence,* **CAR / BOAT / FIRE / HORSE GAG**, &c.

**GOING HOT!** · A pre-**ACTION** warning that a stunt (or **S.F.X.**) is about to be performed.

**(ACTION) BEATS** · Individual stunts that together form a **SEQUENCE.**

**SELL** · To make a **GAG** convincing. ("*Hey, can you sell it a little better?*") To **SELL OUT (FOR THE SCENE)** is to give a stunt 110%.

**GET AIR** · To maximize the height (and therefore the effect) of a jump, fall, &c.

**YARD SALE** · A (convincingly) chaotic stunt — named after the skiing term for a fall that leaves equipment strewn across the piste.

**N.D. / UTILITY** · Any **NONDESCRIPT** gag (e.g., a car swerving out of the way) or stunt player (e.g., Man #3 who is punched by a cop).

**BURNED** · When an N.D. player has performed so many (UTILITY) stunts in a scene or movie that they cannot be used again (no matter how elaborate the disguise).

**HONG KONG** · A style of (martial arts) stunt work popularized by Sammo Hung, Jackie Chan, &c. Characterized by wide angles; long, uncut sequences; inventive use of location-based props; and little if any CHEATING.

## CAMERA TERMS

**PRACTICAL** · A stunt performed **FOR REAL** *or* **IN CAMERA**, rather than **CHEATED** with C.G.I. Approvingly known as, **PUTTING THE BUDGET IN FRONT OF THE CAMERA**.

**HOSE IT DOWN** · To saturate a complex or costly GAG with multiple cameras — including, drones, GoPros, and even cellphones.

**ONE AND DONE** · A stunt executed in a single take. *A.k.a.*, **SHOOTING THE REHEARSAL**. *Similarly*, **ONER** · An extended sequence shot in one go. Some apparent oners are actually multiple takes artfully choreographed, filmed, and edited to camouflage cuts. E.g., using a gun's muzzle-flash to hide a **BODY SWAP** between actor and double; or following the trajectory of a punch with a **WHIP PAN** to allow a stunt player to **RESET** for the next BEAT.

**TEXAS** *or* **COWBOY SWITCH** · Where actor and double swap places during a take, hiding the substitution, e.g., behind a column.

**STITCH** · Where an elegant edit conceals the switch between actor and double.

**OFF STICKS** · Taking a camera off its tripod to follow the action **KINETICALLY**. *A.k.a.*, **RUN & GUN**. *Conversely*, **LOCKED (DOWN)** · A camera **ON STICKS**.

**CAMERA LOCK-OFF** · Where a complex or hazardous sequence is split into **BEATS** that are shot individually using a **FIXED CAMERA** before being **MARRIED** or **LAYERED** in **POST (PRODUCTION)**.

**CLEAN PLATE** · A shot of the stunt scene filmed without actors or equipment; used in POST, e.g., to **PAINT OUT** wires, rigging, &c.

**UNDERCRANKING** · Shooting at a framerate lower than the projection rate (e.g., 18–22 *vs* 24 F.P.S.) to make stunts and fight scenes appear faster, crisper, and more intense.

**SPEED RAMPING** · Speeding up or slowing down the footage of a gag for stylistic impact.

**DOUBLE CUT** · When the same stunt is shown twice or more, from a variety of angles. (A classic of the **HONG KONG** genre.)

**BACK TO ONE** · To **GO AGAIN** from **FIRST POSITIONS**.

Some directors repeat stunts *ad absurdum*, as evinced by the D.V.D. commentary between Brad Pitt, Edward Norton, and David Fincher for their 1999 movie *Fight Club*:[1]

> PITT: Alright, the stunt guy here, no pads on the legs.
> NORTON: I've never been more scared than watching that guy!
> PITT: He does the first take, and everyone's amazed — those stairs are hard! Everyone's clapping, and then we just hear: "**ONCE AGAIN!**"
> NORTON: And he did it eight times!
> FINCHER: No, twelve. I was—
> NORTON: Twelve?!
> PITT: And this is when we were really, truly aware of Fincher's sadism.
> FINCHER: Well, but I gotta say—
> PITT: And what take did you use?
> FINCHER: We used take number one!

**MARTINI SHOT** · The last shot of the day — the penultimate is the **ABBY SINGER SHOT**.

## VEHICLE GAGS

**VEHICLE** *vs* **STUNT DRIVER** · SAG-AFTRA states "a vehicle driver is hired when the level of driving requires *skill* but not *stunt* work" — defining **STUNT WORK** by a range of criteria, e.g., "when any or all wheels leave the driving surface" or "when working in close proximity to pyrotechnics or explosives." (The union deprecates the use of the terms **PRECISION** *or* **PERFORMANCE DRIVER**.)

*Hayley Atwell in a car driven by a stunt player on the set of* Mission Impossible *7, 2020*

**WHEEL MAN** · Informal term for stunt driver.

**PICTURE CAR** *or* **VEHICLE** · Any on-screen vehicle, from vintage ambulances to futuristic hover car. No matter how ancient or obscure, picture cars must be safe, drivable, and reliable: on-set breakdowns are risky and costly.

Picture cars are routinely modified for stunt work or specially built for specific gags. And films often require **MULTIPLES** of the same vehicle, in various stages of distress. (In 2011, *The Green Hornet* used 29 Chrysler Imperials.)

**HERO** *or* **PHOTO** *or* **MONEY CAR** · An authentic, unmodified, **PRISTINE** vehicle.

**CRASH** *or* **STUNT CAR** · A vehicle used for a gag, often stripped of all interior detail and kitted with protective gear, e.g., roll cages, racing brakes, bucket seats, 5-point harnesses, electrical cut-out switches, racing fuel cells, &c.

So safe are many modern vehicles that a panoply of security systems (anti-lock brakes, traction control, stability control, air bags, reversing speed limiter, &c.) must be disabled to enable "dangerous" driving. On occasion, mechanics from the car's manufacturer assist.

Vehicles that cannot be modified may have their engines replaced with "plug and play" **CRATE ENGINES**, e.g., the Chevrolet LS3.

**KIT CAR** · A fake vehicle body, with a **CRATE ENGINE**, used when wrecking a costly car.

**JUNKERS** · Specially built chassis and empty shells used instead of actual vehicles.

**N.D. VEHICLES** *or* **DRIVING** · Nondescript cars that **WIPE** (i.e., drive) **THROUGH** a shot to add background verisimilitude. If near the action, N.D. cars will be driven by stunt drivers; when far from any danger, by supporting artists, sometime using their own vehicles.

**CATCH CAR** · An N.D. vehicle strategically positioned to protect, say, an important monument from incidental damage during a stunt.

**TRACKING VEHICLE** · Any camera-fitted vehicle (e.g., S.U.V., go-kart, motorbike, &c.), driven by a stunt driver and used to film (car) stunts. (*A.k.a.*, **CHASE** *or* **CAMERA CAR**.)

Some are fitted with a **RUSSIAN ARM**: a gyro-stabilized, remote-control crane made by the Ukrainian firm Filmotechnic. In March 2022, to protest Russia's invasion, the company renamed its arm the **U-CRANE**.

**CAR** *or* **BISCUIT RIG** · A stunt-driven platform, rigged for cameras, on which a **HERO CAR** is mounted. A **MIC RIG** is similar, though it uses just the frame of a car.

**POD** · A cage affixed to the roof (or other part) of a **HERO CAR**, from which a stunt driver controls the pedals and steering. **POD**s allow 360° shooting, with minimal obstruction. Pod cars usually require podless **DOUBLES** *or* **CLONES** for wide exterior shots.

**PINCHING OFF** · (Temporarily) clamping the front brake hoses, so the main brake pedal controls only the rear brakes.

*Stunt doubles fight over Mexico City's main square for the Bond movie* Spectre, *2015*

**REMOTE CONTROL** · Vehicles operated at a distance by a stunt driver (in a **PURSUIT CAR**).

**BLIND** *or* **BOOT DRIVING** · Operating a vehicle from an unseen position (e.g., the trunk or back-seat footwell) via a video monitor.

**TEETER RIG** · Allows a vehicle to balance safely over a precipice (with actors inside).

**PIPE RAMP** · An ascending length of metal pipe that, when driven onto at speed, flips a vehicle into a **ROLLOVER**.

Ramps can be fitted with **KICKERS** to give additional height and prevent nose diving. And they can be driven onto **DRIVER'S SIDE UP** *or* **DOWN**, depending on the direction of the desired roll.

**CANNON ROLL** · When a car is flipped into a **ROLLOVER** via a nitrogen cannon.

**DRIVING IT IN** · Committing to a crash at full speed, useful for certain action sequences. For a more natural effect, drivers will **SLIDE IT IN**, i.e., act as if trying to avoid the collision without compromising the effect of impact.

**E-BRAKE** · A hydraulic handbrake wired directly to the rear wheels, allowing for more powerful and controllable turns and **DRIFTS**.

**DRIFTING** · A controlled over-steer, where traction is lost by the rear wheels and held by the front. The effect is a stylish sideways glide with smoking tyres and a growling engine.

**EASYDRIFT / SKIN TYRES** · Grip-less tyre sleeves that enable drifting and sliding at lower speeds and in tighter spaces.

**J TURN / REVERSE 180** · Smoothly transitioning from reverse to forward driving.

**SPIN OUT** · When a pursuing vehicle nudges the side rear-quarter panel of a forward vehicle to spin it off the road. *A.k.a.*, **P.I.T.** (Precision Immobilization / Pursuit Intervention Technique) **MANOEUVRE** used by the police.

**BURNOUT** · Spinning the rear wheels to generate smoke and noise.

**ENDO** · Flipping a vehicle **END OVER END** — often a motorbike that brakes hard and flips.

**T-BONE** · A perpendicular collision. *Also*, **SIDE-SWIPE** · A parallel collision.

**SPIRAL** *or* **CORKSCREW JUMP / BARREL ROLL** · Rotating a vehicle on its axis in mid-air; seen most (in)famously in *The Man with the Golden Gun* (1974), where a remarkable gag is ruined by a swanee whistle sound-effect.

**CAR SKI(ING) / TWO-WHEEL DRIVING** · **POPPING** a car onto its side wheels (using a ramp) and driving it under control.

**DEADMAN RIG / CABLE TIE OFF** · A rigging system that halts a vehicle at an exact spot — used, e.g., to stage a very tight **NEAR MISS** of a pedestrian, vehicle, building, &c.

**PEDESTRIAN HIT / KNOCK DOWN** · Where a vehicle hits a performer. *Similarly,* **CAR HIT**.

**BAIL (OUT)** · To exit a (moving) vehicle.

**PROTECTIVE GEAR** · Depending on the danger of the gag, drivers will wear anything from body pads, mouthguards, and helmets to full fire suits and head-and-neck restraints.

## FIGHTS

**FIGHT COORDINATOR** · Works with the STUNT COORDINATOR to plan and manage entire fight sequences (from HITS and reactions to props and locations).

**FIGHT CHOREOGRAPHY** · Devising (and rehearsing) the individual **MOVES** and **HITS** (i.e., punches, slaps, kicks, &c.) that make up a complete fight **SEQUENCE**.

**STACKING** · Using camera placement to compress the space between the **A SIDE** (attacker) and **B SIDE** (victim), and obscure the point of impact. Stacked hits can be feet apart in real life, yet **READ** as authentic on screen.

**SELLING A HIT** *or* **PUNCH** · Ensuring that the energy of an attack is realistically reflected in the victim's REACTION and **RECOIL**.

**REACTION** · The art of making a hit appear convincing. (*"Never react too soon."*)

**CONTACT** · A hit carefully designed to have actual physical impact. *Conversely,* **CLIP** · Unintended physical contact during a hit.

**EGG ON FACE** · When those in a (large) fight sequence don't have enough to do, and look awkward. (*"I got a bunch of* **EGG** *in that scene."*)

**GHOST BEATS** · Improvised moves that complement the **LEAD** fight scene without interfering with its choreography; a more active way to reduce EGG ON FACE.

Similarly, **STUNT SHUFFLE** · Keeping busy in the background with harmless hand and leg moves while waiting for your turn to fight.

**BRAWL** · A chaotic and seemingly naturalistic style of fighting, characterized by **CHUNKY**, brutal moves; often involving multiple players.

**HAY MAKER / JOHN WAYNE** · An (overly) exaggerated punch. While such cartoonish fighting is no longer fashionable, stunt hits are usually **WIDER** than real-life fights, to allow the camera to **PICK UP** the moves.

**HONG KONG FIGHTING** · Tight and elegantly choreographed fighting, characterized by formal martial arts moves, a rhythmic tempo of hits and blocks, and (often) elements of humour or comic relief.

**SLOW IS SMOOTH, SMOOTH IS FAST** · A mantra that reminds stunt fighters (and actors) that rapid, jerky hits don't register on camera as well as fluent and intentional moves. (*"Pretend you're fighting through molasses"* or *"Move as if you're fighting underwater."*)

**FRAME DROPPING** · An editing technique whereby individual frames are deleted prior to the moment of impact to create a snappier hit; more realistic than simply speeding film up.

**GRUNTS** · The vocal expression of a hit and its reaction. Some sequences require stunt players to grunt out loud, others (e.g., when a performer is doubling ) are performed **M.O.S.** (which might stand for "Mit Out Sound" or "Mute On Sound").

Some performers foreshadow their moves with **GRUNT TALK**, e.g., using the *"Hi"* of *"Hi-Yah"* to alert their victim to the speed and direction of the approaching hit.

**GRUNT PASS** · Where grunts, groans, and other bits of **FIGHT DIALOGUE** are recorded in POST and dubbed in.

**CAMERA MOVEMENT** · Where the camera **DANCES** with the action to add dynamism to a fight, e.g., by tilting or WHIP-PANNING to match the trajectory and velocity of a hit.

**SHAKY CAM** · A hyper-kinetic and sometimes super-close filming style where the viewer is less a spectator to the fight than a bewildered participant — (over)popularized by the *Jason Bourne* franchise.

A slightly less claustrophobic shooting style is **DOCU(MENTARY) CAM**, which follows the fighting from a wider distance.

Hung and Chan's HONG KONG fights are shot with (fixed) wide-angle framing — and resist the urge to cut on every single hit.

## FALLS

Falling safely and convincingly is an elementary skill stunt players master in training. The aim is to match the drama's action realistically while minimizing physical risk.

There are any number of general (**FRONT**, **SIDE**, **BACK**) and more specialist (**HORSE**, **MOTORBIKE**, **STAIR**) falls, and a few falls have earned specific terms:

**HIGH FALL** · Usually one >~40 feet; falls 15–40 feet may be called **LOW HIGH FALLS**. High falls usually terminate in **AIR BAGS** or stacked cardboard boxes (i.e., **BOX CATCH**).

**FLAT BACK** · A fall where the feet are swept away and the entire back hits the deck.

**SUICIDE FALL** · Usually a straight back high fall that approximates a real-life descent (i.e., with little elaboration).

**FACE OFF** · A HIGH FALL performed face first, before flipping over just before impact. (*"Plummeting toward the ground and playing chicken for as long as you can."*)

**PENCIL FALL** · Straight down, feet first.

**SEOCHI FALL** · A sideways head-over-heels leap and fall.

**HONG KONG (H.K.) FALL** · A horizontal double-spin before WRECKING to the ground.

**TANDEM FALL / LOVE ROLL** · A (stair) fall performed by two actors who are interlocked in a fight or otherwise entangled.

**GILLIGAN FALL** · When two stunt performers fall simultaneously.

**PRATFALL** · A fall that (comedically) draws attention to itself.

**TIMBER** · A straight backward or forward fall from an upright position (like a tree).

**WINDOW CRASH** · (Auto) defenestration, usually through frangible **CANDY GLASS**.

**FACE PLANT** · Falling face first without SAVING YOURSELF, usually into well-camouflaged padding.

**TACO FALL** · When a performer lands on their back and rolls their legs up over their head to demonstrate the force of the hit.

**SCORPION FALL** · When a performer lands on their front and arches their heels back over their head.

**WRECK** · An impressive and well-sold fall.

**GROUND POUNDER** · A performer capable of high-energy, big impact falls; one who is willing and able to **CRACK THE CEMENT**.

**SAVING YOURSELF** · There are various ways to **SCRUB OFF** a fall (i.e., reduce its speed and physical impact), including the **TOE TAP** *or* **SLAP OUT**, where a foot *or* hand is momentarily grounded just before impact.

**CLIP** · A fall (or stunt) that ricochets off an object mid-WRECK. E.g., tumbling from a window and clipping a lower balcony as you fall.

**FRAMING OUT** · Using camera angles to obscure the point of impact, thereby hiding safety equipment (e.g., crash mats).

**PICKUP SHOT** · A post-fall reaction, where a gag's impact is acted free from any safety gear.

## RIGGING & WIRE WORK

Rigging is deployed to move actors and stunt performers safely across space — whether flying through the air, spinning in zero gravity, dragging along gravel, or smashing through (CANDY *or* **BREAKAWAY**) glass windows.

Some productions use rigging sparingly and naturally (e.g., to safely stage a simple trip); others deploy it to ensure that the super-heroic seems fleetingly credible.

Known also as **WIRE WORK**, rigging shares techniques, equipment, and expertise with climbing, sailing, rescue, and engineering. Indeed many professional riggers have transitioned from these fields into the film industry.

And although the art of rigging has expanded from ropes and pulleys to computer-controlled winching systems, the science remains doggedly tied to the laws of physics and the complex mathematics of minimum breaking strengths, working-load limits, margins of safety, &c.

*Benedict Cumberbatch* RIDES THE WIRE *for the third season of* Sherlock, *2013*

**PRE-RIGGING** · Scouting a location and working with lighting and **SET DEC**(oration) to plan where the rig is to be constructed and how the ropes will run.

**MICRO** *vs* **MACRO RIGGING** · Small-scale, gags *vs* complex, multi-stunt sequences.

**ROPES / WIRES / LINES** · The cables that suspend and control a performer, constructed from a range of (synthetic) materials. Lines are **TRAVELLED** across a rig; **REDIRECTED** by pulleys, &c.; and **DROPPED** into position.

**TECH / TEK** · Thinner rope used for direct connection to a performer. E.g., 12-Strand Technora, which is 8× stronger than steel.

Tech allows for greater freedom of movement (especially when a player is connected with multiple lines) and reduces **PAINTING**.

Short lengths of tech are called **LEADERS**.

**FIDDING** · The art of **SPLICING** braided and plaited rope, e.g., to join lengths **END TO END**, or to create an **EYE SPLICE** loop at one end. Performed by interweaving the rope's strands using a hollow metal **FID**, and securing the overlap with **LOCK STITCHING**.

Fidding is stronger than knotting, and it ensures a smooth rope of consistent width that can thread safely through rigging systems.

**RIDING THE WIRE** · The art of (inter)acting convincingly when on a line, i.e., moving naturally and not **SANDBAGGING** — unless the gag calls for such dead-weight inaction.

**PULLING / JERKING** · When a performer is pulled on a wire in a specific direction (and at a set speed), e.g., after being shot.

**HAND** *or* **ARM PULL** · When a performer is moved on a line (usually across a short distance) using human effort, e.g., after being hit.

More powerful, controllable, and repeatable gags use compressed-air **RATCHET PULLS**, or mechanical (computerized) **WINCH PULLS**.

**FEATHERING THE LINE** · Subtly manipulating a **HAND PULL** to match the movements of a performer and make a gag look natural.

**FIGHTING THE LINE** · Subtly bracing against the jerk of a line to **SELL** a gag. (The difference between being thrown up and back by a dramatic blast and passively tripping backward like a rag doll over a low obstacle.)

**QUICK POP** · A small wire gag that helps a performer briefly overcome gravity.

**JERK VEST** · A specialist **STUNT HARNESS**, constructed from artificial fabrics like nylon and Spectra. Harnesses are stitched with dozens of load-bearing **PICK POINTS** to which performers are **HOOKED** onto lines with **SHACKLES**, allowing them to be **FLOWN** or **JERKED** at a variety of angles.

There are various specialist versions, e.g., the **HONG KONG HARNESS**, worn only at the waist, to allow for ease of movement; and the **SUPER SWIVEL**, which has gimbals at the hips to allow a player to spin head over heels.

*Shauna Duggins takes a fall for Adrianne Palicki in (and as)* Wonder Woman *(2011)*

**GOOCH WRAP** · A wire gag where the line travels between the legs, e.g., for a **JERK** that spins a player chaotically back heels-over-head.

**BACKING UP PICKS** · Using a second shackle on a harness to secure a **HEAVY PULL**.

**DESCENDER** · A friction device that slows a rope for safe, controlled, and stylish descents.

**TRANSFER** · To travel between two moving objects. E.g., car to car; horse to horse; motorbike to car; helicopter to train, &c.

**MAGIC CARPET** · When a performer runs on a tarpaulin that is towed by a lead vehicle; a **PRACTICAL** way of showing (unusual) speed.

**DRAG** · Where a player is pulled along the ground; sometimes using a **MAGIC CARPET**.

**DEADMAN** · When a player, who is attached by a line to a fixed object, travels at speed until the line runs out and they are **HARD STOPPED** back. ("*The most violent wire gag.*")

**TUNING FORK** · A U-shaped rig attached to a performer's hips and **PUPPETEERED** by the crew. Forks enable a fuller and more natural range of movement, with no face-obscuring wires — and they are often used by actors as well as stunt players.

**PUPPETEERING** · When a performer on a wire or in a **TUNING FORK** has (some of) their movements controlled by the crew.

**AIR AWARENESS** · The art of knowing where you are in space, allowing a performer to land precisely on their mark, facing the right direction, even during the most gyroscopic of gags. (Especially useful in "zero gravity" scenes.)

**SUPERHERO** *or* **THREE POINT LANDING** · A stylized pose that action- and superheroes adopt after descending from a height: back leg kneeling; front foot planted flat; front hand (or fist) touching (or punching) the ground; rear arm elevated for balance and badassness.

**BAG TEST** · Using **DROP TEST BAGS** filled with sandbags, water bottles, &c. to test a rig at the required weight, without risk.

**ROPE MANAGEMENT** · The (not inconsiderable) task of storing, moving, and handling sometimes hundreds of feet of rigging lines.

**GLAZING THE JACKET** · When a rope's synthetic cover melts as a result of friction.

**SAFETY LOGS** · Ropes, harnesses, shackles, and other rigging gear all wear with use, and can be degraded by ultraviolet light, water, and extreme temperatures.

Professional riggers keep detailed logs of the age and use of each piece of kit, ensuring regular maintenance, recertification, and end-of-life renewal. (Such logs are often also an insurance requirement.)

**WIPING WIRES** · Deleting cables in **POST**. *A.k.a.*, **PAINTING OUT**.

## FIRE

Despite advances in C.G.I., the visceral realism of **PRACTICAL** fire gags is still favoured by many directors — even if the sequence is "augmented" in POST. Fire stunts are usually planned, rehearsed, and supervised by a **FIRE COORDINATOR** (*or* **CHIEF FIRE RIGGER**) who answers to the STUNT COORDINATOR.

**LAYERING** · Key to any fire stunt is the safety of each performer, whose skin, hair, eyes, ears, nose, and mouth must be protected from heat, smoke, and flame. Safety is sought by stacking multiple wet and dry fire-resistant layers between flesh and fire. Each coordinator has a preferred sequence of materials, e.g.:

1 .............. CARBONX / P.B.I. undergarments
2 .............. PANTHER FELT welding blanket
3 .............. thick layer of FIRE GEL
4 .............. GASKET SUIT
5 .............. CARBONX garment
6 .............. (FIRE TREATED) costume

**CARBONX / NOMEX** · Trademarked brands of high-performance, non-flammable gear, worn also by steelworkers, welders, fire-fighters, and the crew of oil and gas rigs. *Also*, **P.B.I.** · Flame-resistant polybenzimidazole.

**FIRE GEL** · Non-flammable (refrigerated) viscous goop applied to fabric (and skin) to protect against heat and flame. *A.k.a.*, **ZEL-JEL**, after the brand created by Gary Zeller.

**PANTHER FELT** · A material woven from polyacrylonitrile fibres that can withstand temperatures up to 1,800°F / 980°C.

**GASKET SUIT** · A lightweight (vinyl) **RAIN SUIT** that provides a waterproof barrier between FIRE GEL layers and the outer layers.

**WARDROBE** · The outer wardrobe is the only layer intended to burn, though this too can be FIRE-TREATED for additional protection.

Since natural fibres burn "better" than artificial fabrics (which tend to melt), wardrobe departments often supply wool or cotton stunt versions of synthetic costumes.

**FIRE TREATMENT** *or* **BLOCK** · Spraying fire retardant chemicals onto costumes as a top layer of protection. Some blocks are infused with a fluorescent dye, visible under black light, allowing coverage to be assessed.

**FIRE HOOD** · Made from CARBONX or P.B.I. to protect the head and shoulders; fitted with Pyrex lenses or worn with fire goggles.

If required for a scene, silicone masks and associated wigs in the likeness of a lead actor (or monster) can be worn over the hood.

**HOT SPOT** · An area of heat build up under the protective layers. ("*It's not the flames that burn you, it's the heat!*") Hot spots are a serious safety concern, and they do not instantly dissipate once the fire has been extinguished.

**CHOREOGRAPHY / FIRE DANCE** · Performers carefully plan and rehearse the moves they will make while on fire to safely achieve the dramatic action a scene requires.

**PARTIAL BURN** .............. leg / arm / back
**HALF BURN** .............. bottom / top / back
**BODY BURN** .............. multiple body parts
**JACKET BURN** .............. both arms and back
**¾-THS** .............. legs and JACKET (not chest)
**FULL BODY BURN / FULL WRAP / HUMAN TORCH** .............. entire body engulfed

**NAKED** *or* **SKIN BURN** · One performed using only FIRE GEL. The most hazardous is the **FACE BURN**, which players perform with their eyes shut. ("*You can see the flames through your eyelids.*")

It's dangerous to inhale during a face burn, but skilled performers can sometimes scream.

**OPEN FACE BURN** · One not requiring a HOOD.

**BREATH** · Performers will usually hold their breath throughout the stunt, to avoid inhaling smoke and flame. Longer and more complex gags may require respirators.

**COLOUR-CODED FIRE BURN** · When fuel is mixed with chemicals to change a flame's colour. E.g., lithium for red, copper for blue, and boron for green. Because of potential toxicity, performers will often wear respirators (or the colour will be modified in POST).

**SAFETY TEAM** · Each performer has several dedicated members of safety crew armed with $CO_2$ extinguishers (and soaking-wet towels).

**FUEL** · Complex burns require first a **BASE LAYER** of **RUBBER** *or* **CONTACT CEMENT**, which is **PAINTED** onto the costume; and second, a **FUME LAYER** of flammable **ACCELERANT** (e.g., paraffin, gasoline, diesel), which is sprayed on top. Once the top layer is lit, it will ignite the longer-burning base.

**SEQUENCE** · Different crews have their own running order; one sequence might be:

**ROLL CAMERAS! / FUELLING!**
*instruction to camera crew to start filming*

**SAFETIES READY?**
*wait for verbal confirmation from each member*

**STUNTS READY?**
*wait for thumbs-up from performer*

**LIGHTING!**
*sets performer(s) ablaze*

**GO! / YOU'RE ON FIRE** *or* **UP!**

~ STUNT PERFORMANCE ~
*sometimes accompanied by a verbal countdown of the number of seconds left*

**DOWN! / OUT!**
*performers hit the deck; safety team goes in*

**HOT SPOTS?**
*performers indicate areas of overheating, which are then* **HIT** *with additional* $CO_2$, *or packed with handfuls of* FIRE GEL *under the layers*

**STUNTS GOOD?**
*wait for thumbs-up confirmation*

**CLEAR!**

**DE-PREP** · Removing the protective layers. Even after a performer has been doused with $CO_2$, the fuel-soaked wardrobe layer remains highly flammable. Some jurisdictions require costumes to be **DEGREASED** before disposal.

**DISTRESS SIGN** · The universal sign of fire-stunt distress is to **GO DOWN**, i.e., fall to the floor and **TAP OUT**.

If a stunt involves being on the floor, players will signal distress by tapping out, or adopting a pre-arranged safety pose (e.g., a starfish).

**DURATION** · The time a performer can safely remain alight depends on a range of factors, including the extent of the burn; the formulation of fuel; the thickness of the **FIRE GEL**; the ambient temperature; and the velocity of any wind on location.

Although full body burns lasting over 5 minutes have been performed, most on set gags last 15–30 seconds.

**ELECTRIC MATCH / SPARK KIT / FLAME CANNON** · Some of the many methods of ignition, selected to fit the action (e.g., a dragon scene suggests a **FLAME THROWER**).

**EXPLOSIONS** · Usually the province of the special effects department (which deals with all fire work not involving humans). Stunt coordinators will work with **S.F.X.**, e.g., when performers must react to the force of a blast.

**INJURIES** · While serious accidents are uncommon, minor injuries are a hazard of regular fire work. These include **FLAME** *or* **FIRE LICKS** caused when flame or heat "brushes" fire-gelled skin, leaving a sensitive, red (**SUNBURNED**) patch. Or **SWEAT BURNS**, caused by perspiration trapped against the skin under layers (often in the armpits) that is heated to scalding point. More harmful (2nd-degree) burns are euphemistically called **HEAT BLISTERS**. All injuries are assessed by the **SET MEDIC**; bad burns are treated in hospital.

## STUNT DOUBLES

A **DOUBLE** is any stunt player who **STANDS IN** for an actor.

While obviously vital in perilous situations, doubles also stand in for actors who are frail or injured, and those who, for contractual or insurance reasons, are unable to take even minor risks. As a result, comparatively safe moments of action (jumping on a bed, riding a bike over cobblestones) can sometimes require a double.

Certain actors over-estimate their ability to match the proficiency of stunt professionals — especially when fighting or falling. And stories abound of doubles secretly re-shooting gags that actors *think* they have sold.

But even when highly capable action stars (e.g., Tom Cruise, Charlize Theron) *do* perform their own gags, doubles will often test and camera-rehearse sequences to save time and diminish **KEY-MAN RISK**.

Some actors mesh so well with their doubles that they develop lasting partnerships. E.g., Shauna Duggins {☞ p.220} has doubled for Jennifer Garner for more than 24 years.

And some movies are so complex that more than one double is needed. Keanu Reeves had multiple doubles on *The Matrix* (1999) — one of whom, Chad Stahelski, went on to direct Reeves in the stunt-saturated *John Wick* films.

*Stunt coordinator Tim Trella walks the red carpet at the 2005 Taurus World Stunt Awards*

**1X** · The lead, on-set double for **NUMBER 1** (i.e., the lead actor). If several units are filming at once, there can be more than one 1X.

**KID DOUBLE** · When a smaller (female) adult stunt performer doubles for a child.

**LIMITS** · In addition to looking and acting like their lead, doubles will ensure their stunts match the character's capabilities. Often this involves **TONING DOWN** their fighting or falling skills to make a gag appear plausible.

**FACE REPLACE** · Overlaying a 3.D. scan of an actor's face onto the action of a double (who wears **REFERENCE DOTS** to aid the C.G.I.). *A.k.a.*, **FACE MAPPING**.

**DIGI(TAL) DOUBLE** · Using visual effects (including A.I.) to augment (or entirely replace) the **PRACTICAL GAGS** of doubles; an increasingly controversial industry issue.

## EQUALITY

As with Hollywood (and society) at large, the stunt world is working to address its long exclusion of ethnic minorities and women. Two archaic and offensive practices stand out:

**PAINTDOWN** · "Blacking up" white stuntmen to double "ethnic" or "coloured" leads.

**WIGGING** · Dressing stuntmen as women to double female leads.

One of the greatest challenges for female stunt players is the most prosaic: costume.

Whereas male players can ask wardrobe for 2×-size clothing to conceal their safety gear, female players often have to sell gags in skimpier clothes, strappier shoes, and thinner (or non-existent) protective padding. ("*Try selling a car hit in skinny jeans.*")

Occasionally, coordinators will request a script change to allow for safer clothing: "*Can she take a jacket with her when she leaves?*"

Recently, a reluctance by some writers and directors to depict violence against women has reduced opportunities for female players.

## OSCARS

It's a long-standing source of consternation in the stunt community that the Academy of Motion Picture Arts and Sciences honours neither stunt coordinators nor stunt players.

This omission becomes ever-more insulting as global box-offices are dominated by action and superhero movies that are often little more than breathtaking stunt sequences briefly bothered by banal or implausible plot.

(The first *Mad Max* movie [1979] has 9 stunt players listed on IMDb, and the latest, *Furiosa: A Mad Max Saga* (2024), has ~118.)

It seems both equitable and inevitable that the Oscars will one day recognize stunt performers; in the meantime the Taurus World Stunt Awards honours a range of categories, including Best Fight, Best High Work, Best Work With a Vehicle, and Hardest Hit. ⊙

# Terms of Service

*The secret slang and customer codes of* **RESTAURANTS** *around the world.*

### ESTELLA

MANHATTAN, U.S.A.

**DANCE FOR GRANDMA** · Get your dancing shoes out, perform a tap dance, and wow that guest. *Also*, take care of them with love and kindness, like you would for your grandma.

### LE MANOIR AUX QUAT'SAISONS

OXFORDSHIRE, U.K.

**MRS. A** ........ allergic
**MRS. D** ........ dislike
**MRS. P** ........ preference
**MRS. R** ........ religious food restrictions

**NAY** . No Aperitif Yet | **GT** ....... Garden Tour
**NMY** .. No Menus Yet | **CT** ......... Cellar Tour
**NRY** ... Not Ready Yet | **KT** ...... Kitchen Tour

**SANGERS** ........ a **SELECCY** of sandwiches
**CLINGERS** ........ cling film
**SWANNERS** ........ looks good / tastes good [a take on the French term *soigné*, i.e., elegant]
**YEAH OUI** ... used in agreement or to confirm
**GOLD LABEL** ........ the "good" olive oil
**MISE EN** ........ the prep

**EYES ON** · A request of assistance when you need a second opinion.

**6:10** · A clean down focused in the afternoon that starts off the **CLOSEDOWN** procedure.

**ON GUARD** · *"Who's on guard?"* Chefs who stay in the kitchen to deal with any room service checks while the rest of the team is **OVER THE ROAD** (i.e., on break).

### MICHAEL'S

MANHATTAN, U.S.A.

**CARBS** ........ no potatoes, no toast
**LAWN** ...... chopped salad, chopped extra fine — as if shredded by a lawnmower
**TEXAS** ........ burn it! (for a Texan regular)
**RUDY** ..... a regular who likes his potatoes hot
**BIG BOSS ORDER** ....... when the owner is in

### THE LITTLE OWL

MANHATTAN, U.S.A.

**TWO-HOUR-WAIT FACE**
The doleful look walk-in diners have when told the waiting time for a table.

**SHOW THE LOVE + SPARKLING**
Extra attention, and a free glass of prosecco.

**UNCLE FRANKIE**
A special glass used for complimentary wine — favoured by the owner's Uncle Frankie.

### TURK FATİH TUTAK

ISTANBUL, TURKEY

**SHOW TIME!** · The first guests are arriving.

**SWIMMING** · Signals that someone is struggling **IN THE WEEDS** and needs support.

**ARKA!** · [behind, in Turkish]; used to avoid collisions; *Similarly*, **CORNER!**

**SUS** ("*Table 22, sus.*")
A joking term regarding a diner who appears to be a food critic or health inspector.

**ACT 2** · ("*TBL 51, act 2*") Signal to transfer guests from Turk's courtyard area (**ACT 1**) to the restaurant dining hall. After which, **ACT 3** transfers them to the kitchen tour.

**SPICES** ("*Chef, spices TBL 30, 3pax*")
Signals the kitchen team to prepare a selection of surprise gifts, e.g., house-made olive oil, tarhana, and local spices.

**ALL IN** · Informs the chef on the pass that all reservations are currently in the restaurant.

**MAINTENANCE** · ("*TBL 12, maintenance*")
Alert a service member that a table requires cleaning, water top up, or other beverages.

### SAMMY'S ROUMANIAN STEAK HOUSE

MANHATTAN, U.S.A.

**MR. SCHWARTZ AND HIS NIECE**
Old Jewish man with his girlfriend.

**BIG MACHER**
The one paying the cheque; a big shot.

**MISHPUCHA** ........ regulars, like family
**SHIKSAS** ........ a table of non-Jewish women
**OY VEY** ........ troublemakers

TWEEZER FOOD

## QUAGLINO'S

LONDON, U.K.

**QUAG 1**
Good professional / social status
£100 average spend · ×10 visits

**QUAG 2**
Very influential in his/her industry
C.O.O., C.E.O., Chairman, M.D.
£120 average spend · ×10 visits
Locally influential

**QUAG 3**
Celebrities, investors, A-listers, sports, T.V, press, food critics · £150 average spend
×10 visits (not mandatory)
People of whom everyone needs to be aware

**REGULAR LUNCH / DINNER / BAR**
Been more than four times

**BACCHUS 1** · Wines spend average: £100

**BACCHUS 2** · Wines spend average: £150

**BACCHUS 3** · Wines spend average: £170+

## DON ALFONSO 1890

SANT'AGATA SUI DUE GOLFI, ITALY

*We Italians tend to give nicknames to people, which then replace their real names forever. And, in the kitchen, things can get personal.*

**PLUTO** · A boy at the appetizers who has the moves and looks of Pluto from Mickey Mouse.

**CHECCO LECCO** · Francesco ... from Lecco.

**CAPA DI VACCA** · Because he has a giant *head* and the movements of a *cow*.

**MASTONE** · A master ... who is enormous.

**PISTACCHIONE** · The bald guy in the kitchen whose head resembles a shelled pistachio.

## THE RIVER CAFÉ

LONDON, U.K.

**BRUSKI** · Bruschetta. (Hence, the chefs call themselves the **BRUSKI BROTHERS**.)

## GRAMERCY TAVERN

MANHATTAN, U.S.A.

**L.O.L.** · Lots of Love · A guest who has been super friendly or excited on a previous visit.

**S.F.N.** · Something For Nothing · Any form of generosity, e.g., extra splash of wine, complimentary cake on a birthday, &c.

**BUBBLE GREET** · Pour a complimentary glass of champagne or cider on arrival — usually for an anniversary.

**D.N.D.** · Do Not Disturb · Adopt a reserved or distant service style — usually for business meetings or date nights.

**BE A SWAN** · Move gracefully and calmly (the way a swan glides on the surface) — while also working hard and fast (the way a swan kicks beneath the surface).

**HONEYMOON MARK** · When a couple is holding hands, or deep in conversation, **MARK** (i.e., place) all silverware to the outside of each guest rather than breaking them up by reaching across to mark normally.

**POP THE BUBBLE** · Breaking a meal's flow by intruding while guests are eating a course or deep in conversation. As bad as turning on the lights in a movie theatre!

**RIDE THE WALRUS** · Managing or controlling the restaurant when it's extremely busy (e.g., holiday season.) — as difficult as riding a walrus!

### LE BERNARDIN

MANHATTAN, U.S.A.

**DOWNTOWN / UPTOWN**
Refers to different parts of the hot line. (*"Pick up monk uptown!"*)

### BIBI

LONDON, U.K.

**RUPEE** · V.I.P.

**WELCOME BACK** · Regular guest.

**MOBY DICK** · Big spender.

**MARIAH** · Only visits in December.

**UB40** · Wine pairing, red wine only.

**CHACHA / TAYA** [younger / older uncle] Young / older North Indian guest.

**DOOBA** · Extra sauce.

**MERRYMEN** · Extra hot.

**MULL HOUSE** · Last order in.

**MHIXY** · Vegetarian, but chicken is O.K.

**JOBBIE** · Any item, person, ingredient, &c.

**WET LETTUCE** · Grumpy guest.

**86** · Drunk guest.

**DOWNTOWN** · Run out of prep on a section.

**CHEF MIKE** · Microwave.

**PRESSÉ** · Right now.

**T22** · Warning not to sit highly talkative guests near the chef when he needs to work. (Named after the T2000 in *Terminator*.)

**DUNGEON** · Prep kitchen.

**KING OF THE CASTLE** · Needs a high chair.

**TABLE 101** · The office. (Normally when the chef needs a coffee.)

**KETHI** [gardening] · Herb salad.

**COOKING ON 11** · Highest heat.

**SAMOSA** · Table needs crumbing.

### ARLINGTON

LONDON, U.K.

**B.F.R.** · Breakfast Regular.

**B.I.N.** · Bar if Necessary.

**D.N.R.** · Do Not Ring (up a bill).

**H.W.C.** · Handle with Care.

**T.T.B.C.** · Theatre To Be Confirmed — i.e., time depends on the play's duration.

**T.T.** · Tricky to TURN.

**S.T.H.M.Y.** · Sorry To Have Missed You — when the owner cannot be present to meet valued guests, and so leaves a signed note.

**GINP** · Guinea Pig (used during soft openings for new restaurants).

**MR. BROWN IS IN THE HOUSE** · A code for staff to communicate that there is a small fire, without alarming guests. (Never used.)

### QUINCE & CO.

SAN FRANCISCO, U.S.A.

**SLIMS** · Called out when guests are looking into the kitchen from outside, but can't be seen because of the glare on the glass.

**DON'T JOHNNY DEPP ME** · If two dishes are due at the same time but one cook "jumps the gun" and goes faster than the other. (A reference to *21 Jump Street.*)

**IT'S A** [Tracy] **CHAPMAN**
When a guest wants to go fast.

**KUMQUAT / RADISH / SAFFRON** / &c.
Random fruits and vegetables called out to warn staff to yield to an oncoming guest.

**SLOW TRAIN COMING** · A leisurely diner.

**OFF ROAD** · A spontaneous menu.

**LOVE CATS** · A couple on a hot date.

**BONES IN THE HOOD** · Save the beef bones to take home to Ginger, the dog.

**SCOOBY SNACK** · When the chef asks one of the cooks to make him a snack.

**GRANDE FORCHETTE**
A diner who is going all out! The works!

### TIDE + TIME

MANHATTAN, U.S.A.

**CHEF'S MOM** · When plating for a suspected food critic.

**FULL SEND / SEND IT**
Show them everything we got!

**86 BACON** · Alerts staff that the Dept. of Health is in. (There is no pork on the menu.)

### UBIQUITOUS TERMS

**F.O.H. / FRONT OF HOUSE**

**FAMILY MEAL** · A (hearty) communal meal that staff eat for free before or after a shift.

**CALLOUTS** · Employees phoning in to report they won't be able to work.

**SIDE WORK** · Slack-time chores, e.g., folding linen or doing a [chewing] **GUM CHECK** under chairs and tables. To leave without completing this work is to **SKATE**.

**CUT** · To be released early from a slow shift.

**P NUMBER** · A code that identifies the **POSITION** of each guest at a table, e.g., by their location in relation to the kitchen door.

**AUCTIONING** · Announcing dishes as they are delivered to determine which guest gets which item; a sign of poor **P NUMBERING**.

**COVERS** · The total number of diners.
**OPEN MENUS** · Guests who are yet to order.
**TOP** · The number of diners at a table, e.g., **4-TOP / DEUCE** (i.e., **2-TOP**) / **SOLO**.
**DOUBLE** (&c.) **SEATING** · When two or more groups are seated simultaneously in a section.
**TURN** · A completed seating–leaving cycle.
**CAMPING** (**OUT**) · When diners never leave.
**SCRIPTING** · Telling guests the specials, and **SELLING** dishes the kitchen wants to move.
**TOUCHING TABLES** · Checking in on diners in a section, or across the restaurant.
**DÉGUSTATION** · A multi-course (and usually multi-hour) **TASTING MENU**.
**INTERMEZZO** · A light **PALATE CLEANSER** served between courses.
**GUÉRIDON SERVICE** · Where a dish is cooked or finished **TABLE SIDE**.
**FULL HANDS IN, FULL HANDS OUT!** · Never leave or enter the kitchen empty-handed if food or dirty dishes are waiting.
**CHEF CALL** · When **F.O.H.** needs to speak to (i.e., interrupt) **B.O.H.** ("*Chef,* **MAY I CALL**?").
*Many restaurants have their own versions of:*
**ARTICHOKES** · Attractive (female) diners.
**CUPCAKING** · Focusing on **ARTICHOKES**.
**FIRE TABLE 100!** · Health inspector is here!

## B.O.H. / BACK OF HOUSE

**MEEZ / MISE** (**EN PLACE**) · The orderly assembly of everything required for service.
**EXPO** · The **EXPEDITER** who calls orders as they arrive and checks dishes as they leave — *A.k.a.*, **RUNNING THE PASS** *or* **THE LINE**.
**FIRE** · To start making a dish. *Also,* **RE-FIRE** · To remake an (incorrectly prepared) dish.
**ON DECK** · The dishes a cook has coming up (which may or may not be being prepared).
**HOLD** · To wait before **FIRING** an order.
**DUPE** · The kitchen's duplicate order **CHIT** *or* **TICKET**, hung on a metal **RAIL** *or* **WHEEL**.
**THE LINE** · The kitchen area where food is prepared, and the chefs who work there.
**WALKING IN!** · Alerts the kitchen to a new order to be **STAGED** (prepped) or **FIRED**.
**CALL BACK** · An **ECHO** of confirmation, e.g., **HEARD! / YES CHEF! / OUI CHEF!**
**HANDS!** · Request for help, usually when dishes are waiting to be **RUN OUT** to diners.
**À LA MINUTE** · Anything cooked to order.
**À LA DING** · Food by **CHEF MIKE**[rowave].
**ON THE FLY** · A dish needed **STAT**, e.g., due to an ordering error, a dropped plate, or a **POCKET TICKET** that a server forgot about.

**ALL THE WAY / STRAIGHT UP** · A regular (**REGGAE**) order with no **MOD**(ification)**S**.
**WEARING** · Clarifies an addition to a dish. ("*Burger wearing bacon and* **AVO**[*cado*]*!*")
**FLASH** (**IT**) · To rapidly reheat or extra-cook a dish (e.g., with a butane torch blast).
**KILL IT!** · To **CREMATE** (i.e., overcook) e.g., a burger or steak into a **HOCKEY PUCK**.
***n* OUT!** · *n* = minutes until an order is ready.
**86** · To be out of a dish or ingredient.
**ALL DAY** · A phrase that refers to the sum total of a given dish being made across all **TICKETS**. E.g., if six steaks are on the grill and a new order of two is **WALKED IN**, the count is "*Eight steaks, all day.*" *Also,* used to request a count of what is currently being cooked: "*Can I get an all day on the salmon?*"
**DRAGGING** · A table waiting for one or more dishes. *Or,* when the **LINE** is behind.
**STRETCH IT** · To attempt to eke out an ingredient, sauce, &c. for as long as possible.
**IN THE WEEDS → IN THE SHIT → SUNK** · Various stages of kitchen overwhelm.
**DYING ON THE PASS** *or* **IN THE WINDOW** · Dishes that are congealing under the **HEAT LAMPS** while waiting to be **RUN OUT**.
**VULTURES / SEAGULLS** · Servers who scavenge on food that **DIED ON THE PASS**.
**WIPE & SELL / RIMJOB** · To clean the edges of a dish before sending.
**TWEEZER FOOD** · Absurdly meticulous, delicate (and pretentious) fine dining. ◎
**SOIGNÉ** [elegant] · Fine-dining term for immaculate food, presentation, service, &c.
**SHOE**(**MAKER**) · An incompetent cook.
**S.**(**O.**[**T.**]**S.**) · Sauce (On [The] Side).
**F.N.G.** · Fucking New Guy.
**BEHIND! / CORNER! / ABOVE! / KNEES!** (*combined with* **HOT! / SHARP! / HEAVY!**) A warning shouted when approaching (and **SWINGING** something hazardous).
**MAKE A HOLE!** · *Get out of the way!*
**LOW BOY** · A below-counter fridge.
**OPA! / DOESN'T GO THERE! / FUMBLE! / GRAVITY CHECK!** · Various wisecracks called out when something is dropped.
**TIGHTEN UP!** · Get your **MISE** together!
**DISHIE / DISHPIG**(**GY**) **/ DISHDOG / POTWASH / SCRUB MONKEY / PLONGEUR** Names for those toiling in the (**DISH**) **PIT**.
**FORBIDDEN SOUP** · The murky dishwasher liquid that collects in upturned pots and pans.
**SPACE PUSSY** · Steel wool for cleaning pans.
**FUCK-IT BUCKET** · A container for soiled rags. *Or,* a **BIN** for dishes dirtied after close. ⊙

# Rock of Eye on Savile Row

*The vocabulary of* **BESPOKE TAILORING.**

## THE ROW

Located east of Regent Street, north of the Royal Academy, and parallel to New Bond Street, London's legendary **SAVILE ROW** is just 875 feet long. Yet ever since the 1800s, **THE ROW** (as it is affectionately known) has been the Mecca of bespoke tailoring — a toponymical thoroughfare as instantly metonymic as Wall Street, Fleet Street, or Broadway.

The Row proper is home to such storied names as Gieves & Hawkes, Dege & Skinner, H. Huntsman & Sons, and Chittleborough & Morgan, but its imprimatur extends to the **GOLDEN MILE** of Regent Street, Bond Street, Piccadilly, and Hanover Square. For example, Anderson & Sheppard has outposts on Old Burlington Street and Clifford Street, and Montague Ede tailors on Hanover Street.

Below are the three types of suit, in reverse order of (quality and) customization:

**READY TO WEAR (R.T.W.)** · Mass-produced **OFF-THE-PEG** suits — described by the trade as feeling **DEAD** rather than **ALIVE.**

**MADE TO MEASURE (M.T.M.)** · A suit made from a pre-existing **BLOCK PATTERN** that is **CUSTOMIZED** (to a greater or lesser extent) according to customer preference and build.

**BESPOKE** · A suit made entirely by hand. The Savile Row Bespoke Association lists various membership requirements, including:

› Produce all bespoke garments from an individually cut paper **PATTERN** that has been made by a **MASTER CUTTER**
› Typically create a two-piece suit with at least 50 hours of hand work
› Offer a choice of at least 2,000 fabrics

In addition to their quality, bespoke suits are distinguished by their **CHARACTER**, the subtle and charming human signatures that define anything made by hand and eye.

## PERSONNEL

Although the proverb "It takes nine tailors to make a man" likely refers not to toiling tailors but tolling church bells, a bespoke suit can indeed pass through nine expert pairs of hands:

**SALESMAN** · Employed by larger houses to run "client liaison" — i.e., establishing the specification of the garments required, and assisting with the selection of **CLOTH.**

In smaller houses this role will be undertaken by the **CUTTER.**

**CUTTER** · Takes the client's measurements, creates the **PATTERN**, and cuts the cloth.

The only client-facing tailor, and often the only salaried tailor (the others are freelance).

Some houses divide the job between **COAT** and **TROUSER CUTTERS** for efficiency (and, cynics say, to make it harder for a cutter to leave, since "*they only know half the job*").

**TRIMMER** · Responsible for preparing the suit's additional elements, e.g., linings, canvas, buttons, zips, thread, &c.

Usually the lowest-paid position, and seen as a stepping stone to more expert work. ("*The best way to get a job on the Row is to have one.*")

**MAKER** · Responsible for stitching the cut cloth at each stage of fitting. Most houses outsource this work to freelance tailors, allocating each element of the suit to a specialist:

› **COAT MAKER**
› **WAISTCOAT MAKER**
› **TROUSER MAKER** (*A.k.a.*, **STRIDER** / **DRUMMER**)

**FINISHER** · Responsible for the final fine details, e.g., lining, buttonholes, maker's label.

**PRESSER** · Responsible for all **IRON WORK**, i.e., using heat, steam, and pressure to stretch, shrink, and smooth the cloth to give a garment shape, fit, and crease-less elegance.

*The Old Burlington Street windows of Anderson & Sheppard (est. 1906)*

## BESPEAKING

Every house takes a slightly different approach to making a bespoke suit, but the basic workflow is as follows:

### 1. CONSULTATION

The first contact with a new customer (or the return of a regular) establishes the required garment (suit, jacket, overcoat, &c.) and the desired cloth, as well as a myriad of **STYLING** details (from lapel widths to trouser turn-ups).

### 2. MEASUREMENT

Depending on the garment(s) required, new customers will have 25–40 measurements taken (from **SHOULDER WIDTH** to **INSIDE LEG**). **CHECK MEASURES** will be taken from returning clients to assess changes in weight, posture, and physical capabilities.

Cutters take measurements in their own personal order — which is usually the order of the cutter to whom they were apprenticed. And, in the process, they will dispassionately assess a client's **FIGURATION** (i.e., posture, physique, and silhouette).

As Cabrera and Flaherty Meyers noted in *Classic Tailoring Techniques*:

> In order to get an uncensored picture, the tailor keeps the client away from the mirror during these observations. The temptation to suck in the stomach and stand up straight for the mirror, is too strong. If the tailor were to note that version of the body, the suit would fit only in front of a mirror.[1]

Figuration uses an array of discreet codes, e.g.:

**T.T.** .................. thick through (i.e., chunky)
**P.P.** .................. prominent posterior
**T.H.T.H.** .................. thick thighs
**SWAY** .................. hollow back
**H.F.** .................. head forward
**E.** .................. erect
**B.L.** .................. bow-legged
**P.T.** .................. pigeon-toed

How a garment is to be used will also be established, e.g., a cutter might inquire, "*Will sir be dancing?*" to establish how high and tight a dinner suit's **SCYE** (armhole) should be cut.

### 3. PATTERN DRAFTING

Armed with this array of anthropometrical data, the cutter **DRAFTS** the **PATTERN**, i.e., transfers a client's measurements onto (thick brown) paper, using rulers, **SQUARES** {📷 6}, tape, pre-drawn **BLOCK PATTERNS**, shears, and most significantly …

**ROCK OF EYE** · Measuring, drafting, and cutting **FREEHAND** — using the instinct and experience gleaned over years.

Rock of eye is the most subtle and storied element of a cutter's craft. The art is "*to get the* **RUNS** *right*," i.e., ensure that the chalk lines from measure to measure are accurate, smooth, and elegant. ("*If you make the pattern pretty, it will be a nice coat.*")

**TAKING A PUFF** · Using the outline of an existing pattern as the template for a new one.

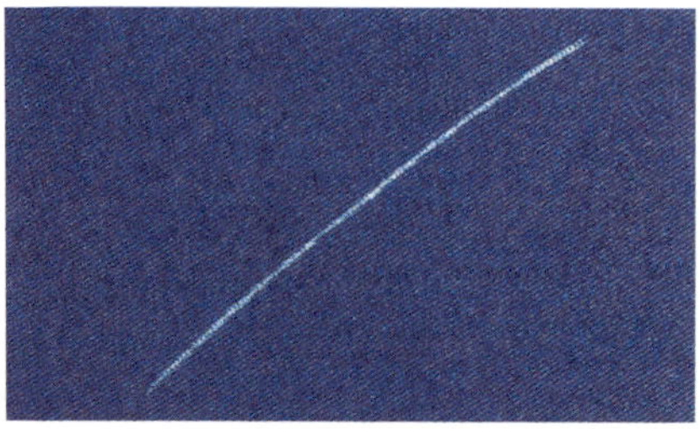

1. **TAKE IN**

2. **LET OUT**

3. **DRAW IN** (i.e., **BRIDLE**)

4. **STRETCH**

5. **SHRINK**

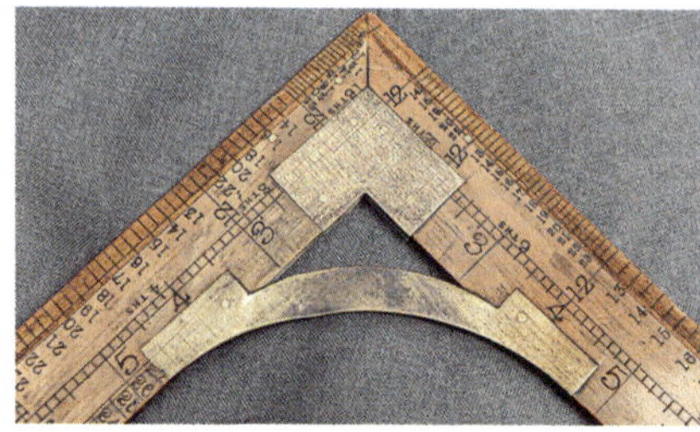

6. **SQUARE**

7. **BUNDLE** *wrapped in* **SELVEDGE**

8. **BASTE FITTING**

9. *A tweed* **BUNCH**

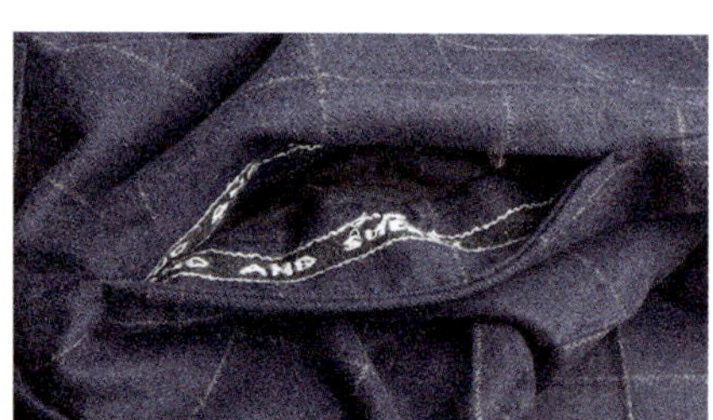

10. **SELVEDGE** *inside a trouser pocket*

### 4. STRIKING

When the paper **PATTERN** is **MARKED** onto the cloth with chalk and cut out with shears.

Cutters will arrange the elements of a suit in a good **LAY**, i.e., one that combines economy of fabric with **ALLOWANCES** for adjustments. (**LAYING OUT** is more challenging with larger clients, **D.B.** coats, and complex patterns.)

When making a cut, cutters will ensure the tips of their shears close at the very edge of the mark, to ensure accuracy — and save cloth.

**CHALK** · **WHITE** chalk is the standard, with **BLUE** used for measures on the left, and **RED** *or* **YELLOW** for measures on the right.

Some cutters use different colours to illustrate client peculiarities (e.g., **DROPS**).

A range of standard chalk marks {e.g., 📷 1–5} is used to communicate adjustments to makers and pressers, illustrated opposite by Antonia Ede of Montague Ede.

Star-shaped marks are used to emphasize key cut-lines (e.g., shoulders) in case chalk lines fade or are **BRUSHED OUT** during handling.

**FIT UPS** · Excess cloth left over from **STRIKING**, which is added to a **BUNDLE** for the **MAKERS** to create flaps, pockets, facings, &c.

**INLAYS** · Extra fabric left in seams to allow for fittings adjustments and after-sale alterations as clients become more or less *"prosperous."*

(The expression **NO INLAYS** means: No room for error.)

**BUNDLE** {📷 7} · A fabric or paper-wrapped parcel, prepared by the **CUTTER** or **TRIMMER** for the **MAKERS**, containing the cut cloth, **FIT UPS**, and other required elements (e.g., buttons, zip). Bundles are often tied with lengths of **SELVEDGE** {📷 10}.

**PATTERNS** {📷 23} · Once used, **PATTERNS** (*A.k.a.*, **GODS**) are labelled and archived.

As a result of tradition (and superstition), paper patterns are *never* thrown away, and so a returning client requiring a new suit of the same or a similar cut can skip a fitting or two.

If a client should die, their patterns are respectfully annotated with a **BLACK CROSS** and **RE-RACKED** in perpetuity.

Especially paranoid or competitive cutters will mark their patterns with deliberate errors (e.g., adding an inch to the back **BALANCE**) to foil anyone attempting to poach their clients.

## FITTINGS

In decades past, bespoke suits required as many as 5 or 6 fittings; most houses now work with 3 or 4, especially when fitting regulars.

The entire process can take anything from 12 to 16 weeks, depending on the backlog of the house and the complexity of the commission. (Rush jobs will usually be accommodated, at a commensurate cost.)

### 1. BASTE FITTING

Where the client first tries on the **SHELL** or **SKELETON** garments, which have canvas but no lapels, lining, pockets, or buttons and are temporarily **BASTED** (*or* **TACKED UP**) with long stitches using thin (white) cotton **BASTING THREAD** {📷 8}.

Once the cutter has carefully marked any required adjustments with chalk and pins, the garments are **TAKEN BACK TO THE PATTERN** — i.e., **RIPPED APART** and **SMOOTHED** with an iron — before being sewn again from scratch.

Any alterations made to the **SKELETON** will also be **MEMORIALIZED** on the original paper **PATTERN** for future reference.

(**PATTERNS** with a jumble of such alterations were once known as **CLAPHAM JUNCTIONS**, after Britain's busiest railway interchange. Patterns marked up by many hands are **SPAGHETTI JUNCTIONS**, after a complex road layout in Birmingham.)

### 2. FORWARD FITTING

Where the coat is semi-complete with facings, pockets, and darts sewn in, and other seams (e.g., shoulder) **BASTED**. If major changes are required at this stage, the customer may be asked to return for a **RE-BASTE** fitting.

### 3. FINISH BAR FINISH / FIN-BAR-FIN

An optional fitting some houses use to finalize specific details, e.g., sleeve button position.

### 4. FINAL FITTING

More often than not, the delivery of the **COCKED** (i.e., completed) **CONFECTION**. Occasionally any minor adjustments required will be made there and then.

**AFTER-CARE** · Houses offer a range of post-sale services — alterations, repairs, pressing, cleaning, stain removal — both as a source of revenue and to secure long-term relationships.

## CLOTH

Although houses will cut any cloth a customer desires, the Row customarily favours British cloth, for reasons of quality and sustainability, as well as look, feel, and tradition.

(As one old-school Yorkshire cloth manufacturer said of his Italian counterparts: "*They make cloth to watch, we make cloth to wear.*")

**WEIGHT** · Traditionally measured in ounces, suiting cloth has become much lighter over the years, thanks in large part to central heating.

| *Description* | *Oz.* | *Season* |
|---|---|---|
| **PAPERWEIGHT** | 6–8 | tropical summer |
| **LIGHTWEIGHT** | 8–10 | summer |
| **MEDIUM** | 10–12 | perennial |
| **MEDIUM HEAVY** | 12–13 | autumn |
| **HEAVYWEIGHT** | ≥13 | winter |

(A recent shift to paying **SALESMEN** with commission has led to accusations of upselling or mis-selling, e.g., when a heavyweight client is sold paperweight cloth that the cutters and makers know will neither flatter nor last.)

When selecting a cloth, a client may be asked if they **RUN HOT**, i.e., are prone to perspiration.

**THREE-SEASON WEIGHT** · A suit that feels comfortable in spring, summer, and autumn.

**W.F.B.** · Cloth that is suitable for Weddings, Funerals, and Bar Mitzvahs.

**BUNCHES** {📷 9, 21} · Swatch sample books.

Bunches are usually arranged by type and weight of cloth, and boldness of design, e.g.:

› **CLASSIC** · The most timeless and popular colours (black, blue, grey) and patterns (pinstripe, Prince of Wales check, &c.).

› **SEMI-FANCY** · Rather more daring colours, chalk- and rope-stripes, and patterns.

› **FANCY** · The most eye-catching cloths — including **SHOUTERS**, i.e., colours and patterns that pique a client's interest (even if they end up picking a more staid **CLASSIC**).

**DOG** · A cloth that doesn't sell. ("*We all have dogs in our collections; the secret is not to let them become a kennel.*")

**QUANTITY** · Cloth is sold in these lengths:

| | |
|---|---|
| **HALF PIECE** | 30–35 metres |
| **FULL PIECE** | 60–70 metres |
| **CUT LENGTH** | as requested; see below... |

The length of cloth required for a garment will vary by house style, required design, pattern complexity, and client size; below is a guide:

| *No turn-ups* | *Metres of cloth* | *Turn-ups* |
|---|---|---|
| 3.1 | TWO-PIECE SUIT | 3.3 |
| 3.2 | D.B. SUIT | 3.5 |
| 4.5 | THREE-PIECE SUIT | 4.7 |
| 2 | COAT | — |
| 1.3 | PAIR OF TROUSERS | 1.5 |
| 2.8 | KNEE-LENGTH OVERCOAT | — |
| | +0.4m for **PATTERN MATCHING** checked cloth | |

**RIGHT** *or* **FRONT SIDE** · The finished side of the cloth that faces outward. *Conversely*, the **WRONG** *or* **BACK SIDE**, on which the **PATTERN** is **STRUCK IN**.

**NOBLE** *or* **EXOTIC CLOTH** · E.g., cashmere; cashmere + silk; linen; linen + silk; silk; &c.

**ONE WAY CLOTH** · Cloth with a nap running in one direction (e.g., velvet, corduroy, some flannels and checks) that is rotated accordingly, depending on the desired texture and appearance (**SHADING**) of pattern and colour.

Houses cut **ONE WAY** as standard — i.e., with the nap running in a consistent direction across every garment — unless a customer supplies an insufficient length.

Certain cloths (e.g., corduroy) may be cut **AGAINST THE NAP**, if brightness of colour is more important than smoothness of texture.

(Some cutters will spin a coin on the cloth to determine the direction of a subtle nap.)

**SUPER NUMBER** · Defines the "maximum fibre diameter" for cloths made from pure new wool, ranging from **SUPER 80** (19.75μ) to **SUPER 250** (11.25μ), according to the International Wool Textile Organization.[2]

Cloths with higher super number tend to be finer, softer, cooler, and often lighter — yet are not necessarily of higher quality or better suited to a particular garment or client. Indeed, many cutters consider super numbers a distracting marketing gimmick. ("*The most expensive bottle on the wine list won't necessarily suit your taste or meal.*")

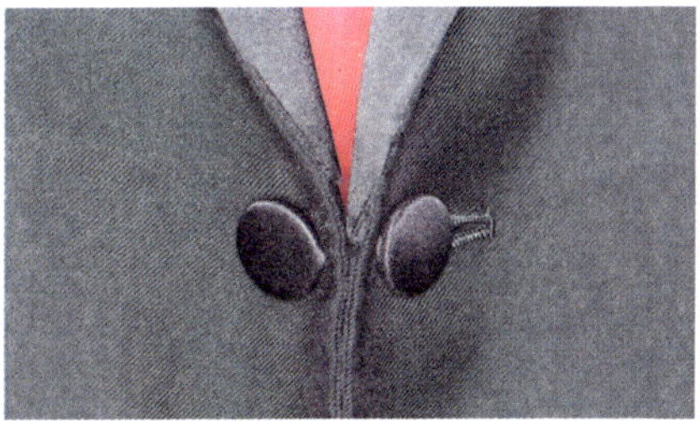

11. **BUTTERFLY BUTTONS**

12. **NIPPLE BUTTONS**

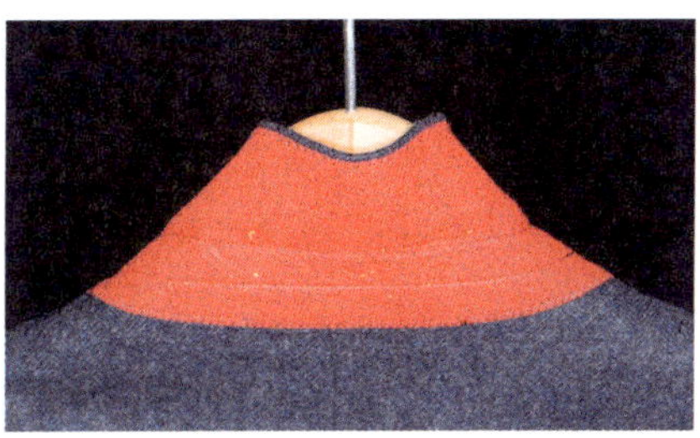

13. **MELTON**

14. **FROGGING**

15. **PROLE GAP**

16. **BARCHETTA POCKET**

17. **WATERFALL & CONTRAST**

18. **WORKING** *or* **SURGEON'S CUFF**

19. **SIDE ADJUSTER**

20. **MAKER'S LABEL**

21. *A selection of* BUNCHES

**LOCKING** · When cutters examine the cloth to check for defects before use.

Manufacturers go through painstaking processes of **PERCHING** (inspection), **BURLING** (removing foreign matter, loose threads, knots, and thick, fabric **SLUBS**), and **MENDING** to ensure their cloth is free from defects.

If lengths contain minor faults, these may be indicated with coloured **STRINGS** (e.g., white for weaving damage, red for dying error) that will be noted by the cutter and avoided.

Cloth with **NO STRINGS** (**ATTACHED**) is faultless.

**SELVEDGE** · The narrow [self+]edges running down either side of a length of woven cloth. Added to: ensure the weft does not unravel; add tension and prevent **COCKLING**; and promote the manufacturer and their design.

Selvedges are also used as a guide when cutting lengths, to ensure the cloth is perfectly **SQUARE** (i.e., cut true) when **PRESENTED** to the cutters and bundled for the makers.

Some houses incorporate the selvedge into their trouser pockets {📷 10} or heel tapes as a subtle indicator of craftsmanship.

**DRAPE** · How a cloth hangs.

**HAND / HANDLE** · The quality and feel of a cloth; that which has a "*good hand*" will "**MAKE UP** *beautifully*."

**LUSTRE** · Cloth with an elegant and pleasing finish. *Conversely*, **SHINE** · A finish that looks untidy, gaudy, or cheap.

**DEAD** · A complimentary term for **ROBUST** cloth that **LIES FLAT** and lends itself to being tailored. *Conversely*, **LIVELY** · Cloth that "*moves around*" as it is handled, making it harder to stitch and press.

## COATS

Only potatoes and donkeys have jackets; suits have **COATS** — whether they be **SINGLE-** or **DOUBLE-BREASTED** (**D.B.**).

**BUTTONS** · The number of buttons on the front of a coat will dramatically alter its look:

› **ONE** · Common in dinner jackets, some have **BUTTERFLY** buttons that come together but do not overlap {📷 11}.
› **TWO** · The bottom button is not fastened.
› **THREE** · The bottom button is not fastened; the top is optional.
› **THREE-ROLL-TWO** · A less structured, three-button coat where the lapel rolls down to the second button. *A.k.a.*, **NAPLES** cut.

D.B. coats offer an array of buttons (e.g., 6×2, 6×1, 4×2, 2×1, &c.) where the formula is:

TOTAL BUTTONS × FASTENING BUTTONS

Even when two buttons fasten on a D.B. suit, only the top button should ever be secured.

**NIPPLE BUTTONS** · Show buttons placed high and wide on a D.B. coat {📷 12}.

**WRAP** · The quantity of overlapped fabric in the front of a D.B. coat; 5¼" is standard. The **DEEPER** the wrap, the smaller the opening.

**SHOULDERS** · The line of a coat's shoulders is key to a suit's fit and silhouette.

Traditionally, American shoulder lines are straighter and boxier; whereas Italian coats have a more natural, fluid slope. Savile Row coats, influenced by hunting and military attire, tend to sit between these two archetypes.

The junction of shoulder and sleeve-head has a dramatic effect on the silhouette. Shoulders can be **SOFT** *or* **NATURAL** (i.e., smoothly sloping); **ROPED** (with various weights of padding); or **PAGODA** (dramatically arched).

Since not all clients have a horizontal shoulder line, **LEFT** *or* **RIGHT DROPS** are (gently) equilibrated with **PADDING** (e.g., wadding).

**LAPELS** · There are three standard coat lapels:

› **PEAKED** · Featuring pointed edges that angle up toward the shoulders, associated with formal wear and D.B. coats.

› **NOTCHED** · Featuring a small, triangular cutout where the lapel meets the collar, commonly found on business or casual suits.

› **SHAWL** · A smooth, rounded lapel, most often seen on dinner and smoking jackets.

**CUFFS** · Coat cuffs may be cut narrower if the client wears barrel-cuffed shirts or wider to accommodate French cuffs — and the modern trend of absurdly bulky wristwatches.

Turnback cuffs (on dinner jackets) are a distinctive feature favoured by certain clients, e.g., Ian Fleming {☞ p.284}.

**VENTS** · Vertical slits at the back of a coat, which allow for ease of movement. ("*One, two, or none.*") Although the style for lounge-suit vents ebbs and flows, by tradition: riding coats take a single vent; D.B. coats take two; and dinner jackets take none.

**MELTON** · A coat's structural undercollar, named after melton wool — a dense, tightly woven fabric with a felt-like finish {📷 13}.

**RECOIL PAD** · A (removable) pad of soft material fitted at the chest of a shooting jacket to absorb the impact of a firearm.

**CLEAN** *vs* **COMFORT** · The tension between a coat that hugs a client's contours (i.e., is **CUT TO THE BODY**) and one that flows casually.

**DRAPE CUT** · A classic Savile Row look, pioneered by Anderson & Sheppard, characterized by higher and tighter arm holes, less-structured internal canvassing, cut on the bias; a rolled (**CARDIGAN**-style) lapel; and additional cloth at the chest that allows for relaxed movement and extended reach.

**SMOKING JACKETS** · Velvet coats, with or without ornate braid **FROGGING** {📷 14}. Traditionally worn for warmth and fume-protection when smoking; now more commonly sported as a more casual form of evening wear.

**BALANCE** · Generally, the equilibrium of a garment as it is worn. More specifically, the fit of a coat from back to front. Adjusting a coat's **FRONT** *or* **BACK BALANCE** to match the posture of the client is vital to a good fit.

**COLLAR GAP** · The inelegant chasm between collar and neck; a sign of a poorly **BALANCED** coat. *A.k.a.*, the **PROLE GAP** {📷 15}.

**PIGGED** · When too-heavy collar lapels curve swinishly forward. *A.k.a.*, **PIG'S LUG** *or* **EAR**.

## POCKETS

Coats can have any number of **IN**(side) and **OUT**(side) pockets, of varying type, e.g.,

› **PATCH** · Pockets stitched onto the surface of a (casual) coat; usually wide and capacious. Newly popular due to the unstructured look of Neapolitan tailoring.

› **FLAP** · Pockets cut into a coat and covered with a strip of fabric. Traditional flaps are **STRAIGHT** (i.e., horizontal); more stylistic (and, when equestrian, **HACKING**) flaps are **SLANTED** at a 15°–25° angle — i.e., "*Up an inch, down a half.*"

› **JETTED** / **WELTED** · Flap-less "slit" pockets providing a clean silhouette.

› **BELLOWS** / **CARTRIDGE** · Capacious and gusseted **PATCH** pockets, used primarily on shooting and safari jackets.

› **TICKET POCKET** · A narrower out-pocket positioned above (and in the style of) the right hip pocket. (Not always flattering for the more diminutive client.) Historically used for tips, tolls, and tickets; now mainly for show. When *inside* a coat, such pockets are **TICKET LEFT** *or* **RIGHT FACING**, depending on the handedness of the client.

**INSIDE POCKETS** · Coats can be made with any number of internal pockets, from the standard **INSIDE BREAST** to special additions for pens and spectacles — which may be lined with Selvyt to keep the lenses clean.

One recent popular request is for an inside pocket cut to fit a Nokia 3310, used by many City boys as a "dumb" work phone.

**CHANGE POCKET** · A patch-pocket-within-a-pocket, designed to stop coins jangling.

**BREAST POCKET** · A **WELT**, **PATCH** (or, occasionally, **BELLOWS**) pocket set over the heart; used for handkerchiefs, pocket squares, &c. Some houses sew a **WORKING BREAST-POCKET** whereby excess (lining) material may be plucked out of the pocket to create an accent. (Incidentally, pocket squares should complement a tie, but not match it.)

**BARCHETTA** · A breast pocket curved like the prow of a boat; popularized by Neapolitan tailors. (The word means *small boat* in Italian.) {☞ p.15} Some Row coat makers decline to stitch such a bold innovation. {📷 16}

## BUTTON(HOLE)S

In contrast to their machine-made cousins, **HAND-MADE BUTTONHOLES** are cut *before* being stitched, which adds to the complexity and jeopardy.

(**TAILOR'S**) **TWIST** · Special button silk. ("*It takes ten metres of twist to finish a coat.*")

**GIMP** · Stiff cord that is hand stitched around a buttonhole to lift it elegantly from the cloth and give it structure and strength.

**DOUBLE WORKING** · Sewing a buttonhole so the inside is as finished as the outside. Used, e.g., on a **THREE-ROLL-TWO** coat. Double worked buttonholes are naturally much stiffer.

**SHANK** · A tightly wrapped **STALK** of thread that lifts a button from the face of the fabric. Thicker garments (e.g., overcoats) need longer shanks to allow the cloth to pass underneath.

**BEESWAX** · Tailors coat their **TWIST** in beeswax to strengthen the thread, reduce friction, prevent tangling, and improve precision.

**KISSING** · Sleeve buttonholes where the buttons are just touching. *Alternatively*, **WATERFALL** · Where the buttons overlap {📷 17}.

**SURGEON'S CUFF** · When a coat has **WORKING** cuff buttons (i.e., that can be unfastened). Named after the coats made for military surgeons who would roll back their sleeves to treat the wounded {📷 18}.

For generations, surgeon's cuffs were a defining feature of bespoke suits. But now, when even Uniqlo coats have working buttons, we must reassess Tom Wolfe's 1965 awe:

> Real buttonholes. That's it! A man can take his thumb and forefinger and unbutton his sleeve at the wrist because this kind of suit has real buttonholes there. Tom, boy, it's terrible. Once you know about it, you start seeing it. All the time! There are just two classes of men in the world, men with suits whose buttons are just sewn onto the sleeve, just some kind of cheapie decoration, or — yes! — men who can unbutton the sleeve at the wrist because they have real buttonholes and the sleeve really buttons up.[3]

**SHAM** *or* **FAKE** · Buttonholes that cannot be opened; sewn for ornament and economy.

Coat sleeve buttons farthest from the cuff are often sham, so they can be removed should the sleeve need to be lengthened.

**CRUSHED BEETLE** / **CAT'S ARSE** · A poorly sewn buttonhole. *A.k.a.*, **DEAD SOW'S EYE**.

**CONTRAST THREAD** · Stitching buttonholes (and other details) in a colour that stands out. The colour can be subtle (picking up from the base cloth) or deliberately ostentatious {📷 17}. The latter is a recent fashion — borrowed from Italy, and frowned upon by the "*Never wear brown in town!*" gang.

**TONE ON TONE** · Stitching (and other details) designed to blend in with the base cloth.

22. *The basement workshop window of Huntsman (est. 1849), on Savile Row*

## DRUMS [TROUSERS]

**FLY** · Perhaps surprisingly, most Row trousers are fitted with **ZIPS** — because **BUTTON FLIES** are fiddly to fasten and tricky to keep closed (especially if less than entirely sober).

**SECOND PAIR** · Because trousers wear faster than coats, ordering two pairs is a wise investment (assuming they are worn alternately, and cleaned together, with the coat).

Some cutters suggest that one pair is formal (with pleats and turn ups) and the other is casual (plain front and hem).

If trousers become worn or shiny at the seat, the **FORK PIECE** can be replaced.

**HALF** *or* **FULL LINING** · The amount of (silk) lining inside the trouser leg; half is standard.

**BRACE TOP** · Fitted with buttons for braces, and cut looser at the waist. *Conversely,* **STRAIGHT TOP** · Fitted with **SIDE ADJUSTERS** {📷 19} or elasticated **DAKS** top buttons.

**BELT LOOPS** · Suit trousers will generally not include these, though casual trousers might.

**RISE** · The difference in length between the inside and outside leg.

**TURN-UPS** · Whether to have **P.T.U.** (Permanent Turn-Ups) on a pair of trousers is a matter of preference, as is the width (though the standard is currently 1¾"). By tradition, dinner suit trousers do not take turn-ups.

**PLEATS** · Single, double, or triple folds tailored into a trouser leg to enhance fit, comfort, and hang.

**BREAK** · How the trouser hits the shoe, ranging from: **NO BREAK** (where the fabric hangs flat) through to **QUARTER**, **HALF**, and **FULL BREAK** (where it buckles markedly).

Fuller breaks have a vintage feel; no breaks (or Thom Browne trousers that hang above the ankle) currently look contemporary.

## BUSINESS

**TRUNK SHOWS** · Several times a year, cutters on the Row abandon the safety of Mayfair and travel around the world to service existing clients and drum up new trade.

In decades past, when **CROSSING THE DAMP POT** (i.e., steaming to New York) took three weeks, cutters measured clients on the way out, and struck patterns on the way back.

Huntsman currently lists trunk shows in 24 locations, from Beijing, Bangkok, and Seoul, to Jeddah, Kuwait, and Dubai.

**ANONYMITY** · Aside from Huntsman, which never stitches a **MAKER'S LABEL** {📷 20} into its garments, there are two reasons why houses on the Row keep their work anonymous:

› It is commissioned, **WHITE LABEL** work, e.g., for a luxury brand.

› The client's demands were so meretricious or gaudy that the house demands deniability to protect its reputation.

23. *A rack of* PATTERNS

**SCRIBBLING** · Stories abound of (apprentice) cutters hiding jocular notes in the lining of coats. Andersen & Sheppard once recalled a suit from the Prince of Wales (now King Charles III) to quash rumours that someone (possibly Alexander McQueen) had inserted something untoward; nothing was found. [4]

**PIG / PORK** · Garments that have gone so wrong they must be **KILLED** and **REMADE**. Over time, racks of **COLD PORK / DEAD PIG** (stored in a **KILL CUPBOARD**) are amassed, waiting to be adapted for other clients.

From time to time, larger houses hold **PORK SALES** so that apprentices (and others) can buy these problematic garments at a discount to alter for their own use.

**BOOT / MONEY** · For generations, it was a point of aristocratic pride to pay one's tailor late (if at all), and a principle of the trade never to pursue debts. Times have changed.

Now — when a *basic* Savile Row two-piece bespoke suit in a standard fabric costs £3,500–£6,500 — houses will ask for a 50% deposit, with the balance to be paid on completion.

As a result, the Row experiences recessions on a slight time delay, since clients who fall on harder times simply leave their (half-)finished suits to linger on the rack until they are back again in funds.

**LOGS** · Freelance MAKERS, FINISHERS, and PRESSERS submit a weekly **LOG** of the work they have completed that, if received by Thursday lunchtime, will be paid on Friday.

## TAILORDOM'S SNIPOCRACY

It's easy to forget that, while bespoke suiting is now the province of the wealthy, until relatively recently all clothes were made by hand. And although the Row has long been home to the finest houses, London was replete with smaller shops and journeymen tailors, often working in cramped conditions for poverty pay.

The unique culture of tailordom is reflected in a vocabulary that has all but vanished.

**KNIGHT OF THE SHEARS** *or* **THIMBLE / NIPSHRED / PRICKLOUSE / SARTOR / SCISSOR-MAN / SEAM-BITER / STAB-RAG / SNIP-CABBAGE / NEEDLE-JERKER / STEEL-BAR DRIVER** · Nicknames for tailors. *Also*, **SCHNEIDER** · From the German: to cut.

**BOARD** · The bench where tailors toil. *Also*, to have experience. ("*I was* **ON THE BOARD** *at Dege & Skinner for five years.*")

**ON THE BACK SEAM** · Being hard-up for money. *Or*, taking a quick nap on the BOARD.

**MUNGO / CABBAGE / CRIB / PEAKING** · Cloth left over from a job. (**COLLECTING CABBAGE** to use or sell was a traditional perk of the job.) Some cloth manufacturers donate their mungo to tailoring students.

**BROKEN SUIT** · Wearing elements of a suit as individual garments (e.g., a suit coat with jeans) is not necessarily a *faux pas*, though the risk is that they wear at different rates.

**PINTS ROUND!** · Yelled when someone drops their shears — for which the punishment was buying a round of drinks. (*"Every time you drop your shears, a tailoress dies."*)

**BARRING** · A way of acknowledging that your criticism of someone else applies also to you, e.g., "He's put on weight, *barring*." If this catchword is not added, colleagues will draw attention to your hypocrisy by **WHISTLING**.

**PINKED** .................. to have done good work
**MARKED UP** ...... to have someone's measure
**CHUCK A DUMMY** .......................... to faint
**POOR HAND / SORE FIST** ....... to sew badly
**CUTTING TURF** ........................ poor work
**MEPHISTO** .................... workshop foreman
**MIKE** ................. to look busy while shirking
**MOGING** .......................................... lying
**DAMP RAG** .............................. a pessimist
**SHINING** .......... blowing one's own trumpet
**IN THE DRAG** .... to be behind on your work
**PELT** ............................ to sew (too) thickly
**SKIFFLE** ........... a hurry-up job; to work fast
**TROTTER** .......... a (foot) messenger; a gofer
**EASY STITCH** ....................... a pleasant job
**HIPPLE** ............ good pay for **EASY STITCH**
**BASTING UP A SNARL** .... stirring up trouble

**WASHING** · A dressing down from a client (*A.k.a.*, a **SNOTTING**); *Or*, to criticize forcefully the work of another tailor.

**GRAB YOUR TURTLES AND NANNIES! IRONS DOWN!** · Cockney rhyming slang: Turtle [doves = gloves]; nannie [goat = coat].

**DEAD HORSE** · Making a garment that has already been paid for in full.

**GETTING THE NEEDLE** · Pricking yourself while stitching (and the resulting irritation).

**MOGUE** · To tease or leg-pull. The rule on the Row used to be *"No mogueing about trade!"*

**SLOP TAILOR / SPRINGER UP** · A ready-to-wear tailor, whose suits are poorly made — i.e., **BLOWN TOGETHER**.

**MANGLE / IRON TAILOR** · Sewing machine. Most bespoke tailoring is hand-sewn, but machines are used for **LONG SEAMS**, e.g., inside and outside leg, and wasitband. Such work is said to be **BICYCLED**.

**ON THE COD** · A (post-payday) drinking session during which tailors bemoan **LEGS AND ARMS**, i.e., *"beer with no body."*

**LAD OF WAX** · A tailor whose suits slip on.

**PIPECLAYING** · Concealing faults in a work. *A.k.a.*, **HIDING THE SNOBBERY**.

**STAND OR FALL** · A cutter who is forced to take on sewing jobs, e.g., during a **BALLOON** · An idle period with no work.

**LIVERPOOL TAILOR** · An itinerant tailor who **WHIPS THE CAT** — i.e., goes door to door among private houses in search of work.

**MAKING YOUR (OWN) COFFIN** · Risking your reputation by overcharging.

**CUTTING YOUR OWN FLAP** · Looking after your own interests.

**CODGER / BUSHELMAN** · Alterations or repair tailor. *Hence*, **CODGE** · To do bad work.

**MOUSE IN THE STRAW** · An antisocial (or non-union) workmate.

**CONNAUGHT MAN** · A stray piece of cloth accidentally left inside a garment.

**FLY WASTE** · Strands of odd fabric that fly around the factory during manufacture and are accidentally incorporated into the weave.

**LEFT FOREPART / HIP STAY / STAY TAPE / MARM PUSS** · A tailor's wife.

**JEFF** · A master (one-man-band) tailor who would **C.M.T.** (Cut, Make, and Trim) a suit.

**KIPPERS** · Female tailors (**TAILORESSES**) who *"go around in pairs"* for safety.

**CORK** · The boss — whose arrival would be heralded by a warning call of **SMALL SEAMS!**

**BLIND** *or* **PRIVATE STITCH** · To sew without showing the mark. *Also*, **RANTERING** · To conceal a seam.

**UMSIE / UMSES / UMS** · General term for any apprentice who has not been around long enough to warrant learning their name. ⊙

# Tekesi!

*From as early as the 1940s, and catalysed by a desperate need for transport during apartheid, commuters in Black townships across South Africa developed an informal system of hand-signals to indicate their desired destination to a honking multitude of independent minibus taxi drivers.*

*Despite advances in technology, millions still make daily use of these* **TAXI HAND SIGNS** *— some of which are demonstrated below by the artist and anthropologist* ***Dr. Susan Woolf,*** *whose study of the gestures was featured on a set of commemorative South African stamps in 2010. (Tekesi means "taxi" in the Southern Bantu language Sesotho.)*

In addition to communicating specific locations, many signs also indicate a general direction:

**CITY CENTRE**

**NEXT T-JUNCTION**

**JUST AROUND THE CORNER**

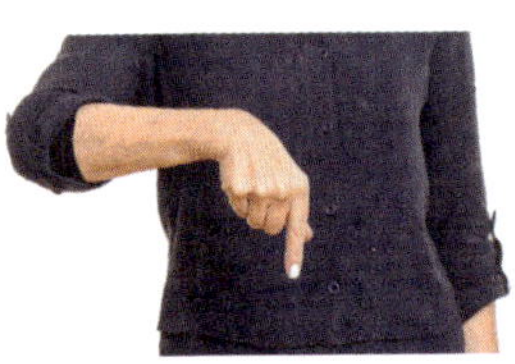

**LOCAL**

**VERY CLOSE**

**SHOPPING MALL**

**I HAVE NO MONEY**
*Drivers sometimes take passengers unable to pay the fare, accepting small coins as "petrol money."*

**UNDERNEATH THE NEXT BRIDGE**
*Indicated by moving the lower hand back and forth.*

**SHO'T LEFT** [short left]
*Indicates that the commuter needs just a short ride to a local destination.*

*Taxi passengers alight in Sandton, South Africa, 2018*

Some of the signs used to indicate specific locations have very specific topographical etymologies:

**DIEPSLOOT**
*Indicated with an undulating wave-like gesture — a reference to the bumpy bridge-crossing one experiences when entering Soweto via Diepsloot.*

**MARABASTAD**
*Indicated by miming castration (with the upper hand as testicles and the lower as a blade) — a reference to the 2001 mutilation and murder of a local taxi driver.*

**KLIPTOWN**
*Indicated by wafting one hand in front of the nose while flagging down a taxi with the other — a reference to (and protest against) a notorious local garbage dump.*

Below are the stamps Dr. Woolf created for the South African Post Office. They depict her paintings of the hand signals, accompanied by a novel form of graphical representation she developed that was thermographically embossed onto each stamp so that the gestures might be "read" by the blind.

# Beltway Bible

*A brief glossary of* **AMERICAN POLITICAL LANGUAGE.**

## PEOPLE

The progression of **D.C. FAME:**

**FAMOUS FOR WASHINGTON**
So, not very.

**DESTINATION**
A notable person toward whom everyone at a D.C. party gravitates.

**PRINCIPAL**
The senior player in any given context.

**PERMANENTS / THE ESTABLISHMENT**
Immovable edifices of D.C. society.

**P.O.T.U.S.** ................... President of the U.S.
**F.L.O.T.U.S.**................ First Lady of the U.S.
**V.P.O.T.U.S.** ......... Vice President of the U.S.
**S.L.O.T.U.S. / S.G.O.T.U.S.** ..... Second Lady / Second Gentleman of the U.S.
**S.C.O.T.U.S.** ........Supreme Court of the U.S.

**GREYBEARD** · A "venerable" Washingtonian brought into a campaign to act as the "adult."

**SHERPA** · A **GREYBEARD** who guides a nominee through a confirmation process.

**EARPIECE** · A member of a security detail (this can inspire **EARPIECE ENVY** in others).

**FORMER** · Who trades on an expired job title.

The **HIERARCHY** of political staff:

**SENIOR STAFF / TOPPER**

**SUPER-STAFFER**
An aide who has evolved into a power player or broker in his or her own right.

**AIDE**

**BODY MAN** · A **PRINCIPAL**'s personal aide.

**FLACK** · A spin-spewing **PRESS OFFICER.**

(**PUGNACIOUS**) **FIREBRAND** · An asshole. *Also*, **MOUTH BREATHER** · A stupid asshole.

**RAINMAKER** · Anyone who can draw crowds and, more vitally, cash. ("*Making it rain!*")

**CLOSER** · The rare person who actually solves problems. *A.k.a.*, **FIXER.**

**HAPPY WARRIOR** · A politician with a mien that defaults to joy; applied to Kamala Harris, Tim Walz, and Ronald Reagan — whose 1984 campaign advert "**MORNING IN AMERICA**" became shorthand for political optimism.

**SKUTNIK** · An individual called out, e.g., during a State of the Union address. Named after Lenny Skutnik, who, in 1982, Reagan cited as a model of heroism for rescuing a plane crash survivor from the Potomac.

**R.I.N.O. / D.I.N.O.** · Republican / Democrat In Name Only.

**SQUISH** · A **RED-ON-RED** insult for overly liberal conservatives who should "*grow a spine.*"

**CUCK(SERVATIVE)** · How the extreme right attacks centrist conservatives who fail to embrace their racism, sexism, and blood-and-soil white supremacy. {☞ **MANOSPHERE** p.262}

**BARSTOOL CONSERVATIVE** · Young, male, libertarian, anti-progressive, Trumpians, associated with the website Barstool Sports.

**CRUNCHY** · Those who practice sustainable, healthful, and low-consumption living. *Hence*, **CRUNCHY CONS** · Right-wingers amazed to find fulfilment in such progressive clichés.

**LET *x* BE *x*** · The belief (hope) that a politician might **CUT THROUGH** if they could just shake off the spin and be true to their nature.

**IT IS WHAT IT IS / IT'S JUST *x* BEING *x*** · A catch-all justification for any D.C. outrage.

**TITLE CREEP** · Why a receptionist in D.C. can be called **CHIEF OF STAFF.**

**STRATEGIC ADVISER / PUBLIC AFFAIRS CONSULTANT** · An unregistered lobbyist.

☜ *President Donald Trump speaks with reporters on the South Lawn, 2019*

*JD Vance grants a* **HALLWAY INTERVIEW** *at the U.S. Capitol, 2024*

**FIRSTNAMELASTNAME.COM SYNDROME** · The proliferation of personal media brands.

**SHOP** · Faux-folksy name for [1] an office within a bureaucracy ("*the comms shop*"); *Or* [2] a small lobbying or consulting enterprise.

**THE [NAME] GROUP** · An eponymous lobbying or consulting **SHOP**. Often a solo operation. *Also*, **[NAME] STRATEGIES** · Like a **GROUP**, but with actual employees.

## MEETINGS

| *Euphemism* | *Reality* |
|---|---|
| **CORDIAL** | cold |
| **ROBUST** | rude |
| **HEATED** | hatred |
| **SPIRITED** | shouting |
| **FULL AND FRANK EXCHANGE** | swearing |
| **REAFFIRM COMMITMENT** | failure |

**PULL ASIDE** 📷 · An informal (though often artfully planned) interaction between two or more **PRINCIPALS**, during a larger event.

**BRUSH BY** · More casual and fleeting than a **PULL ASIDE**, but usually no less strategic.

**WALK AND TALK** · Where principals chat informally, e.g., on the way to a **FAMILY PHOTO** (i.e., a group shot of summit attendees).

**(KEY) TAKE-AWAY(S)** · That to which every event, speech, document, &c., gets distilled.

**READOUT** · A sanitized, media-friendly summary of a private meeting or phone call.

**SPECIAL RELATIONSHIP** · Any omission of this Churchillian phrase in **READOUT** of Anglo-American relations risks instant speculation of a rift. *Similarly*, France is inevitably flattered as America's **OLDEST ALLY**.

**THE ASK** · A favour or request; usually the real reason for seeking a meeting. *Similarly*, **COFFEE?** · Code for a meeting about something other than work, usually (career) advice.

## ROOMS

**HOLD** · Backstage area at an event.

**GREEN ROOM**
T.V. anterooms, where guests mingle.

**SPIN ROOM**
Where post-debate "analysis" is inflicted on the press.

**WAR ROOM**
A place of presumed decision making.

**GRAND BALLROOM / TERRACE**
Some of the public areas at Mar-a-Lago (i.e., **THE WINTER WHITE HOUSE**) where members may casually interact with Trump.

Any **S.C.I.F.**, i.e., Sensitive Compartmented Information Facility. {☞ p.118}

The best room — other than, perhaps, the **SIT(UATION) ROOM** — is **THE OVAL**.

**GREEN ROOM THEFT** · Using on-air something clever a fellow T.V. guest said backstage.

## INTERNAL PROCESS

**CALL ON** · [1] Courting attention by demanding others **TAKE ACTION**. [2] Associating an opponent with something unsavoury, by calling on them to denounce it.

**SOCIALIZE** · To get accustomed to a new idea. ("*Let's socialize this with senior staff.*")

**RUN(NING) TO GROUND** · Actually to complete a task. ("*Chad ran it to ground.*")

**FLAGGING** · Passively transferring responsibility. ("*Flagging this for your attention.*") *Also*, **PASSING** · Fobbing work off to another desk. ("*An action passed is an action completed.*")

**LITIGATE** · To avoid or resolve (bureaucratic) conflict. ("*I need to litigate that with counsel.*")

**SLOW WALKING** · Obstruction by lethargy; once a tactic, now the (legislative) norm.

**HIT THE WAVE TOPS** · To touch briefly only on the key points, to save time in a meeting.

**FOOT STOMP** · To emphasize a point you (or someone else) just made; seemingly derived from the teaching trick of unsubtly stressing material that is likely to be included in a test.

## JOURNAL(ISM)ISM

**JOURNALISMISM** · A PROCESS STORY on journalism itself. {☞ p.256}

**PROCESS STORY** · A piece that focuses on **HOW THE SAUSAGE IS MADE**, with which politicians collaborate even as they condemn.

**HOT TAKE** · A click-courting rapid-response, boosted with adjectives like **FIRE** and **SPICY**.

**SNOWFLAKES** · Short-lived stories that melt quickly. *Conversely*, a story with **TRACTION**.

**MAKE NEWS** · Meta term for the release of actual information; if accidental, a GAFFE. ("*I'm not going to make news on that today.*")

**GAFFE** · As defined by Michael Kinsley: "When a politician tells the truth — some obvious truth he isn't supposed to say."

**GOTCHA QUESTION** · One an interviewee hasn't prepared for; often relating to the **REAL LIFE** concerns of **ORDINARY PEOPLE**, e.g., "*What's the price of a gallon of milk?*"

**(MERELY) ASKING THE QUESTION** · A journalistic dodge for raising an objectionable issue. *Similarly*, **QUESTIONS (ARE) BEING ASKED**, i.e., by the reporter's straw man.

**HALLWAY INTERVIEW** 📷 · When politicians are chased down the corridors of power: some provide comment, others fake cellphone calls.

**COCKTAIL PARTY INTERVIEW** · Media access grudgingly granted at social gatherings.

**NARRATIVE** · The way a story unfolds. Politicians are regularly called on to **CHANGE THE NARRATIVE**, or criticized for allowing a **DANGEROUS NARRATIVE** to **TAKE HOLD**.

**CONVENTIONAL WISDOM** · "*Always more conventional than wise.*"

**ACCESS JOURNALISM** · When proximity to power trumps holding it to account.

Epitomized by the **BEAT SWEETENER** / **SOURCE GREASER** · A sugar-coated profile (**PUFF PIECE**) written by a journalist angling for future favours from its subject.

**ENTREPRENEURIAL JOURNALIST** · One whose personal brand is more powerful than their publisher's. *A.k.a.*, **SUBSTACK STAR**.

**CATCH AND KILL** · Purchasing the exclusive rights to a scandalous story and burying it to protect (one of) the parties involved.

**TICK-TOCK** · A minute-by-minute account of an event / meeting / scandal / disaster / &c.

**STEP-BACK PIECE** · An article on the reaction to the reaction. *A.k.a.*, **THUMBSUCKER**.

**30,000 FT** · The altitude at which THUMB-SUCKING commentators (assume they) fly.

**(KEEPING *x*) IN PLAY** · To sustain interest in a person or event to **GIVE A STORY LEGS**.

**ANOTHER BITE OF THE APPLE** · Extending or advancing an old story that a journalist (or editor) thinks requires renewed attention.

**CATEGORY KILLER** · A definitive feature or **THINK PIECE** that effectively precludes rival follow-ups. *Conversely*, **NEWSMAKERS** · Major pieces that impact the wider discourse.

**THE FULL GINSBURG** · Appearing on all five Sunday morning political shows on the same day (A.B.C., C.B.S., N.B.C., Fox, C.N.N.). Named after William H. Ginsburg, who achieved this feat in 1998, representing Monica Lewinsky. In April 2013, Marco Rubio brought off the **FULL MARCO**, adding in Univision and Telemundo.

**GETTABLE** · Persuadable; said of politicians, pundits, celebs, or other **TALKING HEADS**. *Hence*, **GOOD GET** · Eventually persuaded.

**NERD PROM** · Obligatory nickname for the White House Correspondents' Association annual dinner, and its various satellite parties.

**EARNED MEDIA** · That published by a third-party without payment. *A.k.a.*, **FREE MEDIA**. *Conversely*, **PAID MEDIA** · E.g., commercials, billboards, direct mail, influencer marketing.

**TIME IN THE BARREL** · A politician's turn for intense media (and OPPO) scrutiny.

**BIRD-DOGGING** · When grass-roots activists publicly ambush politicians with questions or attacks, hoping to force them to **MAKE NEWS** on camera. E.g., in 2011, Mitt Romney was goaded by heckles about taxation into saying that "corporations are people."

## STRATEG(ER)Y

**STRATEGERY** · Coined in a 2000 *Saturday Night Live* sketch that spoofed the malapropisms of George W. Bush, the term is now used (self-deprecatingly) to mock overly convoluted or self-conscious political machinations.

**FOUR-DIMENSIONAL CHESS** · An (ironic or TROLLING) re-framing of incompetent or incomprehensible political acts as too subtle and sophisticated to be understood by mere mortals. *Similarly*, **9-D CHESS**.

**TROLLING** · Making deliberately provocative or offensive (online) comments to bait responses, distract debate, drive public opinion, wrong-foot opponents, amplify notoriety, &c.

**PERMISSION STRUCTURE** · A narrative that empowers voters to overcome personal doubts and/or social pressure and adopt a previously unthinkable position. (E.g., it was hoped that Liz Cheney's endorsement of Harris would allow squishy Republicans to vote Democrat.)

**OPPO(SITION RESEARCH)** · Dirt-digging on opponents. **SELF-OPPO** attempts to find out what enemy oppo will uncover about you.

**RAT FUCKING** · Originally college slang for dorm-room pranks and hijinks, the term now describes the dirtiest of political **DIRTY TRICKS**, from surveillance and harassment to cancelling meetings and stuffing ballot boxes.[1]

**BANK SHOT** · An indirect political manoeuvre (e.g., Republicans attacking Hunter Biden to discredit Joe and downplay Trump's legal travails). Named after the basketball (or pool) shot where the ball is bounced off the backboard (or cushion) into the net (or pocket).

**RED MEAT** · Popular/-ist rhetoric or policies, designed to **ENERGIZE THE BASE**. Recently, the Right has taken the concept literally, claiming the **CLIMATE HOAX** left wants to ban red meat and force voters to eat bugs.

**THE BASE** · Those who will vote for you — if they vote at all. Hence the importance of **GET OUT THE VOTE (G.O.T.V.)** strategies.

**OPTICS** · How a political event is perceived, irrespective of its substance or intent.

**LIPSTICKING THE PIG** · Hoping positive OPTICS will camouflage existential flaws.

**MUDSLINGING** · Low-level (and indiscriminate) attacks intended to overwhelm the opposition (and drive the electorate to declare **A PLAGUE ON BOTH YOUR HOUSES**).

**GISH GALLOP** · The rhetorical technique of overwhelming an interview or debate with an endless stream of lies, half-truths, unsubstantiated claims, and irrelevances. (Named after the creationist Duane Gish, who was a master.)

**DOUBLE HATERS** · Voters who dislike both candidates (e.g., Trump *and* Clinton in 2016; Trump *and* Harris in 2024) and **SIT OUT** the election, or vote for a third-party candidate.

*Barack Obama in a* **PULL ASIDE** *with Shinzo Abe at the* A.P.E.C *Summit, 2016*

**HORSESHOE** · The theory — attributed to Jean-Pierre Faye [2] — that the extreme political left and right are not at opposite ends of a linear spectrum, but closely aligned in opposition to the centre, both in views (hatred of mainstream media and "global elites") and tactics (direct action, intimidation, violence).

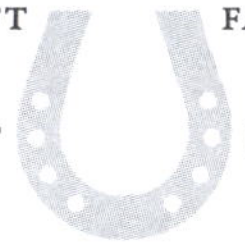


**HIPPIE PUNCH** · When moderate leftists criticize radical leftists to gain credibility with centrists. *A.k.a.*, **PUNCHING LEFT.**

*Similarly*, **SISTER SOULJAH MOMENT** · When a politician condemns a radical member of their coalition to pacify the mainstream. (Named after Bill Clinton's 1992 repudiation of a controversial race-related statement by rapper Sister Souljah, *A.k.a.*, Lisa Williamson.)

**RADICAL FLANK EFFECT** · How a cause is positively and negatively impacted by the acts of its most extreme advocates. E.g., Extinction Rebellion's vandalism of art undermines the climate cause for some, but for others makes more moderate positions seem attractive.

**OVERTON WINDOW** · The shifting frame of political and social acceptability, by which more marginal ideas enter the mainstream. Named after its originator, Joseph P. Overton.

(**DEMOCRATIC**) **BEDWETTING** · The (left-wing) tendency to let timidity and pessimism drive decisions; attributed to David Plouffe.

**DOG WHISTLE** · Using coded language to transmit extreme messages understood (only) by sympathizers. As the Republican strategist Lee Atwater explained in 1981:

> By 1968 you can't say "N*****" — that hurts you, backfires. So you say stuff like forced busing, states' rights, and all that stuff. [3]

Nowadays, unleashed politicians and pundits deploy the **AIR HORN** and **SAY THE QUIET PART OUT LOUD** with pride and even glee.

**BORKING** · To thwart a political opponent through relentless dissection of their policies and personality (or character assassination, depending on your perspective). Named after the campaign that kept Robert Bork off the Supreme Court in 1987.

**SWIFTBOATING** · Smearing an opponent's military record, by accusing them of **STOLEN VALOUR** (i.e., misrepresenting, overstating, or inventing one's military service).

Named after the vicious "Swift Boat Veterans for Truth" attacks on John Kerry's (multi-Purple-Heart-winning) Vietnam War record during the 2004 U.S. presidential race.

**MURDER BOARD** · An intense interrogation session used to prep and stress-test candidates prior to debates, confirmation hearings, &c.

*Hillary Clinton proving* **SELFIES** *are the new* GRIP AND GRIN

**AUDIENCE OF ONE** · Specifically targeting the (perceived) insecurities of an opponent. In 2024, the Lincoln Project wasted millions on ads that failed to "get into Trump's head."

## POLLING

**OVERNIGHTS** · The first-night results of a two- or three-night poll.

**QUICKIE / FLASH** · An instant poll, used to assess the impact of an event or GAFFE.

**ROGUE POLL** · Notwithstanding this term's technical, statistical definition, it usually just means "*Any poll I disagree with.*"

**PUSH POLL** · A political smear disguised as a poll, e.g., canvassing voters with the question "*Do you support Biden's one-child policy?*"

**TRACKING** ....... question(s) asked over time
**EXIT** ................. polls of Election Day voters
**INTERNALS** ......... a candidate's private polls
**SLOPE / TREND** ....... the trajectory of a poll

(**CROSS**) **TABS** · Data that go beyond the **TOP LINE** headline into **GRANULAR** breakdowns by race, age, education, sex, income, &c.

**FAM / FAV** · Familiarity and favourability — i.e., basic tests of public **SENTIMENT**.

**UPSIDE DOWN** · When a candidate's **UN-FAVES** outweigh his or her **FAVES**.

**POLL AGGREGATOR** · One who assesses (and weights) a **BASKET** of polls based on variables like past accuracy, transparency, &c.

**HERDING** · When pollsters manipulate or **SMOOTH** their methodology to match existing polls in order to avoid embarrassing **OUTLIERS**; the consequence is an artificial convergence of numbers that can shape media coverage and, in turn, voter behaviour.

## MISCELLANEOUS

The progression of **ILLNESS** euphemisms:
**IN GOOD SPIRITS** (seriously ill)
**RESTING COMFORTABLY** (unconscious)
**GRAVE** (prepare the obituary)
After **GRAVE**, brace to hear
"*My wife and I were* **SADDENED**
(or **DEEPLY SADDENED**) *to learn ...*"

**ME WALL** · An array of photographs featuring **GRIP AND GRINS** with **PRINCIPALS**.

**SHARPIE** · The autograph pen of choice for politicians; a **BODY MAN** essential.

**WASHINGTON READ** · Scanning the index of a newly released political book for your name.

**D.C. SCALP STARE** · Looking over your interlocutor's head for someone more important.

**BAKED IN** · When personal or political scandals become neutralized by familiarity.

**WHAT I'M HEARING** · "What I think." *Similarly*, **PEOPLE ARE SAYING** · "What I say."

**WALK BACK / CLARIFY** · To recant a GAFFE.

**GOLDWATER RULE** · The (now quaint) ethical ban against psychiatrists diagnosing public figures without consent or a consultation.

**WEST WING SYNDROME** · The fantasy that politics was once (and should again be) like Aaron Sorkin's love-letter to competent liberalism. *Also*, the temptation of hacks and flacks to compare themselves to *West Wing* characters (usually Sam, Toby, Josh, and C. J.).

Even Barack Obama was not immune: In 2013, he said that Sorkin "writes the way every Democrat in Washington wished they spoke."

*Similarly*, political **JOURNALISMISM** has been impacted by pop culture, from the crusading idealism of *All the President's Men* to the "gonzo" excess of Hunter S. Thompson's *Fear and Loathing on the Campaign Trail '72*.

**THREE-LETTER AGENCY** · Winking name for the C.I.A., which in turn calls the White House **OUR FRIENDS DOWN THE STREET**.

**CURIOUS** · Jokingly "confessing" to a potential and uncharacteristic political attraction. ("*I'm R.F.K. Jr. curious.*") An adaptation of the sexual orientation term "bi-curious." {☞ p.194}

**PILLED** · The 1999 film *The Matrix* introduced the idea of **BLUE** and **RED PILLS**: the former a sedative that keeps mankind docile, the latter a truth serum that exposes our enslavement. This trope gained political traction initially among the alt-right, for whom being **RED-PILLED** means perceiving the dark, misandrist, and deep-state forces that control the media, culture, finance, law, &c. {☞ p.262}

Now threadbare with conspiratorial overuse, the term is jokingly used when embracing something new or unexpected: "*I was Kamala curious ... but now I'm Kamala pilled!*"

**REALITY DISTORTION BUBBLE** · The impact of hearing only confirmatory opinions, e.g., in one's social-media **ECHO CHAMBER**.

**EXTREMELY ONLINE** · Anyone who uses X (*née* Twitter) more than you.

**MONETIZE** · What used to be "selling out."

**RED MIRAGE** · When Republicans appear to take an early electoral lead, because less-populous rural G.O.P. precincts declare faster than denser, urban Democratic precincts. (And because Dems are more likely to vote by mail.) The shrinking of this "lead" as election nights progress is known as the **BLUE SHIFT**.

**WAG THE DOG** · When politicians embark on foreign military action to deflect from domestic trouble. Popularized by the film based on Larry Beinhart's 1993 novel, in which a Hollywood producer is hired to fabricate a war to distract from a political sex scandal.

**SHOW BUY** · A political (T.V.) advert created and (minimally) aired to generate buzz and UNPAID MEDIA. {☞ p.277}

**ROLLING THE TAPE** · Playing video footage (on T.V. or at a public event) to prove a point and/or impeach an opponent.

**SPOTLIGHT RANGER** · One who only performs when observed by (and to please) their seniors; a military term, now used for political underlings who merely curry favour.

**LAWFARE** · Political use of the legal system, i.e., when the other team sues (or prosecutes).

**LOW / HIGH PROPENSITY VOTERS** · Those who are eligible to vote, and usually don't / do.

**LOW INFORMATION VOTERS** · Those who vote guided by fleeting signals ("*vibes*," even) rather than considered political analysis. (E.g., voting for Bill Clinton because he "*played the sax on Arsenio Hall*," or Trump because he's a "*successful businessman.*") Usually deployed by the centre-left to denigrate those who vote for (populist) right-wing candidates.

**HORSEFLESH** · The raw potential of (untested) candidates. As Roger Stone said of Trump: "I was like a jockey looking for a horse ... He was like a prime piece of political horseflesh." [4]

**STEMWINDER** · A speech that is either **BARNBURNING** or boring — depending on the writer. (It technically means the former).

**WORKING THE REF** · Aggressively attacking journalists, debate moderators, media titles, &c. to dissuade critical coverage in the future.

**LANDING TEAMS** · Small groups sent into federal agencies after a presidential election to facilitate the transition. These are followed by **BEACHHEAD TEAMS** of temporary political appointees, who work from inauguration until Senate-confirmed officials are in place.

**PEARL CLUTCHING** · Feigning indignation; the political equivalent of Captain Renault's *Casablanca* declaration: *"I'm shocked, shocked to find that gambling is going on in here!"*

## TRUMPISMS

The presidencies of Donald J. Trump introduced a new chapter to the Beltway glossary:

**AMERICAN CARNAGE** · What Trump saw from the lectern of his first inauguration. His solution was an **AMERICA FIRST** policy, designed to **MAKE AMERICA GREAT AGAIN.**

**ALTERNATIVE FACTS** · Coined by Kellyanne Conway to justify lies about the size of the crowd at Trump's 2017 inauguration. *Conversely*, **FAKE NEWS** · Trump's description of the **MAINSTREAM MEDIA**, which he denigrated as **THE ENEMY OF THE PEOPLE** — echoing Lenin, Stalin, and Mao.

**FLOOD THE ZONE** · A strategy of chaos and disorientation, defined by Steve Bannon:

> The real opposition is the media. And the way to deal with them is to flood the zone with shit. 5

**SCARAMUCCI / MOOCH** · An 11-day period: the duration of Anthony Scaramucci's tenure as White House Communications Director.

**CRYING MEN** · An endless parade of "big, strong guys" (coal miners, steel workers, police officers, ranchers) approach Trump with "tears in their eyes," call him "**SIR**," and thank him.

**EXECUTIVE TIME** · Scheduling euphemism for the hours (8–11 A.M.) Trump spends daily watching T.V., making calls, and tweeting.

**COVFEFE** · On 31.5.2017, Trump tweeted, "Despite the constant negative press covfefe." This obvious typo was spun into a conspiracy taken seriously by QANON loons. {☞ p.38}

**NICKNAMES** · Trump has the feral talent of a playground bully in finding nicknames that stick, from *Crooked Hillary* (Clinton) and *Sleepy Joe* (Biden) to *Shifty* (Adam) *Schiff* and *Cryin' Chuck* (Schumer). He often uses his rallies to audition nicknames (*Tiny D*, *Ron DeSanctimonious*), yet occasionally struggles to land *le mot injuste* (*Crazy Kamala*, *Laffin' Kamala*, *Comrade Kamala*, *Kamabla*).

**THREE-WORD-CHANT** · Surfing the wave of the **U-S-A** chant, Trump's rallies echo to:

› **BUILD-THE-WALL** · A reference to Trump's pledge to construct a Mexico–United States barrier, and **MAKE MEXICO PAY FOR IT.**

› **LOCK-HER-UP** · A threat to jail Hillary Clinton for various (imagined) crimes.

› **DRILL-BABY-DRILL** · A pledge to increase oil, natural gas, and coal production.

› **STOP-THE-STEAL** · A BIG LIE rallying call used in 2020, but created by Roger Stone for the 2016 Republican National Convention.

› **FIGHT! FIGHT! FIGHT!** · Trump's defiant cry, declaimed with a raised fist, just after an assassin's bullet grazed his ear on 13.7.2024.

› **DRAIN-THE-SWAMP** · An undying metaphor for slashing D.C. bureaucracy (deployed by Ronald Reagan *and* Nancy Pelosi) that was weaponized by Trump to attack the ...

**DEEP STATE** · A shadowy cabal of anti-Trump federal employees. Defeats are always caused by the deep state; victories are won despite it.

**VERY FINE PEOPLE ON BOTH SIDES** · Trump's description of the neo-Nazi goons and counter-protesters at a white supremacist rally in Charlottesville, Virginia, in 2017.

**STAND BACK AND STAND BY** · What Trump told the neo-Nazi Proud Boys in April 2020, when invited to condemn them.

**PERSON. WOMAN. MAN. CAMERA. TV.** · Words that Trump was proud to have remembered as part of a cognitive test in July 2020.

**THE BIG LIE** · The false claim that Democrats stole the 2020 election.

WE'LL SEE WHAT HAPPENS

**KUNG FLU / CHINA VIRUS** · Terms Trump used to accuse China of unleashing Covid.

**LET'S GO BRANDON** · On 2.10.2021, during an interview with the victorious N.A.S.C.A.R. driver Brandon Brown, an N.B.C. sports reporter claimed that a crowd chant of "Fuck Joe Biden" was actually "Let's Go Brandon." This unlikely phrase was instantly meme-ified into a gleefully anti-Biden, pro-Trump slogan.

**NEVER TRUMPERS** · Prominent Republicans who vocally oppose(d) Trump — including, at one time, JD Vance, who in 2016 privately wondered if Trump is **AMERICA'S HITLER**.[6]

**TRUMP DERANGEMENT SYNDROME** · The accusation that the **HATERS**, **LOSERS**, and NEVER TRUMPERS are perforce delusional.

**ANTI-ANTI-TRUMP** · Those who (claim to) support Trump only because the alternatives (e.g., Biden/Harris) are worse.

**TRUMP TRADE** · Stock positions adopted before and after the 2016 and 2024 elections to profit from Trump's pledges on taxes, tariffs, deregulation, crypto, immigration, &c.

**PROJECT 2025** · A 922-page "policy guide" released in 2023 by the Heritage Foundation that offered a blueprint to dismantle the "administrative state" in Trump's second term.

**M.A.H.A.** · The CRUNCHY, science-sceptical movement to Make America Healthy Again.

**CHILDLESS CAT LADIES** · In a 2021 interview JD Vance signalled sympathy with the manosphere {☞ p.262} by disparaging:

> ... a bunch of childless cat ladies who are miserable at their own lives and the choices that they've made and so they want to make the rest of the country miserable, too.[7]

**THE WEAVE** · Trump's term for his anecdotal and periphrastic style of public speaking:

> If you just read a teleprompter, nobody's going to be very excited. You've got to weave it out. So you — but you always have to — as you say, you always have to get right back to work. Otherwise, it's no good. But the weave is very, very important. Very few weavers around.[8]

**BLUE-ANON** · A left-wing version of QAnon {☞ p.38} that pushes copium conspiracies, e.g., that the Trump assassination attempt was fake; that **#TRUMPCHEATED** in 2024; &c.

**SANEWASHING** · The accusation that parts of the media report Trump's rambling speeches, radical rhetoric, and incoherent policy statements in such a way as to normalize them.

**VERY STABLE GENIUS** · Trump's assessment of his own emotional and mental capacity.

**WE'LL SEE (WHAT HAPPENS)** · Trump's go-to answer/analysis — which has the effect of hinting at, yet not committing to, action. ⊙

# A Vexillology of Pride

*A field guide to one of the most universally recognized socio-political symbols of our age.*

**PINK TRIANGLE**

**GILBERT BAKER PRIDE**

**7 COLOUR**

**6 COLOUR**

**PHILADELPHIA PRIDE**

**PROGRESS PRIDE**

**INTERSEX-INCLUSIVE PRIDE**

Perhaps the earliest gay pride symbol was reclaimed from the Nazis, who forced tens of thousands of homosexual concentration camp inmates to wear a downward-pointing pink triangle badge on their uniforms.

In 1973, the West German gay liberation group *Homosexuelle Aktion Westberlin* reappropriated this stigma as a mark of defiance, and soon the pink triangle (either side up) became synonymous first with gay and lesbian rights and then, in the 1980s, with solidarity for those infected with H.I.V.

In 1978, Harvey Milk, one of America's first "openly gay" elected officials, encouraged the activist, artist, and designer Gilbert Baker to create a flag for the eighth annual San Francisco Gay Freedom Day Parade (now known as Pride).

Naturally, Baker was aware of the pink triangle, but argued "we needed something that was positive, that celebrated our love." And so he turned to traditional vexillology:

> I thought of the American flag with its thirteen stripes and thirteen stars ... I thought of the vertical red, white, and blue tricolor from the French Revolution and how both flags owed their beginnings to a riot, a rebellion, or revolution ... I thought how most flags represented a place. They were primarily nationalistic, territorial, iconic propaganda ... Gay people were tribal, individualistic, a global collective that was expressing itself in art and politics. We needed a flag to fly everywhere. [1]

Combining the post-diluvian rainbow ("I do set my bow in the cloud, and it shall be for a token of a covenant between me and the earth," Genesis 9:13) with the colours of S.F.'s exuberant nightlife, Baker gave each stripe a significance:

| | | | |
|---|---|---|---|
| Hot pink | SEX | Green | NATURE |
| Red | LIFE | Turquoise | MAGIC |
| Orange | HEALING | Indigo | SERENITY |
| Yellow | SUNLIGHT | Violet | SPIRIT |

A surge in demand after Milk's murder on 27.11.1978, led to a shortage of hot-pink fabric, and so a seven-colour version was sewn. And in 1979, the turquoise was dropped and the indigo swapped for blue to create the iconic six-colour flag. [2]

In 2017, the PHILADELPHIA PRIDE flag added black and brown stripes to represent communities of colour. In 2018, Daniel Quasar created the PROGRESS flag by incorporating the TRANSGENDER flag. And in 2021, Valentino Vecchietti added the yellow field and purple circle of the INTERSEX flag to create an INTERSEX-INCLUSIVE version.

☞ *An Intersex-Inclusive Pride flag on Regent Street, London, marks Pride Month, 2024*

## OTHER PRIDE FLAGS OF NOTE

*Although many of these flags are long-established and widely recognized, others are far from mainstream. As a result, some of the definitions, colours, attributions, and symbolic explanations given are tentative and/or disputed.*

**LESBIAN · LABRYS FLAG**
*Designed by* SEAN CAMPBELL *in* 1999
Violet · *Symbolic of Sappho*;
Inverted black triangle · *Reference to the "antisocial" badges used in Nazi concentration camps*;
Double-headed labrys axe · *Symbolic of strength and autonomy*

**LESBIAN** [one of several]
*Designed by* EMILY GWEN [?] *in* UNKNOWN
Dark Orange · *Gender non-conformity*;
Orange · *Independence*; Light orange · *Community*;
White · *Womanhood*; Pink · *Serenity*;
Pastel pink · *Love and Sex*; Dark Pink · *Femininity*

**GAY MEN (TRANS INCLUSIVE)**
*Designed by* UNKNOWN *in* ~2019
Green–turquoise · *Community, healing, and joy*;
White · *Gender non-conforming, non-binary, transgender*;
Blue–purple · *Pure love, fortitude, diversity*

**BISEXUAL**
Attraction to more than one gender
*Designed by* MICHAEL PAGE *in* 1998
Magenta · *Same-sex attraction*;
Lavender · *Attraction to both sexes*;
Blue · *Opposite-sex attraction*

**PANSEXUAL**
Attraction regardless of gender
*Designed by* JASPER V [?] *in* ~2010
Magenta · *(Attraction to) women / femininity*;
Yellow · *(Attraction to) non-binary*;
Cyan · *(Attraction to) men / masculinity*

**POLYSEXUAL**
Attraction to several genders
*Designed by* UNKNOWN *in* [?] 2012 [?]
Pink · *(Attraction to) women / femininity*;
Green · *(Attraction to) non-binary*;
Blue · *(Attraction to) men / masculinity*

**TRANSGENDER**
A gender identity different from the sex assigned at birth
*Designed by* MONICA F. HELMS *in* 1999
Blue · *Traditional masculine*;
Pink · *Traditional feminine*;
White · *Neutral, undefined, non-conforming, or transitioning*

**NON-BINARY**
Identifying outside traditional male or female categories
*Designed by* KYE ROWAN *in* 2014
Yellow · *Non-binary*; White · *Many or all genders*;
Purple · *Binary, fluid, or blended male and female*;
Black · *Agender*

**GENDERFLUID PRIDE**
A gender identity that changes over time and by circumstance
*Designed by* J. J. POOLE *in* 2012 [?]
Pink · *Femininity*; White · *No gender*;
Purple · *Androgyny, Masculinity + femininity*;
Black · *All other & third genders*; Blue · *Masculinity*

**GENDERQUEER** (& **NON-BINARY**)
Umbrella term for various non-binary, non-normative identities
*Designed by* MARILYN ROXIE *in* 2010–11
Lavender · *Androgyny, and queerness*;
White · *Agender and gender neutrality*;
Green · *Identities outside of the binary*

**INTERSEX**
Having biological traits not conforming to typical male or female
*Designed by* MORGAN CARPENTER *in* 2013
*The colours deliberately avoid referencing gender stereotypes; the plain circle symbolizes wholeness, completeness, and potential*

**POLYAMORY**
Consensual non-monogamy with multiple partners
*Designed by* JIM EVANS *in* 1995
Blue · *Openness & honesty*; Red · *Love & passion*; Black · *Solidarity (with those who hide their relationships)*; π · *P(i) for polyamory*;
Gold · *emotional (not physical) attachment*

**ASEXUAL**
Not sexually attracted to people of any gender
*Designed by* the ASEXUAL VISIBILITY AND EDUCATION NETWORK *in* 2010
Black · *Asexuality*; Grey · *Those in a grey area of asexuality*;
White · *Sexuality*; Purple · *Community*

**DEMISEXUAL**
Sexual attraction that depends on a prior emotional bond
*Adapted from the* ASEXUAL PRIDE FLAG *in* ~2010
Black · *Asexuality*;
Grey · *Those in a grey area of asexuality*;
White · *Sexuality*; Purple · *Community*

**STRAIGHT ALLY**
*Designed by* UNKNOWN *in* LATE 2000s
*A subversion of the controversial (and some say homophobic) black and white striped* STRAIGHT FLAG; *the Pride flag rainbow colours form an A that represents the allyship of heterosexual people with the* L.G.B.T.Q.+ *community*

# Hold the Front Page!

*The (increasingly archaic) lingo of* **NEWSPRINT** *and* **TABLOIDESE**.

## TABLOIDESE

Some of the terms associated with the rough and tumble of British **TABLOID** journalism:

**MARMALADE DROPPER** · A story so stunning that readers will let fall their breakfast condiment. *A.ka.,* a **FUCK ME, DORIS** story.
E.g., *The Sun*'s 2005 front-page **SPLASH** of Prince Harry wearing a swastika armband.

**REVERSE FERRET** · When a paper suddenly (and silently) changes its editorial position (or front page story) in response to fresh facts.
Attributed to Kelvin MacKenzie, editor of *The Sun* (1981–1994), who gave stories a 1–3 star **FERRET RATING** based on the discomfort they caused their target, asking: "Whose bum can we put a ferret up?" [1]

**SPOOF** · An innocuous front page run as the first edition to prevent a **FUCK ME, DORIS** being **LIFTED** (i.e., ripped off) by rivals.

**SPOILER** · A story run to undermine or steal the thunder of a competitor's scoop.

**KNOCK DOWN** · To demolish another paper's story. *Or*, to cut a piece down to size.

**STAND UP** · To establish a story's accuracy (to the satisfaction of the paper's lawyers).

**BASH OUT** · To write quickly, on deadline.

**BUY UP** · To pay for an exclusive interview or story, i.e., **CHEQUEBOOK JOURNALISM**.

**RIDDLE IT** · Transforming a headline into a question on a story you can't fully **STAND UP**.

**DOG'S DICK** *or* **COCK** · Exclamation mark. *Also*, **SCREAMER / SHRIEK / ASTONISHER / SQUEALER / BANG / STRIKER**.

**MONSTERING** · Targeting an individual (or organization) for relentless, daily humiliation.

**PUT A KILT ON IT** · To find a Scottish angle for any story. E.g., when Donald Trump fell ill in October 2020, the *Ayr Advertiser* ran: "The owner of the luxurious Ayrshire resort has tested positive for Covid 19."

**BLAGGING** · (Illegally) obtaining confidential personal information (e.g., bank statements, medical records) through **IMPERSONATION** or via **BUNGS** (i.e., bribes), **BIN DIVING**, phone hacking, &c. *A.k.a.*, the **DARK ARTS**.

**SIDEBAR OF SHAME** · The right-hand column on the *Mail Online* website, famed for its salacious stories and **SAUCY** thumbnails.

**KNOBBLY MONSTER** · Tabloid term for an **ELEGANT VARIATION**: a synonym used to avoid repetition. E.g., referring to pork pies as "pig-packed parcels" or Ozempic as the "trendy semiglutide injectable." ("Knobbly monster" was a **SECOND MENTION** for "crocodile.")

## TABLOID TROPES

**PHEW, WHAT A SCORCHER!** · Obligatory (and ironic) heat-wave headline. Temperatures are always compared to **SUN-KISSED** locales ("*It's hotter than the Sahara!*") and/or visually illustrated (e.g., frying eggs on the pavement). "*But make the most of it!*" — because a **COLD SNAP** is ushering in **ARCTIC CONDITIONS**.

**SINCE RECORDS BEGAN** · Suffix appended to (weather) data to add historical heft.

**TROUBLE IN PARADISE?** · Photo caption for celebrity couples looking anything other than doe-eyed. *Or*, if one partner is papped **WITHOUT THEIR WEDDING RING**.

**HORROR** · Mandatory prefix to all violence (e.g., **HORROR ATTACK / STABBING**). *Also*, **TRAGEDY** · Mandatory suffix for accidents: (e.g., **LAKE / BALLOON TRAGEDY**). All of which lead to an **OUTPOURING OF GRIEF**.

The Sun's *Prince Harry* MARMALADE DROPPER, *13.1.2005*

**HELL** · Any form of **MAYHEM** (i.e., delay), e.g., **HOLIDAY / AIRPORT / STRIKE HELL.** *Also*, a **TELL-ALL** story: **MY BOOZE HELL.** *Also*, whenever plucky Brits are **BANGED UP** abroad: **MY** [foreign country] **PRISON HELL.**

**NOW** · A headline word that instantly conveys exasperation: **NOW They're Banning Milk!**

**THAT** · A word that turns any story into a soap-opera plot, e.g., **THAT Dress Is Back!** *or* **How THAT Kiss Ruined My Marriage!**

**BODY-LANGUAGE EXPERT** · A dubiously qualified pundit whose "analysis" of celebrity behaviour "reveals" subtle, hidden clues that coincidentally match the paper's editorial line.

**ETIQUETTE EXPERT** · A pompous popinjay whose *arriviste* advice on "manners" is either gauchely pretentious or blindingly obvious. ("*Five foods you should never eat on a train!*")

**LIPREADER** · One who puts words into the mouths of celebrities and royals, safe from contradiction. ("*Lipreader reveals Meghan Markle's one-word 'order' to Prince Harry.*")

**EXAM RESULTS** · Invariably illustrated with photos of (blonde) schoolgirls jumping for joy — common also in many broadsheets.

**NUMBERS** · Wherever possible, stories should include a subject's age, salary, and property value. ("Jane Smith, 49, a civil servant earning £88,000, set fire to her £550,000 bungalow.")

**STUNNING / ADORABLE / DAZZLING / &c.** · Various sycophantic adjectives used to soften the blow of reproducing a celebrity's Instagram photos — especially if they **LEAVE NOTHING TO THE IMAGINATION.**

**LOOKS UNRECOGNISABLE** · When stars are papped going about their everyday lives — especially if **MAKE-UP FREE.** {☞ THEY'RE JUST LIKE US p.99} *Or*, when **PLUS SIZE** celebs **SHED THE POUNDS**. *Or*, after an **INCREDIBLE** *or* **DRAMATIC MAKEOVER.**

**W.A.G.s** · The Wives And Girlfriends of professional athletes, whose antics and antagonisms provide endless, "glamorous" fodder.

**CANCER** · Everything in tabloid-land "*may* give you cancer" — from ill-fitting bras and broccoli to crayons and cod-liver oil. Usually there is at least a sliver of science behind such claims, but the onslaught of oncogenes does rather overwhelm. In recent years, the risk has shifted depressingly to **DEMENTIA.**

**CONTEMPORARY ART** · Scepticism toward modern art quickly descends into derision if it involves government funding, non-traditional materials, the Turner Prize — or all three.

Tabloid-approved art includes Old Master paintings and **HYPER-REALISTIC** drawings that cannot be part of some snide artist's trickery. ("*Can you believe it's not a photo?*")

**GRAFFITI** · Degenerate vandalism — unless, for some reason, by Banksy. {☞ p.164}

## CONCISE TABLOID–ENGLISH DICTIONARY

Though designed for brevity, TABLOIDESE has evolved into an ironic sociolect, where headlines like **Shamed Love Rat In Death Plunge** both inform readers and invite them to feel part of a clique.

**AMPLE ASSETS** ... large breasts
**AXE / CHOP** ... discontinue / sack
**BABY BUMP** ... visible signs of pregnancy
**BACK ON** ... when a romance is **REKINDLED**
**BARELY OUT OF HIS *or* HER TEENS** ... ≥20
**BLAST / SLAM / RIP / RAP** ... criticize
**BLAZE / INFERNO** ... fire
**BLOW** ... disappointment
**BLUNDER** ... mistake
**BOFFIN** ... scientist / any qualified expert
**BOUNDER / CAD** ... posh womanizer
**BRANDED** ... described as / called
**BRAWL / FRACAS** ... not quite a fight
**BRAZEN / SHAMELESS** ... caught on camera
**BREAKS SILENCE** ... gives an interview
**BUNGLING *x*** ... *x* who got caught (e.g., thief)
**BUXOM / BUSTY** ... large-breasted
**CAGED / BANGED UP** ... imprisoned
**CHAOTIC SCENES** ... not quite a riot
**CLOBBERED** ... required to pay tax, or a fine
**COMPO** ... financial compensation
**COR!** ... prefix for anything mildly **SAUCY**
**COSIES UP TO** ... sits next to
**COUGH UP** ... to pay (grudgingly)
**COY** ... ignored our (shouted) questions
**CURVY / VOLUPTUOUS** ... tolerably fat
**DEATH PLUNGE** ... fatal fall
**EYEING** ... looking to buy
**FIGHTING FOR LIFE** ... in intensive care
**FLAUNTS HER FIGURE** ... wears a bikini
**GIANT** ... any big business (e.g., oil giant)
**GYM-HONED** ... acceptably muscular
**HALF NAKED** ... wearing a bikini
**HAS BEEN SPOTTED** ... i.e., by the paparazzi
**HELL HOLE** ... foreign prison
**HIKE** ... to raise prices, taxes, &c.
**HITS BACK** ... responds to
**HUNK** ... a sexy **FELLA**
**JET SETTING** ... any foreign travel
**JIBE** ... mild insult or criticism
**LAGS / CONS** ... (British) prisoners
**LAMBASTED / SLAMMED** ... criticized
**LOVE NEST** ... site of a **NIGHT OF SHAME**
**LOVE RAT** ... male adulterer
**MECCA** ... any popular location (rarely Mecca)
**MUCH-LOVED** ... reasonably popular
**MYSTERY FRIEND** ... unidentified lover
**NICKED / COLLARED** ... arrested
**OUR BOYS** ... British armed forces
**PENPUSHER / JOBSWORTH** ... bureaucrat
**PLEDGE / VOW** ... promise
**PLUNGING** ... a dress that reveals ample assets
**POSH TOTTY** ... attractive lady **ARISTO**[crat]
**POURED INTO** ... wearing a tight dress
**PROBE** ... investigation
**PROFESSIONAL FUNNY-MAN** ... comic
**QUIZZED / GRILLED** ... questioned
**REVELLERS** ... non-violent drunks
**SAGA** ... a long-running (celebrity) story
**SHAKE UP** ... a change of personnel
**SHAMED / RED-FACED** ... embarrassed
**SHOWS HIS *or* HER FUN SIDE** ... smiles
**SHUNS** ... avoids
**SPAT / WAR OF WORDS** ... a public **ROW**
**SPLASHES OUT** ... spends money
**STEPS OUT IN** ... wears
**STUNNER** ... a sexy **LASS**
**SVELTE** ... acceptably thin
**SWEARS BY** ... uses / is paid to promote
**TAKES A SWIPE AT** ... criticizes
**TEMPTRESS / SIREN** ... the cause of adultery
**TIGHT-LIPPED** ... declined to comment
**U-TURN / CAVE IN** ... change of mind
**WAIF-LIKE** ... almost anorexic
**WORRYINGLY THIN** ... anorexic

### INEVITABLE ADJECTIVES

Apologies *are always* ... **grovelling; fulsome**
Communities ... **close-knit; on edge; rallying**
Criminals ... **brought to justice; on the run**
Falls from grace ... **dramatic; very public**
Footage / photos [of a crime] ... **chilling**
Lifestyles ... **lavish; luxurious; swanky**
Muscles ... **rippling; hulking; killer**
Rows ... **bitter; acrimonious**
Stock markets ... **soaring; plunging; rallying**
Rumours / speculation ... **circling online; rife**
Suburbs ... **leafy; quiet and unassuming; posh**
Temperatures ... **soaring; plunging**
Tensions ... **mounting; running high**
Tirades ... **foul-mouthed; X-rated; furious**

**ROMP / BONK / PORK / SHAG / ROGER** ... to **GET ONE'S LEG OVER** / have **NOOKIE**
**SAUCY / SIZZLING / STEAMY / RAUNCHY / EYE-POPPING** ... acceptably pornographic
**DIRTY / FILTHY / SEEDY / VILE / SMUTTY / SHOCKING** ... unacceptably pornographic

## STORIES

**INVERTED PYRAMID** · The classic structure of a news story, where the vital facts come first, followed by details of diminishing importance. In theory, an editor could cut the final **PARS** of such a story with little news impact. The (U.S.) pyramid usually follows the format: **LEDE → NUT GRAF → BODY → KICKER**.

**LEDE / LEAD** ["*leed*"] · The opening, encapsulating sentence(s) of a story. As George C. Bastian wrote in 1923: "News leads should be simple, brief, compact, vigorous, attractive."[2]

Journalism's cardinal stylistic sin is to **BURY THE LEDE**, e.g., by not mentioning until the sixth graf that the story's subject is a penguin. Not much better is the **SUITCASE LEDE**, into which every possible fact is awkwardly packed.

That said, as Michael Kinsley noted: "Once you have the lede, the rest is just typing."

**ANECDOTAL LEDE** · Taking the reader on a (personal) scenic detour before getting to the damn point. *Similarly*, **DELAYED DROP** · Deliberately BURYING THE LEDE, e.g., to build suspense, or set up a joke.

**NUT GRAF** · A section that follows the LEDE, adding key detail and relevance. Once known at *The Philadelphia Inquirer* as: 'You may have wondered why we invited you to this party."

**BODY** · The main text of an article.

**KICKER** · A cute, humorous, or poignant twist that neatly ends a piece. *Or*, words added to amplify a headline ("*Shock Confession*"). *Or*, an additional, engaging subhead.

**5 WS** · The **WHO**, **WHAT**, **WHEN**, **WHERE**, **WHY** (and **HOW**) of a story.

**ANGLE** · The approach a reporter takes to a story. E.g., after a bridge collapse, focusing on the engineering failure, or the victims' stories.

**N.I.B.** · News In Brief · A 50–150 word story. *Also*, **ODD / BRIGHT** · A 2–3 PAR quirky piece.

**SPLASH** · The front-page **LEAD**. The second most important piece is the **BACKYARD**.

**SIDEBAR** · A box of text or graphics run next to a story to add context, explanation, &c.

**PACKAGE** · A piece comprising multiple stories, photos, graphics, &c. Used to cover election results, terror attacks, budgets, &c.

**HOOK / PEG** · Something that makes a story timely, and therefore justifies publication. (And why journalists are flooded with tendentious press releases prior to Valentine's Day, Women's Day, Pride Month, &c.)

**FOLO** · A **FOLLOW UP** to an earlier piece.

**LEADER / EDITORIAL** · Unsigned pieces that give the publication's opinion on a story.

The **THIRD LEADER** in the London *Times* is often more flippant in topic and tone.

**OP-ED** · A guest-written opinion piece; the term comes from *The New York Times*, where such pieces run *opposite* the *editorial* page.

**SERVICE PIECE** · Any kind of **HOW-TO**. Often disdained by serious journalists, hence the joke disclaimer: "*Not afraid to be servicey!*"

**ABOVE** *or* **BELOW THE FOLD** · A description of a story's significance based on its position in relation to the front-page fold of a broadsheet.

On the web, the fold becomes the **SCROLL**.

## FORMAT & LAYOUT

**BROADSHEET** · Both a newspaper's size, and a description of its highbrow or heavyweight style. (*Hence*, **HEAVIES**.) E.g., *The Australian*, *The Wall Street Journal*.

Although *The Guardian* and *The Times* are journalistically broadsheets, they both shrank to tabloid size for financial reasons; the term they sometimes prefer is **COMPACT**.

**BERLINER** · A mid-size paper (315×470 mm) that sits between tabloid and broadsheet; popular with European papers, e.g., *Le Monde*, *La Repubblica*, *El País*.

**MIDDLE MARKET** · Papers that blend populist stories and hard news. E.g., *The Daily Mail*, *The Times of India*, *USA Today*.

**TABLOID / TAB** · Both a newspaper size (around half that of a BROADSHEET) and a description of a punchy style and populist outlook. E.g., *The New York Post*, *The Advertiser*.

*Boris Johnson plays nice with the* DOORSTEPPERS, *2018*

**RED TOPS** · British tabloids with red MASTHEADS, and roisterous personalities. E.g., *The Sun*, *The Daily Mirror*, *The Daily Star*.

**SUPERMARKET TABLOIDS** · The most sensationalist American (weekly) papers, e.g., *The National Enquirer*, *Globe*.

**MASTHEAD** · The title of a publication (*A.k.a.*, **NAMEPLATE / FLAG / TITLE-PIECE**).
*Also*, the hierarchical list of editorial, production, and management staff, as well as key contributors — more common in magazines.

**EARS / LUGS / PUGS** · A front page's top-left and -right corners; used for promos and ads.

**HAMPER / ATTIC** · A (horizontal) front page story (that appears above the LEAD story).

**SKYBOX / SKYLINE** · A teaser that appears above, next to, or just below the MASTHEAD.

**SEAL** · A front-page text block that shows the **EDITION** (**EARLY**, **MIDDAY**, **CITY**, **LATE**, &c.). Some papers use numbers or asterisks.

**HED** · A headline, traditionally designed to inform; increasingly written to intrigue. A **BANNER HED** dominates the front-page.

**DEK** · A subhead that summarizes a story and engages the reader.

**STICK** · A stub of copy. *Or*, in a broadsheet, a column that runs the full length of a page.

**FURNITURE** · The fixed elements of a page's layout, e.g., date, **FOLIO** (page number), &c.

**STANDFIRST** · Introductory copy below the HED — often in a distinct typographic style.

**REEFER / REFER** · When a piece refers to a related story (on a different page).

**BYLINE** · The credit to a story's author(s). Notably, *The Economist* does not print them.

**SHIRT-TAIL** · Bylines added to the end of a piece, e.g., "Additional reporting by." *A.k.a.*, **TAG LINE**. *Or*, a relevant short piece appended to the end of a longer, related story.

**DATELINE** · Indicates the location of a story's reporting. E.g., on 14.4.1945, *The New York Times* ran a story with the dateline: ABOARD PRESIDENT ROOSEVELT'S FUNERAL TRAIN.

**GRAF / PAR** · Abbreviations for paragraph.

**CUT LINE** · A picture caption (which should pithily encapsulate the story).

**PULL QUOTE** · A quote from the body copy, enlarged for emphasis and/or visual appeal.

**JUMP(LINE)** · When a piece is **CONT. ON P.×××** to allow more stories on the front page. (Sometimes enclosed in a **MORON BOX**.)

**BASEMENT** · The lowest story on a (front) page — often amusing, quirky, or off-beat.

**LITERAL** · A seplling mistake. (Any *horrific* **TYPO** or factual error is a **HOWLER**.)

**FRONT** *or* **BACK OF BOOK (F.O.B. / B.O.B.)** · The place where magazines (who refer to themselves internally as **BOOKS**) run shorter pieces. Longer features appear in the **WELL**.

**T.K.** · Indicates that copy is still To Kome.

**C.Q.** · A note (like [sic]) alerting an editor that an unlikely fact (or spelling) is accurate. Possibly from *cadit quaestio* [the question arises].

**-30-** · A code (American) journalists append to copy to indicate the end of an article.

**W.O.B** · White On Black **HED**, or other text.

• **BLOB PAR** · One of these.

**CROSS HED** · A subhead within a column; used for visual appeal and/or structure, e.g.:

## MISCELLANEOUS

**BELOW THE LINE** · Online ~~abuse~~ comments from valued readers.

**DOORSTEPPING** · Approaching the subject of a story (or their family) at home (or work), to give them an opportunity to "have their say."

Canny media players will demonstrate how utterly relaxed they are by delivering mugs of tea to the waiting **PACK**.

**DEATH KNOCK** · **DOORSTEPPING** a grieving widow(er) to get quotes (and family photos). (Occasionally, death knockers find themselves actually breaking the news to the bereaved.)

**CANINES** · It is journalistic malpractice not to name any dog that is mentioned in a story.

**SPIKE** · To **KILL** a commissioned or completed piece. Named after the metal desk spikes on which unwanted copy would be impaled.

Depending on the contract, spiked writers may be paid a (reduced) **KILL FEE**.

**CHURNALISM** · Lazily regurgitating press releases, or other forms of P.R. **HAND OUT**.

**SNAPPER / MONKEY** · Photographer.

**POOL** · Where an event gives access to a small number of reporters and snappers, whose work is distributed to other organizations.

**COPY APPROVAL** · The (widely deprecated) process of giving the subject of an interview or story the right to see (and edit) it prior to publication. Sometimes justified as the only way to obtain a (celebrity) scoop.

**COLOUR SECTION** *or* **PIECE** · One that focuses on description and impression rather than **HARD NEWS**.

**BEAT** · The topic a journalist covers — from the broad (politics) to the specific (biotech).

**CORRESPONDENT** · A journalist working at a distance or abroad (e.g., Moscow correspondent); *Or*, a senior writer covering a specialist **BEAT** (e.g., security correspondent).

**CONFERENCE** · (Multiple) daily meetings of senior editorial staff, at which the content and layout of the day's paper is decided.

**BACK BENCH** · Senior journalists who make the final editorial decisions on a day's paper.

**EMBARGO** · Because newspapers need time to write stories, review books, &c., they are often given material that may not be used until a specified date and time.

**BREAKING AN EMBARGO** to fabricate a **SCOOP** is considered bad form.

**FISKING** · A savage (and/or witty) point-by-point rebuttal of another journalist's piece; named after the foreign correspondent Robert Fisk, who was a common target of such attacks.

**SET AND HOLD** · To write and typeset an **OBIT**(uary) for later use.

**MORGUE** · Old term for a paper's clippings library; now a place where **ADVANCE OBITS** are kept for rapid post-mortem publication.

**OFF-STONE** · When an edition is sent to the printers, and can no longer be changed.

**BANGING OUT** · To serenade a departing colleague with a cacophony of thumped desks; the tradition dates to the days of moveable type, when the banging was more metallic. ⊙

# The Manosphere's Dread Game

*The* **MANOSPHERE** *is a metastasizing ideological confederacy that combines* **TOXIC MASCULINITY** *— denigrating all but the most alpha of males, and* **VIOLENT MISOGYNY** *— dismissing women as little more than potential mates. In the midst of this are* **INCELS** *— who are utterly alienated from romantic love;* **PICK-UP ARTISTS** *— for whom seduction is simply a numbers game; and* **HUSTLERS** *— who ruthlessly exploit women as pawns and men as marks.*

## X PILLED

It's ironic that so many alt-right and far-right activists preen themselves through the prism of *The Matrix*, since the 1999 movie was written and directed as a transgender allegory by the trans sisters Lana (born Larry) and Lilly (born Andy) Wachowski.[1]

Ignoring (or ignorant of) this inconvenient truth, the radical right bastardizes the film's key plot device, where taking a red pill reveals the reality of humanity's enslavement by intelligent machines, and taking a blue pill returns you to a state of ignorant subjugation.

In the manosphere's twisted interpretation:

**RED PILLED** · To see the "truth" that feminism has transformed men into social, economic, sexual, and political inferiors.

**BLUE PILLED** · To cling to the comforting but false "*Disney*" constructs of soulmates, sexual equality, good guys get the girl, "*Happy wife, happy life*," &c.

**PURPLE PILLED** · To believe in much of the red pill ideology, while having faith that blue pill behaviour can improve life for both sexes.

**BLACK PILLED** · A fatalistic version of the RED PILL that asserts that no amount of MAXXING or ALPHA-aping can turn INCELS into CHADS, so why not simply L.D.A.R.?

## MEN

It's similarly ironic that the manosphere is so fixated on the hierarchy of **WOLF PACKS**, since the theory that wolves are led by **ALPHA** males who dominate lesser **BETAS** has been debunked by its original proponents.[2]

Notwithstanding *this* inconvenient truth, the manosphere delights in stereotyping men almost as viciously as it stereotypes women.

**ALPHA MALE** · The archetypal strong, fit, successful, attractive (Aryan) man: "*Men want to be him, women want to be with him.*" *A.k.a.*, **CHAD** — or if wildly **HENCH** (i.e., fit) **GIGA CHAD**. A Black chad is a **TYRONE**; other racially dubious terms for chad include:

| | |
|---|---|
| **CHADDAM** | Arab CHAD |
| **CHADPREET** | Indian |
| **CHANG** | East Asian |
| **VLAD** | Slavic |

**SIGMA MALE** · A strong, silent, stoic, and solitary **LONE WOLF**, whose self-reliance sets him above even the most superior CHAD. (The invention of the sigma male in ~2010 took many self-proclaimed ALPHAS by surprise.)

**TRADCON** · ALPHAS who disavow womanizing and pick-up artistry in favour of (Christian) Conservative values — not least fidelity.

**BETA MALE** · One subordinate to ALPHAS; a follower rather than a leader; a provider rather than a pillager. In the eyes of an ALPHA, an **A.F.C.** (Average Frustrated Chump).

**ALPHA FUX / BETA BUX** (**A.F. / B.B.**)· The theory that ALPHAS supply strength and sex, whereas BETAS provide comfort and security.

**WIFE GUY** · A (pathetically) uxorious man.

**BETA ORBITER** · One who hovers around STACYS, endlessly and hopelessly.

**SIMP** · A man who expends time and money on women who have no interest in him.

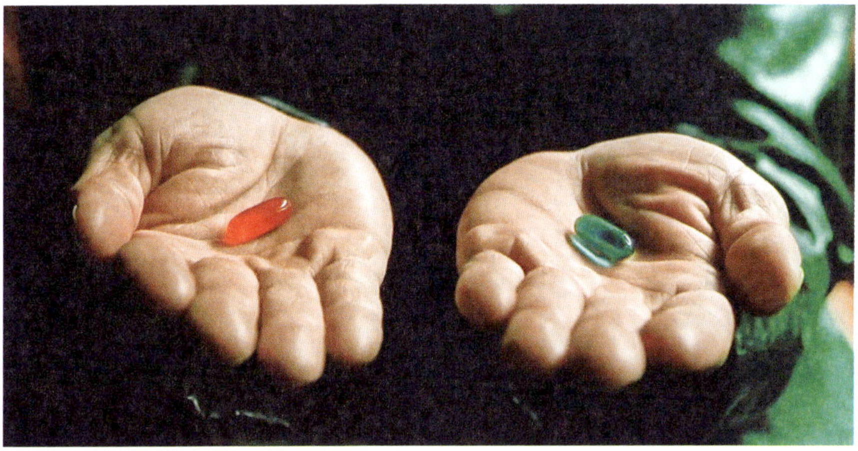

*"You take the* RED PILL *... and I show you how deep the rabbit hole goes."* The Matrix *(1999)*

**CUCK** · Derived from "cuckold" — a man who is ignorant of, tolerates, or is gratified by his partner's infidelity — the term now denigrates any insufficiently **ALPHA** (or alt-right) male. {☞ CUCK(SERVATIVE) p.243}

**SOY** *or* **SOI BOY** · An insufficiently masculine man (whose liberal effeminacy is sometimes blamed on the phytoestrogens in soy milk). *Similarly,* **LOW-T** · A Low Testosterone man.

**NECKBEARD** · An awkward, unprepossessing (pretentious) NERD {☞ p.206} named for the unkempt whiskers that straggle his neck.

## INCELS

**INCELS** [involuntary + celibates] blame their inability to forge romantic or sexual relationships on society's impossible aesthetic standards, its iniquitous misandry, and the **80/20 RULE** where 80% of women are interested only in the most **ALPHA** 20% of men.

Radical incels usually self-quarantine in odd corners of the internet. But once in a while **INCELDOM** hits the headlines — usually when a "frustrated" loner commits mass murder.

Infamously, on 23.5.2014, 22-year-old Elliot Rodger killed six and injured 14 in a frenzied knife and gun attack in Isla Vista, California. Before the massacre, which ended with his suicide, Rodger uploaded a six-minute YouTube video and a 137-page "manifesto" in which he blamed his virginity on girls who "despise and loathe me," and declared "I am the good guy."

Of course, not all incels are violent. But the unconcealed and barely controlled rage that simmers across inceldom is illustrated both by Rodger's nickname — the **SUPREME GENTLEMAN** — and the fact that the incel equivalent of "going postal" (i.e., a furious murder spree) is (jokingly) known as **GOING E.R.**

There are any number of more or less common terms to describe specific types of incel, e.g.:

› **TRUECEL** · One who will remain an incel regardless of any **MAXXING** they attempt.
› **GAYCEL** · An incel who turns to homosexuality out of heterosexual frustration.
› **WRISTCEL** · An incel obsessed with the (effeminate) thinness of his wrists
› **ESCORTCEL** · An incel who pays for sex.
› **WHITECEL** / **ALT-RIGHTCEL** · An incel who embraces white supremacism.
› **MANLET** · A short or physically slight man.

**L.D.A.R.** · Lay Down And Rot · When incels take the **BLACK PILL** and accept their fate.

**LIFEFUEL** · Online content that appeals to incels by denigrating or threatening women. *Also,* **RAGEFUEL** · Content that confirms an incel's worst fears about women and dating. *Also,* **SUIFUEL** / **ROPEFUEL** · Content that encourages incels to take their own lives.

**GRAPE** · An unsubtle code word for rape.

**F.A.** · Those who are destined (or resigned) to be Forever Alone.

CUCK — *the now ubiquitous, catch-all insult for any insufficiently* ALPHA *or alt-right male*

**K.H.H.V.** · A Kissless, Hugless, Handholdless Virgin.

**WIZARD** · Any man who is still a virgin at 30.

**CHADFISHING** · When incels impersonate CHADS online to lure (and troll) STACYS.

**REVERSE RAPE** · How some incels describe women denying (i.e., declining) them sex.

**MOGGING** · When a BETA is dominated by an **A.M.O.G.** (Alpha Male Of the Group). Often in some specific way, e.g., **HEIGHT-MOGGED, WEALTH-MOGGED**, &c.

**ASCENDING** · When incels **DEINCELIZE** by finding love (at which point they risk being rejected by their BLACK-PILLED brethren).

## WOMEN

The manosphere's binary view of women is expressed on a decile scale of hotness and status, where 9s and 10s are desired, and 1–8s derided.

**STACY** · A female CHAD; attractive, popular, socially adept, hyper-feminine, materialistic, vain, &c.

**BECKY** · A woman one rung below a STACY; the female equivalent of a BETA.

**FOIDS** · A misogynistic dismissal of women as merely "Female Humanoids" *or* "Androids."

**WAHMEN / WYMIN / WEEMINS** · (Jokingly) denigrating mispronunciations of "women."

**LANDWHALE** · An overweight woman.

**THOT** · That Ho (*or* Huzz) Over There · A women dismissed as sexually promiscuous.

**R.P.W.** · A Red-Pilled Woman who rejects the "mirage" of equality and "having it all"; recognizes the reality of evolutionary instinct; and seeks commitment (and kids) with the same focus as RED-PILLED men seek control.

**CAPTAIN AND FIRST MATE** · An R.P.W. "dynamic" where women achieve fulfilment through subordinate teamwork to men.

**TRAD WIVES** · Women who proselytize (or cosplay) online for a kaleidoscope of nostalgic Christian, Conservative, Aryan, patriarchal, home-making, home-schooling, maternal, and subservient values. An echo of the Second (and Third) Reich slogan: **KINDER, KÜCHE, KIRCHE** [children, kitchen, church].

**A.W.A.L.T.** · The assertion that All Women Are Like That, i.e., deceitful and manipulative. *Conversely*, **UNICORNS** · Ideal **WIFE MATERIAL**, i.e., loving, faithful. The existence of unicorns implies that **N.A.W.A.L.T.** (Not All Women Are Like That), but the fact that they are mythical creatures speaks volumes.

**D.T.F.** · Women who are Down To Fuck. (The manosphere assumes that all men are D.T.F.)

**HYPERGAMY** · The assertion that women are biologically destined to search constantly for a high(er)-status male — and, the consequent fear that no relationship is ever truly secure.

**ALPHA WIDOW** · A women who never "gets over" her (first) ALPHA infatuation.

## MINDSET

**DREAD GAME** · Manipulatively cultivating compliance, e.g., with public displays of disapproval; inexplicable ghosting; or threats of total abandonment. *Similarly*, **PUSH & PULL** · Alternating affection and alienation to keep a woman disequilibrated, eager, and scared.

Such tactics (are calibrated to) provoke in women **THE HAMSTER** · A frenzied (hamster wheel) of anxiety and low self-esteem.

**M.G.T.O.W.** ["*mig-tow*"] · Men Going Their Own Way · A (toxic) community of (divorced) male **SEPARATISTS** who disavow dating and marriage. ("*The juice isn't worth the squeeze.*") Some become **VOLCEL** · Voluntarily Celibate.

**MEN'S RIGHTS ACTIVISM (M.R.A.)** · A movement that seeks to redress perceived legal inequalities in, e.g., custody rights, workplace discrimination, assault accusations, &c.

**MAXXING** · The manosphere's rebranding of "self-improvement," deployed with any prefix, e.g., **LOOKSMAXXING, GYMMAXXING**, &c.

**TRANSMAXXING** · When INCELS or BETAS transition to women not because of any gender dysphoria {☞ p.193}, but to gain the perceived social and sexual privileges of being female.

**2.D. > 3.D.** · Asserting that online relationships are superior to physical interactions.

**BASED** · Being proud of and indifferent to the consequences of one's marginal ("*politically incorrect*") or extreme opinions. (Sometimes viewed as the opposite of **WOKE**.)

**S.M.V.** · An individual's **SEXUAL MARKET VALUE**, assessed by a range of (superficial and objectifying) attributes, e.g., age, income, looks, social status, sexual experience, &c. (Male S.M.V. usually = looks + security, whereas female S.M.V. = looks + fertility.)

**S.M.P.** · Society's *de facto* **SEXUAL MARKET PLACE** in which "men gatekeep commitment, and women gatekeep sex."

**D.H.V.** · Display of Higher Value that increases your S.M.V., e.g., boasting of exotic travel, or PEACOCKING. *Conversely*, D.L.V. · Displays of Lower Value, e.g., **S.O.V.** · Statements of Vulnerability calibrated to engender empathy.

**PEACOCKING** · Wearing eye-catching attire.

**SOCIALLY ENFORCED MONOGAMY** · Advocating political policies and cultural norms that encourage monogamy — specifically in order to reduce male violence against women.

**ONE-ITIS** · When a (BETA) male over-invests in (the concept of) **THE ONE** (i.e., a "soulmate") who fails to reciprocate his feelings.

**THE WALL** · The age at which women are deemed to pass their biological peak and cease to be desirable to ALPHAS; usually 21–25.

**PASSPORT BRO-ING** · When men go abroad to date or "find love," because they dislike the domestic dating scene; they are looking for a **TRAD** (i.e., submissive) partner; for economic reasons; or because **WESTERN WOMEN ARE BAD** (i.e., independent, feminist, &c.).

Judged by some to be a "macho" rebranding of **MAIL-ORDER BRIDES** (at best) and **SEX TOURISM** (at worst).

*Similarly*, **S.E.A.-MAXXING** · Travelling to Southeast Asia to find (submissive) women. Hence the manosphere's supremacist mantra: **JUST BE WHITE**.

**L.J.B.F.** · Let's Just Be Friends · When women consign (BETA) men to the **FRIENDZONE**.

**SOFT *vs* HARD NEXTING** · Letting a relationship just fade away *vs* ending it abruptly.

**NO FAP / NO NUT** · Abstaining from masturbation or ejaculation as part of a MAXXING or MONK MODE strategy.

**MONK MODE** · Temporarily abstaining from relationships to MAXX one's career, mindset, physique, &c. (The female equivalent is **NUN MODE**.) *Similarly*, **DOPAMINE DETOX** · Abstaining from artificial stimulants (e.g., sugars, shopping, social media) to **RESET** the brain.

**PLATE SPINNING** · Simultaneously dating multiple **PLATES** (i.e., replaceable women).

**MONKEY BRANCHING** · Upgrading to a new partner, using an existing relationship as a pivot — as monkeys swing from tree to tree.

**THE DARK TRIAD** · A trio of antisocial personality traits — narcissism, Machiavellianism, and psychopathy — to which some SIGMAS, ALPHAS, and P.U.A. eagerly aspire.[3]

**N-COUNT** · A tally of one's **NOTCHES** (sexual partners). *A.k.a.*, **BODY COUNT**. A high number is good for men, but bad for women.

**LITERALLY ME** · A dark, alienated, erratic, and psychotically violent fictional SIGMA who appeals to ALPHAS and INCELS, e.g., Patrick Bateman (*American Psycho*), Alex DeLarge (*A Clockwork Orange*), Tyler Durden (*Fight Club*), Travis Bickle (*Taxi Driver*), Arthur Fleck (*Joker*), Thomas Shelby (*Peaky Blinders*).

## GRINDSET

Central to the SIGMA and ALPHA mindset is the belief that men must dominate both their surroundings and themselves, via:

› **HUSTLE** · Finding the most effective strategies for MAXXING, dating, investing, &c.

› **GRIND** · An unending churn of consistent and disciplined work: "*Rise and grind.*"

These two forces are often exploited by a third:

› **GRIFT** · When manosphere influencers NEG *male* insecurity to monetize their books, supplements, crypto, online courses, bootcamps, podcasts, V.I.P. mentee programs, &c.

## GAME

**PICKUP ARTISTRY** (*A.k.a.*, **SEDUCTION SCIENCE**) exploded into the mainstream in 2005, when Neil Strauss published *The Game: Penetrating the Secret Society of Pickup Artists.*

This best-selling book popularized a cynical, manipulative, and volume approach to female seduction, and propelled to minor notoriety a motley crew of pickup artists (**P.U.A.**).

**PICKUP GAME** seemingly hit its high point in the mid-2010s, after which it became dogged by scandal and swamped by dating apps. Yet it still flourishes in online forums, and is finding a new generation of followers on social media, YouTube, and TikTok. Below are some of the game's tenets and techniques.

**SARGING** · Initiating conversation with the aim of CLOSING. ("*The* P.U.A. *lives to sarge.*")

**COLD *vs* WARM APPROACH** · SARGING a stranger *vs* a woman within a known group.

**DAY GAME** · Daytime approaches, i.e., on the street, in a shop, at the beach, &c.

**NIGHT GAME** · Approaching at night, e.g., in bars, clubs, or the streets outside them.

**GUTTER GAME** · A crude, last-ditch (late-night) street approach — often of intoxicated women after the bars and clubs have closed.

**APPROACH INVITATION / CHOOSING SIGNAL** · An indication from a woman that SARGING might be welcomed, e.g., prolonged eye contact, raising a glass in a toast, &c.

**SET** · An APPROACH's structure: e.g., **2-SET** (two girls); **MIXED SET** (men and women).

**OPEN** · How an approach is initiated. A range of strategies are advanced for different SETS:

› **APPEARANCE**: *You look adorable!*
› **SITUATIONAL**: *What's good to order here?*
› **OPINION**: *Do you believe in love at first sight?*
› **REQUEST**: *I need a girl's opinion ...*

Elaborate P.U.A. will OPEN with magic tricks, E.S.P. games, palm-reading gambits, &c.

**FRAME** · The mindset with which a P.U.A. approaches and seeks to engage his target, e.g.:

› **COCKY & FUNNY**: Confident jokiness.
› **AMUSED MASTERY**: Sardonic experience.
› **COMMAND PRESENCE**: Total authority.

**APPROACH ANXIETY** · Overcome with: a strong **INNER GAME** (i.e., mental focus); relentless practice; and/or following strategies like the **3-SECOND RULE**, i.e., immediately acting on attraction before the nerves kick in.

*Manosphere hustlers are simply* NEGGING *other men*

**I.O.I.** · Indicator Of Interest, e.g., smiling, leaning in, &c. *Conversely,* **I.O.D.** · Indicator Of Disinterest, e.g., turning away, walking off.

**FALSE TIME CONSTRAINT (F.T.C.)** · An APPROACH tactic designed to defuse any impression of pressure, e.g., "*Two quick seconds, then I have to go meet my friends ...*"

**NEGGING** · Spiking compliments with insults to charm and disarm, e.g., "*Your hair is great — it would look amazing if you had it styled.*"
*Also*, an action that signals indifference, e.g., scrolling through your phone while chatting.

**1-1 / ISOLATION** · Separating a women from her friends (e.g., at a club) while OPENING.

**WING(MAN)** · A (fe)male friend who assists a P.U.A., e.g., by praising his virtues, or creating opportunity by distracting a target's friends. (Wings are actually told to stand to one side to leave a **CORRIDOR** for women to approach.)

**WHITE KNIGHT** · A BETA who hopes to impress women by "defending their honour" and **COCK BLOCKING** (i.e., impeding) P.U.A.

**INFIELD** · Covertly recording approaches for bragging rights, and/or to "train" other P.U.A.

**SHIT TEST** · A verbal challenge women set to assess a man's ALPHA credentials, e.g., "*I bet you say that to all the girls.*" Countered with strategies like **AGREE & AMPLIFY**, e.g., "*All of them! Only one in a hundred gets the joke.*"

**COMPLIANCE TEST** · A task women set to assess a BETA's passivity, e.g., "*Get me a drink!*" *Or*, a test set by a P.U.A. to gauge passivity, e.g., calling a woman over from across the bar; or getting her to **SPIN** 360° to show off her look.

**KINO** · Manipulatively escalating intimacy via touch; an abbreviation (and bastardization) of kinaesthetics (the study of body movement). *Similarly,* **THE KNEE TEST** · Sitting side by side and touching knees to gauge interest.

**ROUTINE STACKING** · Combining and slowly **ESCALATING** various P.U.A. gambits, e.g.: OPEN → F.T.C. → D.H.V. → NEG → engaging story → *check for* I.O.I. → KINO → &c.

**ABUNDANCE MENTALITY** · The theory that PLATE SPINNING reduces the pressure of approaches, and makes a P.U.A. inherently more appealing. *Conversely,* **SCARCITY MINDSET** · Approaching from a position of desperation.

**CLOSE** · The end of a successful approach, e.g.:

› **(PHONE) NUMBER CLOSE**
› **KISS CLOSE / K-CLOSE**
› **S.D.L.** (Same Day Lay), *A.k.a.*, **F-CLOSE**

**LAST-MINUTE RESISTANCE** · A **HARD NO** immediately prior to (expected) sexual intercourse; some P.U.A. interpret this as **TOKEN RESISTANCE**, i.e., just another SHIT TEST to be overcome by pressure and manipulation.

**EJECT** · To abandon a doomed approach. ⊙

# Doctors & Nurses

*For as long as medicine has been practiced, medical professionals have used euphemism, dysphemism, abbreviation, and slang to save time, speak covertly in front of patients, and sustain an esprit de corps in the face of death and disease.*

## THE HOUSE OF GOD

In 1978, Dr. Stephen Bergman (writing as Samuel Shem) published his hospital satire, *The House of God*, and revolutionized the lexicon of medicine. To this day, medical students seek solace in the novel's gallows humour, and doctors still cite its jaundiced slang:

**GOMER** · Get Out of My Emergency Room · An elderly patient who clings to life despite chronic illnesses and ceaseless interventions. Although "GOMERS *don't die*" they inevitably fall out of bed, hence: "GOMERS *go to ground.*"

**LOL IN NAD** · Little Old Lady in No Apparent Distress.

**ZEBRA** · An obscure (and absurd) diagnosis. ("*[A med student] hears hoofbeats outside his window, the first thing he thinks of is a zebra.*")

**BUFFING** · To polish a patient's chart before **TURFING** them to another service. ("*You gotta* BUFF *the* GOMERS, *so that when you* TURF *them elsewhere, they don't* **BOUNCE** *back.*")

**SIEVE** · An intern who admits too many patients to A&E. *Conversely*, **WALL** · An intern who **MEETS 'EM AND STREETS 'EM**.

* * *

Of course, *The House of God* is but one source of a deep well of slang that helps medical professionals endure their punishing conditions.

Some terms are commonplace (e.g., **WALKY TALKY** · Ambulant and responsive); many are dubious (e.g., **GROLIES** · *Guardian* Reader Of Limited Intelligence in Ethnic Skirt). But the vast majority of those still in use are shared in private — out of respect for patients, and fear of litigation. Few now would dream of saying (let alone writing in the notes) the kind of slang that was bandied about in generations past (e.g., **T.T.F.O.** · Told To Fuck Off).

## PAEDIATRICS

**F.L.K.** · Funny Looking Kid · Who may well be accompanied by **F.L.P.** (Funny Looking Parents) or a **G.L.M.** (Good Looking Mum). *Similarly*, **L.L.P.** · Looks Like Parents.

**PARENTECTOMY** · What is required when the most significant problem is the parent(s).

**4-WALL TEST** · If a child touches every wall of the consulting room, consider A.D.H.D.

**N.P.S.** · New Parent Syndrome.

## NURSING

**THE Q WORD** · The superstition that saying "*It's quiet*" will instantly avalanche the workload.[1] (Akin to saying "Macbeth" in a theatre.) Applies also to the words **SLOW** and **BORING**.

**CODE YELLOW**.......... urinary incontinence
**CODE BROWN**.............. faecal incontinence
**POONAMI**..CODE BROWN HORRENDIOMA

**DIGGIN' FOR GOLD** · Manual disimpaction of rectal stool.

**NURSING DOSE** · A more generous than prescribed dose of a drug given to calm a patient and/or avoid bothering a (sleeping) doctor.

**ROTATER** · A patient so complicated (or annoying) that nurses take turns with their care.

**P.I.P.** · Pyjama Induced Paralysis · When ambulant patients forget they can actually walk.

**3-H** · High, Hot, and a Helluvalot · The holy trinity of a successful enema.

**COUNTER TERRORIST** · A demanding family member who vexes the nursing station.

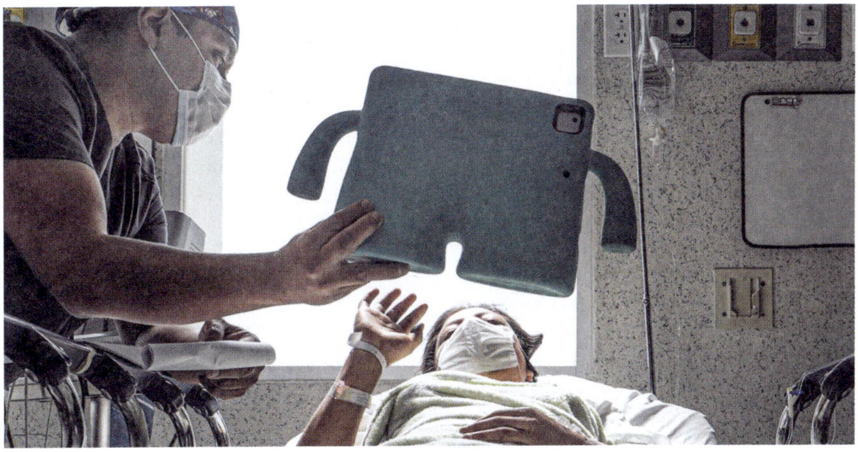

*A new mother speaks to her family via iPad during* THE BADNESS *of Covid*

## PATIENTS

**(L.O.L.) F.D.G.B.** · (Little Old Lady) Fall Down Go Boom · Used for any slips or trips. *Also*, **L.O.L. L.O.L. / L.O.L.**[2] · Little Old Lady Lying On Linoleum. *A.k.a.*, **NAN DOWN**.

**STATUS DRAMATICUS** · A deeply histrionic patient. *Conversely*, **STATUS PATHETICUS**.

**HONDA** · Hypertensive, Obese, Noncompliant, Diabetic, Asshole/ Alcoholic.

**D.S.P.** · Day Shift Problem. ("*Keep 'em alive 'til 7:05!*") *Similarly*, **N.S.P.** · Night *or* Next Shift Problem.

**F.M.P.S.** · Fluff My Pillow Syndrome; when a patient demands **T.L.C.** · Tender Loving Care.

**D.S.B.** · Drug Seeking Behaviour. Often indicated by unsubtle and well-known signs, e.g.: "*I have a very high tolerance to pain, doctor.*"

**WALLET BIOPSY** · Ordering unnecessary and expensive tests or procedures.

**THERAPEUTIC WAIT** · Ensuring obnoxious (non urgent) patients are not seen in a hurry.

**S.O.C.M.O.B.** · Standing On the Corner, Minding my Own Business; the standard explanation for any extremely shady trauma.

**BUDDY** *or* **HOMIE DROP OFF** · Unexplained trauma victim dumped outside A&E.

## SIGNS

**SUITCASE SIGN** · When a patient arrives at A&E with bags packed, and demands to be admitted. *A.k.a.*, **SAMSONITE SYNDROME**.

**MULTIPLE ALLERGY** · The more allergies a patient reports, the more likely they are (also) to have a psychiatric condition.[2]

**O SIGN** · When a sick (elderly) patient lies with their mouth agape. *Followed by*, **Q SIGN** · When a *very* sick (elderly) patient lies with their mouth agape and tongue lolling out. (According to *The House of God*: "The O sign is reversible, but once they get to the Q sign, they never come back.") *Also*, **DOTTED Q SIGN** · When a fly rests on a patient's tongue.

**CELL-PHONE SIGN** · When a patient who reports 10/10 pain is scrolling Insta. (A 2017 study found that patients using smartphones during their initial surgical assessment were 5× more likely to be sent home on day one.[3])

**CALL BELL SIGN** · [Nursing] The more rings on the call bell, the less urgent the need.

**THROCKMORTON'S SIGN** · The (humorous and scientifically debunked) theory that a patient's penis will point to the side of a hip fracture (or other pathology) on radiographic imaging. *A.k.a.*, **JOHN THOMAS SIGN**.[4]

**TOOTH TO TATTOO RATIO** · A quick and visual I.Q. test. (More teeth than tats is better.)

POSITIVE SHOE SIGN?

**CROSSED LEG SIGN** · The anecdotal belief that patients who sit or lie with their legs crossed were unlikely to be in a critical condition was supported by a 2021 study in Rome. 5

**LIPSTICK** *or* **MCDONALD'S SIGN** · When a patient is well enough to apply make-up or eat a cheeseburger. *Similarly,* **HAM SANDWICH SIGN** · When a patient who reports unbearable pain is curiously interested in lunch.

**GOLDEN HALO SIGN** · When patients briefly rally before death, often offering false hope to their family. *A.k.a.,* **ENERGY SURGE** and, in dementia, **TERMINAL LUCIDITY**. 6

**SUNGLASSES SIGN** · The likelihood that a patient wearing shades indoors (absent a valid ophthalmic or neurological cause) has a personality disorder and/or will be problematic. 7

**TEDDY BEAR SIGN** · The likelihood that an adult carrying "transitional objects" (i.e., stuffed animals) has a personality disorder. 8

**POSITIVE SHOE SIGN** · A trauma that causes a patient to lose one or both shoes is serious.

**POSITIVE NICE SIGN** · The nicer the patient (and their family), the worse the prognosis.

**T:O** · Tube to Orifice Ratio · An instant visual indication of case severity; more tubes is :–(

**PORT / BURGUNDY / ROSÉ / &c.** · Comparing hematuria (blood in urine) to wine colour.

## DIAGNOSTICS

**N.F.[*x*]** · Normal For [*x*] · Where *x* is a region with certain social stereotypes, e.g., "*Normal for Norfolk*" (jokingly) implies inbreeding.

**L.G.F.D.** · Looks Good From Door. *Similarly,* **E.B.O.** · End-of-the-Bed Observation *or* End of the Bed-o-Gram.

**N.Q.R.(I.T.H.)** · Not Quite Right (In The Head). *Also,* **J.D.L.R.** · Just Don't Look Right.

**[LOCATION] SLIM** · Not quite as morbidly obese as might be expected, given the region. ("*With a* B.M.I. *of 40, he's Texas slim.*")

**CURBSIDE / CORRIDOR CONSULT** · Soliciting an on-the-fly opinion from a colleague. 9

**INCIDENTALOMA** · Something discovered while looking for something else, which may or may not prove relevant or malignant. 10

**HORRENDIOMA**...... a horrendous diagnosis
**FASCINOMA** .................... a fascinating case

**DYSCOPIA** · Inability to cope; said of patients who are **ACOPIC**, or otherwise **L.M.F.** · Low in *or* Lacking in Moral Fibre.

**CHAMPAGNE TAP** · A bloodless lumbar puncture (i.e., **SPINAL TAP**).

**T.F.T.B.** · Too Fat To Breathe · Obesity hypoventilation syndrome.

**F.O.S.** ....... Full of Shit (mentally / medically)
**S.A.S.** ....... Sick As Shit
**S.L.S.** ....... Shit Life Syndrome

**MAGIC MIKE** · A patient who is always naked. (*"How good a patient looks naked is inversely proportionate to how often they get naked."*)

**CHAOS** · Chronic Hurts All Over Syndrome.

**FOOSH** · Fallen On Outstretched Hand.

**CHECK UP FROM THE NECK UP** · A psychiatric consultation.

## EUPHEMISMS

**MITOTIC LESION** *or* **DISEASE** · Cancer. *Also,* **ONCOGENESIS / NEOPLASM.** *Rather less euphemistic,* **SPANISH** [dancer = cancer].

**ACUTE LEAD POISONING** · Gunshot wound.

**SNOWED** · Over-sedated; either self-inflicted or medically assisted.

**SUPRATENTORIAL SYMPTOMS** · Those that are "all in the mind." (The supratentorial region of the brain contains the cerebrum.)

**HYPODECKIA** · Not playing with a full deck.

**SUGAR** · Diabetes.

**POOR HISTORIAN** · A patient unable to give a medical history, or list their medications.

**C.B.T.** · Chronic Biscuit Toxicity, i.e., obese. *Also,* **ENHANCED ADIPOSITY / FLUFFY / HYPERCALORIC SYNDROME** / &c.

**NORMAL SALINE RESPONSIVE** · A patient instantly cured by a (placebo) salt-water drip. *Similarly,* **THERAPEUTIC PHLEBOTOMY** *or* **RADIATION** · When symptoms miraculously improve immediately after bloods or X-ray. *Also,* **MAGIC ASPIRIN** · When patients come to hospital for drugs they have at home.

**FAILURE TO SWIM** *or* **NEAR SWIMMING EVENT** · Drowning or severe water-inhalation. *Similarly,* **FAILURE TO FLY** · Fall victim.

**FECAL ENCEPAHALOPATHY** · Having "shit for brains."

**ROUND OF APPLAUSE** · Gonorrhoea, i.e., "*a dose of the clap.*"

**HIGH FIVE / H-4** · H.I.V. *Also,* **RETROVIRAL DISEASE / CD4 DEFICIENCY.**

**VOCAL LOCAL / VERBACAIN** · Soothing words in lieu of pharmacological pain relief.

**T.O.P.** · Termination Of Pregnancy.

**PEEK-N-SHRIEK** · When a surgical procedure unveils a **HORRENDIOMA.** *Which may necessitate* an **OPEN AND CLOSE** procedure.

**V.O.M.I.T.** · Victim Of Medical Investigations and Tests. *Also,* **IATROGENESIS / HEALTH-CARE-ASSOCIATED INFECTION.**

## MEDICAL SPECIALTIES

**SLASHER / AXE / SAWBONES** ....... surgeon (who **HEALS WITH STEEL**)
**CAVEMAN / CARPENTER / KNUCKLE DRAGGER / ORTHOPOD** ....... orthopaedic surgeon
**NOSE PICKER** ....... otorhinolaryngologist (ear, nose, and throat)
**STREAM TEAM / PECKER CHECKERS / ROD SQUAD** ....... urology
**GUTS AND BUTTS** ....... gastroenterology
**VAMPIRE / BLOOD SUCKER / LEECH** ....... phlebotomist
**GASSER / GAS PASSER** *or* **MAN** *or* **WALLAH** (*"Gas on, gas off, fuck off!"*) ....... anaesthesiologist
**BABY CATCHER / CORD CUTTER** ....... obstetrician
**BEAN TEAM** ....... nephrology
**GLAND BAND** ....... endocrinology
**TRICK CYCLIST / NUT CRACKER / FREUD SQUAD** ....... psychiatrist
**DERMAHOLIDAY / SKIN GAME / SKIN PICKERS / BEAUTICIANS** ....... dermatology
(The golden rule of dermatology — **IF IT'S DRY MAKE IT WET, IF IT'S WET MAKE IT DRY**)
**BONE WIZARDS** ....... osteopathy

**SELF-TITRATED** · When a patient decides unilaterally to alter their drug dosage.

**BROMHIDROSIS** · Offensive body odour.

**LIMITED BY BODY HABITUS (L.B.B.H.)** · An exam, scan, or procedure impeded by fat.

**THE BADNESS** · A horrific diagnosis. *Or*, the cumulative mental impact of trauma, cancer, violence, abuse, neonatal death, suicide, &c.

## MISCELLANEOUS

**VITAMIN H** · Haloperidol (an antipsychotic). *Also*, **B52** · The antipsychotic drug cocktail of Benadryl + 5mg haloperidol + 2mg lorazepam.

**TEETH** · Tried Everything Else, Try Homoeopathy.

**TINCTURE OF TIME** · Waiting and seeing. *A.k.a.*, **BENIGN NEGLECT**. (Per *The House of God*: "The delivery of medical care is to do as much nothing as possible.")

**(MICHAEL) JACKSON JUICE** · The sedative-hypnotic agent Propofol that "killed" the King of Pop. *A.k.a.*, **MILK OF AMNESIA**.

**HARD STICK** · A patient whose veins are difficult to locate or puncture. *Also*, a patient who takes curious pride in the fact. ("*I should warn you, doc, I'm a* **TOUGH STICK**!")

**STREET PIZZA** · The consequence of a severe **R.T.A.** (Road Traffic Accident).

**DOUGHNUT OF TRUTH** · C.T. scanner.

**MOCKTOR** · Pejorative term for practitioners who assist doctors, e.g., **NOCTORS** (nurses) and **PHOCTORS** (pharmacists).

**MAFAT** · Mandatory Anaesthesia Fuck-About Time · The pre-operative period when the entire surgical team hangs around for the patient.

**SKINFETTI / ELDERDUST / GERY FLAKES** · A shower of dead skin from an (old) patient.

**SCROMITING** · Screaming while vomiting; sometimes a sign of severe marijuana misuse (e.g., Cannabinoid Hyperemesis Syndrome).

**HEPATOLOGY CONSULT / LIVER ROUND** · Post-work drinks. *Similarly*, **G.I. ROUNDS** · Staff meal break.

**F.T.L.** (Failure To Launch) · Older (or adult) children (living at home) with overly pampering or controlling parents.

**WELL KNOWN TO THIS SERVICE** · A repeat patient. *A.k.a.*, **FREQUENT FLIER**.

**A.T.F.** · Ambulate To Freedom · To kick out.

**M.T.F.** · Metabolize To Freedom · When those who arrive in A&E drunk or high need only to sober up before discharge.

## END GAME

**BASEMENT ADMISSION** · A new patient with injuries or illness **NOT COMPATIBLE WITH LIFE** who is destined for the morgue (*A.k.a.*, in England, **ROSE COTTAGE**).

**CRUMPING** · Going downhill fast.

**(T.F.) BUNDY** · (Totally Fucked) But Unfortunately Not Dead Yet.

**F.T.D.** · Failure To Die. *Similarly*, **O.M.T.D.** · Old Man Trying To Die.

**C.T.D.** · Circling The Drain *or* Certain To Die.

**A.R.T.** · Assuming Room Temperature.

**(N.[P.B.)B.B.]** · (Needs [Pine Box) By Bed].

**T.M.B.** · Cause of death: Too Many Birthdays.

**D.I.B.** · Dead In Bed.

**DISCHARGE TO THE *x* FLOOR** · Where *x* is one higher than the hospital's top floor. *A.k.a.*, **CELESTIAL** *or* **VERTICAL DISCHARGE**. *Also*, **TRANSFER TO WARD 13** *or* **SKY-C-U**.

**T.X. TO E.C.U.** · Transfer to Eternal Care Unit.

**D.C. TO J.C.** · Discharge to Jesus Christ.

[It should be stressed that the majority of the terms above that are still current are used privately, ironically, and as part of a coping culture that (seldom) diminishes patient care.] ⊙

# Agit-Prop / Iconography

*A field guide to the* **SYMBOLS** *that define democratic and demagogic direct action.*

**POTS AND PANS** · Beating kitchenware in clamorous protest has a long and lowly history, dating to before the Middle Ages, when ill-suited marriages would be mocked with a cacophonous **CHARIVARI** of kettles, tin trays, and frying pans.

Down the centuries since, such grassroots **CASSEROLADES** have been deployed across the globe, e.g.: in Myanmar (against the 2021 *coup d'état)*; in France (against pension reform); in Iceland (against the 2008–10 crash); and in Argentina (against banking controls).

During the lockdowns of Covid, people in cities across the world converted a discordance of grievance into one of gratitude, hammering pots and pans in support of doctors, nurses, and other essential workers.

**GUIDO FAWKES / ANONYMOUS MASK** · Created by David Lloyd to illustrate Alan Moore's 1982–85 graphic novel, *V for Vendetta*, the stylized, smirking, and moustachioed mask of the British Gunpowder plotter Guy Fawkes (1570–1606) has been adopted by any number of anti-establishment groups — including the Occupy movement, and the "hacktivist" collective Anonymous.

Ironically, because the most popular version of the mask is based on the 2006 Warner Bros. movie adaptation of the novel, the parent company Time Warner takes a cut every time one of their masks is sold.

**WHITE POWER O.K.** · In 2017, according to the Anti-Defamation League, shit-stirrers on the message boards 4chan and 8chan hatched a plot to pervert the traditional O.K. gesture into a symbol of hate:

> We must flood Twitter and other social media websites … claiming that the O.K. hand sign is a symbol of white supremacy. [1]

The confected symbolism was that the three outstretched fingers symbolized W(hite) and the pinched thumb and finger P(ower).

What began as a sick hoax quickly morphed into a sicker reality, with "white power" O.K. signs flashed not only at far-right rallies but also by military recruits, school kids, extremist politicians, and terrorists.

Infamously, the man who, in 2019, murdered 51 people at two mosques in Christchurch, New Zealand, flashed the newly minted Nazi sign to the cameras at his trial.

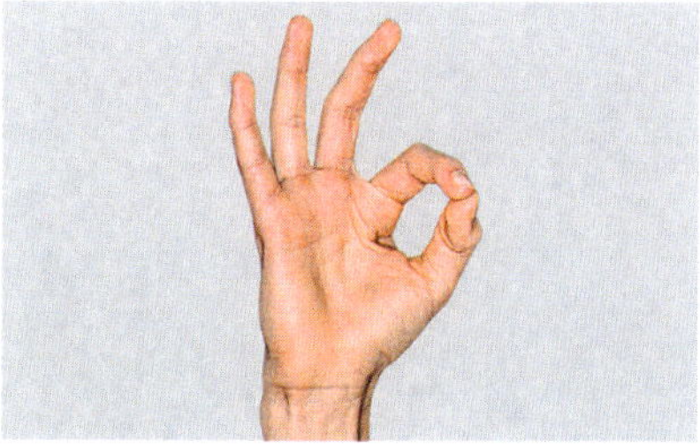

**BLACK POWER SALUTE** · Although the raised fist has long been a symbol of power and protest for anti-fascists, anti-racists, trade unionists, and other activists, its impact on the civil rights movement owes much to the defiance of two African American athletes.

During the 1968 Mexico City Olympics, as Tommie Smith and John Carlos accepted their 200-metre dash gold and bronze medals (respectively), each bowed their head and raised a black-gloved fist as "The Star-Spangled Banner" played.

(Additionally, Smith wore a black scarf to symbolize Black pride; Carlos wore a bead necklace to symbolize Black lynchings; and both men wore black socks with no shoes to symbolize poverty.)

The outrage was instant: the International

Olympic Committee condemned the display, and both men were suspended from the U.S. team, sent home, and castigated by the press.

But the impact was timeless: As President Barack Obama said in 2016: "Their powerful silent protest in the 1968 Games was controversial, but it woke folks up and created greater opportunity for those that followed."

**M.A.G.A. HAT** · Initially suggested by a supplier, the red "Make America Great Again" baseball hat was first worn by Donald Trump on a July 2015 visit to the U.S.-Mexico border.

Its impact was extraordinary: In contrast to the high-gloss branding of his opponents, Trump had found a demotic icon that spanned the poles of classic Americana, from baseball Little Leagues to independent loners, like Forrest Gump. (It was also a novelty that Trump wore his own campaign merch, pairing the M.A.G.A. cap with golf attire and Brioni suits.)

Even now the red M.A.G.A. hat maintains a Rorschachian power to provoke partisan love and loathing with equal ferocity.

At one stage, Trump's campaign was spending more on M.A.G.A. hats than polling; and in 2018, the rapper Pusha T called the garment "this generation's Ku Klux hood."

Weeks before the 2024 election, Elon Musk appeared at Trump's Madison Square Garden rally in a black **DARK M.A.G.A.** hat, with the slogan stitched in an ominous Gothic font.

By way of reply, the Harris campaign unveiled a camouflage cap with HARRIS WALZ picked out in bold orange type — in an attempt to play both on the trend for camo and Tim Walz's rootsy Midwestern background.

**PUSSYHAT** · On 21.1.2017, millions gathered across America — and around the world — to protest against the previous day's presidential inauguration of Donald Trump.

Specifically, these Women's Marches — the largest of which convened in Washington, D.C. — sought to condemn Trump's violent misogyny encapsulated in his "hot mic" admission from 2005: "When you're a star, they let you do it. You can do anything … Grab 'em by the pussy. You can do anything."

The defining, defiant, and mocking symbol of these protests was the knitted, pink, cat-eared "Pussyhat" — conceived by Jayna

Zweiman and Krista Suh, and designed by Kat Coyle — which was made and worn by so many marchers that shortages were reported of vibrant pink yarn.

**TAKING THE KNEE** · On 1.9.2016, before a pre-season game against the San Diego Chargers, the San Francisco 49ers quarterback Colin Kaepernick sought to draw attention to racial injustice and police brutality by kneeling during the national anthem.

This simple and pacific gesture catalysed a storm of controversy: condemned by the right as unpatriotic and disrespectful; embraced by the left as a dignified act of defiance.

Over the years, Kaepernick's genuflection has lost little of its power to inspire. Indeed, for a while the symbol became something of a shibboleth: Athletes politicians, celebrities, and business leaders were all challenged to take the knee in solidarity, and were praised or denounced with equal vehemence regardless of their decision to comply.

**THREE-FINGERED SALUTE** · Although it has origins in the Scouting movement, the three-fingered salute appears to have gained popularity among pro-democracy activists via the novels and film adaptations of Suzanne Collins's dystopian *Hunger Games* series, in which it signals gratitude, admiration, farewell, and solidarity.

An early emergence of the salute followed the 2014 Thai *coup d'état* — after which it was swiftly banned by the military junta. Since then the sign has appeared as a silent anti-authoritarian signal in countries across Southeast Asia.

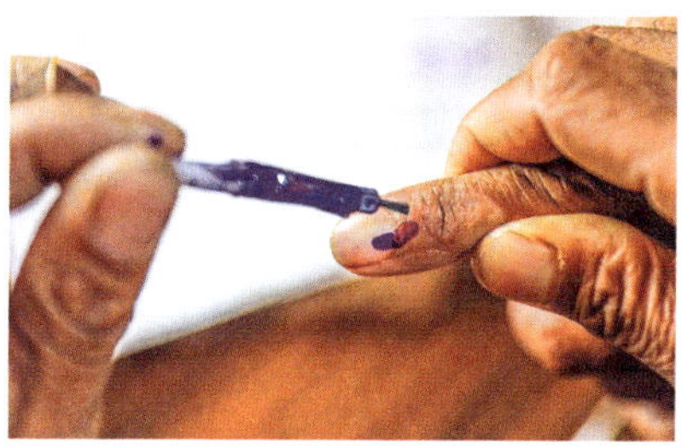

**DEMOCRATIC INK** · In countries without sophisticated voter I.D. systems, an indelibly inked finger is both a precaution against fraud and a prod to participation (akin to "I Voted!" and "I Got Vaccinated!" stickers).

"Voter ink" was pioneered during the 1951–52 Indian general election, and is still in use there today. (Though in 1971, to foil attempts at erasure, India began painting the fingernail bed rather than fingerprint pad.)

While many now raise an inked finger with democratic pride, such a public stain is not without risk. In 2008, Robert Mugabe's goons went door-to-door to find those who had not voted in Zimbabwe's rigged elections. And in 2009, the Taliban amputated the fingers of several voters who had dared to cast a ballot in Afghanistan's presidential election.

**RUBBER DUCKS** · When Thai pro-democracy protesters took to the streets of Bangkok in 2020, the inflatable yellow rubber ducks some activists carried were a form of satirical joke.

But once the government began deploying tear-gas and chemical-laced water cannons, satire became a shield, and the ducks were transformed into colourful symbols of resistance and resilience.

**YELLOW JACKET** · In 2008, a French law required motorists to keep in their vehicles a fluorescent tabard, to be worn in case of emergency. This prudent legislative precaution was subverted a decade later when **GILETS JAUNES** emerged as the unofficial uniform of weekly mass protests across France in opposition to fuel taxation and income inequality.

Although these demonstrations were curtailed by Covid lockdowns in 2020, the yellow jacket remains an easily accessible (and highly visible) accessory to French activism — and it has been adopted by protest groups from Australia to the United States.

**HANDMAID'S TALE** · The 2017 television adaptation of *The Handmaid's Tale* gave physical form to the white bonnets and crimson cloaks that fertile women are forced to wear in Margaret Atwood's award-winning 1985 novel.

Quickly, women took up the simple and startling costume to protest the parallels between Atwood's fictional dystopia and the factual policies of right-wing and theocratic politicians — not least those attacking female healthcare and reproductive rights.

**PUNISHER SKULL** · In 1974, Marvel Comics introduced the anti-hero Frank Castle — a former Marine who witnesses his family being killed by the mob and becomes The Punisher, a brutal, homicidal vigilante.

In ~2011, the Punisher's bleak "death's head" emblem began to be adopted as an intimidatory propaganda symbol by American soldiers fighting in Iraq and Afghanistan. And it soon gained currency with domestic U.S. law-enforcement officers and far-right militias.[2]

Despite attempts by Marvel to dilute its toxicity, the Punisher's skull now represents a vicious mix of lawless law-enforcement and violent white-supremacy; indeed it's likely that at some far-right demos, the Punisher patch has been worn both by protesters and some of the officers deployed to police them.

**BLANK PAPER** · The intolerance of governments across the world has led demonstrators to make their point (and mock their oppressors) by brandishing blank pieces of paper — e.g., in Russia (against the Ukraine invasion), and Britain (against the monarchy).

The power of blank paper protests lies both in its passivity and in the technological challenge it poses for authoritarian regimes. When A.I. text-recognition censorship fails, human censors must individually assess every post containing a blank white square in case they block perfectly anodyne scenes of office life or stationery supplies.

# Influencers Break the Internet

*As tempting as it is simply to dismiss* **SOCIAL MEDIA INFLUENCERS,** *much of our culture dances desperately to their tune. That said, given the rapid rate of online churn, much of their vocabulary seems doomed to enjoy a mayfly's lifespan.*

## INFLUENCERS

Influencers are usually categorized and ranked by their follower numbers — though there are as many definitions of **TIER LEVEL** as there are hustling influencer agencies, e.g.:

**NANO** ..................... *followers* 1,000–10,000
**MICRO** .............................. 5,000–100,000
**MID TIER** ...................... 100,000–500,000
**MACRO** ...................... 500,000–1,000,000
**MEGA / CELEBRITY** ................ 1,000,000+

Nano and micro influencers make up for their lower follower counts with higher rates of trust and ENGAGEMENT. Mega influencers attract **UNPAID MEDIA** (i.e., free coverage online and in the mainstream media). Some campaigns take a **MULTI-TIER** approach, using various tiers of influencer to maximize impact.

**HYPERLOCAL** · A (micro) influencer covering a specific location, who may be engaged, e.g., by a global chain opening in a new city.

**GYMFLUENCER** .............. gym life {☞ p.92}
**FINFLUENCER** .... personal finance, investing
**MOMFLUENCER** ........ pregnancy, mothering
**INFLUENZER** ............... Covid (conspiracy)
**PETFLUENCER** ................ domestic animals
**BOOKSTAGRAMMER** ........... books, reading

**EMPLOYEE INFLUENCERS** · Individuals promoting their employer, or local branches developing their own "personality."

**K.O.L.** · Key Opinion Leader · An influencer whose impact is based not on fleeting fashion but professional expertise in medicine, law, food, business, &c. ("*The professors of social media.*") K.O.L.s would remain potent even if social media evaporated. E.g., Sanjay Gupta, David Attenborough, Malala Yousafzai, Bono.
*Also*, a term synonymous with influencers in China, where K.O.L.s wield significant power.

## CONTENT

Much influencer content mirrors that of the mainstream media (product reviews, interviews, &c.) but some is novel to the medium:

**G.R.W.M.** · Get Ready With Me · A video showing an influencer preparing for an event: from a kid getting ready for school to a star prepping for the Met Gala. *A form of* **B.T.S.** · Behind The Scenes content. *Similarly*, **FIT CHECK** · Itemizing your outfit, for approval.

**GLOW UP** · Documenting a dramatic upgrade in looks, lifestyle, personal development, &c. Such **BEFORE-AND-AFTER**s are usually catalysed by a pressing need (to lose weight, find love) or a looming event (wedding, beach holiday). *Conversely*, **GLOW DOWN** · Rejecting or reversing the cult of self-improvement.

**MUKBANG** · A Korean portmanteau derived from EATING (먹는, *meongneun*) + BROADCAST (방송, *bangsong*) that describes videos of influencers consuming (vast) quantities of (regional, exotic, spicy) food, while explaining the experience. To lure **EYEBALLS**, *mukbang* creators often overeat, eat rapidly, or eat dangerous, unhygienic, or absurdly spicy dishes.[1] *Similarly*, **SULBANG** · Performative online drinking (술, *sul*, alcohol). {☞ COMPETITIVE EATING p.26}

**THIRST TRAP** · (Sexually) provocative content designed to tease and hook scrollers. As (social) media becomes ever-more explicit, there is a sense that "*everything is a thirst trap.*" *Hence*, **THIRST TRAP ANGLE** · A calculatedly coy, flattering, alluring, or titillating camera position, e.g.: coquettish **OVER THE SHOULDER**; revealing **MIRROR SELFIES**; "casual" **DÉCOLLETAGE**; an "accidentally" oiled **SIX PACK**; or **LOW-ANGLE** gym workout videos by **BUTTFLUENCERS**, who just happen to focus always on the gluteal region.

**FLATLAY** · An overhead photo of products laid in a neat (colour-coordinated) grid. Used to illustrate a vibe (*"My summer wardrobe"*); explain a product (a camera and all its accessories); display a range (every cupcake flavour); or tell a story (the contents of a make-up bag).

**STUNT PHILANTHROPY** · Dramatic charitable CLOUT CHASING, e.g., in 2023 MrBeast (Jimmy Donaldson) built 100 wells in Africa, bringing drinking water to ~500,000 people.

**A.M.A.** · Ask Me Anything · Where influencers answer followers' questions to increase **ENGAGEMENT**, evince transparency, humanize their personality, generate content ideas, &c.

**A.S.M.R.** · Autonomous Sensory Meridian Response · Intimate "close-up" audio that triggers a (pleasurable) tingling response.
**A.S.M.R.TISTS** use the technique in everything from make-up demos and **UNBOXING** to dedicated (erotic) **WHISPERING** clips.

**U.G.C.** · User Generated Content · **ORGANIC** content created by **BRAND FANS**, i.e., members of the public who genuinely like and champion a product or service. U.G.C. can be self-generated (ratings, reviews, testimonials), or catalysed by P.R. campaigns.

***x* CHALLENGE** · Once in a while the web is gripped by performative participation, e.g., the "ice-bucket challenge" (where people filmed themselves being doused in ice water, to raise awareness of motor neuron disease). Influencers occasionally innovate such challenges; more often they **BANDWAGON**.

**STREAMING** · When influencers broadcast themselves doing something (e.g., cooking, painting, knitting, watching T.V., &c.) while interacting with an online audience. Millions watch **GAMING STREAMERS** play *Fortnite*, *Minecraft*, *Grand Theft Auto*, &c.

**REACTION** · When influencers film themselves reacting to other content: e.g., music, movies, T.V. shows, or the CLOUT CHASING antics of fellow influencers.

**CLOUT CHASING** · When desperation drives influencers to make **DEGENERATE** content, e.g., harassing celebrities; pranking the public; faking illness; criminal damage; assault; &c.

**UNBOXING** · A capitalist striptease, whereby influencers film themselves extracting products from packaging. Many brands now design packaging with unboxing in mind, deploying Russian doll layering and (unconscionable) quantities of tissue-paper, ribbon, confetti, twine, &c. *Similarly*, **PACKING VIDEOS** · Where brands film their fulfilment logistics.

**SHOPPABLE CONTENT** · Embedding **CLICK THROUGH "BUY NOW"** links into content to turn passive scrolling into active spending.

**TRENDBAIT** · When **TERM-COINERS** spot and hashtag niche trends in the hope of going viral. E.g., #GirlDinner showcased low-effort comfort food that women supposedly enjoy.

**COMMENT BAIT** · Ginning up **B.T.L.** (Below The Line) engagement with cheesy prompts: *"Hey, tell me what you think in the comments!"*

**RAGE BAIT** · Content designed to provoke indignant engagement, from divisive political rants to (culturally insensitive) food misuse.

**APOLOGY VIDEO** · Influencers are forever attempting to ~~make amends~~ save their careers after some (racist, sexist, criminal) outrage by posting on-camera *mea culpas*.
Shot against a low-fi backdrop, prefaced by a deep sigh, and featuring (crocodilian) tears, these formulaic apologies allow influencers to distance themselves from the **DARK PLACE** they were once in (*"I don't know who that person was ..."*) before **TAKING TIME AWAY** from social media to **REFLECT, LEARN, AND GROW**.

**(SHEIN) HAULS** · Videos in which "shopaholics" show off their pre-landfill purchases (from Chinese fast-fashion behemoth Shein).

**ANTI-HAUL / DEINFLUENCING** · When influencers slam overconsumption, or advise their followers to avoid a specific purchase. In 2023, @sadgrlswag said this in a viral TikTok:

> I'm here to deinfluence you. Do not get the Ugg minis. Do not get the Dyson Airwrap. Do not get the Charlotte Tilbury Wand. Do not get the Stanley cup. Do not get Colleen Hoover books. Do not get the AirPods Pro Max. If you do any of those things ... a bomb is gonna explode.[2]

*The National Theatre, London*

## PLATFORMS

*"The influencer landscape is constantly changing."*

This truism applies equally to the rise and fall of influencers, as to the ebb and flow of the platforms they use. (Who still remembers the Covid darling Clubhouse?) And while the media focuses on YouTube, TikTok, X, Instagram, Facebook, &c., other platforms target specific audiences and regions:

Twitch, Discord....... *gaming, game streaming*
Cameo, memmo.me........ *personalized videos*
LinkedIn ........... *business thought-leadership*
OnlyFans, Fansly......... *fan / adult material* [3]
Etsy......... *niche, vintage, handmade products*
WeChat, Weibo, Kuaishou ............... China
Line ............................................. Japan
VKontakte.................................... Russia

**2ND CHANNEL** · When influencers launch a new channel on the same platform to engage different audiences; separate types of content; and/or diversify monetization options.

**POST-PLATFORM** · The growing trend of successful influencers and other content creators (e.g., journalists, historians) transitioning from **FREE-TO-SEE** platforms (Instagram, TikTok, X,) to **SUBSCRIPTION SERVICES** (Patreon, Substack, OnlyFans, BandCamp) where they enjoy greater control of their content, ownership of their audience, and opportunities to monetize both.

## MONETIZING

Few *soi-disant* influencers make money, and fewer still **MAKE BANK**. But the (side) hustle is real, and those with any following will attempt to convert **CLOUT** into comps and cash through **CONTRA DEALS** (i.e., barter) and any number of schemes for **MONETIZATION**:

**GIFTS** · When brands send products to influencers, hoping to inspire free (and favourable) content. *A.k.a.*, **INFLUENCER SEEDING**.

**ATTENDANCE** · When influencers attend and post about an event, either because they are paid or to snag a golden ticket.

**MEDIA FAMIL** · A free familiarization trip for travel influencers to experience and promote a hotel, airline, spa, city, country, &c.

**AFFILIATE MARKETING** · When influencers get paid a commission for every sale their content helps generate — calculated via **TRACKABLE LINKS** and **PROMO CODES**.

**SPON(SORED) CON(TENT)** · When brands plan and pay for (a series of) posts, which influencers (should) identify to their audience.

**PERSONAL (PASSION) PRODUCTS** · Successful influencers occasionally seek to leapfrog sponsorships and collabs by establishing their own consumer brands, selling, e.g., coffee (Emma Chamberlain); chocolate and burgers (MrBeast); beauty products (Jess Hunt); &c.

*Jardin des Tuileries, Paris*

**COLLABORATION** · "Strategic partnerships" where influencers work with existing brands to devise products that (attempt to) merge the winning characteristics of both identities.

**TAKEOVER** · When an influencer temporarily assumes control of a brand's social-media feed(s) and uploads **GUEST POSTS**. An easy way to generate buzz and engagement.

**BRAND AMBASSADOR** · A long-term influencer relationship, covering multiple **CAMPAIGN MOMENTS** across various platforms.

**CREATOR FUNDS** · Cash platforms pay influencers based on their content's popularity.

## VOICE

Influencer success is invariably attributed to **AUTHENTICITY** — and its twin dance partners **TRUST** and **TRANSPARENCY**.

The reality — as we learn from an avalanche of APOLOGY VIDEOS — is that influencers are no stranger to the joke "The key to success is sincerity. Fake that, and you've got it made."

Indeed, it does not take much time online to see that there is a playbook for authenticity — much of which is based upon ...

**T.O.V.** · Tone Of Voice · The personality an influencer projects, which should ideally complement the content they create, e.g., chic, casual, intimate, wacky, authoritative, inspiring, geeky, &c.

**INFLUENCER ACCENT / TIKTOK VOICE** · Just as broadcasters develop characteristic intonations (from B.B.C. English to shock-jock rants), so influencers have coalesced around various medium-specific cadences:

› **SING-SONG** · Using vocal melody to add character to (banal and formulaic) content.

› **VOCAL FRY / GLOTTALIZATION** · A low, creaky, vibrato speech (more common among women) which — though irksome to many — conveys a bored, condescending intimacy that some find charming.

› (**VALLEY GIRL**) **UPTALK** · Where cadences rise at the end of every word / phrase ("*Like? A? Question?*") — both a sublimated affectation and a trick to keep viewers hooked.

› **DRAWN-OUT WORDS *AAAAND* ... AWKWARD PAUSES** · Usually deployed while influencers work out what to say next.

› **MONOTONE** · Often deployed ironically, e.g., when itemizing product specifications.

› **SUPER-FAST** · Many geeky, tech influencers eschew the standard INFLUENCER VOICE by gabbling facts in an enthusiastic stream.

**INFLUENCER VOCABULARY** · Even the briefest excursion online will demonstrate the horrific overindulgence of verbal tics ("*Hey guys!*" "*genuinely*" "*literally*") and vacuous transition words ("*so*" "*like*" "*kind of*" "*well*").

## KEY PERFORMANCE INDICATORS (K.P.I.)

**FOLLOWERS** ........... a **VANITY METRIC** if the followers are fake, or do not drive CONVERSION
**IMPRESSIONS** ...... the total number of times a post has been seen (regardless of ENGAGEMENT)
**COST PER MILLE** ........................ = (total **CAMPAIGN SPEND** ÷ total IMPRESSIONS) × 1,000.
**REACH** .................................................. the number of *individual users* who have seen a post
**ENGAGEMENT** ................ the number of times a post is liked, shared, saved, commented on, &c.
**FOLLOWER GROWTH** ......................... the number of new followers a post/campaign generates
**DEMOGRAPHICS** .. the audience's age, gender, income, &c. (which should match a brand's goals)
**BRAND MENTIONS** ....... tracking how a post/campaign impacts a brand's social-media mentions
**CONVERSION** ..... a campaign's *actual* goal(s), e.g., sales; newsletter sign-ups; app downloads; &c.

## MISCELLANEOUS

**#AD** · Many jurisdictions require influencers to note which posts have been MONETIZED. Some creators — knowing that "#ad" hashtags diminish ENGAGEMENT — will add the note after, say, 24 hours to maximize their numbers while minimizing their regulatory risk.

**I.B.** · Inspired By · A hat-tip to another creator.

**INFLUENCERS IN THE WILD** · An X and YouTube account that documents would-be influencers beclowning themselves in public.

**FACE CARD** · An influencer whose looks are as valuable as a credit card.

**LOOKALIKE AUDIENCE** · Identifying new customers by analysing and then targeting the characteristics of existing customers.

**GHOST FOLLOWERS** · Inactive or **FAKE** accounts that goose an influencer's follower count but do nothing for CONVERSION.

**SOCK PUPPETS** · Fake accounts created by influencers (and others) to manipulate public perception by inflating ENGAGEMENT and/or posting endorsements (or disparagements).

**SOCIAL LISTENING** · When brands scan social media to understand consumer thinking, track influencer activity, spot new trends, and identify threats and opportunities.

**SOCIAL SEARCH** · A (growing) trend, where users turn to social media platforms for data they would previously have sought from algorithm-driven search engines (e.g., Google). *Also*, when traditional search engines incorporate data scraped from social media feeds.

**SCROLL STOPPING / THUMB STOPPING** · Content so engaging it stops viewers in their tracks. {☞ MARMALADE DROPPER p.256}. Like virality: easier to demand than supply.

**F.Y.P.** · A TikTok user's For You Page, i.e., their hyper-personal, algo-driven dopamine drip.

**DOING NUMBERS** · Getting ENGAGEMENT.

**PICK ME GIRL** · A female influencer who seeks male attention (by denigrating women).

**TRENDJACKING** · When corporate accounts race to catch a social-media wave by glomming onto a viral moment: winning if witty, fitting, and fast; **CRINGE** if clunky, off-brand, and slow. Most companies will bide their time for the perfect brand-relevant trend before trying to engage; a few (e.g., Wendy's) are famous for hijacking every viral moment.

**HYPE *or* CONTENT *or* COLLAB HOUSE** · A communal living space shared by (wannabe) influencers who live, work, and create content together. (In 2022, Netflix released a deeply unpopular reality T.V. show called *Hype House*, which tracked nine cohabiting TikTokers.)

**GATSBYING** · A post that targets a specific person (the online equivalent of the parties Jay Gatsby threw to lure Daisy Buchanan). Used in online dating (/ stalking) and by influencers hoping to entice specific potential sponsors.

**TOUCH GRASS** · The need (or injunction) to get offline and experience the natural world.

[BREAK THE INTERNET alludes to the headline on Jean-Paul Goude's semi-naked cover photo of Kim Kardashian, which graced the November 2014 issue of *Paper* magazine — and very nearly achieved its goal.] ⊙

# The D.N.A. of Dr. No(07)

*Almost everything that makes* **JAMES BOND** *"Bond" is to be found in the franchise's first film.* Dr. No *did not simply define an image of espionage that* M.I.6. *is still anxious to disown, it established a* D.N.A. *that, six decades and five Bonds later, still packs an explosive punch.*

*Dr. No* is a simple movie, shot on a shoestring budget, starring a relative unknown, based on the sixth book in a series, and released in 1962 to a mixed critical response. According to the biographer Andrew Lycett, Ian Fleming left an early screening disconsolate:

> But Ian did not enjoy himself, looking sad and distracted as he tried to summon enthusiasm for the carefree, gun-toting character he had created on the screen. [1]

Yet for all these inauspicious omens, *Dr. No* was not just a hit in its own right — grossing over 16 times its sub-$1m budget — it inaugurated one of the most valuable and venerable franchises in cinema history. Almost immediately, Bond became a brand in itself and created one of capitalism's most successful and sophisticated brand-collaboration ecosystems.

Viewing Bond through the prism of commerce is apt, for Fleming's novels glitter with luxury marques. 007, we learn, drives a Bentley; shoots a Leica; wears a Rolex; putts with Penfold Hearts; bathes in Floris bath essence; zhushes his hair in Pinaud Elixi; and smokes cigarettes specially blended by Morland & Co. of Grosvenor Street.

Naturally, not all of 007's tastes are quite so exotic: He uses a Ronson lighter; drinks Gordon's gin; and shaves with a Gillette. Yet no brand was too arcane for Fleming to specify: The elevator in Dr. No's lair, Bond notes in the novel, was manufactured by Waygood Otis.

Fleming was pragmatic about his (unpaid) corporate specificity ("I think it is stupid to invent bogus names for products that are household words"), yet the brands he picked pack a tri-fold punch: as markers of class, as anchors to realism, and as short-cuts to aspiration — initially for a country fogged by austerity, and later for a culture fixated on acquisition.

Key to the brand of Bond, then, is that Bond knows his brands. But what of Bond as a brand in itself?

According to the analysis of Tony Bennett and Janet Woollacott, because the early Bond novels were "installed ambiguously between ... 'literature' and 'popular fiction,'" they had a limited readership that was "largely restricted to the metropolitan literary intelligentsia." [2]

Indeed, in 1955, Fleming considered killing Bond off because the novels paid so little.

Sales picked up in 1957, after the *Daily Express* serialized and strip-cartooned *From Russia with Love*, but it was the release of the *Dr. No* movie that transformed the books — and Bond — into a phenomenon. As co-producer Harry Saltzman said:

> The "Dr. No" book had sold virtually nothing when we made the film. Then I went to Pan and suggested they print an extra 500,000 copies. They laughed at me. And, do you know, in the next seven months, they sold one and a half million copies. [3]

By creating a film that was sartorial, sadistic, seductive, and sly, Harry Saltzman and Albert R. Broccoli dismissed the dichotomy between "literature" and "popular fiction" — giving high-brow viewers a frisson of rough, and cheap-seat gawkers a glimpse of the high life.

Saltzman and Broccoli also coded a brand D.N.A. that would outlast them both — for almost everything that still makes Bond *Bond* is to be found in their production of *Dr. No* ...

* * *

› 00:12 · **GUN BARREL**

It's hard to overstate the impact of *Dr. No*'s opening, which, like a burning fuse, primes the audience for the fireworks to come.

Designed by Maurice Binder, who used a pinhole camera to film down the barrel of a pistol, the sequence actually stars stuntman Bob Simmons, an oddity that wouldn't be rectified until Connery re-shot the scene in 1965 for *Thunderball*.

*Ursula Andress in* Dr. No *(1962) and Daniel Craig in* Casino Royale *(2006)*

This now iconic sequence hits several marks at the same time: It trains the eye to trust the camera; it establishes Bond in the centre of his own stark stage; and it melds action, elegance, tension, and death. It's a strikingly confident kickoff for a neophyte production. Twenty-five films later, and it still has an instant Pavlovian impact.

› 00:27 · **JAMES BOND THEME**
While there are many more ubiquitous audio signatures than Monty Norman's "James Bond Theme" (Intel's bongs, the Netflix "ta-dum," or McDonald's "ba-da-ba-ba-baaa") few are as well-loved or long-lived.

Setting aside its undeniable musical merit, the utility of the Bond theme as a sonic signifier derives, in part, from its interlocking elements: the triumphant 11-note horn fanfare; the lush backing strings and tight horn stabs; the brassy, big-band "Stripper"-esque swing tune; and the pantherine guitar riff (plucked by Vic Flick for a £6 fee), which conjures Bond as completely as Sergei Prokofiev's Peter.

With so many musical cards to play, 007's sonic deck can be shuffled almost indefinitely. Not only can just a few notes from any one of these elements evoke the entire Bond universe, but each has proved adaptable to a range of cultural styles, music trends, and dramatic tasks. Adding depth and longevity to the sonic brand, components of the theme have been woven into every Bond song since Shirley Bassey's "Goldfinger" — some more subtly (Billie Eilish's "No Time To Die") than others (Tom Jones's "Thunderball").

› 00:38 · **TITLE SEQUENCE**
The graphical titles of *Dr. No* are as potent as its gun-barrel opening. And then, as type and shape give way to sensual silhouettes, we get a taste of the "sex" in Bond's "sex and violence" cocktail. It's a testament to Binder's vision that after his death in 1991 (following his work on *Licence To Kill*), *Dr. No*'s titles have been referenced repeatedly, even unto *No Time To Die*.

› 06:33 · **LE CERCLE**
It's apt that we first find Bond in an exclusive casino, since high-stakes gambling is both a metaphor for his fieldwork and best explanation (bar embezzlement) of how he funds so lavish a life.

› 07:59 · **"BOND, JAMES BOND"**
In a flawless detail of sound design, Connery's iconic introduction is not merely underscored by the "James Bond Theme," it's punctuated by the click of his lighter.

This now legendary sequence set a vertiginous bar for every incantation of the spell, as Daniel Craig admitted:

> Saying that fucking line! I mean, if I have to say it, I'll say it once to myself — and then you're on set and you think "I'm fine, I'm fine, I'm fine," and then you say it, and it's like the weight of it. I try to be quite cool about these things, but it's impossible. I don't know how many takes we did at the end of *Casino Royale* but literally there are takes with "The name's Bond" like I'm a 13-year-old whose voice is breaking. [4]

*Bond/Moneypenny byplay, with Lois Maxwell and Naomie Harris*

› 07:59 · **BLACK TIE**
Our first canonical vision of Bond has him in a dinner suit (cut by Anthony Sinclair) that features the same silk turnback cuffs favoured by Fleming {☞ p.235}.

From this scene forward, the silhouette of a black-tied Bond was established as a key brand asset, and every 007 since has appeared in the impractically conspicuous uniform of the gentleman spy. All of which is ironic, given what Fleming told Ken Purdy in 1964:

> I quite deliberately made him rather anonymous ... This was to enable the reader to identify with him. People have only to put their own clothes on Bond and build him into whatever sort of person they admire. If you read my books, you'll find that I don't actually describe him at all. [5]

› 09:39 · **UNIVERSAL EXPORTS**
We discover 007's cover story as he exits an elevator and walks toward the offices of Universal Exports — a joke name that still works because, unlike Britain's actual empire, the sun hasn't yet set on Bond's show-boat diplomacy. As he tells Honey in the novel:

> It's like this. I'm a sort of policeman. They send me out from London when there's something odd going on somewhere in the world that isn't anybody else's business. [6]

Bond's ability to export (fictional) hard and (actual) soft power was celebrated in 2012 when Elizabeth II "leapt" out of a helicopter alongside Craig's 007 to open the London Olympics — a collaboration that illustrated the Crown's (then) confidence and the symbiosis between Bond and Brand Britannia. On Her Majesty's Secret Service, indeed.

› 9:44 · **MONEYPENNY**
As Bond enters M's outer office, he tosses to the hat stand his Lock & Co. trilby — an act of practiced insouciance which alerts Miss Moneypenny that, once again, The Flirtation is about to begin:

> BOND: Moneypenny! What gives?
>
> MONEYPENNY: Me. Given an ounce of encouragement. You never take me to dinner looking like this, James. You never take me to dinner, period.
>
> BOND: I would, you know. Only M would have me court-martialled for illegal use of government property.
>
> MONEYPENNY: Flattery will get you nowhere ... but don't stop trying.

From this 30-second scene, Bond's by-play with M's secretary — played by Lois Maxwell in 14 films — became a much-loved and audience-expected asset.

Moneypenny became a significantly more three-dimensional character in 2012, when Naomie Harris took over the role for *Skyfall* — and promptly (if accidentally) shot James Bond in the chest, on M's direct orders.

› 9:54 · **"007 IS HERE"**
Bond explains his codename in the 1953 novel *Casino Royale*:

> A Double o number in our Service means you've had to kill a chap in cold blood in the course of some job. 7

Any number of theories have attempted to explain the "oo" concept, and Bond's septenarious designation — including the observation that seven "works" as a suffix as it's the only double-syllabled digit. But from Moneypenny's brief aside to M, the concept of a "Double o" with a "licence to kill" became an asset embedded (and trademarked) in the culture.

› 10:50 · **M**
Puffing on a pipe in his wood-panelled office, the head of the British Secret Service is the still point of Bond's whirling world, and a bureaucratic reminder that while 007 may be a secret agent, he's not a free agent.

M's brusque irritation at Bond (despite his manifold mission successes) quickly developed into a much-loved trope — echoing the analytical "magic trick" Sherlock Holmes performs with a yawn whenever a new client steps into his 221B Baker Street rooms.

› 12:28 · **Q**
Although Q is not named in the franchise until *From Russia with Love*, Bond's perpetually exasperated quartermaster is foreshadowed in *Dr. No* by an armourer called Major Boothroyd, who equips 007 with his new gun.

Played for 17 movies by Desmond Llewelyn, Q became so popular he was granted his own catchphrase ("*Now, pay attention, 007!*").

› 13:39 · **WALTHER PPK**
007's Walther Polizeipistole Kriminal is one of cinema's most infamous firearms, on a par with Dirty Harry's .44 Magnum. Yet if it hadn't been for a letter of complaint sent to Fleming by a gun aficionado named Geoffrey Boothroyd, Bond would still be packing his chamois leather holster with a Beretta 418 — "a lady's gun, and not a very nice lady at that."

Over the years, 007 wields a variety of guns, yet few fictional characters are so associated with one brand of firearm. Bond even foreshadows Dirty Harry's "Do I feel lucky?" taunt, when he tells Professor Dent: "That's a Smith & Wesson, and you've had your six."

› 16:17 · **STUNT LOCATIONS**
Although we've already glimpsed Kingston's public streets and private clubs, as 007's Pan American Boeing 707-320 lands in Jamaica, so the scene is set for a world of exotic Bond destinations to come — including Cairo, Las Vegas, Moscow, Monte Carlo, Havana, Venice, Tangier, and even "outer space."

Even if the impact of such "stunt locations" was greater before the era of mass travel, the "Bond effect" on tourism is still seen today. When *No Time to Die* filmed in Matera, Italy, the mayor of the city (pop. 60,000) estimated the "Bond boost" might be worth €12 million.

› 21:58 · **MAKE SURE HE DOESN'T GET AWAY**
Bond's bone-dry quip — tossed as he delivers to Government House the corpse of a goon — is the first of many post-mortem gags that came to characterize the humorous side of 007's sociopathic death toll: at least 370 by one count.

› 24:32 · **SHAKEN NOT STIRRED**
A well-framed product placement shot of a Smirnoff bottle precedes Bond being handed a drink by a hotel steward, who very nearly makes cocktail history by announcing:

> One medium-dry vodka martini, mixed like you said, sir, and not stirred.

In fact, the magic words are first uttered by Dr. No much later in the film. Although 007 only says "shaken not stirred" seven times across the canon — and non-Bond players add another eight — the (trademarked) catchphrase stuck.

› 25:02 · **SPYCRAFT**
Before leaving his hotel room, Bond sets a couple of traps for unsuspecting burglars: talcum powder on his briefcase's latches and a strand of hair spittled across his wardrobe's doors. Later in the movie, he fools an assassin by packing a bed with pillows, and fashions makeshift snorkels from reeds.

Although gumshoe "tradecraft" is more usually associated with the workaday espionage popularized by Len Deighton, Frederick Forsyth, and John le Carré {☞ p.116}, Bond regularly returns to such low-fi tricks, e.g., in *For Your Eyes Only* when Roger Moore ascends a rope by fashioning his shoelace into a Prusik knot.

› 30:55 · **FELIX LEITER**
It's curious that Felix Leiter features in *Dr. No* since he's not in the novel, and he adds little to the plot. One explanation is that a C.I.A. agent helped sell a Limey movie to the Yanks.

However, from *Dr. No* on, Leiter's function to the franchise became obvious: He provides technical, material, and financial support; he offers professional camaraderie to a lone-wolf agent; he reminds the audience that, even if Bond's missions are morally black and white, they exist within a multi-polar grey-scale world; and he demonstrates, more often than not, that one properly dressed British spy is superior to America's vast espionage industry.

› 39:25 · **THE VILLAIN'S LAIR**
Our first glimpse of Dr. No's "lair" — an oversized, dystopian, off-kilter cell — sets the scene for dozens of villainous spaces to come. The man responsible for the "lair look" was Ken Adams, who went on to design a host of similar spaces, including the "war room" in Stanley Kubrick's *Dr. Strangelove*. Adding ironic hum or to these unsettling spaces is the high camp of bustling henchmen and well-signposted health and safety precautions.

› 40:49 · **DEATHCAPADES**
In the novel, Bond is menaced under his sheets by a tropical centipede, and later encounters a cluster of tarantulas in Dr. No's lair. The movie conflates these terrors into a single scene that inaugurated the franchise's exotic (and often absurd) methods of murder, from gold-paint asphyxiation to death by Komodo dragon.

› 46:47 · **GADGETS**
*Dr. No* is lacking in the gadgets that would come to define the franchise (for good and ill). Although in the novel, Fleming describes Dr. No's flame-throwing "dragon" as "just some gadget," the movie's most obvious gizmo is the Geiger counter Bond uses to test Crab Key's radioactivity. Other contenders include the cyanide-laced cigarette with which the hench-chauffeur commits suicide, and Dr. No's bionic prosthetic hands.

It was not until *From Russia with Love* and *Goldfinger* that gadgets become an anticipated asset, and the source of much lucrative spin-off merch. Yet they also created the dramaturgical dilemma of "Chekhov's gadget," for whenever Q issues Bond with a highly specific piece of kit the audience demands it be deployed before the credits roll.

The extravagance of Bond's arsenal was parodied by shows like *Get Smart* and *Inspector Gadget* — and was awkwardly acknowledged in *Skyfall* when Bond meets his new Q:

> BOND: A gun, and a radio ... Not exactly Christmas is it?
>
> Q: Were you expecting an exploding pen? We don't really go in for that anymore.

› 46:47 · **ROLEX**
Little is made of Bond's Rolex Submariner in the film, though it appears regularly from casino to closing scene, somehow surviving Crab Key's decontamination facility. But from *Dr. No* on, 007's timepieces (including Breitling,

*Joseph Wiseman as Dr. No, and Mike Myers as Dr. Evil*

Seiko, Gruen, and TAG Heuer) became key elements of product placement and plot development. The Rolex in *Live and Let Die*, for instance, created a magnetic field capable of deflecting bullets and unzipping dresses.

Although Bond has worn an Omega since *GoldenEye*, his association with Rolex is so resilient that more than a decade later the producers of *Casino Royale* felt obliged to insert this preposterous speed bump of brand clarification between Bond and Vesper Lynd:

> LYND: You know ... former SAS types with easy smiles and expensive watches ... Rolex?
>
> BOND: Omega.
>
> LYND: Beautiful ...

› 49:55 · **CAR CHASE**

While this is not the movie's first car chase, it's the first with Bond at the wheel. From this moment, chases of increasing elaboration became a franchise asset.

Aside from a murderous hearse and a rented Sunbeam Alpine, there are few notable cars in *Dr. No* — certainly nothing resembling the fleet of beautiful and bizarre vehicles Bond would later drive. Although *From Russia with Love* featured a Bentley Mark IV Drophead and a Rolls-Royce Silver Wraith, Bond's automotive identity was properly established in *Goldfinger*, when Q presents 007 with his first Aston Martin.

The 57-year ties between 007 and Aston Martin — celebrated in *No Time to Die*, which featured a DB5, V8 Saloon, Valhalla, and DBS — provides the perfect illustration of how the Bond brand intertwines with its commercial partners: If it's hard to disassociate Aston Martin from 007, the opposite is also true.

› 56:30 · **BOND SONG**

It's debatable whether *Dr. No* has a "Bond song" in the current sense. Penned by Monty Norman, the ballad "Underneath the Mango Tree" features several times in the movie, most unexpectedly when sung by Connery himself.

Yet "Mango Tree" is rarely considered canonical (nor included in the compilations), perhaps because the Bond Theme rather steals the show.

(There are also those who correctly consider the film's true hit to be "Jump Up" by Byron Lee and the Dragonaires.)

› 1:02:21 · **BOND GIRL**

Whereas Bond enters the world in black tie, the first echt "Bond Girl" arrives wearing very little — though Ursula Andress was spared the indignity of emerging from the sea as she does in the novel: naked but for a "hunting knife in a leather sheath at her right hip."

(Curiously, 44 years after Andress strode from the surf, *Casino Royale* featured a strikingly similar set-piece featuring Craig. 📷)

*Dr. No* also toyed with the "Bond Girl formula," as recounted by Roald Dahl (the screenplay writer of *You Only Live Twice*) in a 1967 article for *Playboy*:

> Girl number one is pro-Bond. She stays around roughly through the first reel of the picture. Then she is bumped off by the enemy, preferably in Bond's arms ...
>
> Girl number two is anti-Bond. She works for the enemy and stays around throughout the middle third of the picture. She must capture Bond, and Bond must save himself by bowling her over with sheer sexual magnetism. This girl should also be bumped off, preferably in an original fashion. ...
>
> Girl number three is violently pro-Bond. She occupies the final third of the picture, and she must on no account be killed. Nor must she permit Bond to take any lecherous liberties with her until the very end of the story. We keep that for the fade-out. [8]

The product of this formula has been a pantheon of some 75 actresses for whom a dalliance with 007 proved either a canny career move (Jane Seymour, Kim Basinger, Honor Blackman) or the beginning of the supposed "Bond Girl Curse" (Tania Mallet, Tanya Roberts, Lois Chiles).

› 1:27:27 · **BOND VILLAIN**

> I am, as you correctly say, a maniac — a maniac with a mania for power. ... That is why I am here. That is why you are here. That is why here exists.
> — Ian Fleming, *Dr. No* (1958) [9]

Dr. No is right: Bond exists because maniacs exist — and so the "Bond villain" became vital to the franchise, as well as shorthand for real-life oligarchs and megalomaniacs.

› 1:30:54 · **THAT'S A DOM PÉRIGNON '55**
When Dr. No cautions Bond not to brandish a bottle of Dom Pérignon '55 as a weapon, he is simply setting up the nonchalant reply, "I prefer the '53 myself." From this scene, audiences expected 007 to flaunt a connoisseur's discrimination of everything from brandy ("I'd say it was a 30-year-old finé indifferently blended ... with an overdose of Bons Bois") to saki ("especially when it's served at the correct temperature, 98.4°F").

› 1:32:33 · **I COULD HAVE HAD YOU KILLED IN THE SWAMP**
The reluctance of Bond villains simply to murder 007 at the earliest and easiest opportunity is now a much loved (and lampooned) trope. Its zenith arrives in the movie *Goldfinger* — though the much-loved (and mocked) line never appeared in the novel:

> BOND: Do you expect me to talk?
>
> GOLDFINGER: No, Mr. Bond, I expect you to die!

› 1:49:00 · **THE END**
*Dr. No* fades out (per Dahl's dictum) with Bond about to take "lecherous liberties" with Honey Rider. What's missing from this moment is the tantalizing promise "James Bond will be back," which appears at the finale of many subsequent movies, including the controversially concluded *No Time to Die*, which pledged "James Bond will return."

Of course, in 1962 the producers had no idea if Bond *would* be back, nor that they'd created a masterpiece that would redefine not just espionage and action movies but cinema's relationship to the commercial world.

## DISRUPT ANOTHER DAY

In an era when "legacy" companies of every stripe face disruption from startups, it's notable that Bond has regularly disrupted himself.

The scene was set in 1969 when George Lazenby replaced Sean Connery and proved that 007 was bigger even than "Big Tam." And, as with Doctor Who, the trick still works.

The next disruption was to dump the cartoon campery of Roger Moore for the darker reality of Timothy Dalton and Pierce Brosnan. Such a shift was commercially urgent in the face of competition from Bourne, Bauer, and Batman, and creatively pragmatic in the political context of a post-9/11 world.

Bond had also to contend with the skewer of parody, most notably from Austin Powers. Between 1997 and 2002, Mike Myers's three pastiches systematically dismantled Bond's decades-old tropes with an impact no less eviscerating for being affectionate. As Daniel Craig told *M.I.6. Confidential* in 2012:

> We had to destroy the myth because Mike Myers fucked us. I am a huge Mike Myers fan — so don't get me wrong — but he kind of fucked us; made it impossible to do the gags. [10]

In retrospect, Austin Powers probably saved Bond from himself. The 2002 debacle of *Die Another Day* might have worked financially, but everything the franchise had built was stylistically tarnished when Brosnan jumped the shark by kitesurfing a C.G.I. tsunami. Four years later, Craig's bruised and brooding reboot stripped away the gags and gadgets to recast 007 not as a suave farce but a blunt force.

Yet Bond *is* Bond, and audiences are entitled to have their sweet-tooths sated. Luckily 007's deep bench of collateral allowed Craig to cut on the bias — for example, by saving the name-check "Bond, James Bond" for the final line of *Casino Royale*, and adding this snark:

> BOND: Vodka martini.
>
> BARTENDER: Shaken or stirred?
>
> BOND: Do I look like I give a damn?

Six decades on, and the D.N.A. of *Dr. No* remains popular and potent. Bond has logos, locations, catchphrases, characters, a tone of voice, a look and feel, and a sweeping sonic landscape. He even has a mission statement: to save the world from megalomaniac villains "who think they're Napoleon or God."

So, even when a script stumbles (*Quantum of Solace*) or the action is absurd (*Moonraker*), the foundations laid by *Dr. No* are resilient enough to keep the flag flying.

At the time of writing, it was unclear who might fill Craig's shoes to become 007 № 7; indeed there was talk of a "whole new reinvention." But it would surely be an error to stray far from the formula established in 1962. ⊙

# As You Were, Soldier

*A field-guide to British Army* FIELD SIGNALS.

**READY TO MOVE**
*Rotate hand above waist as if turning a handle*

**DEPLOY**
*Arm extended below shoulder level, waved slowly from side to side*

**ADVANCE / FOLLOW ME**
*Arm swung from rear to front below the shoulder*

**HALT / REST**
*Open hand raised to shoulder (indicate halt length with fingers)*

**GO BACK / TURN ROUND**
*Hand circled at hip height*

**AS YOU WERE**
*Forearm extended, hand open, waved across the body*

**DOUBLE**
*Clenched fist moved up and down between thigh and shoulder*

**LIE DOWN**
*Two or three slight downward pats with open palm down*

**SLOW DOWN**
*Extended arm, palm down, moved slowly up and down*

**CLOSE / JOIN ME**
*Hand placed on top of head*

**OBSTACLES**
*Arms crossed in front of body*

**HOUSE / HUT**
*Hands make shape of roof*

**ENEMY SEEN** *or* **SUSPECTED**
*Thumb pointed down*

**NO ENEMY / ALL CLEAR**
*Thumb pointed up*

**SCOUT GROUP**
*Clenched fist with a raised forefinger*

**SECTION COMMANDER**
*Two fingers held against arm to indicate a corporal's stripes*

**PLATOON COMMANDER**
*Two fingers held on shoulder to indicate a lieutenant's stars*

**ATTACK**
*A chopping movement in direction of the assault*

**MOVE UP**
*Arm swung slowly in direction of movement*

**GIVE COVERING FIRE**
*Weapon brought into aim*

**FORM AMBUSH**
*Hand placed over face, and then pointed to desired location*

**ORDER GROUP**
*Hand mimics a talking mouth*

**CIVILIAN**
*Two fingers formed into a V and held under the chin*

**RECONNAISSANCE**
*Cupped hand held to helmet or eye*

**FREEZE**
*Clenched fist at head-height*

**LISTEN**
*Hand cupped to ear*

**WATER OBSTACLE**
*Make wave shape with hand*

**SPACE OUT**
*Vertical palm moved away from body several times*

**SINGLE FILE**
*One arm extended (above head)*

**FILE**
*Both arms fully extended (above head)*

**ARROWHEAD FORMATION**
*Both arms held backwards (or forwards) at 45°*

**EXTENDED LINE**
*Arms raised to the side, level to the ground*

# Walkie Talkie

*The words of* **PROFESSIONAL DOG WALKERS.**

## TYPES OF DOG

**STREET SNACKER / STREET SWEEPER / SCAVENGER / DUMPSTER DOG** · A dog who eats (anything) off the street.

**PULLER** .......... a dog who strains at the leash
**SEPANX** .... a dog with sep(aration) anx(iety)
**HOOLIGAN** ...... a dog who often misbehaves
**KAREN** .... a female dog who nips other dogs
**CHASER** ...... a dog who runs after everything
**BABY SHARK** ..................... a toothy puppy
**PITAPOTAMUS** ......... a rotund, lazy pit bull

**BRANCH MANAGER** · A dog obsessed with (oversize) sticks. *Also*, **ASSISTANT BRANCH MANAGER** · A (smaller dog) who helps out.

**SHARKIE** · A dog who takes your fingers off as you attempt to give them treats.

**PICK POCKET** · A dog who steals treats out of your pockets or **TREAT POUCH**.

**REFEREE** · A dog who runs alongside a group of playing dogs, but doesn't join in.

**FUN POLICE** · A dog who tries to stop other dogs from playing by barking and/or nipping.

**FURKID** · The canine equivalent of a child, whose owners are **MUM AND DAD**, and whose regular walkers are **AUNT** or **UNCLE**.

**HUMPER** · A dog who "engages" other dogs. *Also*, **HUMAN HUMPER** · A dog who "engages" humans. *Also*, **TRAIN AND CARRIAGE** · Three or more dogs humping in a row.

**MEAT HEADS** · Dogs who crash through foliage completely unfazed by being slapped in the face by twigs and branches.

**LEANER** · A dog who invariably rests against a walker's legs.

**STALKERS** · Dogs who never leave your side.

**FRIENDLY?** · Question exchanged between walkers to check if a dog **PLAYS WELL** with others, or is **N.D.F.** · Not Dog Friendly.

**T-REX** · A dog who is all teeth and paws and will eat anything and everything.

**CUJO** · A very aggressive dog (after the eponymous rabid dog of the Stephen King novel).

**PAPER PUSHER** · A dog who loves to rip up paper, cardboard, newspaper, &c.

**MUD PIGGIES** · Labs and retrievers unable to resist rolling in any mephitic mess of mud.

**THE ZOOMIES** · When a dog runs back and forth in irrepressible excitement.

**SITTER / TESTER** · A dog who refuses to move, often in the middle of a walk. Sometimes coaxable with a **HIGH VALUE TREAT**.

**RESOURCE GUARDER** · A dog who (aggressively) protects its food, toys, bed, owner, &c.

**REACTIVE** · An (untrained) dog who reacts aggressively to one or more stimuli, e.g., skateboards, bicycles, airplanes, other dogs, &c.

**D.I.N.O.S.** · A Dog In Need of Space.

***wah wah wah*** [**TREAT**] ***wah*** · When dogs ignore every command except for key words of canine interest — as in the *Peanuts* cartoon.

## WALKIES

**SOLO** → **DUO** → **GROUP** → **PACK** (i.e., >4) → **MULTI-PACK** (with several walkers)

**SNIFFARI** *or* **SNIFFY WALK** · A **LOOSE-LEASH** walk (i.e., with the lead hanging down in a *J* shape) that follows a dog's olfactory urges without a fixed destination or time limit; said to be mentally stimulating (for the dog).

*A professional walker with a dozen-hound* PACK

**STRUCTURED WALK** · One with a specific training purpose, e.g., establishing a routine; honing technique (e.g., walk to heel); managing **REACTIVITY**; &c. *Conversely*, **UNSTRUCTURED** · A walk for exercise and bonding.

**STINK SPOT** · A nose-attracting pavement stain — often a form of canine **PEE-MAIL** — common on a **SNIFFARI**.

**NOAH'S ARK** · Walking a group of dogs with multiple breed pairings.

**SPLITTING A PACK** · Splitting a large group of dogs into smaller clusters on either side.

**DOUBLE DOODIE** · Two walks in one day.

**PUGGLING ABOUT** · A walk taken with a beagle-pug cross.

**DOGGIE TAKEOVER** · When a pack of dogs on a mission overwhelms a walker.

**BARKOUR** · Dog parkour, e.g., hopping onto benches, boulders, logs, walking on ledges, &c.

**CHECK-INS** · When dogs constantly glance at you (for reassurance) while walking.

**B.Y.O.** · Jobs that require you to bring your own equipment (e.g., poop bags, **BALLOONS**).

**BEANER** · A carabiner to clip leashes together.

**GUILLOTINE / FLEXIE** · A retractable leash.

**GENTLE LEADER** · A muzzle leash — used to halt **PULLERS**, not to prevent biting.

**EASY WALKER** · A chest-harness leash.

**PRONG COLLAR** · One with internal metal spikes that dissuade pulling via pain. *Similarly*, **E** *or* **SHOCK COLLARS** · Those that control a dog through mild electrical jolts.

**FORCE** *or* **FEAR FREE** · An approach to training (and therefore walking) that eschews coercion, threats, intimidation, or pain.

**PAW CONDOMS / BALLOONS** · Rubber boots used in icy conditions to protect paws from **HOT COALS**, i.e., pavement salt scattered as part of the **LAZY PERSON'S PLOUGH**.

**ALPHA UP** · Deploying dominant behaviour to subdue a difficult dog, e.g., **ENTER AND IGNORE**; be the first in and out of a room; don't be cutesy; &c.

**LASSO TRICK** · Leashing a nervous dog by gradually tightening a very loose loop.

**ANCHOR & CONTROL** · Looping the leash around one hand and guiding it with the other.

**VAN TIME** · The time a dog is kept locked in a vehicle while collecting other members of the pack and/or driving to and from a walk.

**BELLY RUB TAX** · The extensive petting some dogs demand before they deign to comply.

**LOCK BOXES** *containing door keys for dog walkers (and Airbnb guests) ... secured at pee level*

**PAW TALK** · The inevitable (and repetitive) small talk into which professional walkers get drawn. (*"No, they're not all mine!"*)

## CALL OF NATURE

**THE BIZ** · № 1 and № 2.

**NUGGET** .......... a minuscule № 2
**DINOSAUR** .......... a voluminous № 2

**GREENIE POOPS**: The consequences of eating a Greenies dog treat.

**RUNWAY POOPER** · One who walks while it poops, rather than staying in one spot.

**PAVEMENT POOPER** · An (**APARTMENT**) dog who will only poop on hard surfaces.

**STICK EATER** · A coprophagic dog. (*"Surprisingly, they never eat their own."*) *Related,* **FRESH OUT OF THE OVEN**.

**NOTHING-YOU-CAN-DO-ABOUT-IT** · Any № 2 that cannot be scooped up. *A.k.a.*, **№ 3**.

**POOPSICLE** · A hard-frozen № 2 — usually discovered **OLD AND COLD**.

**KARMA POOP** · Picking up poop for which your dogs are not responsible (in the hope that others will similarly *"scoop it forward"*).

**MARKER** · A dog who visits every vertical.

## CLIENTS &C.

**BOW WOW** · The initial client meet and greet.

**PAWRENTS** · A dog's owners.

**SHOOTING THE BREED** · When a client aims to raise their dog according to pedigree. (*"The owner is shooting the breed, so please read up on raising a husky."*)

**RESTRICTED BUILDING** · An apartment block that prohibits the admittance of non-resident dogs. This inconvenience sometimes requires a **HOLD** — when a second walker collects and delivers a dog while the rest of the pack waits outside.

**TRACTIVATORS** · Clients who (obsessively) monitor their dog's walks using G.P.S. tracking collars.

**PUPDATE** · An after-walk email sent to the owner that details, for example, whether and where THE BIZ was performed.

**CESARITUS** · Symptom of an owner who is a fan of the "Dog Whisperer" Cesar Millan. (*"He's got Cesaritus, so* ALPHA UP.")

**WHITE COLLAR** · Clients who won't greet you, and don't want to be greeted by you. (*"Just do the job with a smile."*)

**SLUMBER PARTY** · Staying with a dog in the owner's home, while the owner is away. ⊙

# Acknowledgments & References

*I owe an immense debt to two groups. First, a cast of commissioning editors who encouraged my exploration of curious world corners. And second, a panoply of professionals (many of whom requested anonymity) who gave so generously of their knowledge and time.*

*As might be expected, disagreement occasionally arose. (As the joke goes: three experts, five opinions.) I have endeavoured to steer a mid-course through any ambiguity — and, where necessary, have combined contrasting definitions, especially when American and British usage differs. None of those acknowledged below has validated, or is responsible for, the content herein; any errors, omissions, or infelicities are mine alone.*

This book was inspired by five delightful people. First, my wife, **Pavia Rosati**, who, on 29.10.2011, returned home from a party wearing a pin emblazoned with the letters **F.O.J.B.**

This, I soon discovered, stood for **Friend Of Jimmy Bradley**, the celebrated restaurateur behind the Manhattan hotspots The Harrison and The Red Cat. Jimmy used this code (and others like it) in his computerized reservation system to indicate which diners deserved a priority table and some extra love.

The existence of F.O.J.B. set my mind racing: Did other restaurants have similar systems? And, might there be an article in it?

They did, and there was. {☞ p.224}

It is thanks to the encouragement of the great **David Shipley**, then editor of *The New York Times* Op-Ed page, that my first toe-dip in the waters of *Significa* saw the light of day.

I initially explored extending *Significa* into a book in 2014, alongside my then agent, the late and much-missed **David Miller**. But the stars seemed to be unaligned. A decade later I was fortunate to begin working with **Jonathan Lloyd** at Curtis Brown, whose enthusiasm revivified the project.

There is one further link in this chain of gratitude: Iona and Peter Opie's remarkable 1959 book, *The Lore and Language of Schoolchildren*, which I plucked from my parents' bookshelf while a schoolchild myself.

During the 1950s, the Opies (a married couple of non-academic folklorists) interviewed some 5,000 children across England, Scotland, Wales (and Dublin) to collect and compare their nicknames, playground games, counting rhymes, initiation rituals, secret codes, social rules, bets, bargaining, riddles, ciphers, and jokes. To offer just one, small example:

> Sweets are referred to as *comforters*, *goodies* (a common term), *sucks* or *suckers* (*sookies* in Scotland), and *quenchers*. They are also *candies* in Cleethorpes (American influence?), *chews* in Aberystwyth, *trash* in Knighton, and always *spice* in the West Riding ("*Gi'us a spice*"). *Lollies* is also becoming a general term, and so is *gob-stoppers* for "any sweet difficult to chew" ... Bubble gum, the new fad, with its tempting picture card in each packet, was known as *beetle fat*. Other current sweet-shop favourites appear to be the same as thirty years ago, in fact bull's eyes, jelly babies, and dolly mixture, have entered schoolchild language as descriptive nouns.

The genius of the Opies' book is twofold: It takes seriously something usually dismissed as obvious or insignificant, and it pins the thorax of something usually disregarded as fleeting. This is the essence of significa.

I am indebted also to **Dan Milaschewski** at United Talent; **Daniel Bunyard** at Michael Joseph; **Lia Ronnen** and **Danny Cooper** at Workman; **Jon Schott**, **Judith Schott**, **Geoff Schott**, **Oscar Schott**, **Otto Schott**, **Aster Crawshaw**, **Rett Wallace**, **Becca Parrish**, **Sarah Rosenberg**, **James Gibney**, **Harry Macauslan**, **Leanne Shapton**, and all of those thanked below. (Where several key participants in a chapter requested anonymity, it has been granted to all.)

## 5 FOREWORD

▤: Iona Opie, Peter Opie, *The Lore and Language of Schoolchildren* (Oxford University Press, 1959), v, 166 [in Acknowledgments]; Ludwig Wittgenstein, *Tractatus Logico-philosophicus* (Harcourt, Brace, Inc., 1922), 62–63, 149; Maurice Rickards, *This is Ephemera: Collecting Printed Throwaways* (Gossamer Press, 1977), 7; Willa Cather, *Willa Cather on Writing: Critical Studies on Writing as an Art* (Knopf, 1988), 21; [Michael] *Parkinson, The Dr. Jacob Bronowski Interview*, directed by Brian Whitehouse (B.B.C., 1973); Erving Goffman, *Forms of Talk* (University of Pennsylvania Press, 1981), 1; *Jonathan Meades on Jargon*, directed by Francis Hanly (B.B.C., 2018). 📷: Screengrab from *Oxford English Dictionary*, oed.com/search/dictionary/?scope=Entries&q=-significa (accessed 20.12.2024), p.6.

## 8 GONDOLIERS

With thanks to two **anonymous** gondoliers; **Sean Wilsey**; and **Paola Franchi**. Many of the Italian terms cited are written in Venexiàn, the spellings of which, like many things Venetian, are subject to debate. ▤ [1] Mark Twain, *The Innocents Abroad, Or, The New Pilgrims' Progress* (Tauchnitz, 1879), 214. [2] Angela Giuffrida, "Gondoliers wanted: Venice seeks to fill vacancies for city's defining profession," *The Guardian*, 15.8.2024, theguardian.com/world/article/2024/aug/15/gondoliers-wanted-venice-seeks-to-fill-vacancies-for-citys-defining-profession/ SEE ALSO: Rita Vianello, *Il Gondoliere* (Cierre Edizioni, 2011); Luigi "Gigio" Zanon, *L'arte de far Gondole* (Editoria Universitaria Venezia, 2006); Giuseppe Boerio, *Dizionario Del Dialetto Veneziano* (Premiata Tipografia di G. Cecchini, 1856); and the Voga Venezia glossary at vogavenezia.com/glossario-a-b.htm/ 📷 ©: Ben Schott.

## 16 BILLING BLOCK

This piece was first published in the Op-Ed pages of *The New York Times* on 23.2.2013; with thanks to **Trish Hall**; **Aviva Michaelov**; **Jim Ledbetter**; **Suzanne Weinert**; and representatives from the **Writers Guild of America West**; **SAG-AFTRA**; the **Directors Guild of America**; and the **Producers Guild**.

## 20 E.M.P.

A version of this piece was first published in the Op-Ed pages of *The New York Times* on 1.10.2011, with signals demonstrated by the then co-owner of E.M.P., **Will Guidara**; it has since been updated. With thanks to **Trish Hall**; **Aviva Michaelov**; **Sewell Chan**; **Sarah Rosenberg**; **Andrew Chandler**; and **Daniel Humm**. 📷 ©: Ben Schott.

## 22 SNEAKERS

With thanks to **Howie Khan**; **Elliot Crawshaw**; several **anonymous** sneakerheads; and the users of the subreddit **r/Sneakers**. 📷 ©: Abaca Press / Alamy, p.23.

## 26 COMPETITIVE EATING

With thanks to **Crazy Legs Conti**. ▤: The chompetition records are from Major League Eating, majorleagueeating.com/records/ (accessed 1.25.2025). [1] N. Jacobs, M. Bossy, and A. Patel, "The Life and Work of Antonio Maria Valsalva (1666–1723): Popping Ears and Tingling Tongues," *Journal of the Intensive Care Society* 19, № 2 (2018): 161–163. [2] M. M. Blatt et al., "Cerebral Vascular Blood Flow Changes During 'Brain Freeze'," *Federation of American Societies for Experimental Biology Journal* 26 (2012): 685.4–685.4. [3] K. R. Westerterp, "Diet Induced Thermogenesis," *Nutrition & Metabolism 1*, № 1 (2004): 5. [4] M. Steger, M. Schneemann, and M. Fox, "Systemic Review: The Pathogenesis and Pharmacological Treatment of Hiccups," *Alimentary Pharmacology & Therapeutics* 42 (2015): 1037–1050. [5] S. Koprdova, C. Schürmann, D. Peetz, T. Dürbye, F. Kolligs, and H. Koop, "Case Report of Presumed (In)voluntary Capsaicin Intoxication Mimicking an Acute Abdomen," *Case Reports in Medicine* 2020 (2020): 3610401. [6] S. R. Williams, R. F. Clark, and J. V. Dunford, "Contact Dermatitis Associated with Capsaicin: Hunan Hand Syndrome," *Annals of Emergency Medicine* 25, № 5 (May 1995): 713–715. [7] P. J. Gupta, "Consumption of Red-Hot Chili Pepper Increases Symptoms in Patients with Acute Anal Fissures," *Arquivos de Gastroenterologia* 45, № 2 (April–June 2008): 124–127. 📷 ©: ZUMA Press, Inc. / Alamy, p.26, 29; Ben Schott, p.28, 30.

## 32 TAYLOR SWIFT

: [1] Steve Knopper, "Labels Want to Prevent 'Taylor's Version'-Like Re-Recordings From Ever Happening Again," *Billboard*, 30.10.2023, billboard.com/pro/taylor-swift-re-recordings-labels-change-contracts/ [2] Jessica Nicholson, "Taylor Swift Accepts Songwriter-Artist of the Decade Honor at Nashville Songwriter Awards: Read Her Full Speech," *Billboard*, 21.9.2022, billboard.com/music/country/taylor-swift-nashville-songwriter-awards-full-speech-1235142144/ [3] Seija Rankin, "Taylor Swift Reveals Her Biggest Music Video Easter Eggs," *Entertainment Weekly*, 9.5.2019, ew.com/music/2019/05/09/taylor-swift-secrets-album-easter-eggs/ [4] *The Tonight Show with Jay Leno*, season 17, episode 56, aired 2.4.2009, on N.B.C. [5] Mary Elizabeth Andriotis, "Taylor Swift Releases 'The Archer,'" *Teen Vogue*, 23.7.2019, teenvogue.com/story/taylor-swift-releases-the-archer/ [6] D. Horton and R. Richard Wohl, "Mass Communication and Para-Social Interaction: Observations on Intimacy at a Distance," *Psychiatry* 19, № 3 (1956): 215–229. ©: Ben Schott.

## 36 AGIT PROP / Z–A

Elements of this piece were first published by *Bloomberg Opinion* on 27.3.2022. : [1] Charles J. Rolo, *Radio Goes to War* (Faber and Faber, 1943), 137. [2] Walter Kirn, "The Wizard of Q," *Harper's Magazine*, June 2018. [3] Sean Illing, "The future of QAnon, explained by 8 experts," *Vox*, 3.3.2021, vox.com/policy-and-politics/22252171/qanon-donald-trump-conspiracy-theories/ [4] Barry Miles, *Peace: 50 Years of Protest, 1958–2008* (Pavilion Books, 2008), 80. [5] *See, for example,* International Auschwitz Committee, "To B remembered: The sculpture of the International Auschwitz Committee," auschwitz.info/en/b-the-sculpture.html/ [6] Amedeo Bertolo and Marianne Enckell, "La véridique histoire du A cerclé," *Centre International de Recherches sur l'Anarchisme Bulletin 58* (March–October 2002), 12–13. ©: Ben Schott (C.N.D. flag, p.36; X, p.37; C.N.D. graphic, p.38; A, p.39); Sergei Ilnitsky / EPA-EFE / Shutterstock (Z, p.37); Granger / Shutterstock (V, p.37); Robin Rayne / ZUMA Wire / Shutterstock (Q, p.38); David Hartley / Shutterstock (C.N.D. hair, p.38); Public Domain (Auschwitz, p.39).

## 40 LAS VEGAS CASINOS

While this chapter was researched in Las Vegas, much of it applies to casinos across America (and the world). A version of this piece first appeared in the January/February 2016 edition of *Playboy* magazine. With thanks to **Hugh Garvey**; **Amy Rosetti**; the then management and staff of the **Cosmopolitan of Las Vegas**; **Todd Greenberg**; **Michael Shackleford**; **Bill Zender**; **Mark Shumsker**; **Eric Jacobs**; **John Robison**; **Kenny Epstein** & the staff of **El Cortez**; and several **anonymous** dealers at the **Fontainebleau Las Vegas**. : [1] Nevada Gaming Control Board, *Nevada Gaming Abstract 2023*. ©: Ben Schott.

## 56 REALITY T.V.

With thanks to a number of **anonymous** editors and producers, and users of the subreddit **r/Edgic**. [1] Steve Hullfish, interviewer, "Deadliest Catch Editing Team," *Art of the Cut Podcast*, episode 51, June 2020. [2] Dave Quinn, "All the 'Real Housewives' Who Renewed Their Vows — and Whether Their Marriage Lasted or Not" *People*, 9.5.2023, people.com/tv/real-housewives-vow-renewals-ramona-singer-lisa-vanderpump/ [3] Emily Exton "'The Hills' series finale: The joke's on us, apparently," *Entertainment Weekly*, 14.7.2010, ew.com/article/2010/07/14/the-hills-series-finale-the-jokes-on-us-apparently/ ©: M.T.V. / Everett Collection / Alamy, p.57; William D. Bird / Everett Collection / Alamy, p.59; Anon, p.60; WENN Rights Ltd. / Alamy, p.62.

## 70 FATHERS CHRISTMAS

With thanks to **Damian Samuels**; **Stafford Braxton**; and several **anonymous Santas, Mrs. Clauses**, and **Elves**. ©: A.P. / Alamy, p.71.

## 73 BAR SLANG

This piece includes a few entries from one first published in the Op-Ed pages of *The New York Times* on 16.2.2014. With thanks to **Honor Jones**; **Aviva Michaelov**; the staff of all participating bars; **Leo Robitschek**; **Audrey Saunders**; **Sarah Rosenberg**; **Rachel Harrison**; and **Hanna Lee**. ©: Ben Schott.

## 78 OPEN OUTCRY

This piece was first published in the Op-Ed pages of *The New York Times* on 7.4.2008. With thanks to **David Shipley**; **Brian Rea**; and **Ray Carbone**. 📷 ©: Ben Schott.

## 80 FASHION WEEK

A version of this piece was first published in the Op-Ed pages of *The New York Times* on 8.9.2012. With thanks to an **anonymous** cast of models, agents, producers, designers, and photographers. 📷 ©: Ben Schott.

## 86 HORSE RACING

With thanks to the legendary **Barry Dennis**; **Simon Nott**; **Simon J. Walmsley**; and **Oli Shaw**. 📄: [1] *Modern Times: Bookies Never Lose*, directed by Robert Davis and Alastair Cook (B.B.C., 1999), 0:50. SEE ALSO: John McCririck, *John McCririck's World of Betting: Double Carpet and All That* (Hutchinson, 1992). 📷 ©: (Signals) Ben Schott, p.86–88; ANL / Shutterstock, p.87; Rob Jukes, p.91.

## 92 GYMS

With thanks to **Hilary Rifkin**; **Lisa Fleming**; **Blink Fitness**; **Equinox**; **24 Hour Fitness**; and several **anonymous** trainers. 📷 ©: Ben Schott.

## 96 PAPARAZZI

With thanks to **Lionel Cherrault**; **Miles Diggs**; **Aaron Parfitt**; **Brian Harris**; **Jennifer Buhl**, author of *Shooting Stars* (Sourcebooks, Inc., 2014); and several **anonymous** paps. 📄 [1] Matthew Suárez, *Paparazzi Daze: Celebrity Encounters* (Independently published, 2020), 41. [2] Darryn Lyons, *Mr. Paparazzi: My Life as the World's Most Outrageous Celebrity Photographer* (John Blake Publishing Ltd, 2010), 32. [3] Leon Gast, *Smash His Camera* (Magnolia Pictures, 2010), film. [4] Peter Howe, *Paparazzi: And Our Obsession with Celebrity* (Artisan Books, 2005), 45. 📷 ©: David Cooper / Alamy, p.96; Kevork Djansezian / A.P. / Alamy, p.99; Kristin Callahan / Shutterstock, p.100.

## 104 HUNTING / SABBING

With thanks to several **anonymous** hunting aficionados and to **"Ed Howl"** of the **Hunt Saboteurs Association**. 📄: [1] *Report of the Committee of Inquiry into Hunting with Dogs in England and Wales* (The Stationery Office, 2000), 24. SEE ALSO: Mike Huskisson, *Outfoxed* (Huskisson Associates, 1983); Hedley Peek, Frederick George Aflalo, *The Encyclopaedia of Sport* (vol 1.) (Lawrence and Bullen, 1897); Thomas Smith, *The Life of a Fox, Written by Himself* (Edward Arnold, 1897); C. Hare, *The Language of Field Sports* (Country Life, 1949). 📷 ©: Hunt Saboteurs Association, p.105, 109; Jim Gibson / Alamy, p.106; P.A. / Alamy, p.110; Gerard Lacz / Alamy, p.113.

## 116 ESPIONAGE

I am indebted to the spy-writer's spy-writer **Nigel West**, who eliminated error and added depth; **Gita Mooljee**, who added invaluable texture and context; several **anonymous** spooky contributors; and two pleasingly unhelpful insiders from **The Agency**. 📄: [1] "Kaleidoscope (Radio 4)," *The Listener*, 13.9.1979, 339–40. [2] John le Carré, *Tinker, Tailor, Soldier, Spy* (Penguin, 2011), ebook. [3] John le Carré, *The Spy Who Came in from the Cold* (Penguin, 2013), ebook. [4] Barbara Bernstein, "Former C.I.A. Chief Defends Agency Role," *Deseret News*, 5.2.1982. [5]Evan Gershkovich, "Tracking Putin's Most Feared Secret Agency," *The Wall Street Journal*, 12.12.2024, wsj.com/world/russia/evan-gershkovich-russia-putin-arrests-spies-9a75e1c3/ [6] John le Carré, *Smiley's People* (Penguin, 2011), ebook. SEE ALSO: Joseph Goulden, *The Dictionary of Espionage: Spyspeak into English* (Dover Publications, 1986); Ronald Payne, *The Dictionary of Espionage* (Harrap, 1984); Randy Burkett, "An Alternative Framework for Agent Recruitment: From MICE to RASCLS," *Studies in Intelligence* 57, № 1 (March 2013); Henry S. A. Becket, *The Dictionary of Espionage: Spookspeak into English* (Stein and Day, 1986); *Glossary of Intelligence Terms and Definitions*, published by the Intelligence Community Staff for the Director of Central Intelligence (Government Printing Office, 1978); Nigel West, *Historical Dictionary of Cold War Counterintelligence* (Scarecrow Press, 2007); Norman Polmar, *Spy Book: The Encyclopedia of Espionage* (Random

House, 1997); Col. Mark L. Reagan (U.S.A. Ret.), ed., *Terms and Definitions of Interest for D.O.D. Counterintelligence Professionals* (Defense Intelligence Agency, 2011); *Joint Doctrine Publication 2-00: Intelligence, Counter-intelligence and Security Support to Joint Operations*, 4th ed. (U.K. Ministry of Defence, 2023). 📷 ©: Ben Schott.

### 128 SOMMELIERS

A version of this piece was first published in the Op-Ed pages of *The New York Times* on 22.12.2012. With thanks to **Trish Hall**; **Sewell Chann**; **Erich Nagler**; **John Guida**; **Joe Campanale**; **Kimberley Drake**; **Anthony Giglio**; **Paul Grieco**; **Morgan Harris**; **Rita Jammet**; **Pascaline Lepeltier**; **Greg Majors**; **Laura Maniec**; **Steve Morgan**; **Thomas Pastuszak**; **Aldo Sohm**; **Raj Vaidya**; **Dustin Wilson**; and **Eric Zillier**. 📷 ©: Ben Schott.

### 132 CLUBLAND

With thanks to several **anonymous** club secretaries; and **Dr. Seth Alexander Thévoz**, author of *Behind Closed Doors: The Secret Life of London Private Members' Clubs* (Robinson, 2022). 🗎: [1] Dora D'Espaigne, "The Lyceum Club for Ladies," *Lady's Realm* Vol. 16 (May–June 1904), 602–609. [2] Anon., "Clubs and Clubbing," *Cassell's Weekly*, 28.3.1923, 52. 📷 ©: Ben Schott.

### 136 FOODIES

A version of this piece was first published in the March 2016 edition of *Bon Appétit*. With thanks to **Adam Rapoport**; **Julia Kramer**; and **Kristin Eddington**. 📷 ©: Ben Schott.

### 138 HOUSE STYLES

🗎 [1] *Variety*, "Slanguage Dictionary," variety.com/static-pages/slanguage-dictionary (accessed 26.1.2025). [2] Gibbs's essay, "Time ... Fortune ... Life ... Luce," is anthologized in Wolcott Gibbs, *More in Sorrow* (New York: Holt, 1958), 3–19. [3] George Plimpton, ed., *Writers at Work: The Paris Review Interviews, Eighth Series* (Penguin, 1988), 15. [4] Nicholas Coleridge, *The Glossy Years: Magazines, Museums and Selective Memoirs* (Penguin, 2019), ebook. SEE ALSO: W. A. Swanberg, *Luce and His Empire* (Scribner, 1972); James L. Baughman, *Henry R. Luce and the Rise of the American News Media* (Twayne Publishers, 1987); Alan Brinkley, *The Publisher: Henry Luce and His American Century* (Knopf Doubleday, 2011); Peter McKay, *Inside Private Eye* (Fourth Estate, 1986); Sylvia Patterson, *I'm Not with the Band* (Little, Brown, 2016); Brian McCloskey, *Like Punk Never Happened* (blog), likepunkneverhappened.blogspot.com/

### 142 CRESTA RUN

With thanks to **Caspar Hobbs**; **James Sunley**; and **Oliver Jones**. 🗎: Harry Gibson, *Tobogganing on Crooked Runs* (Longmans, Green, 1894); Michael Seth-Smith, *The Cresta Run: History of the St Moritz Tobogganing Club* (Foulsham, 1976); Michael DiGiacomo, *Apparently Unharmed: Riders of the Cresta Run* (Texere, 2000). 📷 ©: Melissa Michel, p.143, 145–146.

### 148 STARBUCKS

With thanks to **Emily Keebaugh**; **Danny**; **Laura J**; **Alice**; **271******; **369******; several other **anonymous** current and former STARBUDDIES; and the users of the subreddits **r/starbucks**, **r/starbuckspartners**, and **r/starbucksbaristas**. 🗎: [1] Melissa Allison, "In person: Terry Heckler, who drew Starbucks mermaid, can't stop sketching," *The Seattle Times*, 19.9.2011, seattletimes.com/business/in-person-terry-heckler-who-drew-starbucks-mermaid-cant-stop-sketching/ [2] Daniela Sirtori, "Why Your Starbucks Wait Is So Long," *Bloomberg*, 10.8.2023, bloomberg.com/news/features/2023-09-20/starbucks-spends-billions-to-slash-wait-times-with-faster-orders/ 📷 ©: Ben Schott.

### 152 COMICS

With thanks to **Davey Jones**. 🗎: G. D. Schott, "Balloons, Tails and Bubbles: Depicting Speech and Thought out of the Brain and into the Clinic," *Journal of Visual Communication in Medicine* 45, № 2 (2022): 76–82.

## 154 AUCTIONS

With thanks to several **anonymous** senior auctioneers. 🗎: [1] Aras Khazal, Ole Jakob Sønstebø, Jon Olaf Olaussen, and Are Oust. "The Impact of Strategic Jump Bidding in Residential English Auctions," *Journal of Property Research* 37, № 3 (2020): 195–218. [2] Alan Beggs and Kathryn Graddy, "Declining Values and the Afternoon Effect: Evidence from Art Auctions," *The RAND Journal of Economics* 28, № 3 (1997): 544–565. [3] Scott Reyburn "The magic behind Sotheby's Freddie Mercury sale," *The Art Newspaper*, 13.10.2023, theartnewspaper.com/2023/10/13/sothebys-freddie-mercury-auction-behind-the-scenes [4] Gillian Ku, Deepak Malhotra, and J. Keith Murnighan, "Towards a Competitive Arousal Model of Decision-Making: A Study of Auction Fever in Live and Internet Auctions," *Organizational Behavior and Human Decision Processes* 96, № 2 (2005): 89–103. [5] Ben Schott, *Jeeves and the King of Clubs* (Hutchinson, 2018), 198. 📷 ©: Stephen Chung / L.N.P. / Shutterstock, p.155, 160; J. C. Tardivon / SIPA / Shutterstock, p.156.

## 164 GRAFFITI

With thanks to **XLS**; **DAPP**; **Connor S.**; **Pete Miser**; and several **anonymous** writers. 🗎: [HEADLINE] "As far as the arm can reach" — NEE; Mark Rosengren, director, *I Write on Stuff* (Standing Passengers, 2006), 0:50. [1] *Graff Files Of Anarchy* (? Toonography Entertainment, ? 2014), 30:40, [2] Philip Thorne, director, *Cope2 — Kings Destroy* (Abstract Video Inc., 1999), 1:20. [3] *Claw Money Miss 17*, youtube.com/watch?v=4G77apHP3VY, 1:14. [4] Robert Moran, director, *Sly Artistic City* (2010), 37:28. [5] Doug Pray, director. *Infamy* (Paladin Entertainment, 2005), 6:00. [6] *Sento TFP, True Style Master* (Montana Colors T.V., ? 2011) youtube.com/watch?v=PAE_VpcVylc, 5.04. [7] Eddie Martin, director, *Jisoe* (Black Us, 2005), 12:04. [8] Erik Doty, director, *Up Here Kids* (*c.*2017), vimeo.com/221017951, 29:30. [9] Gary Glaser, director, *Bombing L.A.* (Glaser Productions, 1989), 29:05. [10] Tony Silver, director, *Style Wars* (Public Art Films, 1983), 47:54. 📷 ©: Louis Berk / Alamy, p.165; Ben Schott, p.167–168, 171–172, 174; (Roll call) Pete Miser, p.167.

## 175 RARE BOOKS

With thanks to the staff of **The Grolier Club**, New York City; **Ben Maggs**; and several **anonymous** bibliophiles. 📷 ©: Ben Schott.

## 180 LONDON TAXIS

With thanks to **Dean Warrington**; **L.D.**; **Paul** and **Brian Thompson**; **Alfie H.**; a rank of **anonymous** cabbies; and **"Gorgeous" George Vyse**, who almost sold me a "lightly used" FX4. 📷 ©: Transport for London / Alamy, p.181; Ben Schott, p.182, 184–185, 187–188; Tony French / Alamy, p.189.

## 190 GESTURE POLITICS

With thanks to **William E. Baroni Jr.** 🗎: [1] K. E. Garrison, et al., "Embodying Power: A Preregistered Replication and Extension of the Power Pose Effect," *Social Psychological and Personality Science* 7, № 7 (2016): 623–630. 📷 ©: Ben Schott.

## 193 S.O.G.I.E.S.C.

🗎: **The Human Rights Campaign**; **Weill Cornell Medicine**; **The Johns Hopkins University**; **The Cleveland Clinic**; **Yale Medicine**; **GLAAD**, notably glaad.org/smsi/anti-lgbtq-online-hate-speech-disinformation-guide/ (accessed 30.12.2024); **The American Psychological Association**, notably its "Guidelines for Psychological Practice with Transgender and Gender Nonconforming People," *American Psychologist* 70, № 9 (2015): 832–864. SEE ALSO: E. Coleman et al. "Standards of Care for the Health of Transgender and Gender Diverse People, Version 8," *International Journal of Transgender Health* 23, suppl. 1 (2022): S1–S259; American Psychiatric Association, *Diagnostic and Statistical Manual of Mental Disorders, 5th ed.* (American Psychiatric Publishing, 2013). 📷 ©: Stefan Boness / Ipon / SIPA / Shutterstock, p.195.

## 196 DIAMOND DISTRICT

This piece was first published by *The New York Times Magazine* on 23.4.2015. With thanks to **Jake Silverstein**; **Luke Mitchell**; **Jessica Lustig**; **Joel Berkowitz**; **Peter Germano**; **Michael Goldstein**; **Jack Groothuis**; **Laurent Landau**; **Leon Megé**; **Eddy Portnoy**; **Martin Rapaport**; **Yves Ringler**; **Kushal Sacheti**; and **Michael Wex**. ¶ Yiddish is rendered using the transliteration system from the YIVO Institute for Jewish Research. ©: Ben Schott.

## 204 CHURCH USHERS

This piece was first published in the Op-Ed pages of *The New York Times* on 19.7.2014. With thanks to **Trish Hall**; **Honor Jones**; **Whitney Dangerfield**; **Filmore F. Gregory**; and **Lillie A. Grant**. ©: Ben Schott.

## 206 FANDOMS

With thanks to several **anonymous** superfans; to the users of the subreddits **r/FanFiction**, **r/furry**, **r/ao3**, **r/comiccon**; and **tvtropes.org**, **archiveofourown.org**, **fanlore.org**, **wattpad.com**, and **fanfiction.net**. : [1] Adam Bradley, "Revenge Of The Blerds" *T* magazine, 28.3.2021, 66. ©: Lee Jae-Won / AFLO / Shutterstock, p.207; Vuk Valcic / ZUMA Press Wire / Shutterstock, p.208; Matias Basualdo / ZUMA Press Wire / Shutterstock, p.211.

## 213 STUNTS

With thanks to **Jeff Wolfe**; **Jason Mello**; **Frank Alfano**; **Alexa Marcigliano**; and several **anonymous** performers. : [1] Brad Pitt, Edward Norton, and David Fincher, commentary on *Fight Club*, directed by David Fincher (20th Century Fox Studios, 1999), D.V.D. ©: Insidefoto / Alamy, p.215; A.P. / Alamy, p.216; WENN Rights Ltd / Alamy, p.219–220; A.F.F. / Alamy, p.223.

## 224 RESTAURANTS

This piece is based on (and includes a few entries from) one first published in the Op-Ed pages of *The New York Times* on 5.8.2012. With thanks to the participating restaurants; **Becca Parrish**; **Sarah Rosenberg**; **Adam Rapoport**; **Rob Newton**; **Ivan Crispo**; **David Loewi**; and **Ruth Palethorpe**. ©: Ben Schott.

## 228 SAVILE ROW

With thanks to **Antonia Ede**; **Michael Hill**; **Robert Charnock** of **Dugdale Bros & Co**; and several **anonymous** cutters and makers. : [1] Roberto Cabrera and Patricia Flaherty Meyers, *Classic Tailoring Techniques: A Construction Guide for Men's Wear* (Fairchild Books, 1983), 18. [2] International Wool Textile Organization, "Regulations for the Fabric Labelling Code of Practice Relating to 'Super S' Descriptions," 1.7.2013. [3] Tom Wolfe, "The Secret Vice" in *The Kandy-Kolored Tangerine-Flake Streamline Baby* (Farrar, Straus, and Giroux, 1965), 254–261. [4] See anderson-sheppard.co.uk/thenotebook/alexander-mcqueen/ ¶ Some of the more archaic trade terms are listed in Arnold Hard, *Hard's Year Book for the Clothing Industry 1952* (United Trade Press Ltd., 1952), 363–391. ©: Ben Schott.

## 240 S. AFRICAN TAXIS

With thanks to **Dr. Susan Woolf**, SEE: susan-woolf.co.za : S. E. Woolf and J. W. Joubert, "A People-Centred View on Paratransit in South Africa," *Cities* 35 (2013): 284–293. ©: (hand signals) Ben Schott, p.240–241; (taxi) Richard Townsend / Alamy, p.241; (stamps) Public Domain, p.241.

## 242 U.S. POLITICS

The bones of this piece was first published in the Op-Ed pages of *The New York Times* on 6.9.2013. It was inspired by **Mark Leibovich**'s splendid book, *This Town: Two Parties and a Funeral — Plus Plenty of Valet Parking! — in America's Gilded Capital* (New York: Penguin, 2013), and co-bylined with him. It has been updated and extensively expanded. With thanks to **Trish Hall**; **Sewell Chan**; **Natalie Shutler**; **David Shipley**; **James Gibney**; and a number of **anonymous** contributors from across the political spectrum. : [1] Lawrence Poston III, and Francis J. Stillman, "Notes on Campus Vocabulary, 1964," *American Speech* 40, № 3 (October 1965): 193–195. [2] Jean-Pierre Faye, *Théorie du récit: Introduction aux "Langages Totalitaires"* (Hermann, 1972). [3] "Exclusive: Lee Atwater's Infamous 1981 Interview on the Southern Strategy," *The Nation*, youtube.com/watch?v=X_8E3ENrKrQ [4] Alissa

Wilkinson, "In Netflix's Get Me Roger Stone, the notorious GOP operative plays both narrator and villain," *Vox*, 6.12.2019, vox.com/culture/2017/5/10/15597328/get-me-roger-stone-netflix-review/ [5] Michael Lewis, "Has Anyone Seen the President?" *Bloomberg*, 9.2.2018, bloomberg.com/view/articles/2018-02-09/has-anyone-seen-the-president/ [6] Gram Slattery and Helen Coster, "J.D. Vance once compared Trump to Hitler. Now, he is Trump's vice president-elect," *Reuters*, 6.12.2024, reuters.com/world/us/jd-vance-once-compared-trump-hitler-now-they-are-running-mates-2024-07-15/ [7] Jennifer Bendery, "JD Vance Dismissed Kamala Harris As A Childless Cat Lady In 2021," *Huffington Post*, 22.7.2024, huffingtonpost.co.uk/entry/jd-vance-kamala-harris-childless-cat-lady-miserable_n_669ea075e4b008fc7de19766/ [8] Bill Barrow, "Inside 'The Weave,'" *Associated Press*, 30.10.2024, ap.org/news-highlights/spotlights/2024/inside-the-weave-how-donald-trumps-rhetoric-has-grown-darker-and-windier/ 📷 ©: The Photo Access / Alamy, p.242; A.P. / Alamy, p.244, 248; White House Photo / Alamy, p.247; Ben Schott, p.251.

## 252 PRIDE FLAGS

📄: [1] Gilbert Baker, *Rainbow Warrior: My Life in Color* (Chicago Review Press 2019), ebook. [2] The Gilbert Baker Foundation, "Rainbow Flag Color Meanings," gilbertbaker.com/rainbow-flag-color-meanings (accessed 22.1.2025). 📷 ©: Ben Schott.

## 256 JOURNALESE

📄: [1] Peter Chippindale and Chris Horrie, *Stick It Up Your Punter!: The Rise and Fall of the Sun* (William Heinemann Ltd, 1991), 106. [2] George C. Bastian and Betty Pier MacDougall, *Editing the Day's News* (Macmillan, 1923), 77. SEE ALSO: Wynford Hicks, *English for Journalists* (Routledge, 1993); Keith Waterhouse, *Waterhouse on Newspaper Style* (Revel Barker, 2010); Nicholas Bagnall, *Newspaper Language* (Focal Press, 1993); Richard Keeble, *The Newspapers Handbook* (Routledge, 2001); and (the hilarious) Robert Hutton, *Romps, Tots and Boffins: The Strange Language of News* (Elliott & Thompson, 2013). 📷 ©: Kay Nietfeld / E.P.A. / Shutterstock, p.257; Aaron Chown / PA Images / Alamy, p.260.

## 262 MANOSPHERE

📄: [1] "Why The Matrix Is a Trans Story According to Lilly Wachowski," (Still Watching Netflix, 2020) youtube.com/watch?v=adXm2s-DzGkQ [2] *See, for example*, davemech.org/wolf-news-and-information/ and iflscience.com/the-term-alpha-male-is-all-a-lie-66483/ [3] M. Dębska et al. "The Dark Triad of Personality in the Context of Health Behaviors: Ally or Enemy?," *International Journal of Environmental Research and Public Health* 18, № 8 (2021):4 113. SEE ALSO: D. Vink et al. "'Because They Are Women in a Man's World': A Critical Discourse Analysis of Incel Violent Extremists and the Stories They Tell," *Terrorism and Political Violence* 36, №6 (2023): 723–739; the websites: **incels.wiki; therationalmale.com; puamore.com; krauserpua.com; daysofgame.com; thomascrownpua.com**; and the subreddits: **r/mensrights; r/PurplePillDebate; r/seduction; r/MensLib; r/NotHowGirlsWork; r/ForeverAlone; r/RedPillWomen; r/MensRights; r/PickUpArtist**. 📷 ©: Landmark Media / Alamy, p.263; Ben Schott, p.264, 267.

## 268 MEDICAL SLANG

*See throughout*, Samuel Shem (Stephen Bergman), *The House of God* (Richard Marek Publishers, 1978). 📄: The following do not necessarily prove the *validity* of the related slang, so much as shed light on its origin. [1] C. R. Brookfield et al., "Q Fever — The Superstition of Avoiding the Word 'Quiet' as a Coping Mechanism: Randomised Controlled Non-Inferiority Trial," *BMJ* 367 (2019): l6446. [2] N. M. Robbins, et al., "Number of Patient-Reported Allergies Helps Distinguish Epilepsy from Psychogenic Nonepileptic Seizures," *Epilepsy & Behavior* 55 (February 2016): 174–177. [3] R. Hoffmann et al., "Clinical Decision-Making: Observing the Smartphone User, an Observational Study in Predicting Acute Surgical Patients' Suitability for Discharge," *Journal of Hospital Medicine* 13 (2018): 21–25. [4] L. Gerber et al., "The 'John Thomas' Sign and Pelvic Fractures — Fact or Humorous Myth?: A Systematic Review and Meta-Analysis," *Journal of Clinical Orthopaedics and Trauma* 10, № 1 (2019). [5] A. Saviano et al., "The 'Crossed Leg Sign' in the Emergency Department (or Tilli's Sign): A

New Semiotic Sign for the Early Evaluation of Patients Accessing the Emergency Setting," *Annals of Emergency Medicine* 78, № 4 (2021): 573–574. [6] M. Julião et al., "Energy Surge: A Deathbed Phenomenon That Matters," *Palliative and Supportive Care* 21, № 2 (2023): 371–375. [7] R. Bengtzen et al., "The 'Sunglasses Sign' Predicts Nonorganic Visual Loss in Neuro-Ophthalmologic Practice," *Neurology* 70, № 3 (2008): 218–221. [8] K. B. Schmaling et al., "The Positive Teddy Bear Sign: Transitional Objects in the Medical Setting," *The Journal of Nervous and Mental Disease* 182, № 12 (December 1994): 725. [9] S. Lowe, "The Corridor Consult," *Obstetric Medicine* 10, № 4 (2017): 155–156. [10] E. Stip et al., "Incidentaloma Discoveries in the Course of Neuroimaging Research," *Canadian Journal of Neurological Sciences* 46, № 3 (2019): 275–279. 📷 ©: Mariana Bae / EYEPIX / SIPA / Shutterstock, p.269; Ben Schott, 270.

## 273 AGIT PROP / ICONS

🗎: [1] Anti-Defamation League, "How the 'OK' Symbol Became a Popular Trolling Gesture," 5.9.2018, adl.org/resources/article/how-ok-symbol-became-popular-trolling-gesture/ [2] Nate Powell, "About Face," *Popula*, 24.2.2019, popula.com/2019/02/24/about-face/ 📷 ©: Ben Schott (Casserolade, p.273; Guido, p.273; White Power, p.273; M.A.G.A. hat, p.274, Pussyhat, p.274; Punisher patch, p.276); Universal History Archive / U.I.G. / Shutterstock (Black Power, p.274); John G. Mabanglo / E.P.A. / Shutterstock (Kaepernick, p.275); Farooq Khan / E.P.A.-E.F.E. / Shutterstock (Ink, p.275); Teera Noisakran / Pacific Press / Shutterstock (Duck, p.275); Marin Driguez / SIPA / Shutterstock (Vest, p.276); A.P. / Alamy (Handmaids, p.276); Vuk Valcic / ZUMA Press Wire / Shutterstock (Paper, p.276).

## 277 INFLUENCERS

🗎 [1] E. Kang, J. Lee, K. H. Kim, and Y. H. Yun, "The Popularity of Eating Broadcast: Content Analysis of 'Mukbang' YouTube Videos, Media Coverage, and the Health Impact of 'Mukbang' on Public," *Health Informatics Journal* 26, № 3 (2020): 2237–2248. [2] @sadgrlswag, *TikTok*, "Deinfluencing you ..." 23.1.2023, tiktok.com/@sadgrlswag/video/7191631951827307822/ [3] S. D. A. Litam et al., "Sexual Attitudes and Characteristics of OnlyFans Users," *Archives of Sexual Behavior* 51, № 6 (2022): 3093–3103. 📷 ©: Ben Schott.

## 282 JAMES BOND

A version of this piece was first published on 9.10.2022, by *Bloomberg Opinion*. With thanks to **James Gibney** and **David Shipley**. 🗎: [1] Andrew Lycett, *Ian Fleming* (St. Martin's Press, 2013), 409. [2] Tony Bennett and Janet Woollacott, *Bond and Beyond: The Political Career of a Popular Hero* (Macmillan Education, 1987), 23. [3] James Chapman, *Licence to Thrill: A Cultural History of the James Bond Films* (Columbia University Press, 2000), 56. [4] *Being James Bond: The Daniel Craig Story*, directed by Baillie Walsh (MGM, 2021). [5] Suzy Menkes, "Secret Agent Man," *T Magazine*, 12.3.2006. [6] Ian Fleming, *Dr. No* (Pan Books, 1963), 91. [7] Ian Fleming, *Casino Royale* (Signet, 1953), 109. [8] Roald Dahl, "007's Oriental Eyefuls," *Playboy* 14, № 6 (June 1967): 86–91. [9] Fleming, *Dr. No*, 131. [10] *MI6 Confidential*, issue 18, vol. 6 (October 2012). 📷 ©: T.C.D. / Prod. db / Alamy, p.283 (left), p.286 (left); Collection Christophel / Alamy, p.283 (right), 284 (right); Pictorial Press Ltd / Alamy, p.284, (left); United Archives GmbH / Alamy, p.286 (right).

## 292 WALKIE TALKIE

A version of this piece was first published in the Op-Ed pages of *The New York Times* on 14.3.2015; it has been expanded. With thanks to **Trish Hall**; **Sewell Chan**; **Honor Jones**; **Jen Parker**; **Aviva Michaelov**; **RuffCity Dog Walking**; **Petaholics**; **N.Y.C. Pooch**; **Dog Walk N.Y.C.**; **Good Dog Walking**; **Agnes & Pavel**; **Tiny Horse**; **N.Y.C. Dog Walkers**; and members of the Facebook group **Dog Walker to Dog Walker**. 📷 ©: David Grossman / Alamy Stock Photo, p.293 ; Ben Schott, p.294.

## A NOTE ON THE TYPE

The body text of this book is set in **ADOBE GARAMOND PREMIER PRO**, designed by Robert Slimbach, and the headlines are set in **NORMAN FAT** from Resistenza Type. ⊙